Preparing for Takeoff

Preproduction for the Independent Filmmaker

Arthur Vincie

Focal Press
Taylor & Francis Group

NEW YORK AND LONDON

First published 2013
by Focal Press
70 Blanchard Road, Suite 402, Burlington MA 01803

Simultaneously published in the UK
by Focal Press
2 Park Square, Milton Park, Abingdon, Oxon OX14 4RN

Focal Press is an imprint of the Taylor & Francis Group, an informa business

Notices
Knowledge and best practice in this field are constantly changing. As new
research and experience broaden our understanding, changes in research methods,
professional practices, or medical treatment may become necessary.

Practitioners and researchers must always rely on their own experience and
knowledge in evaluating and using any information, methods, compounds, or
experiments described herein. In using such information or methods they should be
mindful of their own safety and the safety of others, including
parties for whom they have a professional responsibility.

Product or corporate names may be trademarks or registered trademarks, and are
used only for identification and explanation without intent to infringe.

Library of Congress Cataloging-in-Publication Data
Vincie, Arthur.
Preparing for takeoff : preproduction for the independent filmmaker/Arthur Vincie.
    p. cm.
Includes bibliographical references and index.
1. Independent films—Production and direction. 2. Low-budget films—Production
and direction. I. Title.
PN1995.9.P7V47 2012
791.4302′3—dc23   2012034855

ISBN: 978-0-415-66168-3 (pbk)
ISBN: 978-0-203-58894-9 (ebk)

Typeset in Bembo and Optima
by Book Now Ltd, London

Printed and bound in the United States of America by Sheridan Books, Inc. (a Sheridan Group Company).

Contents

FIGURES

TABLES

Why Prepare?

THE CASE FOR PREP

I mean really, *why*? You've got the script, the money (or credit card), the resources … why not just go *shoot the thing*? It's more fun. And you know the story backwards and forwards, right?

Well, that is an approach to take. There's a lot to be learned from shooting that no book, however well written, can teach you. And now that you're shooting to cards and drives instead of tapestock or film, it's more economical to just shoot lots of footage. Some directors and producers even thrive on the pressure of having to make last-minute decisions. They like the chaos of the just-go-shoot-it style of filmmaking.

However, the vast majority of projects that start this way crash and burn before they ever get finished. As soon as something goes wrong – and inevitably it will – the producer doesn't know what to do except throw money at the problem. Or the director has no idea of how to communicate with actors effectively, so the performances fall flat. Or they beat up on the crew because they don't understand how to lead them. Or the crew end up making decisions about lighting, wardrobe, and production design, but since they don't necessarily have the big picture the film looks rather mismatched or bland.

Pretty soon small problems snowball. The money runs out. The crew and/or cast rebel and leave. The film languishes in post while the editor tries in vain to cut the scenes together into something dramatic. Or the producer manages to finish the film but can't find a distributor because it looks like there was no one at the helm.

As a line producer and production manager, I've worked on a few films like this. Films that will never see the light of day or only got a tiny release. My fellow line producers and I joke about them over beers. But it's really no joke. Someone lost a small fortune – anywhere from a few thousand to a few million. Bridges were burned. In some cases, people were stiffed (I've been among them). Potentially promising careers were dashed. All because the director and/or producer didn't take the time out before the shoot to really think through what they were doing.

So here are some concrete reasons for learning the art of prep:

1. **To diagnose and solve problems before they become expensive and/or time consuming.** If you take the time now to do a proper breakdown and budget of your script, you'll quickly realize that you have a scene that has a ton of extras (which you don't have money for). Or you'll see that most of your film takes place outside, so you'd better make sure to rent umbrellas and tents. If your lead actor has three pages of complicated dialog, maybe you can trim some of it or figure how to make it look visually interesting.
2. **To be able to communicate your vision better.** You'll spend most of your time as a producer and director translating what's in your head into something everyone else can

understand. If you communicate what you want effectively, your crew and cast are more likely to trust you, and therefore work harder for you.

3. **To improve the film.** No matter how good a job the writer did on the script, it's your job to make it into a film. If you wrote the script, you'll have to take off your writer's hat and reshape it into something that's more dramatic, more visual, easier to shoot, and has more layers of subtext.

4. **To cement your authority.** People will be more willing to follow you on the journey if they feel like you know where you're going and how you're going to get there. Know the script backwards and forwards; plan for the various problems that may come up on set; and have an answer ready for aesthetic and/or budgetary concerns.

THE PATH TO PREPRODUCTION

This book will show you how to prep your film. Whether you're the producer or director (or, as is increasingly the case, doing both jobs), you'll learn how to analyze the script, think through the schedule and budget, organize your paperwork, put together the crew and cast, and juggle the gear, vendors, insurance, transportation, and other nuts and bolts.

I'm going to start by assuming that you have at least some financing in place, and that you have a script that you (or the writer) think is in decent shape. The path of preproduction consists of six big steps, broken down into smaller chunks.

1. **Preparing your business:** Starting a production company, picking out the key members of your team (your attorney, business partner, casting director, and possibly an accountant), bulletproofing the script, and putting together a business plan.

2. **Preparing to direct:** Doing a director's script analysis, putting together the materials you'll be presenting to the crew and cast, and preparing a shooting script.

3. **Preparing to produce:** Doing a producer's script breakdown, preparing a schedule and budget for the film, and negotiating with vendors, insurance companies, and unions.

4. **Working with the crew and cast:** Hiring crew, casting, rehearsing, scouting, locking down locations, working with the crew, storyboarding, and shotlisting.

5. **Preparing each day:** Figuring out your day before you get to set, dealing with things when your plans fall apart, and thinking a step ahead of the current crisis.

6. **Preparing for post and distribution:** Figuring out your post workflow, getting the film ready for each stage of post, mapping out a rough marketing and distribution strategy, and preparing your promotional materials.

Each area of preproduction influences the next, so it's important to try and get a handle on all of them. If you don't have your business set up early on, for example, it'll be that much harder to sit down with the director of photography and shotlist. If you haven't done a detailed shooting schedule, there's almost no way you can effectively budget the film.

BEING THE LEADER, AND BEING FLEXIBLE

Your credibility as a leader depends in part on how prepared and organized you are. Uncertainty and doubt creep down from the top of a hierarchical organization. You don't need to know everything, and (believe it or not) you don't need to be right all the time. But you do need to have a real familiarity with the script, the budget, and the schedule. When things change, you need to know what the impact of those changes will be. Being able to shoot from the hip effectively only comes with a great deal of practice.

Good preproduction doesn't *lock you into anything*. Just the opposite. Taking time to prepare your film properly will free you to focus on what matters – what's happening on set – and not get bogged down in problems, doubt, and indecision.

WHO ARE *YOU* IN THIS BOOK?

Not that long ago, the common wisdom was that producing and directing were two jobs that should be done by different people; that you should try to build a team to help make your film; and that distributors would market and distribute your film. Technology, economics, and the retreat of distributors from their traditional roles means that you *have* to do a lot more of the work, including sharing the producing and directing duties. In fact, even if there are two of you (a producer and director) reading this book right now, you're probably both doing a little of each other's jobs already, and taking on a number of other roles as well.

In this new world, directors can't blithely ignore production constraints; and producers can't focus on logistics to the exclusions of creative concerns. And both of them need to pay attention to their audience, to technological change, and to the entire life cycle of the film. So when I address *you* in this book, *you* could be the director, the producer, or the person doing both jobs.

PREP ISN'T LINEAR, THOUGH THE BOOK IS

I had to write this book in a certain order, so that you could follow it and understand prep in a linear, stepwise fashion. In reality, however, you'll be bouncing between different tasks every day, according to the needs of the moment. Because of this, I sometimes have to repeat information across chapters, or refer you backward (or forward) to some data in another chapter. I apologize if this is a bit confusing.

I recommend you skim the whole book just to get familiar with it, even if you're only interested in finding out one piece of the prep puzzle. Even just looking at the section headings will help familiarize you with the way I've structured the process.

WHO THE HELL AM I, ANYWAY?

This book comes from my experience as a line producer, production manager, and director, and from my earlier work in a number of different positions in the film industry (assistant cameraman, production assistant, electric, sound utility, video/audio tech on multimedia shows, etc.). I use examples from films that I've either worked on or know something about (because I know some of the people involved). Most were made for $1M or under; and many were made for less than $200K. I've also budgeted much larger films, up to $10M.

I'm opinionated, and have a particular taste, but I've tried to make it clear when I'm presenting an opinion as opposed to "plain facts."

Table I.1 shows a selected list of the films and television shows I've worked on, and other film-related gigs I've had over the last few years. Many of these films got a small release. A few are still in post.

TABLE I.1 Selected filmography

Film	Role	Director	Producer	Status
Found In Time	Writer, director, producer	Me	Me	Just completed
Caleb's Door	Writer, director	Me	Marilyn Horowitz Lisa Lawrence	In distribution
Helena from the Wedding	UPM, 1st AD	Joe Infantolino	Alexa Fogel Brendan Mason	In distribution
Exposed	Line producer	Burke Heffner	Shashi Balooja Katherine Hinchey	In distribution

(Continued)

TABLE I.1 (Continued)

Film	Role	Director	Producer	Status
The Magnificent Cooly-T	UPM	Stephen Leeds	Pegah Easton Chariya Prasert Leeds	In distribution
Adventures of Power	UPM, NYC unit	Ari Gold	Andrea Sperling	In distribution
The Toe Tactic	UPM	Emily Hubley	Jason Orans Jen Small	In distribution
Goodbye Baby	UPM	Daniel Schecter	Jason Orans Brian Devine Tim Duff	In distribution
Racing Daylight	Line producer	Nicole Quinn	Sophia Raab Downs	In distribution
LL	UPM, 1st AD	Amos Kollek	Amos Kollek	Still in post
Windows	Line producer	Shoja Azari	Shoja Azari Shirin Neshat	In distribution[a]
The Child Within	Line producer, reshoot unit	Luchia Dragosh	Scott Mann	In distribution
Rock the Paint	Line producer	Phil Bertelsen	Dallas Brennan	In distribution
The Empty Hands	UPM	Mahliel Bethea	Mahliel Bethea	In post
Silent Choices	Producer, narrative segment	Faith Pennick	Faith Pennick	In distribution
Company K	Line producer	Robert Clem	Robert Clem	In distribution
The Reawakening	Line producer	Diane Fraher	Jancy Ball	In distribution
The Naked Brothers Band (TV show) Seasons 2–3	Payroll accountant	Various	Kidzhouse Entertainment for Nickelodeon	Show cancelled after Season 3
Lustre	2nd AD	Art Jones	Art Jones	In distribution
Casa Bronfman (doc.)	UPM	Elizabeth Lennard	Elizabeth Lennard	On festival circuit
Silent Choices (doc.)	Line producer, narrative segment	Faith Pennick	Faith Pennick	In distribution
Tribeca Film Festival 2008, freelance 2009–2011	Web production coordinator			
About a dozen or so short films	Varies	Varies	Varies	Varies
ArtMar Productions (production/ consulting/ education company) 1996–2006	Partner		Marilyn Horowitz, partner	
Chaotic Sequence Inc. (production/ consulting company) 2007–present	Partner			

[a] *Windows* was a series of short segments interconnected thematically through the use of windows. Shoja broke the feature up and sold some of the segments to private clients as video art installation pieces.

UPM: unit production manager; AD: assistant director.

Throughout the book I will provide examples from these films and others. In some cases (usually the stories that didn't end well) I've deliberately left names and/or film titles out. I may have to work with some of these folks again, and no one likes seeing their dirty laundry aired openly in print.

ACKNOWLEDGMENTS

This book would not have been possible without the encouragement and help of my many friends and loved ones. To name just a few:

Lauren Mattos, my editor at Focal Press, made a scary process much less so with her encouragement and patience. Heather Carawan read the first draft and made excellent comments. Martha P. Nochimson, my first film professor and friend, was a constant sounding board and helped me figure out the world of publishing. Adam Nadler, writer, editor, and director, proofread and gave me great feedback on the original proposal. Bob Seigel, my longtime attorney and friend, has been a fount of wisdom, and a trustworthy critic and ally. Kat Hinchey, casting director, was a joy to work with on *Found In Time*, and gave me some great notes on the chapters involving casting. Ben Wolf, the director of photography I've worked with for more years than we want to think about, gave me ideas, advice, and support. Debarati Biswas put up with my grumpy behavior, read my work, and helped me see things from a "non-film geek" perspective (thank you Dee, I will turn back into a human being soon, I swear). The editor and sound designer on *Found In Time*, Dan Loewenthal and Quentin Chiappetta, offered encouragement and advice. The cast and crew of *Found In Time* showed me how to have fun in this business again, and contributed some amazing work that hopefully is reflected in the final film. To the cast and crew of *Caleb's Door*, my first film, and especially the executive producer and my business partner for many years, Marilyn Horowitz – thank you for helping me along this path, and putting up with someone who was still learning the ropes. My longtime friends in the film business – Faith Pennick, Anthony Viera, Simeon Moore, Dhimiter Ismailaj-Valona, Michelle Glick Wolter, Verne Mattson, Loren Sklar, Susan Evans, Rick Mowat, and Seth Rochester, to name a few – have become a family.

I've learned something from every producer and director I've worked for, and all the cast and crew I've worked with, so thank you for your wisdom and good company. My mother, Maureen Vincie, and brother, Tommy Loring-Vincie, have always inspired me with their art and their lives. My mother's sharp eye as a photographer, editor, and writer, and Tommy's as an artist, have shaped my own work.

This book is dedicated to the unsung heroes of the film production world, the production assistants. You work hard for little money, less recognition, and sometimes plenty of abuse. All I can say is, I've been there. Persistence and passion really do pay off.

## Chapter 1

The Film Life Cycle

FIGURE 1.1 Arthur Vincie on day 550 of *Found In Time*. (Photo: Simeon Moore.)

Figure 1.1 shows me on the second day of principal photography on *Found In Time*. This is the iconic image everyone conjures up when they think about filmmaking. Studios, publicists, producers, journalists, and directors have hooked us on this image because it's dramatic, and it *does* convey at least one aspect of filmmaking: creating moments between the cast and their environment while on set.

But this picture is misleading. It was taken on the second day of the shoot. But it was also taken on the *five-hundred-and-fiftieth day* of the film's life cycle (give or take a few days). It took a year-and-a-half of *preparation* to get to that point. I was lucky. I've worked as a line producer or production manager on a number of films that took five years to get off the ground.

While production is obviously important, it is not necessarily the most critical to the success or failure of a given film. To see why, let's look at the entire life cycle of a "typical" independent film (Figure 1.2).

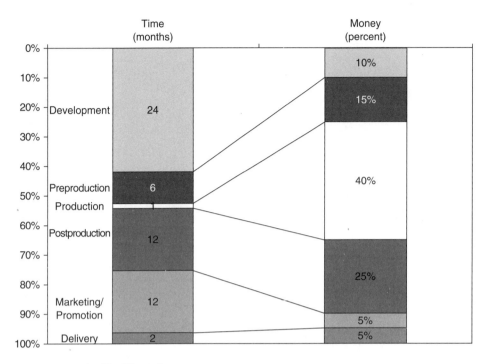

FIGURE 1.2 The film life cycle.

Two things immediately stand out. First, production, while very capital-intensive, occupies only a tiny sliver of the total amount of time spent working on a project. (I'm not including the screenwriting or distribution/promotion phases in this chart. These can stretch on for several years and would unnecessarily complicate the graph.) Second, fixing something during development and preproduction is a lot cheaper than solving it on set. Or worse, "fixing it in post."

So the time for making key decisions – which will, in turn, affect how the money gets spent, and the overall quality of the film – is during development and preproduction. Let's look at each stage of the film's life cycle in a little more detail.

Development. This is the period between coming up with the idea for the story and getting the film "greenlit." The clock starts ticking when you've got a *concrete, written version of your story*. If you're the writer, the clock starts when you've finished at least one draft of your script. If you're optioning a script or adapting a book or other published work, it's when you sign the agreement with the writer. If you're making a documentary, it's when you have an outline (or grant proposal) of some kind that sketches out what you're trying to achieve.

The point of development is to get the main elements of your film together and in top shape: the script, the production company, the financing, the team, and your life. Even if your main source of financing is your credit card (or second mortgage) and you've written a two-person drama that takes place in your uncle's house, you will want to take some time rewriting, thinking about your cast and crew, and getting your life in order. Development can (and usually does) take years.

Preproduction. In theory this starts when the film is "greenlit" (generally when some or hopefully all of the money for the film hits the production company's bank account) and ends on the first day of shooting. In reality there's a great deal of overlap between development and preproduction. It's not uncommon for screenwriting to go on and for major creative decisions (Where? Who? What are we shooting on?) to be made well into preproduction.

Because of this, I generally define the start of preproduction as the moment when you have to start paying your team (or at least signing contracts with them). At this point your team may include only your lawyer, casting director, assistant, producer, and/or director. But once you sign on the dotted line the film becomes real. Now it's *really* time to get it together.

Preproduction on my second film, *Found In Time*, took roughly nine months. On many films, this phase is more compressed – two to three months, tops. I opted for a longer period because I couldn't afford to hire a large staff, and so I could have more time for rewriting and script analysis.

Production. This is the most capital-intensive, viscerally exciting part of the filmmaking process. If you haven't made major decisions by now, they are usually forced upon you by economics. As a director, much of the work you'll be doing with your actors and crew will be grounded in your prep work. As a producer, much of your job will consist of being a glorified plumber in a leaky apartment building. Fix the leak, move on to the next one.

On an independent film (under $1M), the production period rarely exceeds six weeks, and is usually much shorter.

Postproduction. This is where you wake up and realize the difference between the film in your head and the one you actually shot. Hopefully, it's a positive difference. There are still many creative decisions to be made here – particularly for documentaries – but in a sense they are constrained by what's come before. Either you're honing in on your film's core themes during picture/sound editing or you're building something new based on the footage. Usually it's a mix of both.

This phase is like a marathon. It lacks the frantic energy of production but the stakes are higher than during preproduction. When you're in production, you're thinking about several things at once, and each action has multiple dependencies. In post, everything is more linear – you have to finish picture editing before you can begin serious sound design work; you can't do your final conform and output to tape until your mix is done; etc.

If you've done your prep as a director and producer, this phase can actually be fun. You can focus on finding the "happy accident" shots instead of damage control. Postproduction can last up to a year, depending on how complex the film is and your funding situation.

Marketing and festivals. Once your film is finished, it's time to find a distributor for it (assuming that, like most indie features, you didn't have distribution lined up ahead of time).

At this point, your role is that of a salesman. You're here to get your film in front of customers. The customers in this case are *not* ticket-buyers, but distributors, sales agents, and producers' reps. Even if you eventually take up the arduous task of self-distribution, your first stop should be to approach these people, to see if there's a fit.

Festivals, for better or worse, are a major conduit through which to get to these people. Even going to a film market doesn't have the same punch (buyers will wonder why you didn't go to a festival first).

This phase is where a lot of filmmakers understandably burn out. Apart from the fact that it takes a long time – usually at least a year – for a film to go through the festival circuit, it's also very time consuming. If you've put your promotional materials together ahead of time, you can save yourself a lot of headaches.

Delivery. This is what happens after you've signed a deal with a distributor. You usually have one to two months to deliver the materials associated with the film (the deliverables). That often includes several different masters – standard and high definition (SD, HD), DVD, digital tape and files – as well as the sound design sessions, copies of all the contracts, a dialog list, the music cue sheet, and a plethora of other paperwork. Often you'll have to cough up money for a PAL transfer. The bad news is that there will inevitably be something on the list you weren't expecting. The worse news is that you will probably be completely broke by the time you get to this stage, but any promise of money from the distributors will be contingent on getting them what they want first. The good news is that – again – if you've done your prep ahead of time, a lot of the things on this list will already be close at hand.

UNDERSTANDING THE LIFE CYCLE

Common sense suggests that it's less expensive to fix problems earlier on in the life cycle of the film. But the nature of independent filmmaking often works against common sense. Raising money can, by itself, suck up most of your development time. And during preproduction, small immediate concerns divide your attention into little slices, while bigger, more abstract problems requiring concentration get pushed aside.

Also, many filmmakers become seduced by the "movie in their minds." Having also worked as a computer programmer, I can tell you that this same pattern repeats itself among developers. We all have this brilliant vision of what the software should look like and how it will work internally. Then we start coding, and that vision ends up dashed against the messy rocks of reality.

The best way to counteract the forces of financing, attention deficit, and fantasy is to sit down early on and analyze your script. The type of analysis you do depends on your job title, but the end result is the same: you will be able to make decisions that come from a deep understanding of the material.

This leads us to the first axiom of preproduction:

1. All decisions should come from your script analysis.

This may seem obvious, tautological even. But how often have we seen films that suffered from one (or more) of the following?

- Miscast actors
- Thin characters
- Lack of visual coherence
- Bland shots or editing choices, *or*
- Shots that were completely out of place with the rest of the film
- Sagging second acts

Now, you can argue that these are the results of group-think or economic factors. A "name" actor who's wrong for the role may have been the lynchpin that secured the financing. The producer and director dumbed down the script to make it more accessible. There was pressure to keep the film on budget so a lot of the visual "flair" was sacrificed. However, these are the pressures that all films, and all filmmakers, have to deal with. You never have enough time, money, or energy. You will never have the perfect cast, the greatest crew, or the most accessible story since sliced *Star Wars*.

- **Good shots/flair.** Good shots don't necessarily cost a lot of money. On *Racing Daylight* (a film I line produced), the director and producer got a local jib operator to donate his time and his 40-foot rig for free. Yes, free. On *Found In Time* (my own feature), my director of photography mounted the camera on a Glidecam, which added fluidity and motion to what would otherwise have been static shots.
- **Casting.** A "miscast" actor can turn in a brilliant performance, given the right support from the director. Witness Tom Hanks as a hitman in *Road to Perdition*. Or Campbell Scott in *Rodger Dodger*. Or Christopher Plummer in *Beginners* (for which he won an Oscar).
- **Dumbing it down.** *The Dark Knight* was a studio film, and a lot of producers and executives leaned over Christopher Nolan's shoulders. But the results weren't dumbed down. It remains one of the high water marks of the superhero genre. On a more independent scale, *Super, I Sell the Dead, Helena from the Wedding*, and *Tiny Furniture*, all made for less than $1 million, featured very inventive stories and performances. While not accessible to everyone, they weren't completely *inaccessible* either.

So while the pressure to produce bland material will always be there, the opposite is true as well. There are always opportunities to make something more interesting, assuming that the script is solid to begin with. This leads to the second axiom of preproduction:

2. Good filmmaking doesn't have to be expensive, if planned out ahead of time.

There *are* certain inescapable costs. Skilled crewmembers should be paid a decent wage (they can save you money). A more expensive location may be worth it if it comes with less baggage. That "extra" day of shooting will keep you from going into overtime on one of your other days. But if you do your analysis properly, you can figure out how to accomplish a lot for very little.

LONG-TERM PAYOFFS

Some of the things you'll be doing to prepare for your film will pay off during the shoot. Budgeting, scheduling, storyboarding, and shotlisting obviously fall into this category. Getting your cast deal memos signed and your music cleared will have relatively little immediate payoff, but can have a big impact later on. *No distributor will license your film if it contains uncleared music, or if your actors haven't signed release forms or deal memos (or you haven't completed your SAG (Screen Actors Guild) paperwork).* But paperwork is probably the least sexy part of filmmaking. We didn't get into this business to push papers around a desk, right?

This leads us to the third axiom of preproduction:

3. The least interesting things on your to-do list are the ones that have the biggest long-term impact on your film.

Successful producers and directors have agents, reps, lawyers, publicists, accountants, managers, and often spouses who take care of the less "interesting" aspects of filmmaking, so they can do the fun stuff. But at the beginning of your career, you can't count on having these resources. You will have to do at least some of these things yourself. Better get used to it now.

DON'T GET SCARED

Making a film – regardless of genre, length, or content – is one of the most rewarding and wonderful activities you can undertake in your life. You will learn things about the world, about people, and about yourself.

As Figure 1.2 shows, making a feature is a long-term process. You can't do everything tomorrow, and it would be suicide to try. This means that you'll have to adjust to living with your project for a long, long time. But it also means that you *have time* to make good decisions. In fact, your second-biggest asset as an independent filmmaker (after your brain) is time. Structure your time properly, break down the processes into simpler tasks, and you will find yourself accomplishing a hell of a lot very quickly.

QUESTIONS/EXERCISES

1. Using Figure 1.2 as a guide, plot out (on paper or in Excel) a two-to-four year plan for your film. You don't have to list every step between today and the completion of the film, just the big phases (Development, Preproduction, Production, Post, Marketing, Delivery).
2. If you haven't done so already, set a start date for the shoot. Compare it to your chart. Do you have enough time for preproduction?

(Continued)

(Continued)

3. Estimate, in a very rough way, what percentage of each of the following you already have in place:

  a. Funds
  b. Script analysis
  c. Budget
  d. Cast
  e. Crew
  f. Locations
  g. Equipment
  h. Transportation/lodging/food
  i. Post workflow
  j. Marketing/promotional materials
  k. Distribution

Do *not* list anything like the following: "Well, I met this guy who promised he could do *X* service for me for *Y* price," or your cousin saying "Of course I'll come down and help you out on the shoot for a day or two." Such statements mean little unless backed up by real effort or a history of working together.

## Chapter 2

Fixing the Script

FIGURE 2.1 Your script, like this building, is not quite ready to be shown.

SO YOU THINK THE SCRIPT IS READY?

You think your script is perfect. It's wonderful, it's awesome, you could shoot it tomorrow if some-one gave you all the money for it. At least, that's what I thought after I finished the second draft of *Found In Time*. However, this is rarely the case. Scripts are never really done, because their purpose changes over time. It's important to craft your script to fit the needs of the moment, and spend some time on this even before you start your script analysis and breakdown work.

WHAT IS YOUR SCRIPT?

During the financing and development stages, your script is a *sales document*. Your audience is potential investors, the agents/managers of "name" actors, and sales agents and distributors.

It's also a *blueprint* for your producer or line producer to base the budget and (prospective) schedule on. Your audience is your producing partner (or you, if you're doing the budget yourself).

During preproduction, your script becomes a *design document*, pointing the way to your story. Your audience is your casting director, cast, crew, and the agents of prospective cast members. To your assistant director and production manager (or whoever is filling these roles), the script is a *logistical asset*, like a terrain map.

During rehearsal, your script becomes a *scaffold* that your actors will then breathe life into.

During production, your script becomes *the baseline* and is rarely followed with 100 percent fidelity. The script supervisor and editor use the script as the means of comparing what you wanted to shoot with what you actually shot, and try to reconcile the difference in one way or another (either by trying to force the footage to follow the script, or jumping away from the script to fulfill the story).

At no time is the script the story. This may seem strange – what were you writing, if not a story – but the truth is that the story of the film is what's in your head. The script is a vehicle for telling it but it leaves a lot out. This is both bad and good. The bad is that no matter what, your story will always become somewhat diluted in the act of fitting it into the script format. The good is that your cast and crew will fill the gaps and make it into something that may be better than what you could have thought of on your own.

You'll notice that some of these roles conflict. Blueprints are supposed to be specific, as are design documents; but sales pitches are generally more broad, and scaffolds are (as the name implies) rather barebones. But jumping between these different roles is not as difficult as it might seem.

I'm spending time on these seemingly academic points because it's important to put some distance between you and your work. You have to have a certain flexibility (without being overly compromising) in order to rework the script to fit these different roles. And before we dig into these roles, it's important to tune up your script.

THE TUNE-UP PASS

Before you show the script to anyone (except your partner), you *must* fix the following things. It's obvious but I'll say it anyway: *your script is the first real contact investors, agents, distributors – anyone who you want to get to – will have with you.* Just as you wouldn't show up to a business meeting in your bathrobe, you don't want your script to look unprofessional.

Check out the name. A good name can sometimes make the difference between a "meh" and a "hey that sounds cool" response. You need to consider three things: Does the name reflect the story? Is the name catchy, or is it too unpronounceable or abstract? And, is the name too common? *Found In Time* was originally titled *Lost and Found*, which was catchy and reflected the themes of the script. But there were at least eight or nine *Lost and Found* films on IMDb (Internet Movie Database), not to mention *Land of the Lost*, and a ton of other titles that sounded similar. You *don't* want your film to be confused with another one. Just ask the genius who renamed *John Carter of Mars* to *John Carter*. Which one sticks in your mind more?

Grammar and spelling mistakes. I can't tell you how many scripts I've read that had large numbers of typos and errors. Some of these scripts came directly from the writers' agents (who should have been looking out for their clients better).

Breaks in format. Using the wrong font, margins that are too wide/narrow, line spacing, incorrect page numbering – again, I've seen it all. The format is there for a reason (which I'll get into below), and straying from it will only cause you grief.

Inconsistent character names. This is a big one, and it's very hard to keep track of while you're writing. But if you introduce John Beck in one scene as JOHN, stick with JOHN throughout – no JOHNNIE, JON, JOHN BECK, or BECK.

Inconsistent location names. If it's INT. JOHN'S HOUSE – LIVING ROOM, don't switch to INT. LIVING ROOM later on.

Dialog switches. This is a common mistake – you accidentally gave one character's lines to another. I do this all the time, and then my mind mentally inserts the "correct" name when I'm reading the script.

Not introducing characters in ALL CAPS. This drives me crazy. When I'm breaking down a script, seeing ALL CAPS in the description signals the introduction of a new character. If I don't see that, I start worrying that I missed the character in another scene.

Too-similar names. If you have a SAM and a SAMANTHA, you'd better change one of them (Sam becomes Jason). Likewise for place names or objects (your audience will get confused over the difference between an ORAY gun and a RAY gun).

Endless days. If your character has worked at the office, traveled six hours to another city, has another ten scenes, and the sun hasn't set yet – you've written the 30-hour day. This happens all the time, and it's something a lot of folks won't even notice, but whoever's doing your budget definitely will.

Location changes without scene breaks. This drives me *absolutely crazy*. If your characters are in EXT. COURTYARD, and they walk into the interior of the house, that's the end of the scene. Don't continue their conversation without putting an INT. HOUSE scene slug in place. Even if you shoot this as one scene later on, having proper scene breaks helps you figure out how many days you really need certain locations for, what kind of gear to bring along, etc.

Too many scene breaks. You may have a phone conversation or something that might really be a montage. In this case, using INTERCUT instead of starting a new scene with each line of dialog would make for a better read.

Forgetting INTERCUTs. Phone/text/chat conversations should have an INTERCUT somewhere towards the beginning. Most of your readers will not notice if this is missing but your first assistant director (1st AD) will.

Incorrect camera directions. You're not writing a spec script. So you can bend the rules here and put some camera directions in (as long as it doesn't muddy the read – see below). But if you're going to put in directions, be accurate. So:

1. TILT is a camera swivel from a fixed point, along the vertical axis. There is no TILT LEFT.
2. PAN is a camera swivel from a fixed point, along the horizontal axis. There is no PAN DOWN.
3. TRUCK means you're moving the camera on a dolly or other device, but keeping the camera pointed (mostly) in the same direction. There is no TRUCK UP or TRUCK DOWN. I've seen this written sometimes as CRAB LEFT or RIGHT, but this is confusing to a lot of non-film people (what the hell is a crab?).
4. CRANE UP or CRANE DOWN indicate that you're moving the camera vertically without tilting it. I've sometimes seen this written as PEDESTAL UP or DOWN, but again, non-film readers will be confused.
5. PUSH IN means pushing the camera toward the object it's focusing on (on a dolly, jib, crane, or handheld rig). There is no PUSH OUT, PUSH LEFT.
6. PULL OUT means pulling the camera away from the object it's focusing on. There is no PUSH OUT.

These are the most common mistakes I see. They don't kill me but I know a lot of DPs who pull their hair out when they see them.

Overuse of CUT TO or SMASH CUT. This is more of a stylistic choice than a mistake. Some writers like to use the CUT TO or SMASH CUT transition as a form of punctuation, to emphasize a quick pace. But using it too often can actually produce the opposite effect – instead of simply reading the next scene I'm reading the "SMASH CUT." Strictly speaking, a CUT is the default transition from one scene to another, so there's no reason to put it in.

Montage. This isn't a mistake, but it bears mentioning. Whatever you've put in your montage you're going to have to shoot, cull from your other scenes, and/or purchase from a stock library. I've seen films with outrageous, long montages (like the birth of the universe) that were clearly unaffordable or not well thought-out. You might want to leave the montage in for the investors, but be more specific about what you're putting in it once you start thinking practically.

Internal monologues. You can cheat a little bit, but you should try to avoid writing internal character states whenever possible. The characters' internal states will be revealed through dialog and action.

You'll find that once you've gone through this tune-up pass, you'll probably come across some other things that need to be tweaked. Your script will improve and you'll be ready for the next phase.

CREATING THE BLUEPRINT

Now that you've done the tune-up pass, it's time to hand off the script to a line producer, your producing partner, or yourself, to do a breakdown and budget. We'll get into that process in more detail in Chapters 9 and 10, but before you start budgeting your script, take another look at it with the eyes of a line producer.

A line producer looks at a script as a collection of elements – cast members, locations, picture vehicles, lighting setups, props, wardrobe changes, special effects, etc. – that need to be analyzed, scheduled, and budgeted. Seen from this perspective, your script probably has some obviously expensive elements (like that night exterior car chase) and some obviously cheap ones (like two characters sitting in a room talking).

Without fundamentally altering your script, you can maximize the value some of your elements have, and eliminate others that are just costing you money but aren't furthering the story. Here are a few concrete examples:

The one-line character. You have a character who says exactly one or two lines but otherwise sits at the bar as part of the background. Guess what? You now have to pay that person a cast salary, which could amount to a few hundred to a few thousand dollars (depending on your SAG agreement, and including employer fringes). Can you throw those lines to someone else who already has dialog? Do the lines really need to be there in the first place?

The one-scene location. You have a location you only need for one relatively inconsequential scene – the reception area of an office, or the slacker boyfriend's living room. Consider that during production, unless this scene takes up a whole day's shooting, you're also going to have to change locations to shoot whatever else you have on the schedule that day. Anytime you're moving from place to place is unproductive. Plus, you'll probably have to pay a location fee, and buy/rent equipment and props for the location, etc. Can you move this scene to a location you're already using for other scenes?

Tough locations. Airports, courthouses, train stations, subway stations, major bus depots, sports arenas, the observation deck at the Empire State Building … you can certainly shoot in these places, but insurance requirements, bureaucracy, and/or outrageous location fees relative to your budget could put them out of reach. You can try to steal the shots you need, but what happens if they kick you out? What do the scenes add to the story? Can they be set somewhere else? Can you grab an establishing shot as B-roll and then shoot the actual scene somewhere else?

Licensed music. Licensed music is probably the biggest budget sinkhole that filmmakers fall into. If you've written "and then The Rolling Stones' 'Sympathy for the Devil' comes up on the loudspeaker" into your script, you just bumped the budget by $50K or more. You may want to keep the music cue in the script for now to give your investors, cast, and crew some idea of what you have in mind, but be flexible on this once it's time to start shooting. Also, obtaining music rights is a huge time suck.

Licensed footage. Clips from famous movies or television shows will also cost you a fair amount. Do you need these clips at all? Can you re-create them somehow?

Phone conversations. Keep in mind that these have to be shot twice – so you can get both sides of the conversation on camera and intercut later. So if you have three phone conversations in your script, totaling 6 pages, you actually need to shoot 12 pages of dialog. Can you make these in-person conversations? Can you trim out one side of the conversation?

Rooftop scenes. Rooftop vistas can add a lot to the production value of a film, but they're more difficult to shoot on than you'd think – you have to cart all the equipment up (usually some very tough stairs), you're at the mercy of the weather, and the odds of getting clean dialog are iffy (it depends on how exposed the building is to winds). Do these scenes add to the story?

Big crowd scenes. You can probably afford one or two big set pieces in your film, but if you're going from one big crowd scene to another, you may have a problem. Do you think you can shoot all the crowd scenes in one or two days? How many people do you need? Can you take advantage of an existing crowd?

If you have any of these elements in your script, you shouldn't *necessarily* just start cutting them out. But you should be aware that they will cost you something in production (either in time, cash, favors, or all three). If on the other hand you find that they're not doing anything for the story, take them out now before the line producer gets down to factoring them into the budget.

At this point, you should have a script that's error free, and somewhat frugally constructed, so that you can create the budget and breakdown. We'll go into the budget and scheduling process in more detail in Chapters 9 and 10.

CREATING THE SALES DOCUMENT

Once your baby is ready to present to the world, you have to carefully consider who it's going out to, and what you want them to take away from the read.

Your first audience will be investors, actors' agents/managers, and possibly sales agents (if you're trying to get presales). The investors may or may not know much about filmmaking, so it's key that they don't get put off by reading the script. You want to make the script as "user-friendly" to them as possible.

Actors' reps and sales agents are insanely busy people, and it's likely that they will not actually read the script (unless they know you personally or are too small to have assistants) but pass it onto one of their underlings. These underlings have a mountain of scripts on their desk, and go to bed crying at how many they will have to read the next day, and at how many of them suck. These folks *desperately want* to read something good.

Your objective is for your script to be *fast* and *good*. The good part is up to you, but there are a few ways to make the read fast:

1. **Take out excessive camera direction.** It slows down the read and most people (myself included) can't really visualize the directions that well. Or the direction is physically impossible (camera dollies THROUGH THE WALL – *what?*).
2. **Minimize scene transitions.** Your script will be harder to read if it keeps jumping around every 1/4 of a page. Can you consolidate some scenes?
3. **Trim your descriptions.** Go for poetry instead of prose. If your descriptions are longer than three lines, consider breaking them up or losing something. I've had more than one reader tell me that if he sees long paragraphs of description he just turns the pages.
4. **Trim your script.** Before I even read a script I look at how long it is. If it's longer than 110 pages, I start to sigh. If it's longer than 120, I groan. If you find that your script is soaring past 100 pages, it's time to see what you can trim out.
5. **Smooth out the technical talk.** Technical verisimilitude is a good thing, but a little goes a long way. If you find that your characters are talking to each other like they're repeating nuclear power plant operating manual instructions, dial it down a bit. You'll notice that even on more dialog-driven films such as *The Social Network*, with its multiple court cases and programmers talking about code, expositional dialog is interspersed with action. The dialog doesn't get in the way of the action, and yet a lot of information is conveyed in a very short time (especially in the first half-hour, when we learn about Zuckerberg's hacking abilities, how honors clubs work, and the details of the two court cases pending against him).

6. **Make the blocking clear.** When I'm writing I usually keep the blocking pretty sparse. But your investors will want to get some sense of the physical action, so don't be afraid to be specific about character movement, or the choreography of a chase or fight scene. Just don't over-complicate it, either. If you're writing every parry, dodge, and punch of a fight, you're probably slowing down the read.

You want the style to "pop" but not get in the way of the story. Your goal should be for the investor or reader to pick up the script and read it all the way through despite having a full bladder. This may seem like a high bar to aim for, but unless these folks know you, you have to prove that you're worth their time and risk.

Okay, so you've now rewritten/tweaked the script. You can send it out with the business plan (we'll cover that in Chapter 3) to investors. You'll also be sending out the script by itself to agents.

OTHER SCRIPT-RELATED CHORES

Copyright Your Script!

You will definitely want to copyright your script *and* register it with the Writers Guild of America (East or West). You should do these things as soon as you have a finished draft. Some producers like to copyright each draft, but I'm not sure that's necessary unless your script changes radically from the first to the shooting draft.

The copyright office website is: www.copyright.gov. You have the option (finally) of registering and uploading your script over the web through a special fill-in form. The filing fee is lower and you'll save postage as well.

The Writers Guild of America West (www.wgawregistry.org/webrss) and Writers Guild of America East (www.wgaeast.org/script_registration) also offer electronic registration of scripts. Register with the group that's on the same side of the Mississippi river as you (no, really, that's how they divide their coverage regions). Note that WGA registration does *not* carry the same legal weight as copyrighting the script.

Keeping Track of Your Script

Over the course of the rewrite process – which will continue pretty much throughout preproduction and even production – you'll be generating multiple drafts. I recommend starting each draft as a new file, and numbering the draft on the cover page and in the file name. This sounds obvious but I can't tell you how many times I've seen producers send out the wrong draft to an agent because they didn't have a clear numbering system. You can't go by the date modified on the file because you may open an older draft and save it by accident.

I also recommend keeping track of who you've sent the script to, and what draft they read. Some producers I've worked for are pretty fiendish about this – they send out a SASE (self-addressed stamped envelope) with every copy, with instructions that if the recipient passes on the script, they should return it. I've never been quite that organized, but I do keep all the cover letters in a separate folder, and I keep a log of who I've mailed or emailed the script to. At some point during prep, you may find it difficult to keep up with this practice. Honestly, once you've got your cast and crew it doesn't matter as much.

Script Clearance and Rights

I debated about putting this topic at the top of the chapter but figured a lot of people would just jump off a cliff right after reading it. If your script is based on real events and/or people, references brand-names and big corporations prominently, quotes other movies or books extensively, or contains chunks of material developed by someone other than you, have your attorney read it *before* you start sending it out.

Technically, if an event has become a matter of public record, or if the work you're referencing is in the public domain, you can use it without checking for defamation or copyright infringement. So making a film about Jesse James or adapting *The Tempest* is fine. But if your script is about your next-door neighbor Bill who just got into a barfight with a fireman, you may have some work ahead of you.

Prospective distributors of your film will want to know that your script doesn't infringe anyone else's copyrights, defame anyone, or otherwise cause legal trouble for them. You can certainly avoid a great deal of trouble for yourself if you don't write about real people or events. But if your budget allows for it, you should consider hiring a script clearance company to write a *clearance report*. The folks who work at these companies will read your script and look up any character names, references to events, films, books, music, etc. that show up in your story.

If they find any coincidental links between one of your characters, they'll include that on their report. For example, one of your characters is named Joe Screenwriter and he's from Portland, Oregon. During the course of the script he steals from his best friend. They'll see if there are any Joe Screenwriters that live in Portland. If so, they'll tell you. You wouldn't want the real Joe Screenwriter suing you for defamation of character, right?

With the clearance report in hand you can then change or eliminate any potentially troublesome material (let's change Joe Screenwriter to John Producer, or say he's from New York instead). You should file this report along with other important contracts and paperwork that you may have to present to a distributor down the road. We'll cover filing more in Chapter 3.

Your need for a clearance report depends in part on your genre. If you're writing a Shakespeare adaptation, period piece, sci-fi, fantasy, or horror script with supernatural elements (as opposed to some kind of serial-killer story), you're probably okay. But if you're writing a comedy, bio-pic, drama, true-crime, or thriller script, you should at least consider getting a clearance report.

QUESTIONS/EXERCISES

1. Give your script a "tune-up" pass. Make some notes as you're revising.
2. See if you can convince someone to read a section of your script out loud. You can record this session or not. Pay attention to *how* they read it – do they stumble on certain knotty sections, or are there unintentionally funny bits? Does the script seem to drag at points where it should be picking up?
3. If you have a little money in your pocket, give your script to a proofreader just before sending it out. It's possible to proofread it yourself (and thereby save some money or a favor), but you may be too close to it to really evaluate it objectively. I usually hire a good friend of mine, who's also a writer and editor. Sometimes we read each other's work. If you can't afford to pay someone, see if you can barter a service in exchange.

## Chapter 3

Preparing Your Business

FIGURE 3.1 Keeping track of money.

LEARNING BUSINESS AS AN ARTIST

In the days of the studio system, the executives were the businessmen, and they hired the filmmakers to be artists. By leveraging economies of scale – building reusable sets, purchasing equipment that could be used on multiple films, and hiring teams of craftsmen – they were able to produce films on an assembly-line model. These were some of the best films ever made, and every nation has copied the Hollywood model. The downside of having the businessmen run the show is that, as a filmmaker, you had to work within their guidelines. If you wanted to be independent – good luck. United Artists was founded by directors who were fed up with this system.

Today, however, Hollywood works on the freelance model. You're hired on a job-by-job basis (season by season if you're on TV and you're lucky). Studios subcontract out the actual *filmmaking* to production companies. Some of these companies further contract out the work to smaller entities. This makes it possible for filmmakers to make projects that are riskier, and fill a niche audience. However, it also shifts the burden of running the business onto you.

So if you want to be a filmmaker, you also have to be a businessperson, or at least act like one. But despite what you may have heard, running a business can be fun. So let's dig into what's involved.

WHAT BUSINESS ARE YOU IN?

Simply put, you're in the *intellectual property business* – you license intellectual property rights in exchange for money. In your particular case, the intellectual properties in question are your films. More broadly speaking, you're in the business of making money, because money funds your filmmaking.

Note that this is different from what you may define as your *work*. You work as a writer, producer, or director (or some combination of the three), making the films that you will eventually sell. This is a subtle but key difference. As a filmmaker, you wake up every morning because you want to make good films. As a business owner, you want that film to be salable in the film marketplace. This may create some tension, which is why a lot of people partner up, with one handling the creative work and the other dealing with the business. But this tension can be constructive. Having commercial constraints on your work keeps it from becoming self-indulgent (with rare exceptions, a four-hour-long film will not only be difficult to sell but boring as well). Having the creative impulse pushing back against business sense can also lead to breakthroughs – many genre films are much more creative, heartfelt, and even political than they might at first seem.

With only so much time, energy, and money available, you have to decide where to put your resources so that they will further your business *and* your work. This may mean turning down a job that has nothing to do with your business, *unless* that job pays a terrific salary, which can help finance your film (or at least give you development money). On the other hand, taking a lower-rung position with a film company may earn you less money but give you the opportunity to learn and make contacts that will help your business down the road.

I make these kinds of decisions every day. Do I help out my friend for free on his short, so he'll owe me one (or maybe because I owe him one)? Do I turn down a budgeting job because it will take up time I need to promote *Found In Time*? Do I guest-lecture at a film school, which won't pay much but which could result in (again) some work down the road? Or is it too much work to prepare notes and a lesson plan right now?

You want to make your business serve your needs, and not take over your work. So you shouldn't make a film simply because you think it will be commercial if you don't also genuinely like the script. At the same time, you want to make sure your work is not distracting you completely from your business. So don't go off into the wilderness to do your script analysis work and completely neglect paying your bills.

YOUR BUSINESS, FROM 30,000 FEET

Okay, so you run a business. What does that mean? What do you do now? And when do you do all this?

First, you need to actually set up your business. It's best to do this before you start raising money for the film, but some steps (like setting up your LLC) can wait. If you've already tackled one of these steps, congratulations! Just skip ahead to what you haven't done yet.

1. Set up your ongoing development company.
2. Put your office together.
3. Find your partner and war council.
4. Put the business plan together.
5. Form and set up the production company.
6. Care for and feed your company.

I can sense already that a few of you are skipping past this chapter to the more fun stuff. I urge you to at least skim the next few pages.

Before we get too deep into what these individual steps mean, it's important to talk a little bit about what kind of companies you'll need to form, and why you need to form them at all.

WHY FORM A COMPANY?

So, why form a company in the first place? Why not just do business with other people as you, Jill or Joe Filmmaker? The short answer is that it's essential to separate you as an individual from the business that you're driving – it's analogous to the earlier work vs. business discussion. A company provides a vehicle for this, because it's considered a separate legal entity from you. The longer answers are:

Simplicity of accounting and taxes. On the surface of it, your accounting and taxes just got a lot more complicated – you now have to keep separate books, file new sets of returns, and keep your personal expenses and income separate from that of your company. However, without this structure, it'll be almost impossible for you to separate one batch of receipts out from another, or determine whether money you received was for one project or another.

Formality. Your investors want to know that there's a formalized structure in place before they write checks. The rules of corporate behavior and investor rights are well-understood.

Respectability. Most investors, banks, crew, cast, or distributors won't take you as seriously as an individual as they will a company. This is crucial when it comes time to raise money, negotiate with agents, hire people, and deal with distributors.

Taxes, Part I. Your development company and the film's production company will most likely take a loss (on paper) during their first few years of operation. The IRS and state tax departments won't look askance at this, and will allow you to deduct a fair number of expenses. However, if you declare business losses on your personal return for more than a few years, they'll consider your business activity a "hobby" and won't let you deduct it (or worse, audit you for it).

Taxes, Part II. If you earn money as a freelancer (and not as a regular employee), you're responsible for the entirety of your social security contributions (that's 15 percent of gross income), and you're likely going to be taxed at a higher rate in general. Your company, however, doesn't pay social security contributions at all. Unless you take a salary as CEO of your company (which doesn't make sense unless you're earning more than a certain amount of money), you've just received an effective 15 percent raise.

Protection from liability. This is also called the "corporate veil." Except under certain circumstances – like defrauding your investors or running off with the payroll – your personal assets can't be attacked in the event of a lawsuit. This may seem like a distant possibility, especially if you're working with friends, but in our litigious society it's a real possibility that by the end of making your film, someone will be upset enough to sue you.

Contractual freedom. Any contract you enter into will be between your company and the other party, so you aren't personally bound by the conditions of the contract. Your film will most likely become a Screen Actors Guild (SAG) project, which means the production company will have to sign an agreement to produce the film under SAG rules. Any entity that signs this agreement becomes a signatory for the life of that entity.

Down the road, however, you may end up producing a reality TV show. If you signed up with SAG as an individual, they will ask that you hire SAG actors for the show. If your film production company signed up with SAG but you (personally) did not, then you can go form another company to produce the reality show without having to sign with SAG.

Defined exit process. At some point, all businesses end or close shop, though they can outlive their founders. You'll stop working with your partner at some point, or they'll want to buy out your interest. Or your film may not get off the ground. Or if you're really lucky your business will be attractive enough to be bought by another company. Company structures provide a means for making these kinds of endings graceful and resolving the disputes that can sometimes happen.

DIFFERENT TYPES OF COMPANIES

So, now that you're sold on the idea of forming a company, it's important to distinguish between the different types of corporate structures out there. There are quite a few, and the rules for each differ somewhat from state to state.

A *sole proprietorship* is an unincorporated business. If tomorrow you decided to print stationery calling yourself the president of "Famous Directors" and opened a bank account as Your Name DBA ("doing business as") Famous Directors, but did nothing else, you'd be operating a sole proprietorship. The big advantage of a sole proprietorship is that you have very little additional paperwork to deal with, and only one extra form to file with the IRS.

The disadvantage is that you're personally liable for all decisions, contracts, and expenses, taxable at the personal level for all income. You'll also never be able to raise capital outside of your family. Some companies, agents, and vendors won't deal with you at all.

While it may seem tempting, my advice is to *not* work as a sole proprietorship.

A *general partnership* is what you get when two or more people run an unincorporated business together. They share equally in the profits and losses, and are equally liable for any contracts they enter into.

In my opinion, this is the worst of all worlds, because there's more work to do to keep the books separate, and you'll still suffer the same problems when it comes to raising capital and deducting taxes.

Note that if you're working with a producing or directing partner, you'll want to form a partnership agreement, but you don't want to form a general partnership – you're better off using a subchapter S corporation (see below).

A *subchapter S corporation (S-Corp)* is a formalized structure designed for small businesses. You buy shares in your company and can also sell them to private individuals (though not, in most states, other companies). Profits are (mostly) distributed based on stock ownership.

Shareholders must elect a board to run the company. In practice, you elect yourself.

The corporation is separate from you in terms of liability and taxes, but there's a "flow-through" mechanism so that, without taking a direct salary (which would then be subject to taxation), you can move money from the corporate accounts into your own.

If you're making most of your money as a freelancer, then this is the best option for your ongoing business entity. The amount of filing paperwork is relatively minor, and the tax forms aren't too painful. You can have between 30 and 70 shareholders, depending on the state (they just buy stock in the company).

A *subchapter C corporation (C-Corp)* is designed for big businesses – like the ones you see traded on the stock exchanges. They can issue multiple classes of stock and have other companies as shareholders. The protection from personal liability under a C–Corp is pretty close to bulletproof. However, this entails a great deal more paperwork (both when setting up the company and maintaining it) and is really overkill for your small business.

Limited liability partnerships (LLPs) and *limited liability companies (LLCs)* are hybrid structures that sit somewhere between corporations and partnerships. These companies usually have two classes of partners (or members, in the case of LLCs). General partners run the company and make decisions, and have more liability for anything that goes wrong. They then sell shares of the company to investors, who become limited partners. Limited partners take a more passive role – they put in money and take out profits, but generally leave the running of the company to the general partners. They also have more protection from lawsuits.

An LLP is taxed as a partnership – income and expenses go back to the partners. An LLC can be taxed as a corporation.

LLPs are especially suitable for certain classes of professionals who want to form companies – lawyers, architects, accountants, and possibly doctors. LLCs are great for film productions. Your investors become limited members, and you (and your partners, if any) become managing members. *I would recommend forming an LLC as the production entity for the specific film you're working on.*

There is more paperwork involved in setting up an LLC than an S-Corp. But the advantages outweigh the disadvantages. Firstly, your attorney won't have to spend a lot of time crafting the LLC documents you'll need to have ready for investors. Secondly, investors are familiar with the LLC structure.

501c3 non-profit organizations are companies (of any of the above types) set up to run a charity; a religious, educational, or arts organization; a school; or an amateur sports club. They are exempt from federal, and most state, taxes. They take donations from investors without any expectation of giving back a profit to them. The investors deduct the donation from their income taxes.

The paperwork is a bit more cumbersome, and there are generally more restrictions on the kinds of things you can and can't do as a non-profit.

Many documentary filmmakers, especially those making social-issue films, think that their best bet is to form a non-profit company. However, the problem comes when it's time to sell the film. The film either has to be given away for free or any income received for it has to only cover costs. As a general rule, non-profit companies are ill-suited to film production.

A more productive avenue is to find a fiscal sponsor – a non-profit that can accept donations on your company's behalf, and then funnel those funds to you. This is covered in more detail later in this chapter.

There are a myriad of other types of companies, but if I list and describe them all you'll probably sue me for extreme boredom. The important types for your purposes are the S-Corp and the LLC.

SETTING UP YOUR BUSINESS

You'll be setting up two companies. One will be your ongoing development company, and will survive the current film. This entity is where any money you make as a freelancer in the film world should go to. You may also produce some shorts, music videos, podcasts, or other non-union projects with this company. But it's not a good idea to produce a feature (whether doc or narrative) under it. This company will most likely be an S-Corp, though you could also work on an unincorporated basis for a while (see below).

The other company will produce the film. This company's sole product will be your movie, unless you're going to use it to produce a slate of projects.

Which Type to Choose for Your Ongoing Development Company

Which type of organization should you form for your day-to-day film business? Table 3.1 shows a quick checklist. If you find yourself mostly in the "A" column, I'd suggest waiting on forming a company until you're a little further along.

On a day-to-day basis, you won't notice much of a difference between being an individual and operating a company. But you'll be able to deduct more expenses from your taxes as a business (part of your phone, utility, and rent or mortgage, if you're working from home; some of your car usage);

TABLE 3.1 Figuring out which type of business you should form

	Unincorporated/ Sole Proprietorship	S-Corp
How do you earn most of your income?	Regular employee	Freelancer
Are you spending a lot of money developing your film business?	No	Yes
Do you work from home?	No	Yes
Do you have producing partner(s)?	Just me	At least one other person

and you'll have more access to credit. You can also freelance as an incorporated entity, which, as I mentioned earlier, means that you'll be taxed on your income at a lower rate.

Chaotic Sequence, Inc. is my S-Corp. I'm the sole shareholder at the moment. When I do budget and script breakdowns for producers, work as a production manager or line producer, write for hire, or do pretty much anything as a freelancer, Chaotic Sequence gets the check.

Chaotic Sequence also buys all the office supplies and computer gear, picks up my cellphone and broadband internet bill, and pays a chunk of my rent (for my home office). Whenever I have a business-related meal or pitch meeting, or end up ordering in so I can eat from my desk while working, the company picks up those tabs as well. All of these expenses are in turn deducted from the Chaotic Sequence, Inc. income. So the company only gets taxed on the net amount.

I keep two sets of bank accounts and credit cards, and generally segregate business from personal expenses. At the end of the year my accountant files one set of tax returns for myself, and one for Chaotic Sequence.

Which Type to Choose for Your Film Production Entity

Usually, you'll want to form an LLC. You and your partners will become managing members and any investors you bring in will become limited members. The LLC has become the standard corporate structure for film production companies.

There is a significant exception. The filing and (in some states) publication fees associated with forming an LLC can be steep. If you don't think you'll ever get investors apart from some family and friends – if your film will essentially be self-financed – then you may instead want to form an S-Corp. This is a bit unorthodox but becoming more common as film budgets have shrunk and more projects are being self-financed.

Found In Time LLC is the company that I set up to produce *Found In Time*, my feature film. This company is the rights-holder for the film, and was also the insurance policy holder, the Screen Actors Guild signatory, and the contact for all equipment vendors. I'm the managing member of the film (and also an investor), and I have several limited members who invested in it.

Chaotic Sequence, Inc. loaned money to Found In Time LLC at several points, most of which the latter paid back. Found In Time LLC also used Chaotic Sequence Inc.'s office space and office equipment, which Chaotic Sequence could have charged for the use of. This is in fact how many film producers survive – they not only take a salary when working for hire on a film but charge the production company for the use of their equipment, staff, car, and office space.

While this all may seem like shenanigans – especially if you're talking about two companies that are both run by you – it is quite legitimate. You have to treat each company as a separate entity, because the IRS and most of the rest of the outside world already does.

SETTING UP THE BUSINESS – PICK A STATE

So let's get back to our steps. Let's say you've decided to form your S-Corp. What do you do first?

The first thing is to pick which state you'll be basing your S-Corp out of. Each state has different rules, filing fees, and tax rates. Some states, like Delaware, are particularly "corporate friendly." Most people incorporate in their home state.

However, if you incorporate outside of your home state, you have to set up a mailing address in the state you're filing in. This could mean renting a PO box and having the mail forwarded to your home. You also need to register your business in your home state as a *foreign corporation*. Yes, it's strange.

The other big thing is that your company will be governed by the laws of the state you've incorporated in, and if any kind of lawsuit comes up you'll have to show up in the court of that state.

To date, I've started two New York and one Delaware S-Corps. The taxes and the filing fees were higher in New York than in Delaware. Even after renting a mailbox, my short-lived Delaware corporation was cheaper to maintain. My advice is to compare your state's corporate taxes and filing fees with those of Delaware, Nevada, or other "corporate-friendly" states. Apple, Inc. is incorporated in Nevada, despite having offices and plants across the world.

CREATE THE COMPANY!

Finally, you're ready to incorporate. Here are the steps to follow:

1. Come up with a name.
2. Do an entity title search.
3. File the state application.
4. File the federal application to get an EIN (entity identification number – like a social security number for a business).
5. Once the certificate of incorporation and EIN forms arrive by mail or email, go to the bank and set up a basic business checking account.

Naming your business. You can have endless discussions about what you should name your business. Should it be general – "Amalgamated Development, Inc." – or very specific – "Independent Films 'R Us"? A memorable title can leave a great impression. Some people argue that "Film" or "Production" should be in the title somewhere to indicate what your business is about – brand recognition *is* important in business.

I would argue that putting "production," "film," "producer," or any other *too-specific* word in your company can limit you in the long run, unless you can combine it with other more interesting words/phrases. You may end up producing more transmedia or webisodic projects down the road, in which case having a name like "Handy Films" may seem kind of silly. Some companies have very visual or conceptual titles – "Red Car," "Sherpa Productions," "Gigantic Features," and "FilmGym" are examples. While two of these companies use those specific words I just mentioned, they do so in interesting ways.

Think about what you want to achieve, what strikes you emotionally, and what your strong suits are creatively/technically. This can lead to some good titles. Don't rush this process! Once you've incorporated, you're stuck with your company's name for all intents and purposes.

The state doesn't care what you do with your company, incidentally. I've done computer programming jobs under Chaotic Sequence, Inc. I sent out a different letterhead and invoice to the programming clients, but all the checks went to the same account. It's natural that a company may branch out into other areas, and you may have other skills that you're going to get money for along the way.

I picked Chaotic Sequence because it seemed to embody both my strengths and filmmaking itself. Filmmaking is this seemingly chaotic process that somehow "lines up" in just the right way. This paradox plays itself out at many other levels (the arrangement of pixels on a monitor, when seen too closely, will appear chaotic; but watching the arrangement in sequence from a viewing distance will reveal the story). I also seem to be good at organizing "noisy" information. It took me about two weeks to settle on a name.

Beware of titles that are too similar to existing companies. You don't want to get confused with another company! Finally, come up with a bunch of alternate titles, in case your first choice is already taken.

Title search? You'll want to do a title search before you incorporate. This way, if the name of your intended business name is already taken by another company, you can pick one of your alternate titles before you file. Each state, buried deep in the bowels of its website, has an online entity search tool (sometimes called a corporate entity search tool). It's free and it doesn't take long.

Filing the state application. Every state has a website where you can download the forms, read through the instructions until you fall asleep, and fill out the incorporation paperwork yourself ... or you can use one of several online services that do the boring work for you and charge you a fee. While it's generally good to do things yourself, this is one case where the latter option works out better. Most of the charge goes to cover the state filing fees that you'd have to pay anyway.

Inc-It-Now (www.inc-it-now.com) is probably the most popular site. Go online, pick out the type of company you want to form and the state you want to form it in, and check off various options. Don't bother with the bells and whistles or the rush delivery services. Just get the basic package plus the *executive corporate outfit*. While this last item will seem extravagant – it can add up to $70 to the fee including shipping – it's money well-spent.

In a couple of weeks you'll receive a state filing certificate along with a black beauty (what they call the executive corporate outfit) – a big, black binder containing copies of all the filing forms, along with the stock certificates for the company, a corporate seal for you to use, and some boilerplate documents. I usually use the black beauty for other important documents (like tax forms, EIN application, etc.).

Get your EIN. In order to file corporate taxes, you'll need an EIN. This is like a social security number for corporations. You can file for one for free by hitting up the IRS' website, https://sa2.www4.irs.gov/modiein/individual/index.jsp, and filling out the form. Don't be intimidated by the warning at the beginning – it's just a reminder that by using the government's website you're consenting to have them put some cookies on your machine (without which the form won't function). If you don't feel comfortable with this, there's a link to download a printable copy of the form.

You'll usually get a "provisional" EIN from the website as soon as you fill in the form. Then you'll get a snail-mailed slip with the permanent EIN a week or so later. Unless something very unusual comes up, your provisional and permanent EIN will be the same.

Set up your accounts. Now that you have all your paperwork together, you can apply for a business checking account. Get the cheapest one you can find. You'll also want to get overdraft protection and a line of credit (if possible) so you can make purchases without having to worry immediately about cashflow.

Congratulations, you're in business.

PUTTING YOUR OFFICE TOGETHER

The temptation a lot of people have when they start a new business is to spend a lot of money on an expensive desk, a brand new computer, filing cabinets, embossed letterhead, and an office. *Please don't do this.* Your advantage as a small business is that you're unencumbered by overhead (large staff, management, office, equipment), so you can make decisions quickly and easily. Your disadvantage is that you don't have a lot of capital to spend. So spend it wisely.

These days, all you need for your office is:

1. A flat surface
2. A laptop
3. A filing cabinet
4. An external backup system of some kind
5. A printer
6. A broadband connection
7. A cellphone
8. Business cards and letterhead
9. Some bookkeeping software

Flat surface. The flat surface can be your desk, a plank across your lap, a table at a café, or whatever works for you.

Laptop. I recommend a laptop over a desktop because you'll need to be mobile, especially during production. Working from home can also be tremendously difficult, due to the distractions of pets, family members, television, and/or the bed.

Filing cabinet. Get the cheapest two-drawer cabinet you can afford. You can always expand later. But you'll need someplace to put the tremendous volume of paperwork you're about to produce on your film.

An external backup system. Whether you go for a cloud-based approach, or hook up a USB hard drive to your laptop, or go old-school and burn data DVDs, you need something to protect your data in case the worst happens and your drive crashes. A good rule of thumb is that you should multiply the data that you want to back up by 10, to get the size of the drive you'll need to buy. Retrospect (www.retrospect.com) has a number of good, affordable backup software solutions.

Printer. I would recommend spending the extra dollars on a good laser printer. Even in this day and age I find myself printing a lot of scripts, schedules, callsheets, budgets, and other items on every film. Don't just look at the initial pricetag – look at the cost per page. A cheap inkjet will cost you a small fortune, because the ink cartridges have such a limited (200–400 page) lifespan. Paper is also a factor. My laser can handle pretty much whatever cheap stock I throw at it, whereas my inkjet is a lot more finicky. I do have an inexpensive, lightweight multifunction inkjet (printer/copier/scanner) that I tote with me on shoots, and print color photos on.

Broadband connection. Whether you get this as part of your cable package, rent it separately, or steal your neighbor's, just make sure it's adequate. I've usually found that the bottom-to-middle tier is fine for streaming video.

Cellphone. Landlines are wonderful, but they don't offer enough value for me to offset the price.

Business cards and letterhead. I recommend getting good quality business cards, but in small quantities (500 as opposed to 1000). Most people exchange information electronically now, but there's still a need for business cards, and nothing screams "amateur" like cheap-feeling ones. Several online services, including Vistaprint (www.vistaprint.com), offer affordable prices on small runs. And no one seems to care about embossed stationery anymore. Just design something that you can save as a Word (or OpenOffice) template file, so you can print it out whenever you need to.

Bookkeeping software. This is an area where, unfortunately, you'll have to spend some money. There's only a couple of small-business standards, QuickBooks and Peachtree. You can limp by for a bit with a spreadsheet or design a database (if you're clever) but building a true double-entry bookkeeping system will take away time from your business. I picked QuickBooks because almost all the production companies I know use it, as does my accountant.

Keep your overhead low. Most small businesses are killed within the first few years because they can't get ahead of their baseline costs (rent, phone, utilities, etc.).

GET YOUR WAR COUNCIL TOGETHER

You can't do everything yourself. Even if you could, the results would be uneven. When you first start out, you'll need some help along the way. Meet your war council. These folks will act as your advisors and support system, and will help take your business to the next level.

So, who should be on your war council? It depends mostly on your skill set. Are you a computer geek? Then maybe you don't need an IT person. Are you an accountant? Then maybe you just need to retain another one occasionally, rather than have an ongoing relationship with one. But for the rest of us, here's a brief list of who you need:

1. An attorney who specializes in entertainment law
2. An accountant (even if s/he only does your taxes once a year)
3. A tech support geek
4. A graphic designer – for your letterhead, website design, and other communications needs
5. An agent and/or manager

Attorney. I can't stress enough the importance of having an attorney whose specific expertise is in entertainment law. This is a broad domain that covers intellectual rights, music licensing, securities, labor/employment rules, union contracts, and a number of other areas. Also, your attorney will most likely be able to connect you to crew, equipment houses, and other people they've dealt with.

Accountant. Your accountant can be someone who just does your taxes at the end of the year, or who comes in and reconciles your books periodically. This depends in turn on your budget and how comfortable you are with QuickBooks and financial management. I would argue that, if you can deal with the day-to-day bookkeeping yourself, you'll be better off. You'll have a deeper understanding of your true financial situation, and you'll save some money. On the other hand, if your idea of accounting is to keep all your receipts in your wallet or desk drawer until they're an unrecognizable mess, it may pay to invest in a monthly bookkeeper.

IT geek. You can't operate your business without your hardware, software, and peripherals working properly. Add to this the need to set up a website, put together a database for your contacts, and manage the rather large amount of hard drive storage you'll need to purchase over the next few years, and it can be quite a task.

Are you up for it? If so, great. If this isn't your area of expertise, then either get good at it or hire someone who does it for a living. At least have a person you can make 911 calls to when your hard drive crashes. I'm lucky in that I've been fixing and running computers since I was a teenager, and programming on and off for twenty years. But I still reach out sometimes to other people when I'm stymied by things.

Graphic designer. You may only need this person to help design your letterhead and website; or you may need this person periodically throughout the filmmaking process (to make on-screen graphics, film titles, posters, postcard art, etc.). You're looking for someone who "gets" your business and can take whatever sketches you have and make them really pop.

Agent/manager. It may take a long time to find this person, but there's no reason not to look now. If you have a body of work already – a couple of spec scripts, some shorts or commercials you've done – you could do worse than to send out some query letters and try to get an agent or manager now. They can only help you when it's time to get your film together.

The best way to find your war council is through word of mouth. Start with any film people you know. Ask around about who's the "go-to" attorney in the low-budget arena. When they couldn't get Final Cut Pro working on their computer, who did they call? Who did their taxes last year?

Most cities, counties, and states have a film commission office which can give you the names of local production companies and vendors to call. Call these companies up for referrals. You'll get a few polite "whatever, we'll get back to you" responses, but some people will take the time out to talk to you.

Online sites such as mandy.com have directories of film professionals. If you live near the local chapter of the Independent Film Project (ifp.org) you can join for a small fee and attend their seminars on film production, financing, and distribution. If you have to spend a chunk of change, invest in an IMDbPro membership (imdbpro.com). If you know what films have shot near you, you can find full crew/cast listings and, in some cases, contact information by looking up the titles on the site.

The attorney is probably the first person you want on your team. She may be able to refer you to the other folks you need. The effort of building your council will also teach you a lot about the local film landscape.

BUILDING YOUR BUSINESS PLAN

Whether you're looking for investors or will be putting your film on a credit card, you'll want to prepare a business plan. There are several excellent books written on the topic already – I recommend Louise Levison's *Filmmakers and Finance: Business Plans for Independents*. So I'm only going to cover a couple of points about the process.

Essentially, a business plan consists of several parts:

1. An executive summary of the rest of the plan
2. A synopsis of the film and bios of the key personnel
3. For non-film investors, an overview of the film production and distribution landscape
4. How you intend to market and distribute the film, given part 3
5. A summary budget of the film
6. A best-guess set of income projections, based on comparable films and your own financial analysis

If you have the money or know where it's going to come from, what's the point? Given that it can take a lot of work (1–2 months) or money (the going rate for having someone else do it is $3500+), why bother? The short answer is that you will learn a lot about your film, from both a creative and business standpoint.

First, you'll learn where your film fits into the overall marketplace (and if it does at all). Are there distributors that have handled films similar to yours? Are there other films that have similar budgets and genres, and how well did they do? If you notice a sharp drop in overall revenue for low-budget horror films made between $500K and $1M, then maybe you should make sure your budget doesn't go over $500K.

Second, you'll figure out a distribution strategy for the film. Did these other comparable films do well in festivals, or were they direct-to-DVD titles? Perhaps instead of spending a lot of money on festival fees, you should aim to find a sales rep. Is there an audience you can get a hold of through grassroots marketing? Maybe hybrid or self-distribution is the answer. Thinking about where your film will end up will help shape the script now.

You'll also be gathering promotional materials that you can re-use later on. Your concept art can become part of your web design. You can reference the comparable films when discussing the "look and feel" of your film with the cast and crew. The bios can go into your press kit and the website.

Along the way, you'll be collecting data on cast, crew, and companies – who worked with whom – that may come in handy when it's time to pick your own team. Finally, the budgeting process will get you thinking about how much your film really will cost.

I don't think I dread anything more than writing a business plan. But I'm always glad I did it, because at the end of the process I learn more about the film business and where I fit into it.

FORM THE PRODUCTION ENTITY

At some point, you'll want to form the production entity for the film. The steps are similar to the ones you took when you started your ongoing company:

1. Pick a state.
2. Research a name.
3. File the initial paperwork.
4. Apply for an EIN.
5. Set up a separate bank account and credit cards, and possibly an escrow account.
6. Publish (this only applies in certain states).
7. Apply for a resale certificate.
8. Put together the operating or shareholder agreement.

Instead of starting up an S-Corp, you'll most likely be starting up an LLC.

It's a good idea to wait on forming your production entity until you actually have some investment money, or are pretty sure you're going to get it.

Let's skip ahead to step 5, setting up a separate bank account.

Setting Up the Bank Accounts

One of the decisions you need to make is whether you'll have an *escrow* setup as part of your financing. The basic idea is that you set a minimum amount that you have to raise before you can go into production. Until that time any monies you raise go into an escrow account. You won't be able to draw from the account until you reach your minimum, at which point you've "broken escrow."

Once you break escrow, you can transfer funds from the escrow account into the production checking account, and then write checks from this account for your various expenses.

This arrangement protects your investors – if you fail to reach your financing goal, you can give the money back to them. The escrow break point should be at least enough to get through production and maybe a rough cut. So if you're trying to raise $200K, your escrow break might be $120K.

This arrangement has become less and less common over the past few years for projects with budgets of less than $1M. Most projects at this budget level are funded by friends and family of the filmmakers, so the trust issues aren't as relevant. Also, the producers usually need funding right away to start the ball rolling, while still raising money.

Try to get an overdraft on the standard account. This will give you a reserve in case you have to write some emergency checks and things get a little tight. You'll also want to apply for four credit cards:

1. One standard Visa or Mastercard with a decent limit ($5–$10K for a $200K film), that you can give to your production and costume designers. They'll need these in order to do buy-and-returns.
2. One debit card linked to the production checking account.
3. One AMEX card, for charging larger items. American Express offers discounts on office supplies, FedEx, and other services. Just keep in mind that the balances need to be paid off every month.
4. One standard Visa or Mastercard with whatever limit you can get. This will be the main production company card.

Try not to use your personal credit cards, or those of your ongoing development company, to charge film-related expenses. It'll just make for problems later on when you're trying to reconcile where money was spent and charged to what account. It's better to write a check to your film entity (either as an investment or loan), and pay the expenses out of the film entity account.

Finally, apply for a line of credit. This may be difficult to get. You may find yourself in a position where you need to spend money on something – scouting, casting, copies of your business plan – and you haven't broken escrow yet. In those situations (or in an extreme emergency) it's good to have access to the line of credit.

I recommend investigating credit unions or smaller regional banks. They tend to charge lower fees and have most of the conveniences of larger banks. Most belong to ATM networks so you can withdraw money without paying ATM fees. Some even pay you small amounts of money every year. Nerdwallet.com has a searchable database of credit unions.

Spend some time getting to know your corporate bank staff, if your local branch has one. You may need to ask them for help down the road. At one point during preproduction on *Found In Time*, one of my investor's checks hadn't cleared yet, but I had to pay for a location rental. I called my banker and explained the situation. She looked at my account on her system and saw the incoming check, so she allowed the checks I'd written to clear.

Publishing

This is a nice piece of graft for newspaper publishers, but in Nebraska, Arizona, and New York, once you've formed an LLC, you need to publish official notice of its formation in at least two periodicals, for a specific period of time. This law is ancient and now mostly helps fund newspaper and periodical publishers. If you don't do this within 120–180 days of forming your company the state may suspend it, which means you technically can't do business, open a bank account, etc. In a worst-case scenario the state will reject your tax returns and treat any income/outgo as applying to the personal returns of the members.

In each state that has this ridiculous rule there's also an ad agency that specializes in these types of placements. Even though you'll have to pay them a premium they can often get you cheaper listings than you would be able to find on your own.

Plan to spend about $800–$1300 on this. The list of acceptable publications varies by county, so in some cases the local publication rates can be very expensive. Your attorney will most likely know the best advertisers. A quick web search will also reveal some "advertisers" but tread with caution. Some are just scammers.

Keep in mind that incorporating in another state won't save you – if you plan on doing business in New York, Nebraska, or Arizona, you still have to publish in that state.

Apply for a Resale Certificate

Your film production company should pay little to no sales tax on goods and services bought in-state. Why? Because your company is using them to produce a film – a product – and you'll be paying sales tax on any distribution income you receive. As far as the state tax department is concerned, you're a manufacturer – you buy components, put together your product, and sell it to a wholesaler.

You can thus exempt your company from paying *most* sales taxes. There are exceptions, and they vary from state to state. In many states, hotels, gas, and some auto rentals are still subject to sales tax. In order to make your LLC exempt, you have to apply to become a reseller. This is (thankfully) a fairly straightforward process in most states. Visit your company's state tax website (or the tax section of their official state government site). You're looking for an application for a "Sales Tax Certificate of Authority." This gives you the right to collect sales tax on goods you sell, since you'll be paying them back to the government. It also exempts you from paying sales tax on anything you plan on either reselling directly or (in your case) incorporating into something else you're going to resell. Most of the forms can be filled in online.

In a week or so you'll get a cute certificate that will have a very important number on it. It'll look something like Figure 3.2. The number (which may or may not match your EIN) is your resale ID.

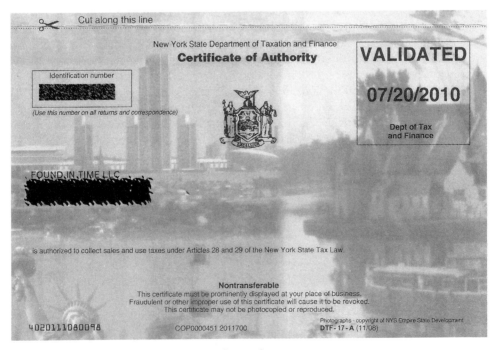

FIGURE 3.2 The "Found In Time LLC" resale certificate.

In Chapter 12, we'll discuss how to use this certificate, along with the resale certificate form, when you're setting up your equipment vendor accounts.

Once you become a reseller, most states will require you to file quarterly sales tax returns. Most of these can also be filed online, and since you won't be selling anything anytime soon, you can fill them out pretty quickly.

Putting Together Your Shareholder/Operating Agreements

Now you have to structure your LLC so that it's film-investor friendly. Even if you're the only investor in your project right now, you still have to put together the legal framework for handling the flow of monies into and out of the company, how profits will be allocated, and who's driving the boat. You may get lucky and find someone who wants to kick in a really large sum. It's good to have the paperwork ready for that person to sign.

An LLC has two agreements, usually prepared and bundled together: the operating agreement, and the subscription agreement (often the latter is an appendix of the former). The operating agreement lays out the structure of the company – where it's formed, who the managing members are, what the purpose of the company is, what the budget of the film is, what the risks are, the rights and liabilities of the limited members, etc. The subscription agreement lays out the terms of the subscription or enrollment of the investor in the company.

When an investor hands the LLC a check, s/he is subscribing to or enrolling in the company, and becomes a limited member. This is analogous to buying stock in a company, except that buying more stock doesn't equate to having more control – the investors remain limited in terms of both their actions (they can't take the film away from you) and liabilities (they can't be sued because of your mistakes).

The combined operating/subscription agreement typically runs about 25–40 pages and is full of rather horrifying language describing the risks involved in investing in films. You have to leave this in there but can sometimes ask your attorney to soften it a bit. Most of the investors I've worked with understand the risks before they've signed the checks and don't really need to be told.

As you can imagine, you really can't prepare this document yourself (unless you're a lawyer). This is usually the point at which you'll call upon your attorney to become the production legal counsel on your film. This leads to the chicken-and-egg issue: how do you pay your attorney to start working on the film while you're still trying to raise money for it?

You'll have to go into your pocket and cough up a retainer. This is one reason to set up those lines of credit I mentioned above. The retainer doesn't have to be a huge amount of money. Entertainment attorneys are well-versed in these types of problems and will work out a payment schedule with you. The retainer should be included in the film budget. You can either pay yourself back from the investment pool, or let the retainer become part of your investment in the film.

You'll typically bring your attorney onboard as the production legal for the whole film (so they'll produce most if not all of the contracts you'll need), for either an hourly or flat rate. If you have a "name" in your cast I recommend the flat rate. The amount of time your attorney and the actors' agents will spend passing the cast agreement back and forth will burn hours.

If you're confident that you can handle the more standard contracts (crew and vendor agreements) yourself and you don't have a "name" in your cast, you might be okay with the hourly. But most of the time the hours pile up and you'll pay about the same amount either way.

Self- and Friend-Financing

The LLC is a well-understood structure for financing and producing films. But they can be expensive to set up, and may not be necessary *if*:

1. The only investors are going to be private individuals, and US citizens *and*
2. The budget of the film is really tiny ($30K–$120K) *and*
3. The total number of investors will not rise above that allowed by the laws of your state (in New York, you can only have 70 investors in a single S-Corp).

If all three conditions apply to your situation, then you should consider forming another S-Corp instead. This will require your attorney to fashion a slightly different type of shareholder agreement. In an LLC, leadership is independent of the size of your subscription. In an S-Corp, generally whoever has the most shares gets the most decision-making power. If you're both the filmmaker and the main investor, that's fine, but if you're not, then you don't want to cede control of the film to your biggest investor.

This conundrum can be solved in a number of different ways – through stock ownership (you reserved 51 percent of the shares for yourself and set aside 49 percent for the "public"), or through clauses in the shareholder agreement.

I sometimes think I should have formed an S-Corp for *Found In Time*, because the money that I spent on publications and filing documents would have been better spent on the project itself.

CARE AND FEEDING OF YOUR BUSINESS

There will certainly be times, especially when production gets closer, that you'll have to pay more attention to actually making your film. But during prep, it's important to also put some time aside to think strategically about your business. You need to do three things to keep your business going:

1. Think strategically.
2. Stay on top of your bills and paperwork.
3. Keep up your business "appearance."

Strategic Thought

You can't delegate this to anyone else. But it doesn't have to be a chore. Just spend some time reflecting critically on what you're doing at the moment, and make sure that it lines up with your long-term goals.

Everyone has a different process for doing this. Some people like to keep a big chart up on the wall, others maintain a journal, still others post a to-do list to a cloud app. I like *the weekly meeting* – at least once a week, have a twenty-minute meeting with yourself (and your partner, if you have one) and ask the following questions:

1. **What did I do for the business?** Did you hire a casting director? Look at resumes? Open your bank account? Tweak the script? Make some contacts? Now's the time to brag.
2. **Am I doing anything that will take me further from the business goals?** Did you get sucked up into somebody else's problems? Get distracted by a 12-hour *World of Warcraft* playdate? Procrastinate on something? Now's the time to fess up and see if you can untangle yourself.
3. **Are the business and film in line or out of whack?** In the heat of the moment, it's possible to make a decision that might be good for your film (like signing on a "name") but bad for your business (promising him/her more than you can afford). Alternately, are you spending all your time on your business and not getting a chance to work on the film itself?
4. **Am I putting too much time into my business and neglecting my family/friends/ fun?** You are your primary business asset, at least right now. If you're getting burned out, you need to schedule some fun time. Save your energy and your apologies to friends and family for production.

Limiting the meeting to twenty minutes will keep you from making too big a deal of it. When I had a business partner in my last company, we tended to have this meeting over dinner. Now I usually have this meeting with myself and my cat on Monday evenings. I don't talk out loud (most of the time) but I do think and jot down notes for a good twenty minutes.

Paperwork and Bills

I don't know anyone who actually enjoys working with bills and paperwork, though sometimes I'm very satisfied when I'm *done* handling them and my inbox is empty for that cruelly short time span. Many of us probably went into film because it seemed like a good alternative to shuffling papers across a desk.

In any event, you'll want to find a system of organizing your bills that accomplishes five main objectives:

1. Your bills get paid on time.
2. Your critical papers (like your resale cert) don't get lost.
3. Your personal, development company, and production entity paperwork stays separate.
4. You can find what you need within a couple of minutes at the most.
5. You can maintain this system easily.

You may hit upon the right system immediately, or you might find yourself getting frustrated and having to try other things. Here's what I've done – it may work for you as well.

Go paperless. I signed up for paperless statements for nearly all my bills. This cut down on my clutter ten-fold.

Keep accounts in QuickBooks. I keep all my credit cards and checking accounts in QuickBooks, and download and import the activity files from each card vendor's/bank's website. This took a little setting up but it was very much worth it. Now I let the computer do the boring part of entering and reconciling expenses, and I just categorize them.

Autopay all the way. In exchange for surrendering a little bit of control, I've put all my bills on autopay through either the vendor or my bank. I've avoided a lot of overdue fees and interest rate bumps, and saved myself a few ulcers as well.

Binders for short-term storage. I have one binder for Chaotic Sequence, one for my personal bills and papers, and a third for Found In Time LLC. Each binder is divided into sections, one per bill, bank account, or vendor (like my accountant or cellphone provider). Every other month, I clean out my inbox, sort out the bills, 3-hole punch them, and put them into the appropriate section of the binders.

Receipt envelope. This is for cash and credit card receipts that may be deductible. I empty my wallet about once a month, putting most of the receipts into the envelope. At the beginning of the following year, I go through the envelope and categorize the receipts that are deductible, then put them back, seal the envelope, and start a new one.

File cabinet for long-term storage. Once a binder is full (it usually takes a year or two), it goes into my filing cabinet, where it rarely sees the light of day again. You have to hold onto corporate records for up to ten years and personal records for six. Every couple of years I empty the filing cabinet into a cheap cardboard filing box, label the box with the years (e.g. 2005–2006) of the contents, and put the box away in the closet.

My accountant does my taxes. This is something I just don't have the brainpower for. I keep everything in QuickBooks as best as I can, but especially given the number of returns I have to file (two film production companies, one development company, and one personal), it's too much work to do myself.

Maintaining this system takes me only about two or three hours a month. During preproduction and production, I spend more time on it, but that's pretty normal.

Keeping Up Appearances

This will be covered in more detail in Chapter 5, but it bears some mention here as well. Once you've set up the online and print presence for your business – your LinkedIn, Facebook, Pinterest, and Twitter accounts, website, and your stationery – it's important to keep them updated. Likewise, you'll want to update your bio every few months to reflect the current state of your work. If you surf the net you've probably seen more than a few production company websites with very outdated information, graphics from ten years ago, or broken links.

You may have to delegate this work to a web/print designer, or do it yourself, but don't neglect it for too long. I usually update the Chaotic Sequence home page once a month, and the other pages every couple of months. The *Found In Time* site is updated at least once a month with a new blog entry. The social media accounts are updated anywhere from daily to weekly, depending on how busy things get.

PUTTING IT ALL TOGETHER

Your business is there to serve your creative, career, and financial needs. If you prepare your business properly now you'll be able to focus more energy on your film work later when you'll really need to. Also, the business sense you'll learn now will serve you well throughout your career.

QUESTIONS/EXERCISES

There are no right or wrong answers. The goal is to better understand your film and your work as part of your business.

1. Write down what you consider to be your film work. Are you a writer, director, producer, actor, DP – or a combination of these?
2. What kind of business do you want to be in? Do you want to produce and sell genre films? Dramas? Comedies? Do you see yourself sticking to indie features, or branching out into commercials, webisodes, or other forms? Do you want to make projects for a specific niche audience?
3. How will your current film further your business goals? Will it show off your writing talent? Will it be a way of connecting to the niche audience you identified in #2, or are you aiming for a broader release strategy?
4. Think of some company names. Find the entity search tool of your home state's corporate tax website.
5. If you personally know anyone who's gone through the process of making a feature, call or email him/her up and ask for a little bit of business advice – take him/her out to lunch. You may also get an entertainment attorney referral out of it.
6. Hit up the IFP website (ifp.org) and see if there's a branch near you. You can see if there are any upcoming seminars. Usually they're pretty cheap. Take one and see if you like the crowd and the organizers. It may be worth joining.

## Chapter 4

Working with Other People

FIGURE 4.1 It really does take a village.

COLLABORATION AND LEADERSHIP

As the producer and/or director, you're the leader – the top dog in a hierarchical stack of departments, grouped by expertise. You say it, and it shall be done. At the same time, you're a collaborator, a part of something that's bigger than you, which you also serve as well as orchestrate: the film. Any successful leader knows that she's only as good as the team supporting her. By the same token, the team will take its behavioral and ethical cues from the leader.

By and large, leadership is emphasized over collaboration in our society. While we admire teamwork in sports, business, and filmmaking, we celebrate the director, coach, or CEO. The cult of Steve Jobs is a good example – the man was not a professional programmer, designer, engineer, or even (from what I can tell) a particularly good businessman. He was able to somehow wrangle people from these different disciplines, and get them to work together to create some amazing, game-changing products. But who were the team members (apart from Steve Wozniak)? Can you name any of them? Hopefully, Jobs did.

Communicating with other people, sharing ideas, offering guidance and constructive criticism, instilling an ethos of honesty and accountability, listening to complaints (and following up on them), organizing the efforts of different groups, disciplining troublemakers – these are a few of the things that good leaders do. If you're a little shy, used to working alone, or are not used to leading people, don't worry. Leadership and collaboration are learned toolsets, not inborn traits.

What follows is a crash-course on how to develop leadership skills. It's good to start now, because once you've started hiring people, you won't have a lot of time to get up to speed. We're going to analyze, in a very abbreviated way, what leadership consists of:

1. Preparing yourself for the leadership experience
2. The different styles of leadership
3. What motivates people
4. The five big tasks of leadership
5. Handling group dynamics
6. Applying all this to the real world – hiring, communicating, rewarding, and (sometimes, unfortunately) firing people

The main goal is to be able to lead your team and make the film without becoming either a tyrant or a doormat. In truth, being a leader is like playing a role. You have to understand the needs of the character and of the larger group, then develop a performance that meets those needs.

THE LEADERSHIP EXPERIENCE

The first images a lot of people have of film directors or producers are the classic ones: the director blasts orders into a megaphone while sitting in a high chair. The producer sits behind a very expensive desk and shouts at underlings. We either secretly welcome the idea of becoming that person ("now they'll listen to me!") or promise ourselves never to turn into that kind of leader ("I won't be like those _____s"). Real leadership, however, doesn't require a higher chair or bigger desk. It does require a bit of insight, perspective, and some mental adjustments, especially if you've been a worker bee up until now.

The biggest difference I found was that being a leader *feels* completely different from being a worker. I'd had job responsibilities in the past but nothing that really prepared me for being at the head of a small army.

First, you have to realize that the buck really does stop with you. If something needs to be done and there's no one else around or willing to do it, it becomes part of your job.

Second, you may find leadership to be a lonely task. You may have to make unpopular decisions – like pushing for another hour of work, or going for another take, or asking for last-minute changes to the main character's wardrobe. You may get called names or made fun of behind your back. If you're working with your friends or spouse, the relationship may feel the strain. This is normal. As long as it doesn't get out of hand, a little stress and even name-calling is okay.

Third, you have to divide your time into smaller chunks and distribute your attention when working with other people. You'll have to say "no" or "I'll get to that later" more than you might ordinarily, just to keep your head above water. You'll also have to find a way to balance your own need for concentration with other people's need for your input.

Fourth, you have to disentangle your ego from your film. If you don't, you run the risk of making really bad decisions. History is replete with rulers who brought their countries to financial and social ruin through their big egos: making statues honoring themselves, treating the treasury as their personal wallets, warring with their neighbors to get more land or because their ancestors insulted each other – you get the idea.

On a film I line produced, the director had us build some flywalls inside of an apartment so as to enable him to get a "perfect shot" that had been in his head for a long time. The shot turned out so-so because we didn't really have the money or time to pull it off properly. You have to make decisions that are best for the project, which may mean accepting input from other people, working with the environmental variables you have, and/or giving up on something you really wanted. Usually what you get in return, however, far outweighs whatever you're giving up.

Last, you have to learn how to delegate. You don't want to dump too much on the people who you depend on, but you can't assume responsibility for everything either.

THE MEGA-TASKS OF LEADERSHIP

So what does a leader actually do? The job boils down to five fundamental "mega-tasks." You probably flit between these tasks without knowing it, and most of the time, you don't have to be conscious of which one you're performing.

- **Outline a vision**, in as concrete terms as possible, about the film. In your case, writing the script, the business plan, the budget, the director's vision statement.
- **Attract and align people** to that vision. Attract investors. Hire your crew and cast. Rehearse. Meet with your crew.
- **Help your team** achieve that vision. Provide your crew with the gear, money, and time they need. Make design and budget decisions.
- **Eliminate obstacles.** Pay off the loud neighbors, fire people who are too insubordinate, solve crises as they come up.
- **Stay on track.** A conductor keeps the orchestra in touch with the overall score. You should keep the crew and cast in touch with the film you're trying to make.

All the activities you'll be doing during the shoot should *significantly* advance one or more of these mega-tasks. This is a good sanity check – if you're worrying over fine-grained details, like which bagels you should buy for craft services, you're probably not doing that more important rewrite (this is where delegation comes in).

LEADING THE TEAM

We've talked about adjusting to the experience of leadership, and made it more clear as to what you're actually supposed to do as a leader. So how does this play out in real life? Let's go through the steps of leading the team, starting with you and moving outward.

What You Should Always Be Doing

Be prepared. This is what this book is all about. You will be judged as a leader in large measure by how prepared you are. People will feel more confident of your abilities if they see that you've given thought to the details.

Be on time. If you're late, it gives everyone else permission to be late. If you're late once on set for a good reason, that's one thing, but if you're late every day, that's a problem.

Be calm. Everyone will look to you for emotional cues, whether they admit it or not. Stay calm in the face of problems or challenges, and your cast and crew will as well.

Be communicative. You can have the best plan in the world but if you don't somehow get it across to your cast and crew, there's no chance they'll be able to pluck it from your brain.

Be concise. People are busy. Try to get your point across quickly. Don't go into detail if you don't have to.

Apologize and move on. If you're wrong about something, say you're sorry, fix what you did wrong, and move on. If someone else is wrong, give them the opportunity to apologize but don't dwell on it.

Remember names. I'm terrible at names. I work extra hard to overcome this – I play word association games, try to repeat the name back to the person (this works better than you'd think), and/or write it down if I can. You also want to remember *everyone's* names – the agent's assistant, the receptionist at the camera rental house, the janitor at the location you're shooting at. When you call me by name, it's an acknowledgement that I'm also a person and not just a job function. It makes me want to help you and engage with you as a fellow human being.

Present opportunities, not favors. You're not asking people to do you a favor. You're offering them an opportunity to be part of a good project; to earn a little money; to help their careers; to work with other people who can help them; and/or to invest in an interesting venture.

Be thankful. You're providing people with opportunities, but always let people know – honestly – when they've done a good job.

Be quiet. Anyone can talk. A really good leader knows when to listen. Not just to other people, but also to your own gut instincts. Listening doesn't mean saying yes to everything that everyone wants. But it gives them validation, which is often what they really want in the first place.

Be decisive. Don't get bogged down on small decisions – make them quickly. They can (usually) be reversed if it turns out that you were wrong. If you need a minute, ask for one, but don't freeze up (especially on set). People will lose confidence. This is where being prepared will pay off – most decisions will be easier to make *and*, if necessary, undo.

Be safe. Apart from worker's compensation insurance, most safety measures are pretty cheap. Hire a stunt coordinator, rehearse scenes adequately, make sure people get enough turnaround between days, etc. Apart from practical reasons (like not wanting to fall behind schedule to deal with an accident), demonstrating that you care about everyone's safety will make people feel better about working on your film.

Keep the budget to yourself. Don't show your complete, detailed budget to anyone outside a specific "inner circle." That usually means your partner, attorney, line producer, unit production manager, post supervisor, and production accountant. If an investor specifically asks for a detailed budget, give it to her, but otherwise just hand her the topsheet. Budgets aren't necessarily fair – some departments will be given more money than others – so the last thing you need is to be taken to task or questioned on a given line item. And investors from outside the film industry may not really understand the budget at the detail-level anyway.

What you should do is show each department head its own budget. In the case of the director of photography (DP) and production designer, tell them the budget of *all* the departments that are affected by them as well (for production designers, this would include the art, props, set dressing, set construction, greens, and scenic departments; for the DP, this would include the camera, electric, on-set FX (maybe), and grip departments).

Keep your own emotional council. Part of being at the top is that you can't expect sympathy from the other people on your team. That's one reason it's good to have a partner or a war council. You'll need to have someone you can unburden yourself to.

Leadership Styles

So *how* do you lead other people? We all grew up with authority figures: parents, principals, preachers, teachers, policemen, politicians. Some were very good leaders, others – well, not so much. Unfortunately, it's easier to see where the bad leaders go wrong than see how the good leaders do their work. I've tried to identify a number of leadership "styles." This is a very simplified way to look at things.

By threat. Unfortunately, this is the one we remember too well. You follow a bully around so he won't beat you up. This is probably the least effective way of leading people in the long run, because most people will immediately find ways to circumvent you, quit, or give you the minimum output to keep their jobs.

By virtue of position. This is a variation on what your parents probably told you. "Because I said so, and I'm your mother." This does work sometimes but it should be used sparingly.

By rational argument. You try to build a rational case for what you're asking for. Sometimes people don't need to know the reasons why you're doing what you're doing, or don't care. At other times, it's exactly the right strategy.

By reward. "Because if you do this, we'll get ice-cream afterwards." Who doesn't like ice cream? Paychecks are nice too. A good credit is also helpful. A reward doesn't have to be cash – sometimes it's the chance to work on a great script.

By encouragement. Coaching, mentoring, parenting, and gently pushing people to do their best.

By example. Your teacher showed you how to do it, then asked you to repeat what she just did. Sometimes it's better to show than to tell. Also, your behavior sends out cues as to what's acceptable. If you're consistently 10 minutes late, then it's okay if everyone else is. If you're asking people to jump into the pool, you should be the first one in the water.

By humor. Sometimes telling a good joke and keeping the set light will get everyone off on the right foot. Or being willing to be made fun of.

By experimentation/process. Rather than tell someone to do something, you explore the process together. Try this, or let's go back to that. The effort is collaborative. You make people feel like they're a part of the team rather than a cog in the wheel.

By exhaustion. "I don't care. Do whatever you want."

By delegation. You make people individually responsible for the results or how they get there.

By micromanagement. Also all too common. You tell someone what you want, then check in on them to make sure they're doing it right.

By listening. You lead by asking what others are looking for, finding out how you can fit into their workflow, and adapting to circumstance. Therapists and actors ideally listen more than talk.

Whether you know it or not, you probably have a style you gravitate towards. If you're a bit shy, perhaps you listen more than command. If you're very giving, you probably lavish rewards on people. If you're a little more intellectual, perhaps you explain the hell out of everything.

The best thing is to try and expand your repertoire, and learn how to tailor your styles to different people, circumstances, and states of sleep deprivation. There are definitely times when you need to explain your actions, and others when you need to tell them what you need done and let them figure it out. There are times when you need to encourage people, and others where waving a paycheck or a beer around is exactly what's called for. There are even times when you're going to have to fire or dress down people to keep everyone else in line, but these should be regarded as "nuclear" options.

How do you figure out the right way to lead people in a given situation? Partly, it's a question of listening to them, and figuring out why they came aboard. You can't assume that everyone's in love with your film the way you are. Each group of people (investors, actors, crew, vendors, distributors, agents) has their own motivations and needs.

Leading Your Investors

Film investors are somewhat romantic by nature. It's still pretty damn rare to make your money back on an independent film. Most people invest because they want to be part of something more interesting than a hedge fund. Or because they want to enter the field themselves. Or because they believe in you. As a group, you can say that they're motivated by *adventure* first, then by *money* and maybe *safety*.

Safety? Well, yes. Adventurous people will climb a rope bridge. But not if it's clearly broken. So part of your job will be to sell the adventure of investing in your film without it appearing to be a foolish risk.

Sell the steak. Some investors are really interested in helping you tell your story. They're easy to talk to because you can always come back to the script.

Sell the sizzle. Other investors want to get in on the ground floor of what looks (to most outsiders) like a fun industry. Tell them about the production process, invite them to the set, send them crew t-shirts and/or other paraphernalia.

Talk business. Be prepared to talk in terms of financial projections (remember your business plan).

Stay in touch. Stay in constant contact with your investors, after they've invested in your film. They can help you enormously down the road, often in unexpected ways – they may be able to help you again (financially or otherwise) if they feel that you've taken their contribution seriously.

Leading Your Cast

"Most people run away from intense situations. Repo men run *into* intense situations." This is from Alex Cox's wonderful 1984 film *Repo Men*, and while the character is talking about his profession, he could just as well be talking about actors. Most of us run away from or bury our emotions. The actor's job is to run towards emotion – to get to the truth of their character. This is hard work. Actors need to be treated with some care. They need to feel that they're in a *safe* but *challenging* environment. Ideally, you're something like a coach/fan/good parent. You have to push them to dig deeper, but make it clear that you won't let them look foolish onscreen. Money is secondarily important to the majority of actors because most – over 90 percent – will never be able to live exclusively off their acting.

This applies whether you're the producer or the director, by the way. As a producer, you may have some difficulty dealing with agents, but don't let it spill into your relationship with the actors.

Do your script analysis. As a director, the main way to make the cast feel safe is to do your script analysis before you start casting, so you can feed them raw bits of information for them to chew on.

Talk in terms of process as opposed to results. As the coach, you point them in the right direction but let them work out the destination.

Provide the comforts. As a producer, you'll be keeping the actors safe by providing necessary comforts – a decent holding area, private rooms or at least screens, healthy snacks – and by staying on top of the paperwork with their agents. Don't let them get caught in the vortex of production.

Leading Your Crew

From the crew's perspective, the cast gets the glory – the screen time, the adoration and support of the director, and sometimes a very nice payday. Meanwhile, the crew does all the less than glamorous work. To some extent, they're right. Their motivations are more polyglot. Some will be motivated by a need for *credits* and a *career* jump; others want a *challenge*; still others are *loyal* to their department heads. Generally, the more experienced the crew member is, the more she'll be motivated by *money* and/or the *need to work*. I've taken on jobs that didn't pay well in part because I couldn't stand staring at the walls of my apartment any longer.

To appeal to this rather mixed group, it's best to keep things simple:

Pay everyone on time. This should go without saying, but I can't tell you how many times I've lined up to get my check only to find an excuse from the producer. Nothing will make your crew abandon ship faster than the feeling that they're going to be exploited.

Understand the budget dance. When you're talking to an experienced department head about his/her budget, they will often assume that you're holding something back in case they go over. Or alternately, they'll inflate their cost estimates just a little bit to cover their butts, in case something really does go over what they expect it to.

If you've known the person for a while, you should be honest about what's in the budget, and tell her that "yes, this really is what's earmarked for your department." If you're working together for the first time, it's probably inevitable that you'll be playing the game a little bit. So if the wardrobe budget is really $13,000, tell the costume designer that it's $12,500 – since she's probably assuming that the real number is $14,000 anyway and she's planning to spend $13,000.

Talk in terms of results. For the most part, your crew members know more than you do about their respective disciplines. Just tell them what you want, and let them figure out how to get there. There may be some specific instance where you need to show them how to do something, but it's pretty rare.

Decisions are final. Sometimes it's great to have a spirited, creative debate. On the set of *Bonnie and Clyde*, Warren Beatty and director Arthur Penn argued every day. They liked the conflict and the resulting energy and ideas. But once you've decided on something, you have to bring the conversation or debate to a close. Don't keep it open for further discussion.

Offer to help. Sometimes it's good to get your hands dirty. If there's something that needs carrying, or something that you have skills with, offer to lend a hand. The crew will appreciate it, even if they say no. Sometimes I make the coffee after lunch. Other times I'll take out the garbage. I do this partly because it needs to get done; partly because it sends the message that no one should be above doing the chores; and partly because it genuinely helps cement the relationship between us. Understand that there's a fine line between helping and getting in the way, and that on a union shoot, you may not be allowed to invade someone else's turf.

Delegate. On the other hand, there are times when you really have to split your attention in too many places, and you need to prioritize. It may take a couple of days of working with your crew before you know who you can delegate what tasks to.

Leading Your Vendors

You might not think of vendors as being part of your team, but they are. A good vendor can help you out of technical jams, refer crew folk your way, and in rare cases invest in your film (either in kind or in cash). On the other hand, leaving a bad taste in a vendor's mouth can spoil your future relationship with them.

Listen to your crew. DPs and gaffers typically have a "short-list" of vendors they like. It's good to get quotes from these vendors. But do your own research as well. Their vendors may not be competitive on price initially, or may not want to work with you if you're too small for them.

Find the go-to guy. In every shop, there's someone who's been there for a while, who knows the ins and outs of the place. Find out who that person is.

Tell them they have some competition. You don't have to be rude, but you can mention that you're taking bids from multiple sources. That can sometimes get them to reduce their quotes.

Service has value. When you're comparing vendors and quotes, you should think about the hidden cost of bad customer service/repair. There's one company I tend to rent camera gear from pretty consistently, even though they're a little more expensive. The reason is that their tech staff know how to prep camera packages properly, are quick to answer questions, have saved my bacon out in the field a few times, and so ultimately kept me from losing time (and therefore money) on set.

Look out for the long term. Squeezing every drop of profit from your vendor's quote will not endear you to them when you come back for your next project. At some point, you have to decide whether the deal is damaging your long-term relationship – and whether that matters.

Leading Your Distributors/Agents

Distributors can't be "led" the same way you lead your crew and cast. They're bigger than you, and they're in a different business altogether – they license intellectual properties (either scripts or completed films), repackage them, market them to consumers, and sell the experience of watching them. It's often too onerous for them to actually make films. They have essentially "outsourced" that task to you, the producer.

The best way to lead distributors is to prepare for their eventual presence in your life. Don't wait for them to come up with artwork and a marketing campaign. If you know the market for your film, start communicating to that market right away (we'll talk about this in the next chapter). Start figuring out now what the deliverables for your film might be, and make sure to include as many of them as possible in your budget.

Jon Reiss, in his seminal book *Think Outside the Box Office*, argues that filmmakers need to budget 50 percent of their financing towards marketing and distribution. While this is a tall order and probably out of reach for a lot of indie filmmakers, it's a clear sign as to what you should expect from a distributor (that is, not much).

Research distributors. This can be difficult because of the shifting distribution landscape. In the year or two it will take you to make your film, some of these distributors will go under, change focus, or get absorbed by other companies. Is there a distributor that handles films in the same genre as yours? Who have you heard good things about?

Sales agents and producer's reps are somewhat different animals. Sales agents represent films at markets, taking a bundle of them and trying to get different distributors in different media windows to license them. So you have sales agents that only take narrative films to TV markets, others that specialize in foreign sales, still others that work more with docs, and so on. Their compensation is tied to how much they can sell your film for, so they have more direct incentive to get you a better deal. Sales agents are empowered to make deals on your behalf.

Producer's reps, on the other hand, are more like advisors. They take some compensation up-front, and a commission on any sales. They too specialize and have particular tastes. They pitch your film to distributors, and work with you to get the best deal for the film (which may not always be the most lucrative). They can also help you navigate the festival circuit, recommend sales agents, and generally give you good advice on distribution. Producer's reps have a longer-term stake in you as a client.

On the surface, it looks as though the sales agent, by virtue of having a more direct incentive, will get you a better deal. But consider that a "better" deal on paper could be costly in other ways. An exclusive deal with a small cable company in Germany that blocks you out of other territories, or streaming sales, may mean more money in your pocket now, but missed opportunities later. And a producer's rep, by virtue of thinking long-term, may help you make connections that won't be as remunerative but could result in more widespread distribution or a solid connection.

In either case, you lead these folks by spelling out what your ideal goals are for the film. You also lead them by preparing your deliverables and your marketing materials ahead of time.

Leading Your Advisors

Your advisors are your war council, as well as your friends, family, mentors, and other people in your "inner circle" who you confide in. These are the folks whose support is essential, and yes, you have to lead them as well.

The first thing is to be picky about who enters your inner circle. You don't want people who are dealing with a lot of drama in their lives, or who are out to pursue conflicting agendas. This doesn't mean you cut off all contact with your crazy friend who's great to hang out with – it just means that maybe he's not the person you talk to when there's a crisis. Even if he knows *a lot* more about filmmaking than you do.

The second thing is to cherish and honor the folks who are in your inner circle. This does not require grand gestures. Buy your best friend a book. Take your spouse out to dinner just before you start serious preproduction. Most of all, stay in touch with these folks throughout the process, even when you don't need them. And be ready for them when they need you.

These are all common-sense suggestions, but they can be quickly forgotten as you head into preproduction. More and more of your time will be consumed by the film, so devote some free time before this happens to making your advisors happy.

GROUP DYNAMICS

During the course of the shoot, you'll be assembling a team of investors, cast, crew members, supporters, advisors, vendors, and even sales/distribution people. To make these disparate individuals work together as a team, you'll create a structure for them. You'll want to aim for a "gestalt" – a particular combination of size, experience level, money, energy, and material – that will best serve the film. Having a million free interns running around sounds great on paper but doesn't work all that well in practice. Neither does having a lot of grumpy veterans, or a domineering director of photography. Here's a way to look at the group structure and consciously aim for creating the right one for the film.

The Group Structure

On paper, a film shoot is like a military company. The executive producer sits on top, followed by the producer, then the director. The director and producer both have department heads who report to them, with some "cross-reporting" going on. The department heads, in turn, are responsible for their staff. Let's call this organization a "nested hierarchy" (Figure 4.2).

The degree of rigidity or formality in this organization – how well-defined the roles are, how many people per department, etc. – is determined by the budget, script, and what the director and producer want out of the project. Smaller crews are like family. Larger crews are like a small corporation. Each has their advantages. I typically group the film crew into one of three "categories":

Run and gun. This is my personal favorite, and a very good choice for $200K-and-under films. The crew should be no larger than 14–15 people. The gear fits into *one* truck (preferably one van). Every department will be understaffed and each department head should help the others out. The cast understands that they may have to "rough it" a bit (most are pretty game). The producers and director have to make decisions quickly, and elaborate camera/art department/lighting work may stretch everyone a bit thin. The shoot is three weeks long, tops; preferably two plus. "Non-essential" positions are eliminated.

30-man team. This is my *least* favorite, because there's usually just enough money around to get everyone to thinking that there's more. The shoot length is 4–5 weeks, and the cast and scripts are generally bigger (with more locations as well). The gear takes up four cube trucks and possibly a fleet of smaller vehicles. You need good people in the production and locations departments to support the rest of the crew; but these departments are often understaffed to make room in the budget.

The real shoot. The crew is 60–80 strong, which is still not enough somehow. But now you can go to more places, build more stuff, and burn more money. Your production staff will need to be experienced enough to support the other departments. You'll have between five and ten trucks, depending on what you're doing and where you're going. Day-playing gear and personnel is essential to staying on budget. You'll be able to attract more experienced people in the crew, and the cast will feel a little better taken care of. The crew positions are more specialized.

As you can see, with each group comes different challenges. A small crew can usually respond more quickly, but can also run out of resources. If your entire art department is one person, they can't really prep tomorrow's set. The danger of a larger shoot is that the logistical tail ends up wagging the creative dog – last-minute script changes, improvisations, or any kind of change in plan can throw the crew for a loop.

Informal Roles Within the Group

In any given group, you'll see some people take on particular informal "roles." Some are positive, but others can be quite dangerous to the project. Some of the more obvious roles are:

The go-to guy. This person has all the answers. Maybe they have more experience than anyone else on the crew. Or they're in a position that lends itself to this role (like being the production manager). If they're genuinely doing it for the film, that's great – the best thing you can do is

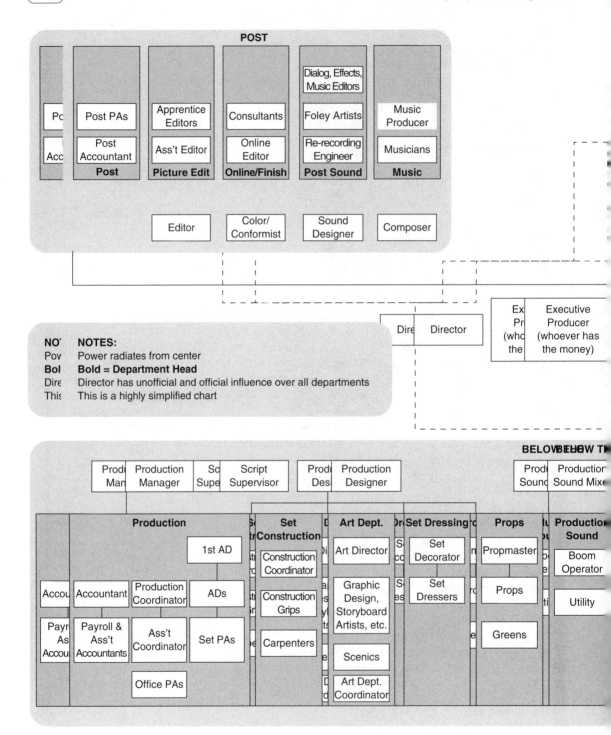

FIGURE 4.2 The hierarchy of a film shoot.

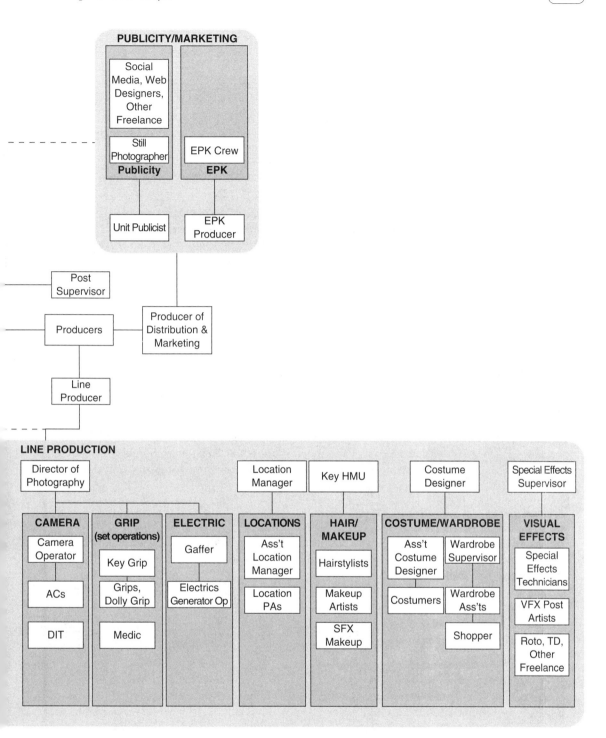

help this person out. If the person occupying this role is really an *alpha* (see below), then you'll have to watch them carefully. Also, if you're the director, you want the cast to turn to you, not the go-to guy.

The fool/joker. Someone is always cracking jokes and being a smart-ass. Every crew should have a joker. It helps leaven the mood a bit and can relieve tension. As long as the joker takes their actual job seriously and doesn't offend anyone, leave this person alone. One exception: making fun of the cast is not cool, unless it really is in good humor and the cast member(s) are okay with it.

The straight man. This is probably you. You'll find yourself the butt of a few well-meaning jokes. Just roll with it and play it for laughs.

The hardass. This person takes everything seriously and won't be messed with. They're willing to be a bit unpopular in order to get things done. This could be you, or it could be your 1st AD (better that it's her). This person may need some "tenderizing" if her attitude is too off-putting.

The spaced-out/slacker/problem child. This is someone who somehow never does the whole job, does it late, does it badly, or just doesn't listen very well to directions. There are several different ways of dealing with this person. You can try to mentor them, put them where they can do the least harm, or fire them.

The alpha/troublemaker. In every group, there's at least one person who resents the hell out of the system, who thinks they can do a better job than you can, or who thinks they're doing you a favor. Jealousy and envy are natural feelings. I've certainly experienced them when line producing other people's films. What counts are actions. Is the person being really insubordinate? Are they challenging you in a non–productive way, or making a point of embarrassing you or making things difficult in general? Warn the person (privately), wait for improvement, and be prepared to fire the person if there isn't any.

These roles are dynamic, and one person may play several at once. If the group is working well as a whole, then you don't need to worry too much about who's doing what. Sometimes it's best to stay out of the way of whatever drama is happening between the crew members. Other times, it's best to intervene (if one person is bullying another).

SOME REAL-WORLD EXAMPLES

At this point you should have some very abstract, fundamental ideas of what leadership entails. To make this more concrete, let's discuss – briefly – three real-world examples of how leadership comes into play.

Hiring Your DP

We'll get into this more in Chapter 16, but your DP is perhaps your most critical crew hire. A lot of filmmakers are seduced by a pretty reel, only to end up in production hell because they really didn't spend enough time getting to know the DP.

I went through this on my first feature, *Caleb's Door*. My producer and I hired a DP who had done some very impressive work on a tight budget. But after three days of working together, it was clear that we weren't a good fit for each other. The producers and I fired him and replaced him with a much better DP, Ben Wolf, who I'm still working with all these years later. This cost me a day of shooting and some money from the budget (since we had to pay some kill fee money to the first DP). So consider this position carefully.

Bring more materials to the interview. Bring visual aids – stills, paintings, picture books, clips from other films, sketches – to the interview.

Ask and then listen carefully. Listen to her feedback on the script, the visual aids, and the characters. A few questions you can use:

1. Was there anything that visually popped out at you about the story?
2. Do you see a shooting style in your head?
3. Can you tell me about (this clip from your reel)?
4. Tell me about your last few camera crews – how big were they?
5. How many pages a day do you feel comfortable shooting?
6. Do you enjoy the storyboarding process?

On independent shoots, you often have to move fast, play loose with the storyboards, and accomplish a lot with a small crew. Some DPs are comfortable with this; others really like to work slower and more methodically and will resist you (sometimes mightily) on set when you push for faster results. Better to find this out now.

Talk about movies. Your ideal DP has an encyclopedic knowledge of movies. Ben is a film buff from way back before he even started shooting (I've bugged him to write a book on early Russian cinema). It's very easy to communicate with someone who has roughly the same references as you, and it will give you both a way of recognizing if you've done something that's been repeated *too* many times.

Talk about directors. You might want to ask her about other directors she's worked with (what did you like about working with "X"?), or what she thinks of directors you like. What you want to listen for is the *character* of the answers rather than the substance. Does the DP continually rag on past directors? Do you detect resentment in her tone? A little frustration is okay. A lot could indicate trouble.

Challenge her. If the DP says something you don't agree with, try to get into it a little bit. Ask, "why do you say that?" or "what do you mean?" What you want to know is how she handles push-back from you, and how flexible or opinionated she is. Sometimes friction can be creative, other times destructive. Someone who's passionate about their craft will often defend it vociferously, but do they also respect you and your craft?

Do you have chemistry? This is something you know right away, but then spend a lot of time rationalizing about later. Can you envision working next to this person for 12–14 hours per day? You don't have to be friends or even particularly like each other, but you do have to have a comfortable working relationship, one where you have each other's backs.

Handling Conflict on Set

Filmmaking is hard work, and is done by people who are creative, passionate, and sleep-deprived. This is a recipe for conflict. Some is good, some is bad.

Good conflict is when you're arguing about the approach to a particular shot, or about some technical detail. You want to frame it one way, the DP disagrees, you both talk about the various options, and the AD turns red and notes that this is taking too long. An actor resists your direction and does something you don't like. Usually, you just haven't been specific enough or you're not seeing the scene the same way. So you go back and forth for a bit about it until you see eye to eye.

Make your case but keep your voice level and your body language open (don't slouch or turn away from the person). Consider that the other person may be right. Or you're right, but you haven't explained things well enough. These creative differences can make magic happen. If there's time, try it both ways. Or is there a third path that will combine both approaches?

In bad conflicts people get personal, or bring their internal issues out into the open. If someone starts trying to embarrass or contradict you in a way that makes you appear weak, *don't respond in kind*. Ask politely if you can table the conversation for a bit, or take it somewhere private. If you're a spectator – if the argument is between two people on your team – break it up and tell them to pick it up later on.

Don't have arguments in front of the rest of the crew. If you lose you look weak, and if you win you look like a bully, since you have more power to begin with. If your partner wants to argue with you, *definitely* take it off set. Whenever I see producers and directors arguing with each other I immediately start thinking about how fast I can get my last check or my out-of-pocket reimbursement – just in case the shoot goes to hell.

Once you're in private, argue about *the film*.

Frame the bad behavior or issue in terms of how it's hurting the film, not you. Stress how valuable the person is and how you're sure there's a way to solve this. Don't make it about you, even if the person is insulting you. If it's an actor, he may be taking it out on you because you're their confidant. If it's a crew member, it could be because he's green and needs a little encouragement. In either case, your first response should be supportive and get the focus back on the film.

Don't fall back onto the "director's rule" (the "because I said so") argument unless you feel it's absolutely the only way the person is going to get back to work. Some people respond *only* to the assertion of authority. You generally don't want to work with these people, because filmmaking, at its heart, should be a more "gentle exercise" in authority. While there are plenty of dictatorial directors, they're either backed by more amenable producers, or pay people very well (this is supposedly the case with James Cameron), or have a really solid track record, which attracts talent. As a newcomer, you're not in a position to treat people badly.

Firing People

I've only had to do this a few times in all the years I've been line producing and directing. It's never much fun but it's often saved a shoot from going off the deep end. In the few cases where I've held back, I've always regretted it. So when's it a good idea to do this, and how do you do it? And is there anyone that shouldn't be fired?

First off, save this "nuclear option" for last. Second, you have to separate your ego from the equation. If the DP is challenging you on all your decisions in a bad way, or is deliberately sabotaging your shoot (Tom DiCillo talks about this with regard to the first DP on *Johnny Suede*), you have to replace him. If you just don't get his sense of humor or he's a bit shy or domineering but is delivering great material, then find a way to work together. You don't have to be friends with everyone you work with.

Finally, you have to consider the negative effects of keeping the person on, versus those of firing him. If you fire the person, will you lose money, financing (if it's a "name" cast member), time spent finding a replacement, and possibly additional crewmembers (out of loyalty)? On the other hand, will keeping him aboard create too much tension on set, will you fall behind schedule, and – the acid test – will the end results be inferior?

The best way to fire someone is to do it quickly, explain as little as possible, and do it at the end of the day. This limits the amount of damage the person can do. I think it's better to fire someone in private, but you may want to have your partner or line producer with you. This second person can act as a circuit-breaker in case the firing turns into an argument.

If the "firee" works in a department, then the department head should do it or both of you should talk to the person together. Generally, you want to let the department heads deal with their own staff.

If possible, pay the person out for the day. Don't be stingy about a kill fee (usually the deal memos I do spell out an additional day or the remainder of the week). If the person owes the film something – footage on a drive, petty cash, etc. – make sure to collect it by the end of the day.

The following day, some crew members will be happy about your decision, and others will think you're a monster. The best thing to do is simply to say that "X" is no longer part of the film. Don't discuss the reasons. It's probably obvious to everyone anyway.

THE MYSTERY OF OTHER PEOPLE

Working with other people, and especially leading them, is quite an undertaking. And most of this chapter has dwelled on the challenges, which may make it less appealing. Working with other people can be an absolute joy, and can make the film better. Even if you could do everything yourself, you would be missing out on what other people contribute – their individual tastes and artistry. When you really appreciate and nurture these tastes, the film grows – and you grow as a person as well. Just be as prepared as possible. People respect directors and producers who know the material and their craft.

QUESTIONS/EXERCISES

1. Take a group that you work with often – your department at your day job, your class, your family, etc. Who's playing which of the roles that are mentioned above?
2. Practice pitching your film to friends who will be honest with you.
3. Practice listening. This is harder than you think. The next time you're engaged in a conversation, ask questions, and "mentally tag" the answers. Try to write down the gist of the conversation later on.

## Chapter 5

Marketing

FIGURE 5.1 Your film as a brand.

You need to start marketing your film as soon as you have a completed, polished script. For better or worse, you can't simply make a great film. You're competing with too many other people who are attempting the same thing. To stand out to investors, agents, cast, crew, sales agents, reps, and distributors, you have to convince *them* that it's a great film.

At first glance, marketing seems about as important to filmmaking as the color of your toothbrush is to your teeth. It's window dressing. In one sense, this is true – marketing is about coming up with an enticing skin, so as to make the prospective consumer buy the car, toothbrush, or film. It sometimes bears absolutely no resemblance to the interior of the thing being marketed. But on the other hand, it's how you communicate about your film to the outside world, and so it's vitally important.

Distributors, just like record labels, promised artists that in return for forfeiting a good chunk of their possible profits, they'd take care of the marketing. Distributors organized ad campaigns, merchandise tie-ins, contests, trailers, press releases, junkets, and special events, then deducted the cost from any future profits.

Independent filmmakers can't count on that kind of support anymore. The larger distributors have retreated to their core businesses, which is making broad-appeal "tentpole" films. They perceive that it's too expensive and risky for them to promote more than a handful of "smaller" films that, at best, will not earn more than their expenses back.

Smaller distributors have stepped into the breach, and the array of distribution options (video on demand, cable, streaming, Blu-Ray, micro-cinema) has grown. The problem is that these smaller distributors have smaller budgets for marketing, so more of the burden falls on the filmmaker.

But even a large distributor isn't going to help you much if you didn't plan out your marketing from the beginning. Did you get production stills on set? Do you have a press kit? Do you know what genre your film is? Do you have a poster? If you don't have your materials lined up by the time you start approaching distributors, you're going to have to spend more time and money chasing these elements down.

So, you have to be responsible for marketing your own film. What does this mean, exactly?

THE MARKETING PROCESS

Marketing consists of using several elements in conjunction with each other to find, inform, and motivate a group of people (or companies). Hopefully, this target group goes from being passive to doing something about your film. When you're marketing to investors, hopefully they turn into check writers. When you're marketing to distributors, one of them will turn around and license your film. And when you're marketing to your ultimate audience – the folks who'll watch your film – they'll click on the link, order it, and watch it. The success of your marketing, then, can be measured by what percentage of your audience turn into active participants.

This is *very hard* work. Jon Reiss, Sheri Candler, Peter Broderick, and a few other producers in recent years have argued that it merits the creation of a relatively new crew position, the Producer of Marketing and Distribution (PMD). I don't dispute their wisdom, but even if you hire or partner with someone to fulfill this role, you're still in charge of giving them good material.

So, let's look at each link in the marketing chain:

1. **Elements.** Your script and business plan are the first marketing document (as we discussed in Chapter 2), when you're primarily marketing to investors. Production stills, press kits, a website, a social media presence, trailers, artwork, special events, press releases, and other elements will become more important later on.
2. **Coordination.** You have to make sure that all these elements are sending out the same message about your film. This could also be called "branding" or "identity establishment." You want to make sure that your artwork matches up, your synopses are consistent, and that you're using each element in a consistent, clear way.
3. **Audience.** The group you're marketing to will change over time. At first, you should focus on finding investors (this includes crowdfunders, and people who are donating in-kind services – more on crowdfunding below). Later, cast and crew. Later still, distributors, film festivals, agents, and reps. From day one, though, you should be trying to build a fanbase – people who can carry the word about the film to their friends. Guy Kawasaki, the original Apple evangelist, called this "finding the cult."

Apple is the exemplar of great marketing. Ask an Apple fanboy why he pays a premium for a tablet computer or a smartphone, and he'll point to the logo. Apple was always great at finding the pundits, critics, and bleeding-edge users and making them into true believers.

In building your audience for a given film, you're also – hopefully – creating the cult that will spread the word about your *next* film.

Over the next few sections, we'll talk in more detail about what you'll need to do to set up your marketing campaign so that, by the time you go into production, you'll have a good foundation.

A Special Note on Crowdfunding

Crowdfunding is a relatively new phenomenon that is already having a big impact on the independent film world, so it bears a special note here before we plow further along. Simply put, crowdfunding is a method by which you raise money from a large group of people (rather than going after individual investors). These people donate small amounts (from $10 to $1000) and, in most cases, become donors and fans rather than investors. The actual process is administered by crowdfunding sites, which take a commission on the donations. You set up a page for your film, put your marketing materials on it, and then use every means at your disposal (emails, Facebook, Twitter, etc.) to drive people to the page. The tacit understanding is that you will reward your donors with some kind of goodies (a name in the credits, a copy of the DVD, a t-shirt, etc.), and keep in touch with them as your film progresses.

There are currently three big players in the crowdfunding world – IndieGogo, Kickstarter, and RocketHub – and each have their advantages and disadvantages. By the time you read this, there will probably be a few more companies making a go at it. Crowdfunding is a great way to raise small amounts of cash but isn't really a good "A" plan for financing your entire film. When you factor in the costs of setting up your crowdfunding page, the commissions you'll have to pay on any donations received, and the costs of any of the swag you've promised, you won't make very much money. And you'll be competing against bigger-name directors.

It is, however, a great way to connect to fans. Think of it almost like a DVD pre-ordering model. If you do it right you can have the campaign pay for itself and raise awareness for the film.

The keys to managing your crowdfunding campaign are:

1. Keep the amount to be raised small (no more than $5000 per campaign).
2. Keep the campaign length short (30 days).
3. Understand the commissions that each service charges:
   Each one takes a percentage of the donations.
   The charge vendors (PayPal, Amazon Payments, etc.) also take a processing fee.
4. Update your pages as often as possible with all the content you developed for the other media.
5. Reach out to people as often – but as gently – as possible. You don't want to end up in people's spam folders, but you don't want them to forget about your campaign, either.

If you approach this as a fan-building exercise and not as a financing strategy, crowdfunding can actually work well for you. And some people have raised their entire budgets using it.

Setting Up Your Marketing Process

Before you build a site, start a blog, make a poster, or tweet away like crazy, you have to answer these key questions:

What is my film about? Can I pitch it in two or three sentences? Spend some time thinking about this, go back to the script, and figure out why you wanted to write it in the first place (or option it, if it's not your own script). Imagine you have to tell someone what the movie is about, and you only have a short trip in an elevator to do it in (this is called the "elevator pitch" technique).

You can't build a good marketing campaign until you answer this fundamental question. You can, however, refine the answer over time. After all, the film you make is not necessarily the one you wrote. So don't feel too much pressure to get it right on the first try.

What genre is it in? There are people who argue that genre is dead, and in many ways, it was always a somewhat artificial marketing shortcut. People want to see stories that (a) give them more of what they know, and/or (b) show them something new. These are not mutually exclusive needs. Genre serves as a convenient labeling tool. Is your film a zombie movie, a gay romance, a musical; or some combination of these? Drama and comedy also have genres or subgenres – a comedy can be romantic, stoner, bromantic, buddy, and/or dark. A drama can be a coming-of-age story, a dysfunctional family tale, a period piece … the list is endless. The more you can pinpoint the genres that your script belongs to, the better.

What is the ultimate audience for it? Who wants to see your film? Who has the same sensibilities as you? If you answer "all humankind" then you're being too general. If you answer "white straight single atheist males 25–27 with brown hair and glasses" you're probably being too specific. You probably have some idea, just based on your tastes and those of your friends, of who would want to watch your movie. You can get a little more specific by figuring out who watches similar movies or TV shows. This can take some digging and may not be 100 percent accurate.

Genre is a big help here. You can define your audience in large measure by genres. Who did you make the film for? "Zombie movie aficionados." If you wrote a gay romance zombie musical, you might be able to target a number of audiences. Be aware, however, that audiences are not necessarily additive in nature – the intersection of zombie movie fans, gay romantics, and musical lovers might be fairly small.

My first film, *Caleb's Door*, was originally written as a horror film, then eventually turned into more of a drama with a few spooky moments. This unfortunately had the side effect of making it a more difficult film to market. The dramatic film festivals didn't like it much – they thought it was too mainstream. The horror film festivals wanted more gore. Because there are some faith "elements" in it, a few faith-oriented distributors were interested in it. But that had never been my target market, and ultimately I don't think that audience would have appreciated it anyway.

My new film, *Found In Time*, was always meant to be a fantasy/time-paradox movie. I figured out who among my friends would like these kinds of films, and also asked them about other films they'd seen lately with similar themes. A few titles kept popping up – *Primer, Pi, Source Code, 12 Monkeys*. Doing some research revealed that these films tended to appeal to young males, about 18–35; some of the actors seemed to have broader appeal (women like Brad Pitt and Jake Gyllenhaal, apparently). I looked at IMDbPro and BoxOfficeMojo, read *Variety* and *MovieMaker* articles, and asked some fellow sci-fi/fantasy fans to weigh in.

I can't emphasize this last part enough. If you want to find out who likes your film, try pitching it to someone you think is a "typical" audience member. I know a lot of sci-fi/fantasy/role-playing/comics geeks (and am one myself), so it wasn't hard to find a few people to talk to and pitch the story to. Most of them thought it was solid, and a few later became my first crowdfunders.

Once you've figured out the answers to these first three questions, write them down somewhere. Congratulations: you've just formed the backbone of your marketing strategy. You may have to revise your answers later on, depending on how the film ultimately turns out, but at least you've got a plan of attack.

THE PRIMARY ELEMENTS OF MARKETING

With your first three questions answered, you can put your first marketing materials together. These will include:

1. A longer synopsis of the film
2. Bios of you and whoever's aboard your team at this point
3. Concept art – this can be photos, video, illustrations
4. A teaser. This can consist of practically anything, as long as it tells the audience something about your film. A lot of filmmakers shoot pitches, intercut with some graphics and theme music
5. A "vision statement" about why you wrote and want to shoot the script
6. A short blurb about your ongoing production company
7. Decent headshots of yourself and your team
8. Some metawords that describe your film
9. Your email list

From these primary elements, you'll then assemble:

1. Your business plan
2. A "pitch" slideshow or document (this is sometimes part of the business plan, sometimes separate)
3. A preliminary poster
4. A press kit
5. Preliminary storyboards (possibly?)
6. The film's website
7. Your ongoing production company's website
8. The Facebook page for the film
9. Your LinkedIn profile
10. Your Twitter account
11. Any "guest" accounts/blogs/sites that you're going to take part in
12. Your crowdfunding page (if you're going this route)
13. Your YouTube and Vimeo channels
14. Your e-newsletter

These elements will change over time. You'll have to update your bio and vision statement as you go. As team members come aboard (and others drop out), you'll have to keep their bios current as well.

All this activity *can* also inform your creative work on the film. Some of the concept art will make it into your director's "look-book" (see Chapter 7). And just thinking about these things will sharpen your understanding of the script. So while it seems like a giant distraction, it can be a great boon.

It will take you some time to put all these elements together. Writing a good bio is especially hard. Study other business plans and hit up production company websites to see their marketing efforts.

Let's wade into each of these primary elements.

The Longer Synopsis

You'll want to create two synopses of the script: one that's about 150 words long, and another that's about one page (400–450 words).

The shorter version should basically just expand on your one-to-two sentence pitch. For *Found In Time*, my short pitch was:

> Chris is a psychic who compulsively collects seemingly random objects. Every item he finds today will be needed by someone tomorrow. His gift makes him slip randomly between the past, present, and future. But then he commits a murder in the future. Can he alter his present to prevent it?

So my longer synopsis was:

> *Found In Time* is a fantasy set in an "altered" present-day New York City. Psychics with real powers sell their "wares" on the street, marginalized by society and closely monitored by the dreaded Psychological Police Corp (the "Psychcops"). They lead dark, lonely lives, plagued as much as aided by their gifts.
>
> Our hero, Chris, is a psychic "collector." He compulsively picks up the things most of us throw away or forget – pens, coins, lighters, keys, stones, and other detritus – and sells them to passersby. But every object he picks today will have meaning for someone in the future.
>
> His gift comes with a big downside, however – he experiences his life out of order, "slipping" between the past, present, and future. Chris tries to live a "normal" existence. But when he commits murder in the future, he realizes he has to alter his present in order to prevent it. But how can he do that when he's not even sure of *what time it is?*

What you want to get across is:

1. Genre
2. Basic plot
3. Main character and his/her plight

The shorter you can make it without losing the essence of the film, the better. Be prepared to write a few drafts. I've found that saying the 150-word and 400-word synopses out loud helped a lot.

Bio

Your bio should be no more than one page long. You may want to write a shorter version (a couple of sentences) that will serve as a "byline," but tackle the longer one first.

What should go in your bio? Start with your job description. "XX is a writer/director/producer." What have you made to date? Include that here. Have you won any awards or gotten any recognition (this could include being a finalist in a screenplay competition, having something you worked on in another capacity go to Sundance, and/or participating in a lab)? Definitely include these. Done anything exciting with your life that might be relevant? If you've written a script about mountain climbing and you're a climber yourself, include this as well.

Where did you go to school? This is less important than you'd think but if it was to an Ivy League institution, definitely highlight it.

Any other relevant experience? Have you mostly worked on other people's films, or (if you're still in school) do you TA? How are your technical skills? Have you written articles on or taught any courses in filmmaking? If you already have a production company, what has it produced?

If you're at the very beginning of your career, you may not have a huge list of credits to trot out. That's not a deal-breaker, however. You can always list any other projects that you're working on or have written; just list them as being "in development." If you've worked as a PA on other people's shoots, you can include those or the studios/distributors that were involved.

When I first graduated from film school, I worked on pretty much any kind of project I could get. For the first year or so I flitted back and forth between being a camera operator on low-budget live event tapings, to working as a PA on bigger shoots, to doing video tech for off-off-Broadway theater pieces. My resume was a mess, so I simplified it. "Arthur has worked in various job capacities for ABC, NBC, The Knitting Factory" etc. … Just listing the "big name" channels and companies opened a few doors. Once I'd done a few consistent jobs as a line producer on some shorts, I started putting those credits first, and pushed the PA ones down. Eventually I took out older credits that weren't applicable anymore. You may have to develop multiple versions of your bio that emphasize different skills.

Cajole the other members of your team into giving you their bios. Some folks are better at writing these than others, so be prepared to do a little copyediting. In the best of possible worlds, some of your team will be able to coach *you* with your bio.

Concept Art

A good artist steals a little. A great artist steals a lot. In the quest to be original, we often ignore the enormous resources at our disposal – thousands of years of art and writing, nearly two centuries of stills (with different technologies), over a hundred years of film, sixty-plus years of television. Reproductions of that material are often just a few Google searches and downloads away.

Do you have an idea of what your characters look like? Is there a location in the script or key prop that might make a great poster? Are there paintings or sculptures that capture some of your themes? (Spielberg often references paintings when conferring with his DP, Janusz Kaminski.) Are there other films whose aesthetics you admire?

If you can't find something, create it. I take my inexpensive digital still camera out and shoot landscapes, or set up poster shots on the fly in my office. Some directors I know have hired or begged their friends to pose for poster shots and "tableaus" from the film. Using a combination of clip art, stills found online, and original content, you can create just about anything.

Create or find some music that can convey your themes as well. Resolution is important since you'll be editing these tracks later – if you rip CDs then save them to the highest quality format you can get. If you create the tracks from scratch, save them to WAV files. If you download MP3 files, try to find ones with a 128Kbps or better bitrate.

What you ultimately want to end up with is:

1. About ten to twelve great stills
2. A few video clips
3. A few songs
4. Some possible fonts for use in the title

Keep in mind that you'll want to get your hands on the best-quality files you can, because you'll be manipulating and recompressing the work for different media (print and web) and in various sizes. The end of this chapter includes a quick guide to the differences between web and print graphics, and some suggestions for how to get the best results when acquiring images for both.

Vision Statement

Once you have your concept art together, you'll want to write a brief (1–2 pages of text plus concept art) statement about how you intend to actually shoot, post, and market the script. This should convey both the artistic ideals and business goals you're aiming for. You may have to write a few versions of this for different audiences – your cast and crew will want to know about the creative aspects, your investors might want to know more about the business goals.

Study other art (in whatever media) that you're inspired by. What is it about how the artist(s) put together the work that you find so compelling? How would you shoot the same story? Genre, again, is a great help here, because you can use or break with its conventions, but everyone (at some level) understands how those conventions work. Ultimately, the reader should be inspired to be a part of the film.

Your Company

You had to spend some time pondering this in Chapter 3, but now you should write down a one-to-two paragraph blurb describing what your ongoing production company has done, what you aim to accomplish in the film world, and what your next projects are. If your company is new, include any work that you were a key partner on (writer, director, or producer). Include any future projects that are in your bio. You want your company to come off as a viable enterprise.

You may be exaggerating somewhat, but in truth you're just projecting forward a few years. A lot of thriving businesses started out in a garage or bedroom or basement. You want to communicate your dreams and the energy you have for achieving them.

Headshots

These are a must. You usually want two shots: a close-up of you looking in profile or straight at the camera, and a wider shot of you doing something film-related. The classic looking-through-the-viewfinder shot never gets old, even though directors and producers rarely do this. Watching the monitor with headphones is a good one. I've had a few over the years, depending on my weight, beard level, and experience. Again, get the highest-resolution digital files you can.

Teaser

Since you haven't actually shot the film yet, it's obviously going to be a bit difficult to put together a true trailer or even "teaser" as those things are typically defined. What I recommend you do is to put a "sexy" title sequence together, using some of your concept art, and add some interview footage of yourself and whoever else is on your team. What you want to express in the interviews are:

1. The pitch
2. Your background; stress any kind of recognition you've received for past work
3. Some excerpts from your vision statement
4. Something about the visual style you're aiming for
5. A broad outline of your target audience

Add some of the theme music you created or found as part of your concept art. Set the titles in one of the fonts you found. And you'll want to keep this teaser to six minutes or less, preferably a lot less.

Metawords

You want to come up with a list of ten to twenty metawords, keywords, or tags (a single tag can be multiple words, e.g. "romantic comedy"), that describe the genre, themes, lead characters, people involved, and anything else you can think of that might be related to your film. For *Found In Time*, I initially came up with:

Independent film, indie film, fantasy film, sci-fi, science fiction, time travel, time slip, psychics, psychic vendor, Psychcops, Psychological Police Corp, time paradox, found in time, Arthur Vincie, Ben Wolf

The title is acceptable as a tag, by the way. As with all the other elements, you'll want to revisit this list and refresh it from time to time. If you get a "name" cast member, obviously s/he should go into this list. If your film turns out somewhat differently (genre-wise) than you'd intended, you might want to revise the genre tags.

These metawords will become part of your tweets, YouTube channel, website, crowdfunding page, and Facebook updates (when appropriate). You may want to go back and incorporate a few of them into your bio and synopsis (but only if they fit with the existing text). This will hopefully help drive traffic to your online presence.

Email List

Don't just put every name in your address book, and all your Facebook friends, into this list. Consider very carefully who you think would be interested in your film. You may, for example, want to exclude your day job boss, if you think s/he won't appreciate your independent filmmaking efforts ("oh, that's why you keep showing up late every morning").

You want to start with a seed of between 200 and 1500 contacts, preferably people you know well or at least have met a few times (even if only online). These are the folks who will hopefully become fans, donors, crew, vendors, and/or cast members, and even ticket-buyers down the road.

Ideally, you want to create a database, spreadsheet, or address book (in Outlook or whatever email client you use) containing not just the raw email addresses, but also:

1. First and last names
2. Company names
3. Position/profession
4. Mailing addresses (for postcards/special invites)

5. Phone number
6. Website URLs (for link exchanges down the road)
7. Something about how you met/know them

Keep this information up to date.

Putting the Salad Together

If you haven't figured this out yet, now would be a good time to organize this material on your hard drive so you can find it later. As more than a few of my mentors have said to me over the years, "if it's not labeled it's *lost*." So label your files something meaningful. Keep in mind that if you have interns or people helping you out, they need to be able to make sense of your naming conventions.

You will accumulate *a lot* of files, so I recommend creating subfolders within your main film folder. My *Found In Time* subfolders included:

- **Advertising**
  BusinessPlan
  EPK (electronic press kit)
- **Graphics/ConceptArt**
  Logos
  Posters
- **Media** (for video and audio files)
  WebsiteGraphics

Each of these subfolders contained a mix of Word docs, spreadsheets, and Illustrator, Photoshop, CorelDraw, and assorted other graphics files.

YOUR MARKETING PROCESS

You've got your elements assembled in a few folders on your hard drive. You've got a much better understanding of your film. Now what?

Your marketing process (I hate the term "campaign" but will use it for convenience) is a multi-tentacled beast that reaches out to both web and traditional media outlets to alert people to the presence of the film, and hopefully jump-starts a conversation between you and your audience. This conversation can be as simple as comments on your blog, or as complex as fan fiction, personal email exchanges, and crowd-collaboration on the film itself.

A lot has been written about the changeover from the "old" way of marketing (you push trailers, press kits, pictures, etc. in people's faces) to the new way (you and your fans engage in a conversation). But in truth marketing has always been a two-way street, even if it wasn't paved. Ask any serious sci-fi/fantasy/game fan. Fans have interacted with each other and the show/game creators both online and in "real life" for over three decades.

Case in point: from the beginning, *Babylon 5* creator J. Michael Straczynski recognized the value of the internet as a way of getting the word out about his low-budget but awesome sci-fi space opera TV series. Lacking the deep pockets of Paramount with their (somewhat competing shows) *Deep Space 9* and *Voyager*, Straczynski started talking about the show on various internet forums in advance of the pilot's first airing. He also talked about the pilot and the show in various interviews with sci-fi/fantasy magazines. In 1995(!), one year after the show started, the official website went up. It was later moved to AOL (hey, it was 1996 and AOL was huge back then). The site featured artwork, pictures, and logos that could be downloaded by fans of the show for free, as long as they didn't make any money off them. Fans were encouraged to create their own sites using the artwork.

Straczynski also moderated the fan forums and answered a lot of emails personally, which was pretty amazing. I don't actually know how he slept, since he was the executive producer and chief screenwriter (he wrote nearly all of the show's 100-plus episodes). The results were impressive: the show finished its run in 1998. Some TV movies, comics, and novelizations still come out periodically. The fans still buy merchandise and Blu-Rays, write fan-fiction, and every now and then lobby for a new series.

There are three important takeaways from this example:

1. Straczynski identified early on who would want the show.
2. He worked hard to *personally* forge a connection with fans.
3. He encouraged fans to be active participants.

This is the best-case scenario for your film – that your marketing efforts lead to a deep and ongoing connection to your audience. This effort may extend past this film and into future projects.

Each part of your marketing process should be geared to accomplishing those three goals, even if the individual parts (the business plan) may be aimed for a slightly different audience. While you probably won't be showing the ticket-buying audience your business plan, you want to create the same sense of excitement about and personal connection to the film, and to you.

Figure 5.2 illustrates the different segments of your audience, and how you'll reach each of them.

Let's delve into each marketing "vehicle" in a little more detail.

Poster

Nothing will make a film seem more real in people's minds than seeing a poster for the film, even if said poster is completely fake and only exists on a computer screen. It's like the "after" picture in a before-and-after advertisement.

Many posters feature the faces of the lead actors, which will be difficult for you to pull off, since you haven't started casting yet. Use what and who you have available. Do you have actors you were thinking of casting or who are good friends who will help you out? Do you have some particularly iconic imagery in your concept art stash? Early posters are often more mysterious, giving people a taste without revealing much about the plot (sometimes without even revealing the title). Look at posters for comparable films. You will probably make different poster versions as preproduction progresses.

Storyboards/Illustrations (Possibly)

Professional storyboards can be a great visual aid during preproduction, but can also serve as powerful marketing material. Just like the poster, boards make the film come alive in the minds of the audience. The Wachowski Brothers used storyboards and comics to illustrate their pitch for *The Matrix*. Just the fact that you've had them done will help sell you as a filmmaker.

One caveat, however. Until you have your DP on board and your locations more or less locked, the boards will be of very limited use to you as a director. I would advise *against* making storyboards of the entire script at this stage. Instead, pick out one to three exciting scenes and hire an artist to board them. Or hire your artist to create illustrations of your main characters that would function like production stills.

One final warning: having badly done artwork is worse than having no artwork. If you don't have the illustration skills and can't get good work done (either through favors, barter, or money), skip over this and focus on getting good concept art.

Business Plan and Pitch Doc/Slideshow

I mentioned the business plan back in Chapter 3. While your plan serves a distinct business purpose, it's also part of your overall marketing scheme. Whether you hand it out only to private investors,

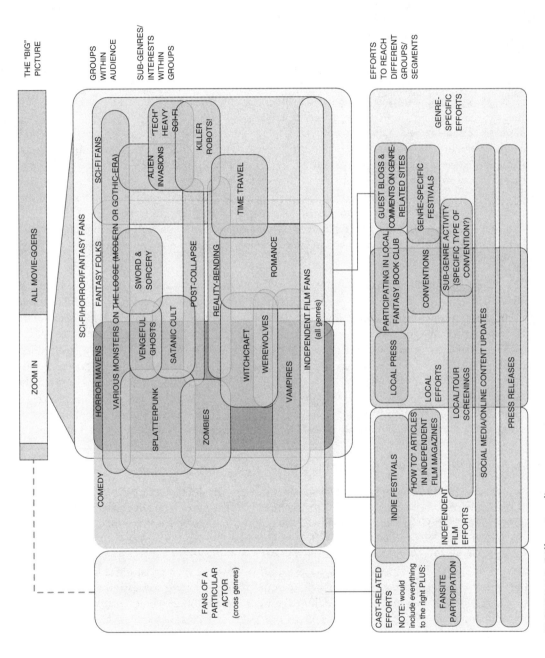

FIGURE 5.2 Different audience segments.

The "BIG" PICTURE

ALL MOVIE-GOERS

ZOOM IN

FANS OF A PARTICULAR ACTOR (cross genres)

GROUPS WITHIN AUDIENCE

SUB-GENRES/ INTERESTS WITHIN GROUPS

SCI-FI/HORROR/FANTASY FANS

SCI-FI FANS

FANTASY FOLKS

HORROR MAVENS

COMEDY

VARIOUS MONSTERS ON THE LOOSE (MODERN OR GOTHIC-ERA)

"TECH" HEAVY SCI-FI

KILLER ROBOTS!

ALIEN INVASIONS

TIME TRAVEL

SWORD & SORCERY

VENGEFUL GHOSTS

SATANIC CULT

POST-COLLAPSE

REALITY-BENDING

ROMANCE

SPLATTERPUNK

ZOMBIES

WITCHCRAFT

WEREWOLVES

VAMPIRES

INDEPENDENT FILM FANS (all genres)

EFFORTS TO REACH DIFFERENT GROUPS/ SEGMENTS

GENRE- SPECIFIC EFFORTS

GUEST BLOGS & COMMENTS ON GENRE- RELATED SITES

GENRE-SPECIFIC FESTIVALS

PARTICIPATING IN LOCAL FANTASY BOOK CLUB

CONVENTIONS

SUB-GENRE ACTIVITY (SPECIFIC TYPE OF CONVENTION?)

LOCAL PRESS

LOCAL EFFORTS

LOCAL/TOUR SCREENINGS

INDIE FESTIVALS

"HOW TO" ARTICLES IN INDEPENDENT FILM MAGAZINES

INDEPENDENT FILM EFFORTS

SOCIAL MEDIA/ONLINE CONTENT UPDATES

PRESS RELEASES

CAST-RELATED EFFORTS

NOTE: would include everything to the right PLUS:

FANSITE PARTICIPATION

56

or put it up on IndieGogo or Kickstarter, it's the first or second (after the script) in-depth contact many people will have with your film.

So in addition to being rigorous and professional, a business plan should also be engaging. Use the synopsis, bio, poster, storyboards, vision statement, and concept art to add some "zing" to the business speak. The layout and choice of artwork is important – it's a clue to your visual style. You want to convey who you are, and what's so special about this film that other people will want to reach into their wallets to either fund it or see it when it's done.

This can be very hard to do, since you can't gloss over the more sobering elements of the business plan. So some people put their efforts instead into a pitch document or slideshow (in PowerPoint or Keynote or some other slideshow creator). The pitch document essentially summarizes the business and creative case for making the film into 25–30 slides that can be presented in-person, viewed online, or read via print-out. You rely more heavily on the concept art and other visual elements, and lighten the amount of text.

The two documents are aimed at investors – including crowdfunders – and not necessarily at the general public.

Press Kit

This is something that you should start building right away, though you're probably not going to release it until the film is at least shot. It's aimed at professionals and semi-professionals – journalists, bloggers, sales agents, producer's reps, distributors, and possibly late-stage investors. It typically consists of the following:

1. A reproduction of the poster
2. Stills from the shoot (you can use concept art until you've shot something)
3. Storyboards
4. A director's statement
5. A war story or two about the shoot
6. Bios of all the key cast and crew, including headshots
7. A full credit list
8. Contact information
9. Links to your site, Facebook page, Twitter account, and any other online sites you have
10. Reproductions of any articles and/or interviews you've done regarding the film (either print or online)

The press kit should exist in two states: as a single PDF that can be downloaded from your site or printed and handed out to people; and as part of an EPK (electronic press kit).

An EPK is a collection of elements that can be burned to CD or DVD, downloaded either individually or in one ZIP file from your website, or viewed directly from your site. The EPK should contain most of the following:

1. A PDF of your standard press kit
2. Print and web versions of your poster and key artwork (DVD covers, postcards, storyboards/ illustrations, etc.)
3. Print-friendly and web-friendly versions of your stills and headshots
4. A standalone synopsis of the film
5. The trailer, usually in H.264 HD (more on this format shortly)
6. Any behind-the-scenes material you've shot and cut together, also in H.264 HD
7. All the links and contact information listed above

You may have to ultimately prepare several different press kits for different audiences.

Since a lot of these elements don't exist yet, you shouldn't worry *too much* about putting the press kit together now. However, it's important to start thinking about and preparing for it now.

The kit, website, and social media presence are the first things the press and industry will see of your film, so they should be consistent with each other design-wise, and also communicate what the film is about. Just the fact that you have a kit signals a certain level of professionalism.

Websites

Even in the age of social media, your websites serve very important functions. Some people are still Facebook-averse, or don't want to wade through status updates to get information about your film. A website is also a good way of sustaining a longer conversation, rather than bite-size updates.

And frankly, Facebook (and other sites) have rather shady user agreements about who owns the content posted on their sites (read the fine print). Also, given that only LinkedIn has survived longer than five years (MySpace, anyone), you will want to have a web base that is stable over the long haul.

You want to create two websites: one for your ongoing business, and one specifically for the film. The elements listed above will become part of the sites' designs. Your audience includes fans as well as investors and industry folks.

A website is really three things working together:

1. A domain name (hopefully you registered these back in Chapter 3)
2. A hosting plan
3. The actual site that people see, developed using one or several platforms

Websites are still, I find, a lot of work to set up and maintain, but they're a bit like parks – neglect them and people will just stop coming by. People want fresh content, so you'll want to pick a site development platform.

Web hosting providers can register your domain name, provide you with a cheap hosting plan, and give you the tools to develop your site. These tools range from awful to decent. You can also roll your own site using whatever web skills you possess (you can, in theory, build a static site using just HTML and maybe a little JavaScript).

Hosting Plan

Web hosting plans have become fairly commoditized over the years. So you should aim for the cheapest package possible that's still reliable. That usually means going for a basic shared hosting plan (where one physical or virtual server is shared by a bunch of websites, each with their own accounts and directories). You usually get a few email accounts, support for PHP/MySQL, WordPress, Drupal, and sometimes another language (PERL, Python, or Ruby), and add-ons for customer tracking and e-commerce. The internet service provider that registered your domain name for you will often give you a discount if you also host your site with them.

Website

You really have four options here:

1. Develop the website on your own using whatever platform you're comfortable with.
2. Use one of your ISP's "one-click" website templates.
3. Use WordPress, Drupal, or some other website framework to build a site.
4. Hire someone to do one of the above-mentioned methods.

I've done all of these at various times, and each option has its pluses and minuses. If you roll your own site, you'll be able to customize it to your heart's content. So if you're a .NET guru or Flash genius, you have the chance of displaying that talent to everyone. Also, you may find it faster to develop in a platform you're already familiar with than learn WordPress or Drupal.

The "one-click" templates have gotten a lot better but, by the time you finish customizing them to something that's close to what you want, you might as well have used one of the other options.

If you're not a web developer, and you want to build something relatively quickly — and have something that other people can maintain down the road — I recommend Drupal, WordPress, Joomla, or another reputable (and free) content management system (CMS).

A CMS provides a framework for managing your web content and design, so you can focus more on creating content, and less on coding and database development. It helps to have a programming background, but by following some tutorials and asking questions on the CMS provider's user forums, you can get a pretty decent-looking site up relatively quickly.

The main advantage to using one of the CMSes (especially Joomla, Drupal, or WordPress) are:

1. **Customization:** Just about any CMS worth anything features add-ons written by fans and professional developers that can customize the look of your site, or add new features (like a photo gallery or video player).
2. **Standardization:** If you ever need someone else to maintain your site, it's easier to find someone with experience with the big three CMSes above, or train them in its daily use, than to find a PHP, Flash, or .NET expert.
3. **Your time:** You have better things to do with your prep time than code. Really.

I built my chaoticsequence.com website on my own using Flash and HTML. Then I ditched Flash and rewrote the site using PHP, CSS, and HTML, with a MySQL database storing the content. I did this while I was still writing the script for *Found In Time*, so it was a "relaxing" exercise. For foundintimefilm.com, I decided to use WordPress for all the reasons mentioned above.

Whatever platform you choose to develop your site in, remember that *good, "legible" design* is more important than *the best code.* Your sites should accomplish five design goals:

1. Tell the user what your business is (in the case of the film, tell the user what the film's about).
2. Present the user with a way of finding information about the film in an obvious way.
3. Offer the user ways to connect with you — via phone, email, social media.
4. Offer the user ways to share your site with others.
5. Do all of this in an eye-pleasing, quick way.

Without digging into the principles of good web design, here's a few tips to consider:

Content

1. Update your content frequently.
2. Interconnect all your websites and social media pages. So your company site should have a link to your film site, and vice versa. Both should link to your IMDb page, LinkedIn profile, Twitter account, the Facebook page for the film and the company, YouTube channel, etc.
3. If you have anything to sell, make sure the user can get to your e-commerce page from every other page on your site (including your home page).
4. Try not to hard-format your content, but use stylesheets to create custom styles.
5. Use your metawords on your site; in both the text and in the header's meta tags. All CMSes have meta tag settings that you can stuff your metawords into.

Design

6. Think of your website in "Web 2.0" terms. This means making sure the user can print, email, and share any page they land on, and can comment on any blog entry you write.
7. Web design has become fairly standardized over the past few years into a "grid" similar in nature to a magazine or newspaper grid. Your site should have the layout elements shown in Figure 5.3, more or less.

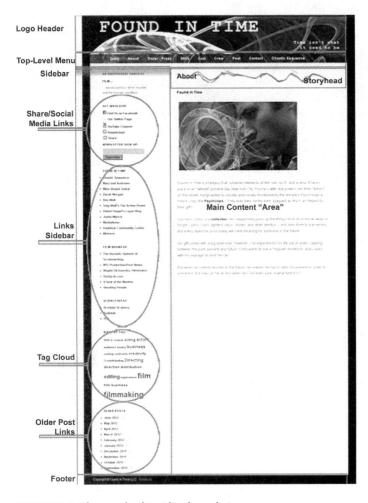

Logo Header

Top-Level Menu

Sidebar

Share/Social
Media Links

Links
Sidebar

Tag Cloud

Older Post
Links

Footer

FIGURE 5.3 The standard "grid" of a website.

8. With the exception of tablet and smartphone screens, you're generally designing for a land-scape layout. Keep your header images and menu bar relatively slender.
9. Skip Flash-based splash pages, they're annoying. Skip Flash altogether if you can help it.
10. Test your site on different browsers, and on phones and tablets.
11. High-contrast type/background color schemes are easier to read (black text on white or vice-versa) than low-contrast schemes (white or yellow on gray).
12. Sans-serif fonts (such as Arial, Verdana, and Univers) are traditionally used for titles, menu labels, and captions. Serif fonts (like Times New Roman) are easier to read. Don't have too many fonts on the page.
13. Keep the look of each site self-consistent.

Media

14. Audio should be turned off by default.
15. Host your video on Vimeo or YouTube rather than on your shared server. These video services are tuned for streaming video, whereas your hosting servers are probably not.
16. Images should support the text, not overwhelm it. If the user has to scroll past an image to get your story, it's too large.

Your film site should contain bios of yourself and the rest of the team, the film synopsis, artwork, the poster, trailer, links to companies associated with the film, and some version of your vision statement.

Blog. You'll also want to create a blog as part of the site, and update it as often as you can stand. This blog will serve as a diary for the filmmaking process. You can also use the blog to promote your teammates' work, talk about issues that are related to themes in the film – anything that you think will give fans a greater connection to the project.

What About Just Setting Up a Blog?

Setting up a blog for a film (as opposed to a full-blown site) is a good option if you just want to dive in and start writing content. Blogger.com will even register a domain name for your site. I used it for *Found In Time* for a while.

However, it became clear fairly early on that I was going to outgrow the "just blog" format – while being an important part of the site, the blog was not the whole thing. Once I hit this wall, I ended up transferring the domain name to my internet hosting service and developed a full-blown site, with a blogging *component*, in WordPress. If you can be patient and set up a full site first, you'll be spared the transfer process that I went through (which wasn't horrible, but was time-consuming).

Social Media

Rather than iterate through the process for creating pages for your film in Facebook, and setting up a presence on all the major social media sites, I'll just touch on the highlights.

All of your pages should contain links to your company and film website (the priority is the link to the film site). Also, while you may not feel comfortable leaving your phone number on these pages, you should at least leave your email address.

Update your social media pages/accounts as often as possible, but not just with information about your film. In fact, you should *not* be too hawkish; it drives people away. Follow the "80/20" rule – talk about yourself 20 percent of the time, and other people's work 80 percent. Be especially careful on professionally oriented sites such as LinkedIn – if people feel that you're spamming them they'll drop the connection very quickly.

Use your metawords in your profile and in your tweets. Make sure every email, bio, and forum response includes the URL to your film's site.

As you hire cast and crew members, make sure to add them to your Twitter feed, and invite them to your film's Facebook page. Be judicious in your invitations to your film's Facebook page.

"Old-School" Web Work

Don't neglect the value of participating in "older" web offerings. Guest blogging, being active in user forums (especially those that have something to do with your film's theme or its genre), and subscribing to and contributing to listservs are all ways to raise awareness for your film.

I subscribe to an online resource called Shooting People, that includes an NYC-centric list-serv, where people can ask and answer questions, post job/classified ads, put up links to various resources (including blogs), and announce their crowdfunding campaign. I've also contributed articles and guest blogs over the years to reelgrok.com (a budgeting site), mixform.com (an online portfolio site for actors and crew), and other services. Participating in online forums that are relevant to your script's genre or theme is a great way to introduce people to your film, without pushing it in their faces.

Vimeo and YouTube

Vimeo and YouTube both offer methods of creating channels through which you can upload and stream your trailer, behind-the-scenes materials, and finished scenes from the film. They also offer various privacy options so you can control who sees the clips. This is very important for when you want to upload videos for feedback and comments, but don't want the whole world to look at them yet. Finally, both offer a way to use those all-important meta tags in your videos, so you can improve your chances of getting hits.

Get to know both services. YouTube has the larger reach, but I personally prefer Vimeo's streaming quality. I used Vimeo for sharing drafts of clips and trailers with select people, and both services for putting up final versions. Try to get people to subscribe to your YouTube Channel. Put any out-of-circulation material you have (older shorts or webisodic work) on the channel to increase value.

A special note on SoundCloud (soundcloud.com): If you have concept/theme/trailer music (that you have the rights to), consider posting it to this service. This can also be an "extra" that you upload to your website.

Email Lists

What you ultimately want out of all these other efforts is a database of contacts, who you can then reach out to when you need to get folks to come to screenings, contribute to your campaign, buy DVDs, and/or become evangelists for your film.

To harness your email list, you'll want to keep it fresh and keep people involved with the film. Sign up with one of several email contact services, and put together a regular e-blast that goes out to these folks. These services offer pre-built email templates (or you can roll your own), contact list management, integrate with social media, and can check your emails for possible "spam" flags (things that will get your email rejected or tossed into a spam folder). I use Contactology, which charges me a flat monthly fee no matter how many e-blasts I send out.

This is time-consuming work. Setting up the initial email template and importing the names took a while. Each blast takes a few hours to write, proofread, and test-send. I also spend at least an hour each month trying to maintain the email list – getting rid of bounced emails and adding new contacts.

Ideally, your blasts should contain short paragraph-long notices about things coming up within the next few days to a month or so. This could include events, play openings, screenings of films, DVD/theatrical/cable premieres, casting/crew notices, mentions of new blog entries, etc. Try to follow the 80/20 rule.

If your film targets a specific niche audience or social cause, your blurbs can be about non-film issues. If your film is about punk rockers, you can include mini-reviews of your favorite bands' new albums, for example.

Always include links to your websites and social media pages. If the list provider has the option to cross-post to Twitter/Facebook, take advantage of this feature. Most services also include tracking tools (ranging from primitive to spectacular) so you can see who's opened your emails, and who's clicked any embedded links.

Most of the email services have tiered pricing structures, based on the number of people in your contact list. Others charge per e-blast. You can usually get a discount if you allow the service to include its logo in your e-blast and/or if you pay for a year in full. Contactology has a good mix of features and is reasonably priced.

OTHER METHODS OF MARKETING

So far I've covered methods that you can use on your own or with a small team. If you want to go further than these tools, you'll have to weigh and measure whether the effort you devote, and the resources you'll have to marshal, will be worth the end result.

Fundraising Events

If you plan ahead, you can create a fundraising event for your film. I've been to several of these and helped organize a few, and they are pretty open-ended in terms of format. Some have featured live music, others a reading of the script, still others a screening of the teaser or the director's previous work. Almost all included some kind of mixer and a raffle to get swag. The suggested donations to these events have ranged from $10 to $50, and raffle tickets tend to sell for $5–$10 each.

You'll need to factor in the following costs:

1. The venue
2. Equipment (PA or projection system)
3. Some behind-the-scenes still photographers and videographers, who can take pictures of the event
4. Whatever live talent you're bringing
5. Drinks and food (usually appetizers)
6. Programs/flyers/copies of the script/business plan
7. Advertising the event
8. Some staff to handle the drinks, take donations, set up, and clean up

A lot of these costs can be rolled up by working with an established venue, such as a bar, music club, theater, screening room, or nonprofit arts center. Leverage whatever favors you have to get people to donate their time and merchandise for free.

If you approach the event with the aim of networking first and raising money second, you'll probably have a better time. My experience has been that these things make money about one third the time and break even another third. There doesn't seem to be a magic formula for success, except that they're more effective if you already have a fan base.

Other Live Events

You can associate yourself and your film with other events. In the above-mentioned punk rock example, do you know of a place that regularly hosts punk rock shows? Do they need help, or a DJ, or would they be interested in screening your teaser between acts? If you have a horror, sci-fi, or fantasy film, reach out to local sci-fi/horror/comics groups and see if they're interested in hosting a teaser screening or maybe a reading.

I've guest-lectured at a few film schools, usually on producing or line producing, and screened some clips from *Found In Time*. I've also screened my shorts at various events, and made sure to bring as big a crowd as possible. Other filmmakers I know direct plays, and so occasionally screen their teasers in advance of the play.

You want to make sure that if you're approaching another organization that your needs line up. For example, bars often have movie screening nights, but they need people to show up and order drinks. If you can bring a crowd through your e-blasts and Facebook notifications, they'll be more receptive to the idea of screening your film.

Product Placement

Product placement can be worthwhile if it's for something that's in your script already. You may be able to get some financing from it or at least cross-promotion. But keep in mind that pursuing it can be a full-time job in and of itself.

To approach a company directly, you'll want to start with the corporate communications department. Every large company has one, even if they call it something else ("community relations," "communications," "publicity"). Make a packet containing the synopsis, your bio, and some kind of pitch explaining how the company's product would fit within your film. They may look at the script. Be prepared to follow up with emails and phone calls. Start this process as early as possible, and be prepared for a certain amount of red tape.

Networking Parties and Events

I've nearly always found these to be a waste of time. The organizers always pick a bar that's too crowded, where the music is cranked up so high you can't hear anything. After being at a few of these I started seeing the same people over and over. Your mileage may vary, however.

Seminars are much better for networking and pitching. You and the other participants are already in a receptive mood, since you're there to learn, and there's usually a "networking" angle built into these events.

Advertising

Paid advertising isn't worth it when you're in preproduction. You may get more hits on your website but those will not generally translate into hardcore or even casual fans. The exception is if you can advertise in a venue that specifically caters to your film's audience. You may also want to advertise for cast or crew on certain online and print venues (mandy.com and *Indie Slate* have crew and cast call listings).

I've advertised my production company in various online directories over the years, but it has seldom led to paying work. I've gotten a lot more work from word-of-mouth.

Link exchanges are more fruitful. Someone puts up a link to your film on their site, and you put up a link to their site on yours. You can each benefit from the other's marketing efforts. Just be careful that you're not exchanging links with a potential competitor.

Transmedia *Is Not* Marketing

Transmedia is a method of storytelling, wherein the story spans several different media, each supporting the other. So you may watch the film, then read a comic that delves into a specific part of the story, then see some webisodes that reinforce another part, and so on. When it's set up properly, each platform strengthens the audience member's experience of the story, rather than divides it. Often the film is an anchor or a very important component, but is not the whole story.

I confess I look at transmedia a little differently than a few of my peers. I see it as a logical extension of sci-fi/fantasy storytelling into the domain of other genres. When I was growing up I watched the *Star Trek* shows and films, read some of the novels and comic adaptations, bought the toys, and played some of the board, card, and computer games. The idea of telling a story across several media, with the main plotline occurring in the film, is nothing new to me. If anything, transmedia seems to use the internet as a "glue" to cross-reference these different story aspects together. My friends and I did the same using pen-and-paper, to try and place different events in the *Star Trek* universe (from comics and the various series) along one timeline.

What it clearly *is not*, however, is a marketing tool, except incidentally – people may pick up the thread of the story in one medium (like the website) and then want to go buy/rent the film. If you have a story that benefits organically from being told across multiple media, then great. If not, don't try the transmedia approach to generate more fans. You will spend a lot of time and energy that would be better spent elsewhere.

CONCLUSIONS

Evangelism

You want to reach out to prospective evangelists – people who can take your message and carry it further. This has always been Apple's strategy. They regularly host events at their stores, and send people to user groups across the country to connect with early adopters who will then walk into work beaming about the latest iPhone. Your evangelists may be members of your crew or cast, who will talk in glowing terms about your film. They may be early crowdfunders.

If you find evangelists, reward them. Send them screeners before you send them anywhere else. Give them credits in the film or at least on the website. Promote any work that they're doing.

Evaluation

All of the above efforts sound like a lot of work. They are. Zoe Keating, who's a successful (and self-supporting) cello player and composer, says she spends about half her professional life making music and the other half promoting it. All the artists, writers, musicians, and filmmakers I know are constantly trying to market themselves and their work.

You will have to evaluate your efforts periodically, and drop activities that don't make sense, and focus more on those that do. Maybe you're better at tweeting than posting blog entries. Maybe you're more visually oriented – so focus on photo sharing.

Maybe you're finding all of this is taking too much time away from actually making the film. At this point, you should consider what marketing activities you can do without, and whether it makes sense to hire a Producer of Marketing and Distribution, or at least a decent assistant/intern.

As mentioned in Chapter 3, you may have to hire a designer for your site and other marketing elements. You may also have to bring on a teaser/trailer editor. In both cases I'd suggest that you see how far you can get on your own, so that the people you hire have some idea of what you're after.

Sincerity

I've consciously tried to avoid the word "branding" in this chapter because I associate branding with many activities, none of them good. You're not stamping your mark on cattle, or plastering your corporate logo on people's butts. You're reaching out to make a solid, hopefully lasting connection with fans.

These fans will pay you back for the effort in one way or another – they'll become evangelists, audience members, donors, crew or cast members, vendors, and possibly even sales contacts. You don't really know where the relationship will lead, so it's best to start off with a clean, sincere effort.

QUESTIONS/EXERCISES

1. Look at the posters of films that are similar in some way to yours. Are there any elements – typeface, contrast, image, color scheme – that unite these posters? Are there any standout posters? Can you use any of the common elements in your own work?
2. Join an online forum that you find interesting, that is related in some way to your film, or that's focused on a subject you have some knowledge of. Read the conversations a bit. Are there questions that are asked that you can answer? Do you have a strong opinion about something that you want to share?
3. Look at the bios of various filmmakers and other arts professionals you admire. Is there a common style to the bios?
4. Start putting all your basic elements – concept art, bios, headshots, etc. – into a word-processing document (could be in Word, OpenOffice, etc. – doesn't matter). This can serve as a template or library for you to dip into when creating your press kit, business plan, website, etc.

WEB VS. PRINT GRAPHICS

Table 5.1 briefly summarizes the difference between web and print graphics.

In general, when putting your concept art and other graphics together, you want to start with files with the highest resolution and print size you can find. You can always downsample (from 300dpi to 72dpi) or shrink an image; it's a lot harder to upsample. So if you're creating or editing

TABLE 5.1 Web vs. print graphics

Characteristic	Web	Print	Comment
Dots per inch	72	150–300	This indicates the number of pixels (dots) per inch. Most monitors, with the significant exception of handhelds and some smartphones, run at 72dpi. Most printers, however, print at anywhere from 600 to 1200dpi for text, with 150–300 considered acceptable for most graphics (though not all)
Colorspace	RGB	CMYK	RGB = Red/Green/Blue, the primary colors of light. The light you see from your monitor is some combination of red, green, and blue values
			CMYK = Cyan/Magenta/Yellow/blacK, the primary colors of most printers
Emphasis	File size	Image quality	Web graphics are optimized for fast download and rendering to your browser. Print graphics are designed to be printed at different scales and resolutions without image degradation
File type	JPG or PNG	TIFF, JPG, PSD	JPGs and PNG files are the standard for viewing photographs or complex images on the web (GIFs, while still around, are more suitable for viewing simpler graphics)
			Printers prefer their graphics in TIFF (no compression) format, but do accept others. There are a number of other formats that professional printers deal with (RAW, etc.) but we won't go into that here

your graphics in Illustrator, PhotoShop, GIMP, or another program, try to save them to 300–600dpi TIFF files, then downsample them later for the web.

For best results with still images, shoot with a DSLR camera that saves to the RAW format. You can also use CHDK (www.chdk.com) to turn your point-and-shoot Canon into a RAW-capable camera. RAW files store the relatively unprocessed data that was read by the camera's sensor. Most image-editing programs can read RAW or include utilities that can read and convert RAW files to high-resolution TIFFs or JPGs.

## Chapter 6

Script Analysis

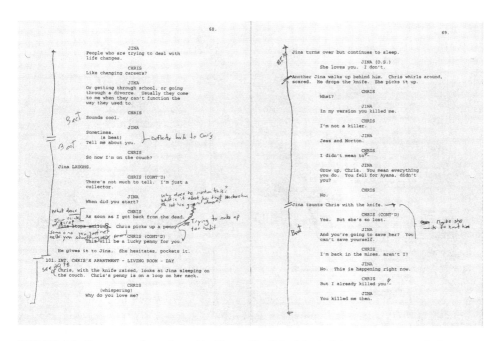

FIGURE 6.1 Two pages from *Found In Time*, after I'd subjected them to some analysis.

You have the movie completely mapped out in your head. What every shot should look like, what every gesture should be, how the whole thing cuts together, even the score. If you've been working on the script for many years, this knowledge is integral to your being. You *are the movie.* Then when you start working with other people, the trouble starts. How do you communicate your vision to others? Worse, even if you explain everything perfectly, other people will refract your words through their own cognitive filters, and the result will still be different from the movie in your mind. Or they'll ask you dumb questions that you will somehow not know the answers to, because … because, hey, wait a minute, I never thought about *that* before!

Until we get to the point where we can hook the writer or director's brain up to a camera (or better, a projection screen), we will be stuck creating a film through a medium, the script. Just like a psychic medium, communication between worlds is never perfect and is subject to interpretation. Your job as a director is to be the psychic, delving into the spirit world of the script and bringing back a cogent, concrete vision – a direction – for the story. Once you have this direction, you will then use it to guide the rest of your decisions, from casting and production design to editing and sound design.

While this description will come across as either romantic or absurd (or both), it's not off the mark. Even if you wrote the script – actually, especially if you wrote the script – you don't have access to all the unwritten assumptions that went into it. So, using the script as your guide, you have to flesh out the full story of your film. Once you have a clear vision of the story in your mind, you can then communicate it to the cast and crew.

A BRIEF DEFINITION

So what does script analysis really consist of? Basically, you sit and read the script (usually many times over), and make piles of notes, drawings, doodles, and highlights. You'll eventually sort these out into the following "documents":

1. **Scene-by-scene, beat-by-beat analysis.** A detailed breakdown of each scene.
2. **Character sheets.** What do the characters want, what do they really need, who do they love, what are the main obstacles in their lives?
3. **A vision statement.** What is the style you're aiming for, what are your goals, what other films are similar to yours?
4. **An internal casting breakdown.** Who are you looking for in real life or even the past who matches the characters in the script?
5. **References.** Photos, books, articles, films, music, and other works that you think would be good reference points and inspiration for yourself, your crew, and your cast.
6. **Shotlist/coverage.** This often comes later, but it helps to have some basic idea of what you're going to need to shoot to cover a scene.
7. **Storyboards.** This also usually comes later, but some people find they're better at sketching things out than writing things down, so if that's the way you work, then great.

I'll be talking about most of these materials in subsequent chapters, but they all have their roots in the analysis you're about to undertake.

Much of this work will be completely hidden from your cast and crew. A lot of it will not survive the production. So you have substantial leeway in how you organize your analysis and the resulting materials, as long as you get the work done. Keep in mind, however, that everyone has a different, preferred way of absorbing information. Some people need to look at pictures; some like to be told stories; some like music, dance, and animation; and others like to read. In your work, be sure to produce material that you can reproduce using each method. We'll cover this in more detail in Chapter 7.

I find that script analysis is an *iterative* process. This is a term I learned from computer programming. You do the same thing over and over again, gradually coming closer in each iteration to the answer you want. In this case, you read and annotate the script over and over again, using what you learned on the last pass to inform the current one, until you have a pretty complete understanding of the story. Before we get started, it's important to explain a few fundamentals.

Story vs. script. The screenwriter wrote the script. But the script isn't the full *story* of the characters. You could say that the story consists of the scenes in the script, plus what happens before the script starts, in between the scenes, and after the credits roll. This could include the lives of people who are very influential on the characters in the script, but who the audience never sees onscreen (or sees only in passing). Good examples of this would include Will's father in *Good Will Hunting* or Detective Somerset's ex-girlfriend in *Seven*.

Text vs. subtext. The story is the text. The rhythms, unconscious desires, and unspoken (though conscious) wishes of the characters are the subtext. The more layers of subtext you can uncover, the better off your film will be. Films as different as *The Hours* and *Serenity* succeed because the characters rarely talk about what's on their minds, but their behavior tells you everything. Even characters who are more self-conscious, like Brad (Jude Law) and Albert (Jason Schwartzman) in *I Heart Huckabees*, communicate the subtext through their behavior. Subtext can also be conveyed through lens selection, color, lighting, set dressing, makeup and hair, sound design, music, and props.

Dramatic action vs. action. Your characters should always be doing *something*. Film is a temporal medium. There is no such thing as standing still (as in a painting, photograph, or sculpture). Even athletes and dancers maintain balance through constant, tiny motions. This doesn't mean that your characters have to beat each other up or run on every page. The characters' action may be completely internal. As long as you can find a way of bringing it onto the screen, then the audience will see and respond to it. In films like *The Myth of Fingerprints*, there's very little "action" in the traditional sense, but there *is* a lot going on. Jim Jarmusch (*Ghost Dog*, *Broken Flowers*, *Dead Man*, to name a few) is the past master of this. *The Dream Life of Angels* and *Godfather Part II* both consist of scenes of characters walking and talking, with very little happening in between. But both are incredibly dynamic and gripping films.

Conversely, films with big action sequences often feel curiously empty, because there is no dramatic action going on. What's dramatic about running away from a fireball or defending yourself in a fight? Anyone would do that. What got the character into those situations to begin with – that's where the *dramatic* action is. What makes Luc Besson (*La Femme Nikita*, *Unleashed*, *The Professional*) a good action writer is that he makes you care about the characters *before* they get beat up.

METHOD

Everyone has a different way of tackling script analysis. It may take a while for you to find your best method. The bulk of this chapter will discuss the methods that work for me. Feel free to use, augment, or abandon them as you see fit. Also, what I'm presenting as a stepwise progression is really a more nonlinear process. You may find that reversing the order of certain steps is more helpful to you.

You can't knock this out in a day or two. Plan on spending some serious time on this. If you find it hard to concentrate for long periods of time (as I often do), break up the work into small segments. Do it during your commute, at lunch, early in the morning, at night – whenever you have little chunks of time. But don't wait until a week before the shoot.

Step 1: The Informal Reading

Nothing will help you get started more quickly than having the script read aloud by other people. Especially if it's your script. Chances are you've been living with this story for a *long* time, and consequently you can't see some of the flaws and bumps anymore.

Try to keep the reading simple. Invite some friends over, grab some drinks, snacks, and food. Divvy up the parts among some of your friends. The remainder will be the audience. Someone should also read the narration (preferably not you). You can assign more than one role to a single person, as long as they aren't both speaking in the same scene. Have your friends read the script out loud, without interruption. Afterwards, have a no-holds-barred discussion about the good, the bad, and the ugly.

Some people argue for having real actors read the parts. I agree, for the most part – they have insight into character research and development. Often they can come up with unexpected suggestions or will interpret the material in a very interesting way. The flip side is that actors can sometimes make a line sound better than it really is. And it's difficult to ask professionals to come over for free (I have sometimes paid actors for readings, depending on how strapped I was at the time; and I always try to feed them well).

Some people record the readings (either on video or audio). I would argue against this. Non-actors usually stiffen up if they know that they're going to be recorded. Actors will often try to make it a performance. Neither reaction is helpful. Take notes and listen as hard as you can. This is also good practice for what you'll be doing a lot of during the rehearsal process, and directing in general.

What are you trying to find out?

1. Does the dramatic action meander a bit too much? Are there "dead" scenes?
2. Is there a character that's out of place, or isn't well-defined yet?
3. Are the stakes high enough?
4. Does anyone (the audience or the readers) care about the characters?
5. Are there problematic lines of dialog (lines that don't make any sense or are difficult to say)?
6. Is the audience following the story or did you lose them at some point?
7. What surprised *you*? What was problematic for you?

The best way to deal with feedback is to nod, tell the person giving it that that was a great idea, and ask them for more. People will often, at first, try to be polite and will not want to hurt your feelings with their real opinions. You may have to gently encourage them to be more honest. Try not to get defensive (this is very difficult). Remain engaged in the feedback process – don't zone out.

What you're looking for are *patterns of feedback*. If two people disagree about a particular story point, then chances are that it's a taste issue. But if everyone (or a substantial portion of the audience and/or cast) keeps chiming in on the same points, then you've got issues that you need to address. If everyone has something positive to say about a particular scene or character, then you're onto something. People are very good at spotting *symptoms*, but they may not know the causes. The trick is to take their feedback, backtrack to the underlying cause, and make the adjustments in the script.

Step 2: Post-Reading Corrections

Armed with the results of your reading, go through the script and see if you can pinpoint the strengths and weaknesses that the audience hinted at. It gets harder to solve script problems the closer you get to a "final draft," so do it now while the script is in a somewhat more "flexible" state.

Typically, the problems fall into three broad categories:

1. The first act fails to set up the characters' motivations.
2. The second act stakes don't go high enough.
3. Your main character is too passive, apathetic, or mean.

These are interrelated issues. Usually solving one of them can go a long way towards dealing with the other two. I don't have a catch-all strategy for dealing with these problems – it varies from script to script – but they all occurred in *Found In Time* and in my specs. I think I know why.

In some ways we all fall in love with our heroes and heroines, and it hurts to write them into a corner, and watch while they get beaten up. But audiences need this to feel connected and rooted to the hero; if things are too easy, they lose sympathy. Even Superman had his Kryptonite. And too often we forget that apathy (and passivity) are usually just masks. Holden Caulfield from *Catcher in the Rye*, Yossarian in *Catch-22*, Hamlet, Bond in *The Quantum of Solace*, Matthew and Maria in Hal Hartley's *Trust*, Lisbeth Salander in *The Girl with the Dragon Tattoo* – these heroes affect apathy, sarcasm, ironic distance, passivity, or some combination of all the above, but are in truth deep believers. Optimists in cynic's clothing, if you will. So if your character comes off as too apathetic, chances are you haven't found their core belief yet, the heart that they shield with their apathy.

Often you'll find that what you considered to be a "camera-ready" script isn't really ready. At this point, you should bring the producer into the discussion (or talk to yourself, if you're also the producer). You may need to do a major rewrite, or at least a tweak. Don't say "we can fix it in preproduction." Your first target audiences for the script are investors, actors' agents, and possibly other production companies. These folks are very busy, and you only get one shot at their attention. If you go out with an inferior product, you aren't helping your cause.

Step 3: Icon Pass/Free Association

Read the script, and keep some kind of notebook close by – smartphone, pen and paper, whatever. If you want, write on the script in the margins. Write down associations that come to you while you're reading the script. These could be allusions that the characters make in their dialog, a piece of music that would work very well with the scene, or an image or sound that strikes you as somehow appropriate to a character. Other things you'll want to jot down or highlight include:

1. Iconic images and sounds that are either mentioned in the dialog (metaphorically or literally) or are part of the description
2. Dialog passages that could be converted into actions, or vice-versa
3. Character backstory elements

Your goal is to start thinking about the script as a film – a visual and auditory experience that unfolds in time. Often writers get caught up in the technical details of telling the story, and forget that the medium is about *showing* as much as *telling*. A line of dialog can be replaced with a good reaction shot. Or an image that keeps cropping up in dialog can be shown rather than talked about. A good example of this is the barn-building sequence in *Witness*. There is very little dialog in this sequence, but the action is about much more than the obvious subject. The Amish build their barns together, as a community. John Book (Harrison Ford), despite his affectation as a cynical cop, desperately wants to be a part of a community, so he throws himself into the work. In *Cold Souls* neither the "soul exchange machine" nor the various "soul image" scenes are explained. The machine's shape and color serves as a powerful icon for the film. The scenes where the characters see inside their own souls lack dialog altogether. Yet they perfectly attest to the inscrutable, poetic nature of the soul – in a way these elements are the "soul" of the film.

Alternately, something that's shown (obvious) can be hinted at in dialog instead (subtle). In monster movies, the less you see of the monster the scarier it is. In *Paranormal Activity*, the characters' verbal reactions to seeing the spooky goings-on is what gives the film its impact.

Sounds and musical cues can also set the tone for a film. I often write to nonvocal music. Sometimes I try to actually think of the back and forth between characters as a song or dance of sorts, adhering to a particular rhythm.

Try not to rule out any associations, no matter how absurd they may seem initially. Often, some of the most memorable scenes in a film are the ones where the tone is borderline absurd, where incongruous elements are juxtaposed. *Blue Velvet* features several moments like this, such as when Frank (Dennis Hopper) beats up Jeffrey (Kyle MacLachlan) while a girl dances atop a car to Roy Orbison's "Candy Colored Clown." In *Memento*, Leonard (Guy Pearce) has to put together his reality based on the images and sounds he receives at the present moment, without any "script" except his extensive tattoos to guide him. The results bounce back and forth between comedy and drama, often in the same scene.

One of the side effects of this step is that you'll start accumulating the elements of your director's scrapbook – a collection of sensory data (other films, poems, songs, stills, paintings, etc.) that you can draw on when communicating your vision to the cast and crew.

Step 4: Beat by Beat, Scene by Scene

In Step 3, you looked at the big picture, gently teasing out the deeper elements within the script. This time around, you'll go through the script line by line, scene by scene, sequence by sequence, and really get to know your story at a molecular level. This will inform all future discussions about casting, scheduling, art direction, sound design, editing – in short, pretty much everything that you as a director will be involved with. *So don't rush this.*

Go back from the top, and read through the script again. I usually mark up the script with a pen and highlighter, and fill out a form by hand, but you can do this however you want. Here's what you'll be looking for and doing.

Beat by Beat

The first thing is break each scene into beats. A beat can be defined as a single topic of subtext, usually reflected by a change in dialog, a shift in the physical action, or both. You and I may start a conversation by talking about the weather, then chat about our jobs and how much they suck, then say goodbye. The introductory remarks would constitute one beat; the conversation about the weather a second; and the "anti-boss" diatribe a third. There may be some conversation in between the beats, which define the transitions.

What connects the beats together is the *objective* each character has in the scene. An objective can be stated as:

What do I want you to do for/feel towards me?

What's important here are two things: (a) that the objective involves *someone else*; (b) that the feeling or action verb is *concrete and actable*.

- I want you to love me.
- I want you to forgive me.
- I want you to hit me.
- I want you to feel sorry for me.
- I want you to pay me.
- I want you to hire me.
- I want you to have sex with me.

Notice the rather extreme nature of these objectives. If we actually ran around telling each other that we wanted them to hit us, pay us, or have sex with us, society would quickly fall apart. So we hide our objectives and cloak them in ordinary dialog until they become the subtext of our conversations.

In a script, dramatic action is created when the characters' objectives conflict with each other. For example, if my objective is to get you to *hire* me, your objective should be to *get rid of* me. The scene then becomes a battle of wills between the characters.

Each beat, then, can be seen as not just a change in topic, but a change in the *strategy* used by each character to get what s/he wants from the other. It's rarely the case that all the characters simultaneously start a new beat. Usually the person who's losing the conflict starts a new beat. Or the person who wins the objective may start a new beat with a new underlying objective.

Assuming my *objective* is to have you *love* me, during the course of a single scene I may try the following *strategies*:

- **I will compliment you:** "My, you're looking lovely today."
- **I will protect you:** "Here, let me get that for you, I'm taller."
- **I will bribe you:** "Let me take you to dinner."
- **I will seduce you:** "Do you want a backrub?"
- **I will brag about myself/lie to you:** "Yeah, after I graduated *summa cum laude* I traveled to Thailand and fed the poor."

Exceptions. Sometimes, the objective should be *very* simple. If your character is hungry, maybe all he wants to do *is eat breakfast*. Then the drama of the scene comes from having him stand in an endless line at the deli, only to have the person in front of him counting out exact change in pennies. *American Splendor* features a scene similar to this: Harvey Pekar (Paul Giamatti) waits forever at the supermarket check-out, while the woman in front of him argues over coupons with the cashier.

This scene is the final breaking point in his life – he goes home and starts writing his comics as a way of expressing his anger and frustration.

So don't be afraid of making the objective very simple and physical. Sometimes it's more effective to give an actor something like this rather than a more psychological, abstract objective.

What ties the scenes together into the larger story are the characters' *arcs*. This is the change that the character goes through over the course of the story. Generally, your hero undergoes the most obvious transformation, but all of your characters should undergo some kind of change, no matter how minor. The change has to be something that can be *felt* and acted upon, so it can't be too abstract.

Some directors and actors want to go further, and find the characters' *spine*. Some people use the two phrases interchangeably, while others argue that there is a difference between them. To me it boils down to *change* vs. *constancy*. If the arc is the *change* that the character undergoes, the spine is the collection of traits and behaviors that are *constant* and don't change. The arc and spine serve as connective tissue, and can keep you thinking about the big picture and not getting too bogged or "beat"-en down in moment-to-moment concerns.

Note that when you're talking to your cast, you may or may not want to get this technical with them. Some actors really benefit from it, whereas others will want you to give them something physical to do and they'll supply the motivation. Others respond better to visual cues (hence the scrapbook). Part of the point of your script analysis is to develop *several points of attack* so you can switch your communication strategy with each cast member.

Figure 6.2 is a visual way of representing the scene/beat/objective/arc.

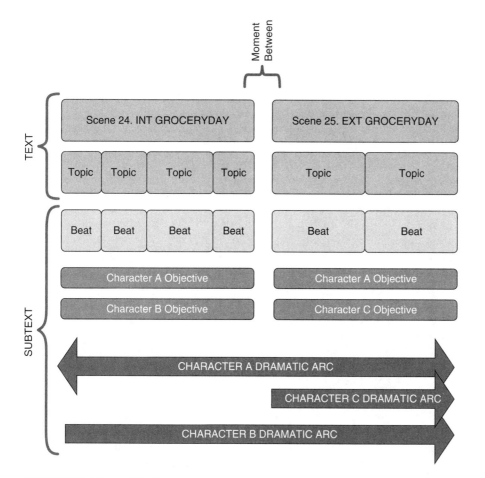

FIGURE 6.2 A layered look at scenes.

Since you're starting with the surface – the script – and working your way inward, you'll probably find it easiest to look at the actual dialog and action (the text) and then figure out the subtext. I separate the changes in conversational topics with a horizontal line on the script itself. Then I figure out what the subtext – the strategy – is that's driving the topic. Then, after re-reading the scene having figured out the characters' strategies, I come up with their objectives.

Other people prefer to figure out the objective first after reading the whole scene, then "line" the script when they see beat changes. Either way will work. The main thing is that you stay as close as possible to what's actually in the script. If it's not on the script, you won't be able to make a case for it in your analysis.

Judith Weston, in her excellent books *Directing Actors* and *The Film Director's Intuition*, suggests coming up with at least three objectives per actor in each scene. Her idea is that you should give yourself as many options as possible. Since you usually don't have much time to work with your cast before you shoot, you may not know what will turn them on. I agree with this, with the caveat that you should try to prioritize a little bit, and perhaps figure out which objective you're going to try out first.

So, you've lined and marked up your script. Great. Now what?

Divide and Conquer

Now you'll want to go through your script again and look for the following:

Blocking/stage directions. These are placeholders for the real blocking that you're going to work out on set. Unless you really know the locations and the actors you're going to be working with, or have a very specific visual in mind, you should pare down blocking directions as much as possible. You don't want the actors to feel overly constrained. Often, you, the cast, and the DP will be able to come up with something better.

Parentheticals. These are emotional "cheats" that writers put in, to place emphasis on a specific line. Trim these out as much as possible. Actors will often try to mold their performance around them rather than finding their own way of delivering the lines. Often a parenthetical remark can be brought into the description.

Obstacles. These can be physical, mental, or emotional. Often, a physical obstacle will acquire greater significance if it also carries thematic/emotional weight. A good example of this is the scene between Pascal (Ian Holm) and Secondo (Stanley Tucci) in *Big Night*. Secondo, whose restaurant is failing, has come to Pascal, whose competing eatery is booming, for a loan or advice. Pascal tries talking to him, but the desk lamp in his office is sitting directly between them. In one motion Pascal finally sweeps it aside. This little gesture carries a lot of weight – Pascal hides his true face, and Secondo is blinded by wishful thinking. Ideally, the main characters (or their behavior) act as each other's obstacles.

Obstacles can be global (recur throughout the script) or transient (happen only in one scene). In *Gladiator*, the transient obstacles are the German barbarians and the competing gladiators. The global obstacle is Commodus (Joaquin Phoenix) and the system of cruelty and slavery he sits atop of. Ideally the transient obstacle is put in place by the global one. A character's weakness can be their own global obstacle, but this has to be made concrete and actable or it becomes too abstract. Tony Soprano's (James Gandolfini's) self-destructive behaviors in *The Sopranos* – beating people up when he gets angry, sleeping around, provoking his sister – are all physical, real phenomena that highlight him as his own global obstacle.

Moment before. This is absolutely crucial. Two scenes in a script may be separated by seconds, minutes, hours, days, even centuries of off-screen time. What happened in between to the characters? Were they together in the next room having an argument? Were they at their day jobs? Was one asleep? Is the moment before somewhere in the script (it could be 10 pages prior, or occur later in the script as a flashback)? Figuring out the moment before each scene starts will give you a powerful means of dealing with two very common problems in filmmaking.

First, because scripts are rarely shot in order, it becomes almost impossible to keep track of where the characters are in their arcs. Usually you base the schedule around location availability, time of day, and other production concerns. In this fractured environment, you need to be able to anchor the cast and crew to the bigger picture. The moment before helps do this.

Second, talking to the actors about the moment before helps to keep them from playing *the end of the scene at the beginning*. Ideally, a scene consists of a dramatic conflict, with an outcome of some kind (even if the outcome just sets up the next scene's conflict). Since the actors know the outcome of the scene already, it's very tempting for them to start the scene by "playing the end." If you've read a film review that contains spoilers, and then see the film, then you know this feeling. "I know how this scene turns out, the main character isn't really dead, so I'm not going to get all weepy about it." By talking with the actors about the moment before, you'll be giving them new information that takes their mind off the end of the scene.

Love in the scene. Going back to *Gladiator* and comparing it to, say, *300*, which villain is ultimately the more memorable? Despite being depicted as an eight-foot drag queen, Xerxes (Rodrigo Santoro) never achieves real dimensionality as a villain, because we never really get a sense of his purpose. Why does he want to conquer Greece? Does he think the Spartans are a bunch of militaristic, fascist thugs and that he stands for a more democratic, heterodox ideal of empire? Does he love his subjects and feels like he has to fight the Spartans or risk them enslaving *his* people? Is he seeking to honor his dead father Darius? *Who does he love so much* that he would risk taking on the fiercest warriors in the land?

Commodus (Joaquin Phoenix), on the other hand, desperately loves his father Marcus (Richard Harris), and is horribly upset when he sees that Marcus favors Maximus (Russell Crowe). Maximus loves his wife and son (Giannina Facio and Giorgio Cantarini). From these simple ideas – two people loving their families – you end up having a sword-and-sandals movie with real weight.

Your characters – whether they are villains, heroes, sidekicks, or even the one-liner/bit players – have to love someone. Love will make the most heinous villain more interesting, the most "noble" hero more human, and will enliven even the smallest role. The "love object" can be one of the other characters in the scene (who may also be the obstacle, which is the setup of many romantic comedies), or it can be someone who's dead or who the person hasn't directly met yet. One of the funniest sequences in the Indian film *Main Hoon Na* takes place on a train. The hero, Ram Sharma (Shah Rukh Khan), talks to a complete stranger about his half-brother Lakshman (Zayed Khan), who he never knew as a child, and is only now about to meet. Being a military man from a career army father, Ram imagines an upright, noble, bold, studious young man. Of course Lakshman turns out to be a juvenile delinquent who's repeating his senior year for a third time. For his part, Lakshman acts this way because his heart is broken – growing up without a father or brother. They each have a fantasy "love" that doesn't jibe with reality.

The heroine can love one person in one scene and their rival in another. This is also a romantic comedy tactic – often the person you had your heart set on turns out not to be "the one." The characters can love someone that they just met, or have known for years but never thought about. Even if your characters are fighting with each other, they usually love each other (in fact, people who are truly bored or dislike each other don't tend to fight as vociferously). This is *Who's Afraid of Virginia Woolf?* territory.

Loving someone doesn't prevent dramatic or extreme action – just the opposite. A parent casts out a child as a "hard love" lesson (*The Chosen* or *Thor*), a brother kills another brother for betraying "the family" (*Godfather Part II*), a man gets a job he hates to support the woman he loves (*Trust*), a woman sleeps with a horrible man to get money for her brother's college tuition (*Set It Off*).

Sounds/props/"physical images." Apart from the iconic images and sounds that recur throughout the script, you may notice some nifty images that crop up in the dialog, some important background sounds, and/or some props or set-dressing items that the actors can play with.

A good image, sound, or "thing" is something that the actors can immediately picture/hear in their heads. The Statue of Liberty is a great image; "liberty" is not. These images, sounds, and things can help actors get their bearing on a scene. If they're actually *in* the scene they also give the actors something specific and physical to interact with, pick up, look at, listen to, etc.

Facts/given circumstances. The given circumstances are the facts that are actually in the script, plus some "neutral" facts that may not be mentioned directly. A neutral fact would be the character's age, birth order, race, gender, or general physical appearance. If John loses his driver's license in scene 20 and has to drive in scene 120, you can put "lost his license" down as a given circumstance.

You want to give the actor evidence from the script but still give her room to maneuver emotionally. Reminding the actor playing John that he lost his license a while ago will affect how he feels about getting behind the wheel, which will, in turn, affect how he delivers his lines, how fast/slow he drives, whether he hesitates before getting in the car, etc. But one actor might decide that he's afraid of getting caught, and will speed up his dialog (let's get in the car and get out of here) but will drive very carefully. Another actor will decide that John's still mad at losing his license and will speed away. Facts are great because they're tangible and don't involve judgments about the character. Your actor can take a set of facts and build actable choices around them.

What bothers or surprises you. You may find that a line of dialog doesn't seem to be working. Or that a beat seems to be coming too early in the scene. Or that the character did something you didn't expect. These are not necessarily things that have to be fixed – on the contrary, they may point up something really important about the scene or the character.

In *Found In Time*, Chris (MacLeod Andrews) explains that he became a psychic shortly after dying of sudden infant death syndrome (SIDS) and being revived. The line came out of nowhere, and it didn't seem to pay off. Introducing something as hefty as SIDS into the script seemed odd. But it turned out to be an important key to understanding the way all the psychics felt. What if all the psychics had acquired their "gifts" after undergoing severe trauma/near-death experiences? How would that make them feel about "ordinary" life? Would they be less afraid of death because they'd already been "to the beyond"? Or would it be something horrible they didn't want to repeat?

This in turn became an exercise I gave to the actors who were playing psychics: to develop (if it wasn't already in the script) or personalize (if it was) these near-death experiences. I believe it added something to their performances.

What you want to end up with is something that looks like the form in Table 6.1. A blank version of this chart is in Appendix B (Figure B.1). Feel free to use your own form. If you have more than three characters in your scene, just use more than one page.

Obviously, you may find that this form doesn't work for you. Invent your own, use a spreadsheet, fill out a notebook – the format doesn't matter. Don't worry about spelling or handwriting (unless you can't read it). Chances are that no one else will see these notes.

Step 5: Tweak and Repeat

It's more than likely that you will have found, after all of these steps, that you need to make some tweaks to the script. Several lines can be excised; scenes need to be trimmed, beefed up, or reordered; or a line of exposition should be added. Do this now rather than wait.

You can still use the materials you've generated up to this point (the script analysis sheets, lists of images, etc.). If the rewrite looks like it will be very significant, then you may, down the road, have to go through some version of the above steps again. However, the script analysis sheets can actually help streamline the rewriting process, so they are by all means still valuable.

Step 6: Thinking About the Camera, Blocking, Editing

Hopefully, the analysis you've done up to this point has led you to thinking about the script in a new way. Instead of seeing words on a page, you've got a whole world in your head now, with complex characters, and a story that's even bigger than the script. Now you can start thinking about

TABLE 6.1 A single-scene breakdown

SCENE #:	**11**		
SCENE:	**INT. JOHN'S APARTMENT – DAY**		
DESCRIPTION:	John and Barney (brothers) talk over breakfast about Jane and Barney's relationship; Jane overhears but enters pretending not to have heard anything. Phone rings – it's Barney's job. He leaves with John.		

	John	*Barney*	*Jane*
Objective:	To have sex with Jane To get Jane to fall in love with him	To have sex with Jane To get to work To get John to settle down	To kick John out of the house To eat breakfast
Obstacle:	Barney	John, because he won't stop talking	John, because he's interrupting their domestic bliss
Moment Before:	John woke up and called his ex-girlfriend – a dude answered	Argued in the bedroom with Jane about "what to do about John"	Argued in the bedroom with Barney about "what to do about John"
Love in Scene:	Jane Barney	John Jane	Barney
Images:	Picture of his ex His sleeping bag in the corner of the living room Kitchen table is a family heirloom	Waking up next to Jane Sound of the shower in the morning Coffee	Coffee Sound of shower Sink full of dishes
Given Circ.:	John hasn't worked in four months John has been living with them for two weeks	Barney gave John some money, and Jane doesn't know about it Barney works at a car dealership	It was John's turn to do the dishes John was Barney's best man at wedding
Surprises?	John says he's looking for work, but in prev. scene he was sleeping in. Has he been looking for work off-screen?		

shooting, blocking, and editing. The script analysis pages and beat markers can help you in several ways, and keep your shotlisting and storyboarding grounded in the drama of the story.

Think in terms of axes of tension. If two people face each other, the axis is the line of sight that connects them – their eyeline, in other words. However you shoot this scene, you usually want to keep the camera along one side of their eyelines and restrain your camera angles so that the characters appear to be looking at each other, or that they're both lined up with the axis. This way the audience can follow the axis without thinking about it. If the eyelines don't match up, there should be a reason – someone or something is in the way (a dramatic obstacle), or one character doesn't want the other to see where s/he is. Otherwise, it will look like the characters aren't looking at each other when in fact they are.

You can use eyeline matching to establish emotional connections between two scenes that are otherwise separated in time and space. A great example of this is in *Blue Valentine*, where Dean (Ryan Gosling), in a flashback from several years ago, looks at the camera after having just moved an old man into a rest home. The film then cuts to a scene several years later, to a shot of Cindy (Michelle Williams). Because the eyelines match perfectly, it looks like a reverse shot. Then you realize that the characters are looking back and forth at each other across the span of their relationship.

You can create an axis of tension even when the characters are not looking directly at each other. Hal Hartley's films *Trust*, *Simple Men*, *Amateur*, and *Henry Fool* all feature conversations where both characters talk to each other but don't look at each other. Often they're looking in the same direction, usually while discussing rather painful things. However, Hartley (and Michael Spiller, his DP) know where to place the camera so as to create the axis properly.

Often, the characters will change their physical position on the transition from one beat to the next, and a new axis will be established. In a police procedural, the detective may realize he's got to get tougher on the suspect, so he moves in closer in the interrogation room. In a gangster movie, the snitch realizes he's about to be killed and runs away. In a drama, the husband realizes his wife has been cheating on him and gets up from the dinner table. In all these instances, the axis breaks off and realigns itself. This is where you have the greatest freedom in terms of cutting and camera movement.

Generally, once you establish an axis, you want to tie your shot choices to it. A common mistake I see in first-time directors is the inclusion of a "cool shot." It's a visual that works great – but it has nothing to do with the tension in the scene, so it just kind of sits there. A good example of this is in *Constantine*, which otherwise features some very good shot choices. An exorcism scene starts with an extreme close up of a cigarette that John Constantine (Keanu Reeves) leaves on the edge of a table. The payoff comes at the end of the scene when he picks up the same cigarette, now burned down to a short butt. The problem with the shot is that, as interesting-looking as it is, it doesn't communicate anything. The time could have been better spent on a reaction shot of Constantine, both before and after the exorcism. Since the shot takes place early in the film, when we've just met the main character, it's even more of a waste.

As you read the script analysis pages and start coming up with possible shots, think carefully about script order. When seeing a location for the first time, you should try to give the audience some sense of the dimensions of the place, and where the characters are in relation to it. *Serenity* features an excellent traveling master that follows Mal (Nathan Fillion) and Simon (Sean Maher) across the entire spaceship *Serenity*, introducing us to one of the central conflicts in the story (Mal as savage vs. the Simon as civilized man), as well as the craft itself. Classic directors who "broke" the eyeline matching rules (Ozu, Kurosawa, Hitchcock on occasion) were usually pretty disciplined at the beginning of their films. Even the cuts across the eyeline serve to familiarize the audience with the space.

The physicality of the script's characters should become more obvious to you at this point. Do you notice how the different characters react to stress? Do they walk around, do dishes, sit down, run away, push people away (literally or figuratively)? While you don't want to overblock the script (see my previous comments), you do want to make note of consistent behavior and see if it can be used thematically. Even if you see that your script consists largely of people sitting down and talking, you can make this *physically* interesting. *Clerks*, *Mallrats*, and *Chasing Amy* feature fairly static shots of actors talking. But Kevin Smith always gives his actors something to do – in *Clerks* Randal (Jeff Anderson) is always playing with something, stealing something from the store, or generally causing problems for Dante (Brian O'Halloran). In *Chasing Amy*, Holden (Ben Affleck) and Alyssa (Joey Lauren Adams) have a conversation while throwing darts.

If you're a really good illustrator, or if you tend to think visually rather than verbally, you may want to storyboard the script at this point, using the analysis you've done so far as a guide. But be aware that until you've hired your DP, scouted your locations, and cast your film, these boards are very speculative in nature. A lot of directors make little "comic strip" boards, using stick figures or quick sketches, sometimes on the script itself.

I like to mark up the script with notes ("insert shot here?") indicating possible setups. Or if I'm pretty sure of how the characters are going to sit/stand/move in relation to each other, I'll draw top-down diagrams indicating actor placement and camera angles. But these doodles and notes are only suggestions.

Step 7: Character Sheets/Bios

Now that you've broken down the script and found the story, it's time to put it all back together and figure out the characters' arcs. Some directors like to write out lengthy character bios. These can be good exercises, but you do run the risk of psychoanalyzing the characters, which will give your actors *less* to work with. If you do create a bio, I recommend sticking to facts and avoiding explanations. Here's a concrete example of the difference between psychoanalysis…

> John has always been haunted by a fear of abandonment stemming from the loss of his father at age 11.

and fact:

> John's father died when he was 11.

The former tells the actor what to feel, whereas the latter gives him the evidence and lets him reconstruct the characters' feelings, thereby making them his own.

Questions and Answers

I do find it helpful to put together a list of questions and answers about the character. I usually start with a standard set of questions:

1. What does John want?
2. What does John need?
3. How would John describe his job?
4. What's the longest romantic relationship he's ever been in?
5. What schools did he go to?
6. What kind of music does he listen to?
7. What environment did he grow up in (city, country, suburbs; big house, small apartment, etc.)?
8. What did his parent(s) do for a living?
9. Does John want to do anything for a living/work besides his current job?
10. Who does John love (even if that person never shows up in the script)?
11. What kind of clothes does he wear?
12. What is his favorite color?

Appendix B features a more complete version of this questionnaire (Figures B.2–B.4). You can add or subtract questions as you see fit. The main point of these questionnaires is to come up with possible, but not necessarily definitive, answers. Ideally, the cast will also bring some answers to the table, and out of the collaboration, fully fleshed-out characters will emerge.

An alternative to answering the questionnaire is to list out significant questions raised by the script itself (which may overlap with the ones above). In *Found In Time*, very few of the characters had last names. So one of my questions was "What is Ayana's last name?" I usually let the actors fill this in. The last names they chose strengthened their bond to the character.

You may want to keep the Q&A sheets and character bios away from your actors. It depends on how much help you think they'll need in creating the character. Some actors can translate bios and Q&As into useful material; others will use them as a crutch, so it's better to give them less than more.

APPLYING THE WORK TO PRODUCTION

Your deeper understanding of the story and characters will inform the production in several ways. In later chapters we'll talk about the vision statement, and about how to translate the analysis into strong visual and audio choices with regard to costumes, props, set dressing, makeup, hair, and sound design. Here are a few things to think about now.

Scheduling

The producer and first assistant director will put together a schedule based on production concerns – consolidating locations and actor days, equipment availability, etc. As a director, you should apply your script analysis work to this process. You have a better sense of what scenes will be harder to shoot from a dramatic perspective. If you have a heavy scene that will tire out your actors, don't schedule it first up or right after lunch. If there's a scene that changes or defines a character in some way, it's probably best to shoot this ahead of another scene where the character has to review what's happened.

Try not to schedule anything at the beginning of the script for the first day of shooting. Both you and the actors will still be getting a handle on the characters, and audiences are more forgiving of lapses in characterization in the middle of the film than they are at the beginning.

Allow "geometrically" more time for scenes involving more than two people. For example, a scene involving two characters could take five setups: one master (1), one close-up (CU) each (2), one tighter two-shot (1), and cutaways (1). A scene involving three characters could take, in theory, nine setups: one master (1), one CU each (3), one tighter-two-shot for each pair (3), a tighter three-shot (1 or 2), and cutaways (1). Four character scenes would take 15: master (1); CUs (4); two-shots of each pair (4); three-shots (4); a tighter-"four" (1); cutaways (1). Obviously, you may not want to cover your scenes completely, but keep in mind that figuring out entrances, exits, and blocking will still take some time.

Visual Design

Now that you have some sense of the iconography present in the script, as well as a deeper sense of the characters, can you translate this into a color scheme? In a film I line produced, *Rock the Paint*, scenes involving the countryside were shot and color-corrected to create a warmer, yellow/orange look. The scenes in Newark were shot in a blue tone that grew darker as the film went on. The director, Phil Bertelsen, and DP, John Foster, made this decision after Phil had sat down with the script for a while. It was a very effective and inexpensive way of conveying the main characters' journey from a rural, somewhat safe environment to one of uncertainty.

There may be a prop or piece of set dressing that says something about your character. On *Helena from the Wedding* (a film I production managed), one of the main characters, Don (Dominic Fumusa), drives an old, reconditioned jeep. The jeep played a large part in both the plot (it kept breaking down) and in what it said about the owner (he was trying to keep his somewhat fragile marriage together).

One of the main characters in *Found In Time*, Ayana (Mina Vesper Gokal), dresses only in black. But she deals with threads and textiles which are themselves very colorful. This clash between her sense of self (reflected in her dress) and her outlook (reflected in her work) gave Mina some good material to chew on, and also gave the costume designer a means of telling her story visually.

Sound Design

What kind of music does your character listen to? What conversations does she pick out at a party? Does the noise of the city or the quiet of the country bother or soothe her? What does her home sound like? These choices can inform the sound design and elevate the drama significantly.

Voice-over can be a very powerful tool, if done correctly. It can reinforce the visuals (as in Terrence Malick's *Tree of Life*) or contradict them to reveal more about the characters (as in Alexander Payne's *Election*). Bad voice-over merely repeats what the audience already knows. If you have voice-over in your script, do you find that it adds to the characters' arcs and subtext, or does it merely rehash the text? If you don't have a voice-over, would it help to add some or would it merely make the script unnecessarily complicated?

PUTTING IT ALL TOGETHER

This is enjoyable work. Try to do it before the madness of preproduction starts. Production concerns tend to overwhelm artistic ones, especially on a tight budget. Your crew needs to be given a concrete sense of what you're looking to accomplish so they can be sure they're on the right track. Your cast needs the scaffolding upon which they can find their characters.

This work will also demonstrate to other people that you're prepared to direct. This is an important component of leadership (see Chapter 4) and casting (which we'll discuss shortly). Finally, it will give you a crucial "big picture" sense of the story. Most of the rest of your job will involve working with people on details. And during the shoot, it will be extremely difficult to think about the big picture when you're trying to move take-by-take and setup-by-setup through your day. Do the work now and you'll always have something to refer to later.

QUESTIONS/EXERCISES

1. Get a copy of a script that you *haven't* written, either a spec that's floating out there or one that's based on an existing film. Imagine that you've just been hired to direct the film. Apply the script analysis steps to two or three scenes in the script.
2. Go to an online dating site and fill out profiles for some of your main characters. Keep your answers relatively concise. In case the site blocks you from saving fictional characters, print screenshots or save them as PDFs – or just copy and paste the questions into a separate document and fill it all out offline. Save yourself some agony and stay away from sites with insanely long profiling questionnaires.
3. Looking at your script, can you think of a color scheme that fits each of your lead characters and their homes?
4. What music do your characters listen to? What music did you listen to when you wrote the script?

## Chapter 7

Gathering Materials

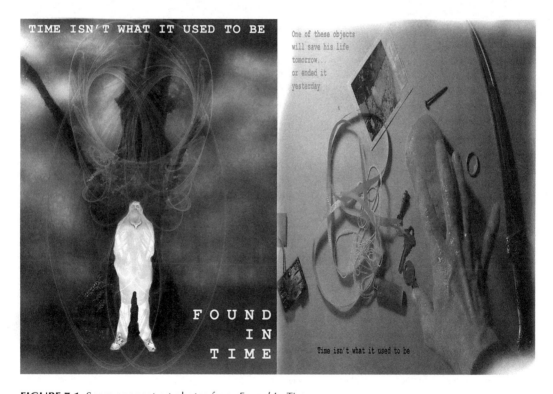

FIGURE 7.1 Some concept art photos from *Found In Time*.

So, at this point you've done your director's script analysis, and hopefully your producer's breakdown. You have a sharp sense of the story you want to tell, and some ideas of how to execute it. The next step on the journey is to translate this knowledge into forms the crew and cast can use.

Since no one has come up with a commercially viable telepathy device, you'll have to put together a "look-book." This doesn't have to be a single document. But it should show in as concrete a way as possible what you want to achieve in your film, and how you want to get there. In a sense, you've been doing this all along in the course of creating your marketing elements, script analysis, and character bios.

COMPONENTS

Your look-book is really a set of items, that you've either created yourself (this is great but isn't necessary) or found:

1. Still images (photographs, paintings, illustrations, collages, etc.) that focus on costume choices, color schemes, architecture
2. Some clips from films, TV shows, or webisodes whose style you like
3. Poetry, books, magazine articles, blogs, and other written materials that are character-based, or focus on one aspect or another of the world of the film
4. Props, costumes, or other objects that are related to your film
5. A vision statement (similar to the one you wrote in Chapter 5) that ties all this material together
6. Some directors like to include storyboards in here

If this looks a lot like the materials you assembled during Chapter 5, you're correct. The goal is also similar – to communicate your vision to others. The key difference is that the look-book is oriented towards your cast and crew, and is more like a guidebook or sketch of the world you want to build.

But you don't want to just shove a whole bunch of stills, clips, and articles at people. You need to be more selective, and also understand the different ways in which people learn.

Learning and Stimuli

Learning is a bit of a magical process. They receive new information, analyze it, integrate it into their existing worldview, and then use it in various ways until it becomes a part of their identity. Some people seem to pick up and recall new things very quickly, but can't put them into practice right away. So I *understood* differentiation and integration in calculus almost immediately, but it took me *forever* to solve test equations. Other people take a long time to digest information (you have to repeat things over and over again), but once they start using it practically they "get it." Learning acting was like that for me; I couldn't really see the beat changes in a scene until I started *acting*, and then it all snapped into focus.

People also vary tremendously in what kind of stimuli they respond best to when learning. There are eight very broad categories of stimuli:

1. **Visuals:** Watching video and looking at stills.
2. **Text:** Reading books, articles, etc.
3. **Non-verbal sound:** Music and environmental noise.
4. **Verbal instruction:** What you got a lot of in school, when the teacher would stand in front of the class and lecture you.
5. **Dialog:** Instead of a lecture, you have a discussion that goes back and forth.
6. **Action:** What you did in physical education class. You mimic the teacher's movements.
7. **Touch.**
8. **Taste/smell:** I'm putting these together because they're so hard to separate.

Since you don't know at this stage who you'll be working with, you'll want to make sure that you have enough material that fits into each of these categories. So, for example, some people will want you to talk about what you want to do. Other people will want you to show them.

Many DPs respond to discussions, but backed up by a lot of visual references. Some actors work better by seeing and then mimicking the blocking you're getting at. You get the idea. Now, how do you teach people through action, touch, taste, and smell? Where do you put that in your look-book?

The short answer is that you *imply* these things. Or you come up with exercises that the actors and crew can do on their own (or with you). A good example of action is physical training. I line produced a film called *Rock the Paint*, and the lead characters – all high-school students – were supposed to be basketball superstars. The director asked the actors to practice basketball as often as possible before the shoot. If you've written a musical, you'd hire a choreographer to design the dances and rehearse the moves with the cast.

Costume designers often work by touch – they pay attention to the drape of clothing on the skin, and the texture of certain fabrics. Some actors require touch to feel like they're really "getting in touch" with the character. I remember playing a soldier in a high-school play. Simply dressing up in my uniform and carrying a prop gun around a week before the first show suddenly made the whole experience more immediate and real, even after a month of rehearsals. So you can provide actors and costume designers with props, or give them some poems or prose samples that use very tactile, concrete language.

If you're directing a film that takes place in a restaurant, you can talk to your actors about how the food tastes, about what it's like to work in the kitchen. There's no faster way to create a strong emotional reaction in someone than talking about a bad smell or taste. The smell or lack of it in certain environments can definitely affect a character's behavior. For *Found In Time*, I wanted to create a dark, oppressive atmosphere in one particular location. I didn't end up having to use these, but I listed all the smells I could think of that would be associated with the place, so I could feed them to the cast if I had to.

GETTING THE MATERIALS

I recommend making as much of the reference material for the look-book as possible, particularly the stills and of course the Vision Statement (more on this below). Something about the process of going out and taking photographs gets me thinking in three dimensions, which is an essential part of blocking. You don't need a very expensive camera to get going, nor do you need Photoshop to tweak the images. There are a few low-cost or free photo-processing applications out – Paint.NET and GIMP, to name a few – that are fully featured. GIMP can even save to PSD files, so Photoshop can read them.

An Example of Shooting Your Own Stills

For *Found In Time* I scheduled some location scouting days about five months before we shot the film. On a couple of the days Ben Wolf, the DP, went with me. We walked through a number of neighborhoods. I had the script and some notes with me, describing what I was looking for. Most of the time we just tried to keep an open mind and take a lot of shots.

About 90 percent of the shots I took were garbage – Ben's photos were far better. But we learned a few key things, namely: (a) what *wouldn't* work location-wise, and (b) what kind of lighting and setting we were looking to achieve. We wanted to make it clear that the story was taking place in New York City, but without referring to the traditional landmarks. We wanted to show all the streetlife of the present-day city, but also present a slightly off-kilter or menacing look.

I also took some of the shots and compared them to other photos I'd shot. This inspired me to put some more stills together that eventually did make it into the look-book.

So, from the scouting shot in Figure 7.2 I was inspired to find one I'd taken a year earlier, shown, after some Photoshop work, in Figure 7.3. I can't tell you exactly what the relationship between the two photos is (apart from the obvious one of the bridge and the park). But something about the desolate, overgrown nature of the first shot led me to think about one of the main characters, Ayana, and her state of loneliness. I later included this shot in the Vision Statement handouts I made for the crew and cast.

Mina Vesper Gokal, the actress playing Ayana, was an art history major, so we spent a lot of time looking at photographs and paintings that reflected her character.

FIGURE 7.2 Astoria in Queens.

FIGURE 7.3 Concept art from the film.

Music

Music is the most immediate way to communicate the tone you're aiming for. Richard Curtis, in the DVD commentary on *Love, Actually*, stated that listening to Joni Mitchell's amazing re-rendition of her song "Both Sides Now" was part of the inspiration for the script. If you think about your own life, you'll probably find music tied to specific memories and emotions. If you play some of that music, you may even feel as though you're traveling back in time.

Your music selections will be especially effective if they cover similar tonal territory. When I was pulling tunes for *Found In Time* I initially amassed a collection of about one hundred or so tracks, covering every genre from rockabilly to classical. Eventually, I settled on about a dozen pieces, including a couple of Arabic oud pieces, two songs by avante-rock singer/songwriter Rebecca Moore, *Te Deum* by minimalist classical composer Arvo Pärt, and Berlioz's *Requiem*. While this still seems pretty chaotic, all of these pieces had a certain "minor key" sensibility in common. Together they didn't quite make up an organic score, but they were evocative enough for the actors.

It's great if, along the way, you find tracks you think will work for the score. But the focus should be on finding music that's inspirational, that the characters might listen to in the world of the film. Music should ideally be keyed to certain characters. You don't necessarily have to tell an actor that a given piece of music is for his/her character, but it helps if you can associate the character to the song.

Video Clips

This is difficult work. What you want to do is find a few clips or films that convey what you're going after. But you don't want your actors or crew to completely ape the style of these films. The clips should simply serve as points of inspiration. So when you're watching films, you want to pay more attention to the form (how the story is told) – and less to the content (the story itself). This is not always possible and you shouldn't try too hard to separate the two. Films have so many elements – camerawork, acting, lighting, editing, sound design, costume/production design – that it's hard to pull apart what makes a given scene or film great.

I usually start with the films I listed in my business plan, but ditch them very quickly. Often the subject matter is either too close or too different. I'm looking for material that matches *the intended style execution.* For this reason, it can sometimes be helpful to look at films outside your script's genre.

Some people watch films with the sound off to focus on the visual elements. I know a few directors who've ripped DVDs of classic films and tried to re-edit key scenes, to try and understand what makes the pacing work. Other people make a note after each cut and go nearly frame-by-frame through scenes.

My own approach is much less rigorous. I pick out a few films that I like that have some surface similarity to my script, or whose technical work I admire, and try and figure out *why* I think these films would be good things to show the cast and crew. I usually look at colors, textures, and camerawork first, editing second, sound third, and performances last.

Getting input from other people is invaluable at this point. My DP, editor, and attorney always have some good suggestions – the three of them each have an encyclopedic knowledge of film, and have different enough tastes that I'll get a nice variety of samples to sift through.

Text

Poems are the best texts to use, hands down. They're compact, quickly read, and are open to interpretation. The ambiguity inherent in the form can lead to some great discussions. Having said that, poetry does require some effort to read and fit into your film's themes. So I usually end up choosing only a couple of poems to use in the Vision Statement.

If one of your characters has a particular profession, obviously you'll want to copy some reference materials that can help the actor understand what s/he's talking about. If your film takes place in a particular milieu or subculture, find a magazine or Wikipedia article that can give the cast and crew a little background.

I try to avoid citing plays or novels. It's too easy for the cast and crew to get lost in the story and concerns of these works and stray too far from your own. An actor who I'd cast in *Found In Time* (who later left due to scheduling conflicts) kept referencing *The Time Traveler's Wife* novel as a point of reference for the script. After a certain point, it became clear that he was trying to map the *Found In Time* plot and time-travel mechanics onto those of *Time Traveler's Wife*. I eventually had to ask him to kindly leave the book out of the conversation and try to approach the script without referencing it.

Likewise, be careful including overly intellectual works. You don't want to let the cast and crew get too stuck in their heads and lose touch with the sensual world. This is another reason poetry works so well – it is intellectual, sensual, and emotional all at once.

Props/Objects/Working in Three Dimensions

Oliver Stone hired then-retired Marine Captain Dale Dye to put his cast through a version of boot camp, in order to prepare for their roles in *Platoon*. He even had Dye conduct an exercise where the actors had to put one of their own comrades into a body-bag, to give them a sense of what the actual experience was like. This has since become a fairly routine practice in military-themed films and TV shows – the cast of the 2003–2009 *Battlestar Galactica* series underwent similar training. You probably can't afford quite that level of preparation, but perhaps there are other physical experiences or objects you can give the cast and crew.

Any kind of model, prop, or costume that you can buy/borrow/make will be of enormous help to the cast and crew. Nothing beats having an object in front of you that you can touch and examine in three dimensions. You can also organize tours with your cast when you get a little closer to production – not just of the onscreen locations, but also of the offscreen ones as well.

Time is an important dimension to consider as well. Can you find a toy, book, or puzzle that was important to the characters' childhoods? Are there old props that the characters might keep in their closets, out of sentimentality?

Don't forget clothing! Even still images of clothes are a great aid when working with the costume designer. What do your characters wear? Are there colors that they like?

ORGANIZING THE MATERIALS

At this point you should have a variety of materials you can hand out to your cast and crew. If the music doesn't grab one actor, then maybe the stills will. Your production and costume designers will appreciate any visual aids you can bring to the table. Hopefully, some element in this collection will ignite somebody's preferred method of learning.

Your Vision Statement should talk briefly about the style of the film, and mention the musical, textual, and video references. Include at least a few of the production stills. Some directors create a complete book with character and location "looks," color swatches, quotes from poems, photos, stills, preliminary boards, and/or extensive notes on the shooting style. Other directors keep a scrapbook of material that's less organized, and just pull what they need from it to give to the crew and cast. Still others make extensive sketches of the characters and/or settings (Ridley Scott was famous for making "Ridleygrams" to describe the future he envisioned for *Blade Runner*). If you have this kind of talent, that's great.

Ultimately, the book should serve as a guide or stepping-stone to the final film, not the film itself, so don't get too carried away. And keep in mind that this book will change over time and evolve, especially after you've cast the film, hired the crew, and nailed your locations.

WHAT TO LEAVE OUT AND WHAT TO ADD

Keep in mind that your crew and cast will be coming to you with their own ideas, some of which will be better than yours. If your look-book is *too complete* and "airtight," they may not feel that they have as much to contribute, and so may ironically find it less engaging. Also, people can only take so much information at a time before getting overwhelmed. So you may want to dole things out a little at a time, and/or break up the book into specific departments, rather than hand them a 100-page tome.

You also want to avoid getting too intellectual in your Vision Statement. If you have very intellectual themes in mind, find a way to express them in concrete terms. People will get confused if your language is too abstract and removed from the sensual world.

On the other hand, you may have to customize the material for each person. My costume designer and I ended up preparing a separate document with photos, and passed it back and forth to each other. My DP and I shared photos and film clips with each other throughout preproduction. The composer, editor, and I passed music files back and forth. So while everyone started out with a copy of the Vision Statement, I kept adding little department-specific items to it.

QUESTIONS

1. What do your characters see on their way to work or home every day?
2. Do they have sentimental objects in their lives?
3. When you think of how you'd like to shoot your film, are there other films that come to mind?
4. Are there pieces of music that inspire you? Is there a piece that summarizes the emotional undertone you're going for?

## Chapter 8

Preparing for Casting

FIGURE 8.1 Preparing for casting.

Casting an independent film is hard, unless you've written your script for a set of specific actors you have guaranteed access to. More often you'll have to reach out past your friends for at least some of the roles. But even if you skip the traditional casting process altogether – if you're just going to offer the roles to specific people – you're still better off if you can do some prep work at this stage. You will come out with a better understanding of the characters and the story.

PLANNING THE INTERVIEW

Casting is a strange process. You will end up making yes/no decisions based on seeing actors for only a few minutes at a time. You will have to infer their level of experience and ability to take direction based on very little evidence. The best hedge against making a wrong decision is to structure the audition process so you know what you're looking for in broad terms, before you even meet the actors.

What you want to prepare are a series of documents, some of which are just for you, and others which you'll share with your casting director:

1. **First casting breakdown.** What are the key psychological, physical, and historical traits of each character? A little like a character bio but more distilled. You may want to share this with the casting director, but it's primarily for you to get you familiar with your character.
2. **Second breakdown.** A more condensed version of the first, which you'll give to your casting director.
3. **Your "dream cast."** Who do you want to play the roles (living or dead)?
4. **Sides.** Scenes for the actors to audition with.
5. **Adjustments.** For each side and each actor, what adjustments can you give between readings? I usually start with the scene analysis sheets I created (see Chapter 6 for details). Your casting director will also come up with adjustments, but it's good to go through this exercise yourself, as it will prepare you for working with the actors on set as well.
6. **Suggestions.** Headshots and reels of actors you'd like to have audition; plays, webisodes, and other indie films that the casting director should see. If you want to cast non-actors, photos of the people you have in mind.

Ideally, all this material came out of your script analysis. If you haven't done the analysis yet, I recommend you do so before you start this prep work.

CASTING/AUDITION OVERVIEW

There's no standard casting interaction between the casting director, producer, and director. Sometimes the producer or director looks at headshots with the casting director. Sometimes the casting director does most of the work. During auditions, either the casting director or director may take the lead with the actors. In some cases, the director isn't involved until the callback phase; in others, the director is more hands-on from the very beginning. Much depends on the skill of the director, the budget, and the experience level of the casting director.

However, the casting process does follow a set of well-worn steps. We'll discuss this in more detail in Chapter 15 (where we'll also get into the producer's side of the process). But this brief outline should highlight how the material you're about to prepare will play a vital role.

1. The casting director reads the script and whatever prep materials the director has already created.
2. The director, producer, and casting director meet and talk about the roles and goals.
3. The director does some more homework (producing the above-mentioned documents).
4. The director hands over the second breakdown, dream cast list, sides, and suggestions to the casting director.
5. The casting director modifies the casting breakdown and sends it out to her contacts (agents, managers, producers, theater/film companies, actors), and to local and national breakdown services (such as breakdownservices.com or actorsaccess.com).
6. She then gets flooded with a deluge of candidates. On *Found In Time*, Katherine Hinchey (the casting director) got over 1700 resumes for a handful of roles. Note that if your film contains nudity or a controversial storyline, this flood could be reduced to a trickle.
7. Using your breakdown sheet and dream cast list; her own contacts, knowledge of acting, training, directors, producers, theaters; and skill at reading resumes and watching clips, the casting director eliminates most of the prospects and adds a few others. The result is a much-winnowed down list of candidates.

8. In some cases, the casting director will present you with the list, so you can make a further round of eliminations. In others, she'll use it to schedule the auditions. In the case of *Found In Time*, Kat passed me between 50 and 80 people each for the leads, and 20–30 candidates for each supporting role. She also placed some of my suggestions into the mix.

9. If you're working on the list with the casting director, you'll group the members of this list into one of four categories: "A" (first choice), "B" (second choice), "C" (third choice), and "X" (no way). Try to get down to 40 actors (at most) per role.

10. The casting director will set up the audition sessions, giving the agents the sides and scripts.

11. During each audition, the actor will come in (hopefully) having at least read the sides and ideally the script as well, and will do a reading of one of the sides.

12. The casting director or director may offer an adjustment, and have the actor read the side again; or they may determine that the actor really isn't right for the part at all. If you're making the adjustments, you'll consult the list you prepared, come up with one that you think will be suitable, give it to the actor, and have him/her read the scene again.

13. Hopefully this process will yield an even smaller set of candidates. Then the casting director will set up callback auditions. Callbacks vary in structure – sometimes you'll cast your lead and then have the other characters read with her. Other times you'll pair people up or have group scenes with different combinations. Sometimes callbacks are unnecessary. Or you may need several rounds of them. The casting director can guide the director in figuring out the best structure for the film.

14. During callbacks, the director (and usually the producer) sit in. The director and/or casting director will give the actors adjustments as needed.

15. Hopefully at this point you'll have found your cast.

A good casting director can help you prepare this material – she can pick out good sides, help you better articulate your goals, organize the process as a whole – but the inspiration has to come from you. The more prepared you are, the more options she'll be able to show you.

THE CASTING BREAKDOWNS

First Casting Breakdown

This is a brief overview of each character, broken down into categories. It's a little different from a character bio, in that you're focusing more on *mapping* the character rather than writing a biography. You may share this with the casting director, or decide to condense it a little bit.

I've listed a sample set of categories in Table 8.1. Since you're probably going to be the only one to see this more detailed version, feel free to alter/collapse/add categories. Also, if a particular category isn't important to you, leave it out.

You could go on creating attributes until you've figured out the character's cavities and fillings. But you want to avoid getting too detailed. This breakdown is just a stepping stone.

Conversely, I'd argue that it's a good idea to create a sheet for each speaking role, no matter how small. You can gloss over certain details if the character plays only a very minor role. But don't skip it altogether.

Second Casting Breakdown

Using the first set of breakdowns as your guide, you'll want to create a table, with one row per speaking role. You want to summarize attributes in this breakdown:

- **Physical attributes:** Name and age range. If these are important, also include: physical disabilities, sexual preference, race, gender, species, body type.
- **Social attributes:** Profession, marital status (married, single, etc.).

TABLE 8.1 First casting breakdown

Category	Characteristic
Physical	Name
	Age
	Species
	Gender
	Race
	Sexual preference
	Height
	Weight
	Hair
	Eyes
	Body type
	Athletic vs. sedentary
	Overall health
	Any allergies or diseases
	Tattoos/birthmarks
Social	Current location
	Describe current apartment/house/shack/etc.
	Profession
	Marital status?
	Family (children, pets, spouses/special friends)
	Does s/he have a passion other than his/her job?
Psychological	Temperament
	Introverted vs. extroverted
	Problem-solving intelligence
	Creative intelligence
	Intuitive vs. rational
	Reflective/introspective vs. active
	What is s/he passionate about?
	What is s/he apathetic about/not interested in?
	What/who does s/he absolutely hate?
	Long-term career/family/political/etc. goals?
Historical	Parents' names/backgrounds?
	Siblings?
	Highest degree in school? General notes on education
	Some notes on childhood
	Notable events in childhood
	Previous relationships
	Previous jobs
	Skeletons in the closet?

- **Psychological/emotional attributes:** Temperament (try to stick to one or two words here), moral compass.
- **History:** Some key element of the character's history.

Table 8.2 shows the cast breakdown sheet for *Found In Time*.

The first breakdown will give you a good idea of what you're looking for. The second gives your casting director enough information to work with, so she can start looking through her headshot files and contacts, and set up breakdown requests.

TABLE 8.2 Cast breakdown for *Found In Time*

#	Character	Age	Gender	Race/Eth.	Profession	Physicality	Emotionality
	Leads						
1.	Chris	20s–30s	M	W	Street vendor (psychic)	Fragile	Brooding, disconnected, fragile
2.	Ayana	30s	F	?	Street vendor (psychic)	Slender	Mysterious, bravura front concealing despair
3.	Jina	30s	F	W	Therapist	Average build	Professional, ambitious, but a fool for love
4.	RJ	40s–50s	M	?	Street vendor (psychic)	Tall, broad-chested	A survivor who puts on a surly front; his heart was gradually beaten down by years of just trying to get by
5.	Morton	40s	M	W	Cop (psychological)	Beefy – bigger than everyone else in the cast	Bully – frustrated at his own stunted career, he takes it out on those weaker than him
6.	Jess	40s	F	W	Cop (psychological)	Athletic	Bully, like Morton, but cares about her partner
7.	Anthony	40s	M	?	Therapist/ psychiatrist	Average	Professional, cool, ambitious. But angry underneath
8.	Ananasi	40s–60s	M	?	Demi-god	Thin, reedy	A trickster – you never know whose side he's on, or if he's joking or serious
	Supporting						
9.	Ring Man	40s	M	?	Businessman	Average	In trouble with his girlfriend
10.	Old Man	60s–80s	M	?	Retired	"Old"	Desperate for some company

(Continued)

TABLE 8.2 (Continued)

#	Character	Age	Gender	Race/Eth.	Profession	Physicality	Emotionality
11.	Nadine	30s	F	?	Lawyer	Average	Professional
12.	Child #1	8–10	M	?	Kid	?	
13.	Crayon Kid	8–10	M	?	Kid	?	
14.	Mother	30s	F	?	Stay-at-home mom	?	
15.	Psych Cop #1	30s	Either	?	Cop (psychological)	Beefy	New to the job, not quite as brutal as Morton
16.	Psych Cop #2	30s	Either	?	Cop (psychological)	Beefy	New to the job, not quite as brutal as Morton

Over- and Under-Defining

Don't *under-define* your casting requirements. You may have a very strong image in your head of who should play which role, but if you haven't made that concrete enough to the casting director, he'll end up setting up auditions with people who are way off base from what you want.

I've set up casting sessions as a producer (on gigs where there wasn't enough money for a casting director), so I can testify as to how frustrating it is to not have enough input from the director. I think he just expected me to figure it out from the script, but scripts are outlines at best. I booked several days' worth of auditions, and didn't even come close to what he wanted.

On the other hand, don't be too rigid in your definitions. Be open to different ideas. The casting director may have someone in mind that you wouldn't have considered but might bring something completely wonderful and unexpected to the table.

Over-defining your characters is just as bad. Especially if you get too fixated on a character's physical attributes (race, age, etc.), you could be closing yourself off to some really good actors. Unless your characters are at a specific point in their lives or there's a reason for them to be of a particular race, it's best to cast a broader net.

So you may have to do a few drafts of this second breakdown before you strike the right balance.

THE DREAM CAST LIST

This is your chance to go nuts. Would George Clooney be a great fit for your lead? Put him down! How about Cary Grant circa 1931? Go for it. Look at the detailed character breakdown sheets you wrote up, then come up with about three or four choices per character. Don't be afraid to go with off-the-wall choices either.

You don't have to provide a lengthy justification for your choices. If your producer starts pushing you to make more commercial choices (or your producer-brain kicks in and argues with you), push back. The purpose of this list is to start the conversation with the casting director, rather than come up with a real "name" list. The dream cast list is based on your artistic considerations, not on reality.

Think about what it is that makes your dream team "right" for the roles. Imagine them occupying the parts and interacting with each other. Can you imagine the chemistry between these dream actors? These seemingly flighty acts of imagination can lead to further insights into the performance you want.

SIDES

It's always a good idea to send your prospective actors (and their agents) a copy of the entire script if you can, but you'll also want to select a series of sides for them to read.

An ideal side is a scene that fits the following criteria.

Length: Two to four pages long. Longer scenes are harder to get through during casting sessions. Shorter scenes don't really reveal enough about the actor's choices. You may end up selecting a long scene and then cutting it off during the auditions. Sides for callbacks can be longer.

Type: Between two characters. Really complex scenes (like five people around a table) are difficult because your casting director or reader will have to read all the other roles. However, there are exceptions. If your script features a lot of monologues, has a lot of "family/crowd" scenes, and/or isn't very dialog driven, then select the scene that you think will best reveal the character or stretch the actors.

Dramatic. The scenes should have some dramatic heft to them. Some would say that climaxes are perfect scenes for auditions. I'm not sure about this. It depends on the script. I sometimes feel that quieter scenes are more of a challenge for an actor, and may be easier for you to evaluate as a director. Most writer/directors have a very vivid impression of the climax of their film, but that can actually impede their ability to evaluate what they're seeing in the audition.

Minimal blocking. If you have a lot of blocking directions, take them out or minimize them. Actors sometimes try to follow these directions too closely, but without the actual environment, it ends up being rather distracting from the meat of the audition. Obviously, if you're casting a dance film you'll need to leave the blocking directions in. And if the actors want to move around during the auditions, that's fine.

No voice-over. Voice-over is a great tool, but it's not good for auditions.

No phone-call scenes. This is really just my own opinion. If your scene takes place mainly in phone calls, then there's no avoiding it (I produced a short film, *Dead Air*, that was an extended father–son phone conversation). People tend to drift mentally and physically while talking on the phone. The exception is if the phone call is vital to the story (think of the phone call at the beginning of *Scream*) – then you should select it.

Minimal parentheticals or other emotional/pacing giveaways. If you have these in your scene, I recommend minimizing them. You'll want to see what the actors come up with instead.

You may have to stitch two scenes together if there's a cutaway in between them, or select only part of a very long scene. In either case, try to make sure that the resulting side has a reasonably well-defined beginning, middle, and end, and stops at the end of a beat rather than in the middle of one. You may also have to delete a one-line character, trim some of the narrative, or otherwise sculpt the scene slightly to make it more audition-friendly.

Try to come up with three to four sides per lead character, and one or two per supporting role. You can use the same sides for multiple characters; in fact this is great! Not only does it save you some work up front, but these sides can be used for callbacks as well.

ADJUSTMENTS

For each set of sides you've created, you want to jot down some adjustments to give each actor you're going to see. Assuming that you did the script analysis work, you should have a good bead on each character's arc within the scene and across the entire script.

However, trying to shoehorn all that information into an audition is too unwieldy and will make most actors' heads explode. What you want to do is come up with a one-sentence note or question that will tweak the actor's performance.

A few good examples of an adjustment are:

Highlighting the moment before. The scene is a love scene between two characters. If you're trying to get a little more tension out of the actor's performance, try this:

"Let's say you two just had a big fight a few minutes ago."

Adding a fact. The scene is an argument between a young couple about to get married. Try:

"Your parents divorced when you were 4 years old."

Asking a question. The scene is a dialog between a patient and a shrink. The actor playing the patient isn't really latching onto the character's underlying despair. Try:

"Have you ever felt abandoned by God?"

Up the stakes. The scene is between a boss and an employee. The employee wants to leave for the day; the boss wants him to stay. Give the actor auditioning for the employee something bigger to fight for:

"You have an interview for a better job you're supposed to be at in twenty minutes."

or:

"You were supposed to meet your girlfriend for dinner about ten minutes ago."

Get physical. The scene is an argument between a cop and his snitch. Put something physical into the scene. It's not something that has to be acted out. You're just looking to see how the actor manifests a strong physical issue in his performance. Try:

To the snitch: "You really have to get your next fix."

To the cop: "You're sore and tired from putting up drywall all day yesterday."

Find the love. The same scene between cop and snitch. Try:

"You guys have known each other for so long, you rely on each other a bit."

"He's the one person you can actually be honest with."

The best adjustment is one that's supported by the script in some way. But ultimately it doesn't matter. An ideal adjustment will accomplish the following:

1. Show you how well (or badly) the actor takes direction from you
2. Give an actor you're already feeling good about (or like but aren't quite sure of yet) some material that will inspire them to tweak their work and bring it even closer to what you're looking for
3. Help *you* look at the actor in a fresh way.

Again, you want to come up with three to four adjustments per scene per character. So if you have 8 roles and 3 sides each, that's $8 \times 3 \times 3$ or $4 = 72$ to 96 adjustments. Yikes! Don't worry – most of the time you're going to have some overlap between sides, and since adjustments are character-specific, one can serve you across multiple scenes. More realistically, you'll end up with about 50 adjustments. That still seems like a lot of work, but keep in mind that you don't have to produce all this overnight – you'll have time between handing off your cast breakdown and sitting down at the audition.

RESEARCH AND SUGGESTIONS

You may have money in the budget to bed-and-board some non-local actors, but it's always good to work with local talent as much as possible. Not only does it create goodwill in the community you're shooting in, but local actors can "get" the nuances right. About half the cast of *Beasts of the Southern Wild* actually come from Louisiana, including the two leads. They knew the way people talk and act in that area in a way that the writer/director (who hails from New York) just couldn't have.

Even if you don't happen to live in an actor-dense city like LA or New York, chances are you have untapped resources close to hand. That could mean a standup comedy club, a community theater group, the local college film or drama department – there are actors nearby. You may even be able to find actors who work in one of the big metropolises but live somewhere nearby. This was the case with *Racing Daylight*. Most of the leads lived or had homes upstate but worked out of New York a lot.

You may have to spend some time scouting out these local resources. Comedy clubs are great spots – standup comics are often very good actors (just think of Robin Williams, Billy Crystal, Eddie Izzard, Jamie Foxx, Steve Carell, and Tina Fey, to name a few). Likewise, don't underestimate local theater groups.

Non-actors can present unique challenges, but can also give very effective performances, as long as they're cast right. Musicians tend to make very good actors, since they're used to performing. They are, however, very bad at getting up early (I'm not kidding).

If there's a performance, stand-up act, film, or play featuring someone you think would be right for the role, go out and see it. Approach the person and find out if they have a reel, resume, or website. Make sure to pass this on to the casting director. Don't make promises – you may be completely enamored of a person's performance, but come to find out that they're actually not a very good actor overall, or can't take direction very well.

HEADSHOTS AND VISUALS

I don't place much stock in headshots. At best they're a way of eliminating people who are completely out of the ballpark. At worst they'll fool you into thinking that someone is perfect when in fact the shot was taken when the actor was younger/heavier/skinnier/etc. Samples of actual work that the actor's done *can* be much more revealing (though it's sometimes hard to separate an actor's performance from the editing, music, camerawork, and other performances, especially if you're looking at a clip reel).

I do, however, find headshots indirectly useful. When preparing my dream cast list, sometimes I'll include a headshot from someone who's physically close to what I'm after. This gives the casting director something more concrete to work with than my breakdown. Some directors I know clip publicity shots, and present these to the casting director as well.

Also, once we're down to callbacks, I find it can be useful to discreetly show the costume designer, production designer, and DP the headshots of the remaining candidates. This gives them some idea of what I'm after visually, and gets them thinking about the design.

CASTING AHEAD

So now you've got a ream of data at your fingertips: a director's script breakdown, a "look-book" full of reference materials, and a bunch of casting notes/docs. What's next? Casting.

But before we dive into that world, we have to track sideways and cover some of the prep activities that tend to fall on the producer's shoulders. The next several chapters, then, will look at the producer's path in prep. Then you'll both (or both sides of your brain, if you're the producer/ director) come back together in Chapter 15. The actual process of casting is typically a very deep collaboration between the producer and director, and is as informed by production concerns as by creative ones.

QUESTIONS/EXERCISES

1. What is the dream cast of your film?
2. Go through the script and pick out one side for each of the lead characters.
3. Using these sides, prepare a set of adjustments to give the actors during the audition process.

Chapter 9

Breaking Down the Script

Scene #: B93
Breakdown Sheet
Sheet #: 147
Int/Ext: EXT
Day/Night: Day
Script Page: 63
Page Count: 2/8

Scene Description: Chris chases Randall, turns and runs away from him
Settings: STREETS/ALLEYS
Location: Mine EXT
Sequence:
Script Day: 100

Cast Members
1.CHRIS
2.AYANA
15.RANDALL AND CARL

Stunts
Ayana shocks Psychcop #2
Ayana beats up Psychcop #1
Psychcop #1 trips over Chris

Wardrobe
Miner Outfit - Ayana
Miner Outfit - Chris
Psychcop Outfit - Add'l
Psychcop Outfit - Add'l2

Set Dressing
"trippable" Garbage
Cardboard boxes

Props
Garbage can lid
Happy Couple Postcard
Psychcop Sticks

Scene #: 116
Breakdown Sheet
Sheet #: 112
Int/Ext: EXT
Day/Night: Day
Script Page: 75
Page Count: 2

Scene Description: The vendors work steadily, until Morton and Jess bully them
Settings: VENDOR STREET
Location: Vendor Street
Sequence:
Script Day: 7

Cast Members
1.CHRIS
2.AYANA
4.RJ
6.JESS
7.MORTON

Background Actors
7.CUSTOMERS #4

Wardrobe
Ayana's black dress
Ayana's blue scarf
Psychcop Outfit - Jess
Psychcop Outfit - Morton

Set Dressing
Mine - random crap

Props
Ayana's spinner/table/cart
Chris Granny Cart/Crap
Chris's "lead" postcard for
Chris's greeting card for Ayana
Chris's postcards
Jess Camera
Jess/Morton smartphone
Miners - IV bags
Miners - Junk
Miners - Mail Pouch
Miners - Notebooks
Psychcop Sticks
RJ's cart/table/stuff

FIGURE 9.1 A typical breakdown sheet, filled out.

Over the next several chapters, we'll be focusing on prep activities that are traditionally considered part of the producer's "domain": scheduling, budgeting, and dealing with vendors, unions, states, and contracts. While they're presented in a linear order, in fact they form a nonlinear, circular process that you'll go back and forth through every day. Every time you adjust the schedule, you'll have to adjust the budget. If this pushes the budget up significantly enough, you may have to renegotiate with a vendor or change your equipment order to bring it back down. If you're signing up with SAG because one of your "must-have" actors is a member, you'll have to revisit the budget again to add in the fringes. This may in turn mean you have to trim a day from your already too-tight schedule. And so on. That's why I put "Thinking Strategically" (Chapter 11) squarely in the middle – because at times, you'll have to step back from this activity and make sure it's all serving the good of the film as a whole.

Everything starts with the script, so your first job is to understand the script at an atomic level. Hence, the breakdown.

BREAKING DOWN THE SCRIPT

If you've already done the director's script analysis, then your script is probably becoming sickeningly familiar to you. However, we'll now be discovering the logistics of your script. There are a ton of books already written on the fine details of script breakdowns and scheduling, so this chapter will focus on the big picture.

Your script is a rough diagram for a complex machine. The breakdown and schedule is a parts list and assembly instructions. Only once you have the script broken down and scheduled can you truly budget it. For this reason, I was tempted to put this chapter in the beginning. But truthfully, there's no ideal place to put this chapter, since you'll probably be doing some version of this procedure throughout the preproduction period.

The process of breaking down, scheduling, and budgeting scripts has changed remarkably little, despite some significant (and welcome) technological advances. Basically, the steps are:

1. Decompose each scene into a sheet listing its constituent elements − cast, wardrobe, props, set dressing, script days, etc. (see below for the full list). Be sure to include elements that are implied but not specifically part of the script. For example, if you have scenes that are set in Tom's bedroom, Tom's living room, and Tom's kitchen, then all of those scenes take place in one location (INT. Tom's House) that you will need to eventually find.
2. Analyze the resulting breakdown, tweak the script, repeat until you feel like you're in good shape.
3. Sort the sheets according to some logical order − consolidating locations, actor days, time of day, stunts, extras, etc. − until you get an idealized schedule together.
4. Take the information gleaned from this process and translate it into a budget.

CHOICE OF TOOLS

If you're going to be a professional producer, then you should go out and beg, buy, or steal a copy of Entertainment Partners' Movie Magic Scheduling and Budgeting programs. They're expensive, though there are academic and upgrade discounts. For better or worse, these programs have been the industry standard for well over a decade, despite sporadic competition. You might as well learn the standard.

If you're broke, you can investigate one of the alternatives on the market − Gorilla or ShowBiz Budgeting. And if you're a little patient (well, a lot, actually), all you really need is a spreadsheet and a word processor. Before there were computers, people used magnetic or cardboard stripboards, paper, and pen (this was actually how I was taught). In order to focus on the strategy behind the breakdown process, I'm going to make reference to specific programs very sparingly.

EXPECT SURPRISES

Scripts are generally more complex than they appear when you're writing them. I worked on a film called *Helena from the Wedding*. The script seemed small enough − eight people gathered together in a cabin to celebrate the new year together. One location, a small cast, two script days. But during the breakdown process, it became apparent that we had a lot of scenes with all eight characters in them. This is not bad, but it takes time to prepare all the actors, so we had to make sure to have an adequate hair, makeup, and wardrobe team. And how do you shoot coverage of all eight characters? The number of angles you need multiplies geometrically with each character you add. We also had four picture cars we had to account for, including a special one (a jeep). Finally, we had to figure out the transportation and room/board for the entire cast (as well as the crew).

These challenges all proved to be solvable, but it was an interesting tale of how even a seemingly simple script hides layers of complexity.

STEP ONE: DECOMPOSE THE SCRIPT

Let's assume that you don't have Movie Magic and that you have to do this mostly by hand. You'll need a pen, a ruler, a printed copy of the script, and a form like the one in Figure 9.2, one per scene.

YOUR AWESOME MOVIE _____

Scene #: _____ Int/Ext: _____ Set: _____ D/N: _____

Length: _____ Script Day: _____ Location: _____

DESCRIPTION _____
_____
_____

Cast Members	Extras	Stunts

Wardrobe	Props	Set Dressing

Hair/Makeup	Picture Vehicles	Animals

Stunts	Visual Effects	Mechanical FX

Sound	Music	Camera

Special Equipment	Comments	

FIGURE 9.2 Breakdown sheet.

It's best to pretend that someone else wrote the script at this point. Read through it and jot down the following, in the appropriate box or line:

Time of day. Morning, Day, Night, Evening. It may not be explicitly indicated in every scene. Personally, this drives me nuts – you should *always indicate* the time of day in a scene header. This will take the guesswork out of the equation. If you wrote something like MAGIC HOUR, EARLY DAWN, or MID-AFTERNOON, put a question mark next to it. You may have to be a little flexible on this.

Length. Pages are measured in eighths. You should always round up.

Scene number. This should be obvious, right? Well, not necessarily.

1. **Phone conversations/texts/emails/chats.** If you have a scene with a telephone conversation and an INTERCUT between the two, *both* sides of the phone conversation should be considered as separate scenes for shooting purposes, so you'll end up filling out two sheets. The first sheet will be John's side of the phone call, the second will be Jane's. Prefix the second scene's number with an "A" (e.g. sc. A11). I recommend you *don't* put the letter *after* the scene number, because when you're trying to label your slate on set "Scene 11A – A take 1" sounds confusing. (The slate will confuse your editor as well.) Another option is to suffix the second scene with a decimal number (e.g. scene #11.1).

2. **Parts of scenes.** If you have one scene that takes place in a really big location – a battleground, for example – you might want to break it up into two or more parts. In this case, fill out one sheet for each part of the scene, and label each sheet with the scene number plus PT and a number (e.g. 11PT1, 11PT2).

3. **Playback of TV or video on set.** If you have an insert shot of something playing on TV, or a videophone conversation, somewhere in your scene, it should get its own sheet. Label the scene number as per the **phone conversations** convention above (e.g. A11 or 11.1). Keep in mind that if the playback is from a popular TV show, you're going to have to pay to license it.

4. **Insert shots of still photos.** If the people in the stills are cast members or extras – in other words, if the production designer is going to have to shoot the still – then you'll want to make a new sheet for each still. Label the scene number with the "A" prefix as per the **phone conversations** convention above (e.g. A11 or 11.1). Make all insert shots at least one-eighth of a page long.

5. **Inside/outside shots.** If you have a scene with a character looking outside from his car, and then a shot from outside the car showing it on the highway, you should probably break it up into two scenes. If the car is parked or we're just moving from an over the shoulder shot to a car-mount, then it can probably be considered as one scene.

6. **Montages.** Remember you wrote those clever montages, way back when you were sitting at your desk? You probably didn't pick apart the images and make each one its own scene. Well, now you'll need to fill out one sheet for each image. Use the PT convention outlined above.

In most of the above cases, the prudent thing to do is to actually break the scene up in the script – especially in the case of #2, **parts of scenes**, then renumber accordingly.

Script day. This is the day in the story that the scene happens in. The first "present day" of your script is usually script day #1, but there are exceptions. If you have a gap of two story weeks between scene 9 and scene 10, scene 10 still takes place on script day #2.

This can get very complicated very quickly, as you can imagine. I usually handle flashbacks by starting them at Day 100, and flashforwards by starting them at 200. Newscasts or "found footage" scenes I start on Day 300. I separate these by 100 to keep numbers from colliding.

There are some significant exceptions, however.

If your "present day" is just a framing device for the main body of a script that takes place "in the past," then script day #1 should be the first day of the script. The "present day" material should start at day 100 or 200 (to keep it from colliding). For example, *Saving Private Ryan*'s first scene – with the older Ryan walking through the graveyard – would be marked as script day #100. The second scene, on D-Day, would be marked as script day #1. If you have a particularly knotty story or one with alternative storylines, then you'll want to consider starting each storyline on a different hundred-count. For example, start Jane's storyline on Day 100, Jack's storyline on Day 200, and so on.

If you have a story that occurs across a very wide span of history (where costume and production design elements would be very different), consider starting each era on a hundred mark, in historical order. For example, scenes taking place in 1400 BC would start with Day 100, those taking place in AD 700 would start at 200, and present-day scenes would start at 300. Whatever system you devise for your script, keep it consistent.

Why go through all this? For starters, your costume designer needs to know how many wardrobe changes each character will have. The production designer and costume designer will need to know what period s/he is trying to capture. It will also help you keep track of continuity, particularly in postproduction. As you change the script closer to production, knowing what day things happened in the story prevents you from creating impossibly long days (see Chapter 2), or from referencing events that have literally not happened yet.

It can also give you some idea of the scope of your script – is it a tight story that takes place within a week? A longer drama that takes place over years or months? Often scripts have a lot of "spaces" between days that aren't noticeable upon a first read. This can feed back into the director's prep – what happened between the script days, or throughout the offscreen portion of a given day?

Interior/exterior. This is not as straightforward as it seems. A car is never a strict INTERIOR, because the car is moving or parked somewhere; by the same token, even a covered porch isn't really just an INTERIOR unless it's on a soundstage. Usually, INT. CAR becomes something else, like INT./EXT. CAR ON HIGHWAY. When in doubt, use INT./EXT.

Set. What room or space your scene takes place in. Try to be consistent – if you have three scenes taking place in John's bedroom, make sure they all say JOHN'S BEDROOM and not JOHN'S ROOM, BEDROOM, and JOHN'S BEDROOM.

Location. One location can contain multiple sets. If three scenes are set in Josh's bedroom, Josh's living room, and Josh's kitchen, then logically they all take place in the location JOSH'S HOUSE. This will help you budget your location rentals, and indicate to your location manager what she needs to be looking for.

Synopsis. Keep this brief. List the major plot event in the scene.

Sequence. Some people like to group a set of scenes together into a sequence. I personally have always found this more trouble than it's worth. But I can see why it would be useful, particularly if you're cutting back and forth between different storylines (you may want to group all the scenes within a given storyline together into a single sequence).

Cast members. List every cast member in the scene, regardless of whether they have a line or not. Each cast member will have a number associated with him/her. The leads usually have the lowest numbers, the supporting characters higher, and the bit players the highest. Movie Magic is *not* very smart about listing non-speaking characters correctly, so don't trust it.

1. **Aging characters.** If you have characters that age, make sure to separate each one into a separate role if the age gap is large enough. In other words, the character Jack at age 10, 20, and 60 will be played by three different actors, so list them as 10-YEAR-OLD JACK, 20-YEAR-OLD JACK, and 60-YEAR-OLD JACK.
2. **Name your characters consistently.** If you've decided on Dr. Ozzy Osborne as your character's name, he should not show up as OZZY OSBORNE, OZZY, OSBORNE, or THE OZZ anywhere else in the script (except in dialog, of course).

3. **Voice-over exception.** If you have voice-overs in your script, I usually find it helpful to break out each character's VOs into separate roles. For example, if CHRIS shows up in your script and is also the voice-over narrator, then you'll want to have separate CHRIS and CHRIS V.O. characters. This will save your AD, actors, editor, sound designer, and script supervisor from being confused. For example, if your character appears in a particular scene *only* via voice-over, you don't want your AD to call the actor in to shoot a scene he isn't in.

Extras/background. List all the extras (sometimes called background actors or BG) that appear in the scene. I usually name the extras by location or event. For example, JOHN'S WEDDING BG or RESTAURANT BG. If you keep coming back to the same location but on a different day, suffix the name with a number. So Friday's restaurant crowd is RESTAURANT BG #1. Saturday's is RESTAURANT BG #2. If you have featured extras, list them separately. So you could have RESTAURANT BG and BAR BG at the same location, for example.

If you know how many extras you'll need, indicate it in the name – e.g. RESTAURANT PATRONS (10). If you don't know, I recommend overestimating or leaving it blank. Keep in mind that the writer may not have actually mentioned extras specifically, but they'll be there (a city street, sporting event, school hallway, or park will usually have extras, for example).

Stunts. Critical to list, even if the stunt is minor. You may not need a stunt coordinator, but you will need to consider the stunt as part of the schedule. A fall, stabbing, shooting, acrobatic move, fight, car crash, or anything that might result in bodily harm could be considered a stunt.

Visual FX vs. floor/mechanical FX. Visual FX are things that will be finished during post-production (like a composite of a ghost, or any kind of greenscreen work). Floor/mechanical FX are completed on set (like fog from a fog machine, or a door closing). If you have a computer showing something on the screen, this can be considered a mechanical effect (even if it requires some visual effects work before the shoot). Sometimes you'll have a mechanical effect that will also be augmented in post. List it in both categories.

Weapons. These will probably require an armorer, a weapon rental, and most likely a stunt coordinator, so don't miss these.

Wardrobe. You want to note extraordinary jewelry or items of clothing. If the character's clothing is nondistinct, you still want to distinguish the clothing that the person is wearing on that script day. For *Found In Time*, the main character, Chris, wore some variation of jeans/t-shirt most of the time. So I simply indicated CHRIS WARDROBE DAY #1, CHRIS WARDROBE DAY #2, etc. By doing this you're helping your costume designer figure out what individual costumes s/he needs to put together for each character. Be sure to mention women's handbags here.

Props. A prop is something you hold in your hand. It's good to be thorough here – prop purchases can take up a significant part of your art department budget. Include little things that aren't mentioned explicitly. If the main character writes at a desk in the scene, then your props list would include a writing instrument and at least a piece of paper, even if you didn't spell this out.

Set dressing. This is anything that decorates the walls, floors, and ceiling, or that sits around (relatively) unmoved by actors. If a sword on the wall ends up being used by your hero in the last scene of the script, then it's really a prop.

Set dressing includes items like signs, billboards, advertisements, or painted-on items, as well as furniture. Here again, you should try to be specific. If you're really not sure what's in a given room, you can use a generic set dressing description (i.e. "College Dorm Room Decoration" or "Nuclear Reactor Control Room Machines").

Makeup/hair. Does one of your characters have a wig? Does he have a moustache he shaves off during the course of the story? Does one of your characters get badly burned? Include any special-effects makeup ("simple" blood effects) or more complicated prosthetic work (dummy hands, severe burns, etc.). If your characters are supposed to look tired, or dead, write in "Tired look" or "Dead look."

Animals. Don't forget these guys. They can have an impact on the budget – they usually have to be rented, along with some kind of handler.

Sound. If you have a specific sound effect, please write it down here.

Music. If your script calls out music cues, list them here. If you don't have a specific song in mind, use "Music Cue #" followed by the number of the cue (in script order). This will help you later when you're trying to figure out how much music you'll need to find/license and/or have composed for your film.

Special gear. If you have to rent a crane or some greenscreen material for a shot, write it in here.

Camera. Fill in this box if you have specific camera moves, or you think you'll be using a specific lens. I usually list **car rigs** here as well.

Picture vehicles. These are cars that are in the film. This should include anything that's featured (e.g. John's Car) or just in the background (e.g. Cars on Highway). You'll also want to include wrecked cars that appear in the scene, and process trailers. A process trailer is a special tractor-trailer that picture cars sit on. It's low enough to the ground that it looks like the actor is driving the car. The trailer is wide and long enough to put the camera and lights in other spots without attaching it to the car. They're also stabilized somewhat for a smoother ride. They're not cheap to rent but can make it possible to get car shots you wouldn't be able to get otherwise.

Comments. Anything that's noteworthy that doesn't fit a given category. For example, if you have a sex scene, you'll want to note the degree of nudity specified (or implied) in the script. If you wrote a musical, you might want to specify that you have a big dance number in a scene.

Once you've broken down the script, you'll know it in intimate (some would say excruciating) detail.

ANALYZE, TWEAK, REPEAT

The first thing you need to do is look through your breakdown sheets and see if there are any inconsistencies or errors. If you started with a breakdown generated automatically by Movie Magic, you'll notice that characters are not always consistently named. Tweak your script, and rename the characters in the breakdown to match.

You may need to renumber the cast members in the breakdown, and number a few other elements as well. I like to number the picture vehicles (if any) and extras.

Also, start looking at the sets, extras, locations, characters, big scenes, and small scenes. Here's what you're looking for.

Sets that can be combined. Do you have three different bathrooms in your script, or five different offices, that all take place in the same location? If so, can you pick one bathroom or office to set all these scenes in? In *Found In Time*, I had several scenes that took place in a doctor's office, and a one-off scene that took place between two doctors in a conference room. Rather than go out and try and find an office *and* a conference room, I simply reset the conference room scene inside the doctor's office. This cut down on the number of sets I had to go find.

Consolidating characters. If you have a group of people in your script (like a set of bar patrons), you'll find that at least one member has no lines, or only speaks once. Can you eliminate this role altogether without changing the scene? If so, you just saved yourself some money and time.

Upgrading an extra. On the other hand, if you have an extra doing a lot of action – but not speaking – then that person should really be considered an actor, not a background player.

Big scenes. How many of these do you have? An independent low-budget film can afford two or perhaps three "big" set pieces. A set piece could be a scene featuring a chase scene or stunt, or a big wedding with a lot of extras, or a club dance number with a ton of dancers. But if you have a lot of set pieces, you're probably looking at a more expensive script than you can afford.

A few years ago I line produced and post supervised a film called *Rock the Paint*. The original budget target was $200K. However, after breaking down the script and seeing that there were six or seven basketball games in the film (including one that ends in a brawl), it became obvious to the producer that this budget was inadequate. Instead we raised the production budget to $400K (which really still wasn't high enough).

Can you consolidate two set pieces? Or can you shoot them on the same day (realistically) using the same elements (cast, crew, stunt coordinators, etc.)? For a film I budgeted featuring seven lacrosse games, we broke out and consolidated all the audience/bench reaction shots into separate scenes. The producer and I figured we could shoot all the audience cutaways on one day for all the games, just by moving the audience around enough to make it look like a different crowd in each game. This would be cheaper than bringing back extras for each game. We also realized that one "game scene" was only a collection of highlight shots, so we scheduled it to be shot as part of another game.

Small scenes. On the other hand, if you have a number of short scenes that take place in different locations, you're also in trouble. Getting twenty locations for twenty short scenes will in all likelihood cost you more than finding two locations that can serve you for ten scenes each. You want to keep moves between locations to a minimum in the shooting schedule, but if you have a bunch of short scenes that require different locations, you're going to lose a lot of time. Can you consolidate the locations somewhat?

Usually in the course of this process, you'll discover some typos, plot issues, or other things that need some clearing up. You may also discover that, despite your best efforts in Chapter 2, you still have some serious problems that need attention. This could include impossibly long script days or scenes that span multiple sets. So you may need to do a quick rewrite of your script. Keep in mind that you'll have to tweak your breakdown to get it back in sync with your new draft.

Once you've tweaked the script and re-adjusted your breakdown, the next thing is to start working on your stripboard.

SCHEDULING

Now that you've turned your script into a pile of sheets, you now need to turn that pile into a set of strips. Movie Magic, Gorilla, and other scheduling programs do it for you. If you're unlucky enough to not have any of these programs, you can use Excel (or OpenOffice, if you're really broke) to do this task. Essentially, each strip should have:

1. The scene number.
2. Scene INT/EXT.
3. Set.
4. Time of day.
5. Synopsis.
6. The cast numbers (preferably in their own column).
7. If you have a lot of extras, picture vehicles, or some other element, put the numbers for these elements in as well.
8. I like to put the script day in (some people don't like this).

What you'll end up with is something like Figure 9.3. The colors are coded to the INT/EXT type, and the time of day. If you're using Excel, I recommend doing this as well. It makes it a lot easier to see at a glance what's going on.

At first, scheduling a film seems impossible. There are so many variables. Where do you start? The first thing to realize is that you don't have to create a perfect schedule, but something that seems

60	EXT VENDOR STREET	Day	1 2/8 pgs.	CAST: 1
	Chris puts the playing cards away, comes across the hanged man	Day 5		BG:
69	EXT VENDOR STREET	Day	4 2/8 pgs.	CAST: 1, 2, 4, 6, 7, 16
	Chris is served with "mine" papers by Jess and Morton; RJ and Chr	Day 6		BG:
71	EXT VENDOR STREET	Day	1/8 pgs.	CAST: 1, 2, 4
	Chris watches RJ walk away	Day 6		BG:
76	EXT VENDOR STREET	Day	6/8 pgs.	CAST: 1, 2
	Chris packs up his gear to go after RJ	Day 6		BG:

End Day # 4 Monday, September 13, 2010 -- Total Pages: 8

8:00 AM CALL

| 70 | EXT VENDOR STREET - FLASHBACK | Day | 7/8 pgs. | CAST: 1, 4 |
| | Chris and RJ talk to each other about when they first met | Day 103 | | BG: |

CITY STREET / STREET

133	EXT ANOTHER STREET	Day	4/8 pgs.	CAST: 1, 5
	Chris walks up to Anthony, gives him a stone	Day 7		BG:
39	EXT ANOTHER STREET	Day	2/8 pgs.	CAST: 1
	Chris walks down the block, picks up stuff	Day 3		BG: 3
41	EXT ANOTHER STREET	Day	3/8 pgs.	CAST: 1
	Chris continues to pick up junk	Day 3		BG:
59	EXT ANOTHER STREET	Day	1 2/8 pgs.	CAST: 2, 5
	Ayana walks by Anthony, they talk, he tries to get her to stay away	Day 5		BG:
19PT	EXT VENDOR STREET	Day	1 4/8 pgs.	CAST: 1, 4, 5
	Chris finds crayons, Anthony shows up	Day 2		BG:
20	EXT ANOTHER STREET	Day	3/8 pgs.	CAST: 1, 2, 5
	Chris walks around the corner, sees Anthony, then sees Ayana, get	Day 2		BG:
109	EXT STREET	Day	1/8 pgs.	CAST: 2
	Ayana walks down the street, shopping cart in tow	Day 7		BG:

MOVE - WEST TWO BLOCKS

26	EXT STREET BY THEATER	Night	7/8 pgs.	CAST: 1, 3
	Chris and Jina get into an argument over his "slipping time"	Day 2		BG:
24	EXT STREET BY THEATER	Night	6/8 pgs.	CAST: 1, 3
	Chris and Jina walk down the block, talk about film	Day 2		BG:

End Day # 5 Tuesday, September 14, 2010 -- Total Pages: 6 7/8

*** END WEEK 1 ***

FIGURE 9.3 A first draft of a schedule.

reasonable and "realistic," that you can use to budget your film with. The "true" shooting schedule will evolve over time, as locations, cast members, and other factors fall into place. Scheduling comes down to consolidating the following elements, in no particular order:

1. Cast
2. Locations
3. Time of day
4. Interiors and exteriors
5. Extras
6. Vehicles
7. Stunts/effects

Every script is its own snowflake (for better or worse), so it's impossible to generalize from the above list as to which is the most important in your case. However, just to get started, I recommend going in this order:

1. Get feedback from the director.
2. Decide on the five-or-six day week, and the "target length."
3. Consolidate locations.
4. Work from day to night.
5. Exteriors first, interiors later.
6. Consider turnaround and creeping crawl issues (see below for details).
7. Decide on the days of your shoot week.
8. Group your remote locations together.
9. Crew considerations.
10. Incorporate company moves and travel days.
11. Consolidate cast.
12. Consider special effects, stunts, children, or other "tricky" stuff.
13. Adjust your page count.

Let's go into more detail about these steps.

Feedback from the Director

Directors will often have some kind of preference for the order they want to shoot things in. Most directors would prefer to shoot scenes in script order, even if that makes for more logistical trouble than it's worth. If you have the kind of script where this can happen (everything takes place in one location over a limited number of days with a small cast) then this *is* worth considering.

Even if you can't accommodate this, see if you can schedule all the scenes for one location in script order. This may complicate your lighting (if you have to go from day to night to day again), but it may simplify your wardrobe, production design, or other concerns.

Many actors would prefer not to shoot the beginning of the script on the first day. The cast may not feel like they're fully in character yet, so the performance will be judged (by both the director and audience) and set at the wrong point.

Directors may want to "save" certain scenes or shoot others in a certain order. On *Helena from the Wedding* the director, Joe Infantolino, wanted to shoot the last scene last, and I think it was the right choice. The scene required the characters deliver an understated performance that revealed a lot of subtext. The actors were terrific, but I think it made their job – and Joe's – a lot easier to have inhabited their characters for two weeks before shooting the scene.

Another important consideration is what pace the director feels comfortable going at. Your budget probably won't permit you to shoot just three or four pages per day. But you shouldn't heap too much on the director's plate either, just because it will cost you extra to rent the location for another day. If you give the director an impossibly difficult schedule, then you could be hurting the final film, which is ultimately more important than the budget.

This is a big sore point between directors and producers. I worked on a film (which shall remain nameless) where the director favored a more deliberate, put-the-camera-on-the-dolly style. The executive producer wanted to make a cheaper, grittier, run-and-gun film. The difference was three days of shooting – 15 versus 18. I felt strongly that we were looking at an 18-day shoot, but the executive producer won the budget argument. However, after all the overtime we went into trying to work with the director's style, we could have paid for two out of the three days, and probably gotten better results.

So while you can't always accommodate the director's requests, you should pay attention to them and try to factor them into the schedule. It's better if you can start out with the dramatic needs leading the production, rather than the other way around.

Decide on the Length and Type of Schedule

Paranormal Activity is the ultimate one-location movie. It was shot in five really long days with a minimal crew and three cast members. I've worked on films shot over the course of five to six weeks, but in the last few years the average micro-budget shooting schedule seems to have shrunk down to two to three weeks – that's 10 to 18 days. You won't know exactly where you're going to land until you do the schedule, but it's helpful to set down a *target* length so you know how to clump your days together. What you're looking for is the sweet spot between the money running out and the film turning out badly.

The first thing you should decide on is between a five- or six-day week. The five-day week means you'll have a full weekend off between shoot weeks. The big advantage is that you'll have more time to think, rest, do your laundry and other critical chores, and catch up with expense reports, payroll, watching "dailies," and so on. You'll also have more time to plan out the next week. Your art department will have one more day to do returns and buy stuff for the following week (they never get a real day off). It's easier to avoid turnaround issues (more on this below). *But* you'll have to pay extra on anything that you're renting by the week or month. You'll also have to take more time off from your day job (if you have one). It will probably be harder to find a crew that will be able to work for the substandard (or no) wages you can offer them, at least for the entire shoot.

On the other hand, the six-day week means that you'll only have one day (technically, 36 hours) between each week of shooting. This means you'll have less time to cram in all the inter-week chores – laundry, review of last week's shoot, payroll, expense reporting, etc. The cast and crew will have less time off as well. *However*, you'll be able to get back to your day job sooner, which could be critical to your financial situation. You'll also pay less for weekly equipment rentals, and your cast and crew will be done sooner so they can go on to their other pursuits.

Having worked on both kinds of shoots, I strongly advocate for a *five-day shoot week*, especially if you're going to be shooting for more than two weeks, and if you're doing most of the producer/director work yourself. The crew and cast need rest, the art department needs time to prep, you need time to think. People's mental and physical performance deteriorates remarkably on the sixth day, so you're not really getting a full day's work out of anyone anyway.

You may not have much choice. On *Helena from the Wedding*, our biggest expense was having to board nearly the entire cast and crew in upstate NY. Just to be able to come in on budget we had to plan for two six-day weeks. On the other hand, *Found In Time* was shot locally. Since everyone was wearing a lot of hats, we *had* to take two days off between shoot weeks just so we could get the next week's props and set dressing ready. Most of the crew, cast, and equipment rates were based on the days rather than weeks of shooting, so the only thing that cost more was the production insurance.

Once you've decided on the type of week, you'll want to figure out how long you want to try to target your schedule for. This is fairly simple. Start by totaling up of all your strips (not the script). Divide the result by six pages per day, round up to the nearest whole number, and see what the result is.

So, for a 88-page script that has two phone conversations and a montage in it – resulting in 93⅜ pages' worth of strips – we get 93.375/6 = 15.563 = 16 days of shooting. That's either 3.2 five-day weeks or 2.7 six-day weeks.

This is not to say that you can afford this many days, or that this is even the ideal schedule. But six pages per day is a "safe" average to start with. It gives you a target to shoot for when you're actually putting the first draft of the schedule together. Once you've done a first draft, you'll have a better sense of whether this target makes sense, and you can adjust it up or down. By comparison, a Hollywood film might shoot three to four pages per day.

Consolidate Locations and Put Day Breaks In

Now you've talked to the director and figured out your target shoot length. You're back to staring at a bunch of color-coded strips on a screen or on your desk. The best thing to do at this point is to simply sort them all by location, set, and scene order. So all of JOSH'S HOUSE scenes should go together, maybe starting with JOSH'S HOUSE – KITCHEN (scenes 6, 13, and 17), then going upstairs to JOSH'S HOUSE – BEDROOM (scenes 4, 5, and 12), then moving to JOSH'S HOUSE – UPSTAIRS STUDY (scenes 27 and 28). Just by doing this, you've gone a long way to organizing the mess.

Now you can start putting actual day breaks into the schedule. Start by putting a day break between each *location* (not set). So you'll have one break between all the scenes at JOSH'S HOUSE and the ones at SCHOOL AUDITORIUM.

This will give you an immediate sense of the *scope* of your script. You may have thought a lot of the script takes place in just two locations. But now you can see that almost half of the script takes place in about eight other places.

Now that you've got each location separated by day breaks, put day breaks *within* each location, using the six-pages-per-day formula above. You don't have to be exact. You can combine *sets* within a single day, and break apart one set over multiple days if necessary. But try not to shoot a set and then come back to it later (though you may have to do this for other reasons, as you'll see below). This will now tell you how long you'll need to spend at each location.

If you have a location change in the middle of the day, indicate this by putting a banner strip between each location's scenes. This strip should say something like COMPANY MOVE TO XXX, where XXX is the new location.

Time of Day/Interior/Exterior

Now your schedule is starting to resemble "clumps" or groups of locations. It's time to order these clumps. To start:

1. Exteriors should go before interiors in the schedule.
2. Scenes should be clumped together by time of day (morning, day, evening, night).
3. Day scenes should be shot before night scenes.
4. Keep your distant locations together.

You can group morning and evening scenes together, because in most cases the audience can't tell the difference between dawn and dusk.

Exteriors should go before interiors as much as possible. This is because despite many technical advances, exterior filmmaking is still weather-dependent. If you schedule your exteriors on day 1 and there's a really bad rainstorm, you can try and shoot a "cover set" – an interior somewhere else – then come back to your exteriors on another day. On the other hand, if you schedule your exteriors on the last day of shooting and you're rained out, you're out of luck and you'll have to add another day to your schedule.

I like shooting the day scenes first because it's generally easier to start shooting on days, then move to nights. People have a hard time getting used to night shooting, especially at the beginning of a production. The other reason for segueing into nights is because of the "creeping crawl" factor, which we'll talk about shortly.

You want to keep all of your distant locations together, and organized by the actual area that you're going to be shooting in. On a film I worked on called *Company K*, we had very widely spaced locations: three days in New Jersey, two in New York, four in rural Pennsylvania, and one in Philadelphia. We started out with the local shooting (New Jersey, then New York), moving from daytime to nighttime scenes. Then we had one day off, and one travel day to rural Pennsylvania (more on this later as well). We shot for four days in Pennsylvania, again going from day to night scenes, then decamped for Philadelphia. We were able to travel, shoot, then bring everyone back home to New York on the last day.

By grouping all the distant locations together, I was able to save money on hotels, gas (fewer trips), and travel days.

You'll notice that sometimes these priorities conflict. If you have five days in a location that includes days and nights, interiors then exteriors, what do you do? Treat the location as a miniature version of the shoot. Schedule your exteriors first, and move from day to night. You may find that you have to focus more on time-of-day than interior/exterior issues, particularly within a single week's shooting, because of turnaround.

Turnaround and Creeping Crawl

Why care so much about the time of day? As the shoot moves on, you'll find that you have to start later and later in the day in order to obey turnaround rules, and give your crew and cast enough rest.

According to SAG and AFTRA, you have to give your cast members 12 hours of time off between each day of shooting. This 12 hours is defined as starting either (a) when they leave the location, if the location is local, *or* (b) when they arrive in the hotel, if it's a distant location.

On a typical shoot day, your actors will be on set for 12 hours, plus lunch (typically a half-hour). So if you have a shoot that takes place in your hometown, and your first day starts at 6AM and ends at 6:30PM (12 hours plus 1/2 hour lunch), you can't start your second day until 6:30AM. Over the course of a five-day week, your call time on set will "crawl" two hours. Once you start your second week, you can reset the call time back again. This two hours can seriously hamper being able to shoot all your daytime-critical material in a decent timeframe. So it's better to move all your daytime scenes up to the front of the week, and then shift towards more evening/nighttime scenes as the week wears on.

If you're on a distant location, the crawl is even worse. Say the hotel is a 20-minute drive from the set. That means that every day you shoot a full 12 hours plus lunch, the call time will creep by 70 minutes (20 minutes of travel each way = 40 minutes; plus the 1/2 hour for lunch).

If you have a lot of nighttime scenes, the same issues apply – you may have to start on nights but add some daytime scenes at the end of the week.

In an ideal world, you'll be able to group your day and night scenes in week-long chunks. If, however, you find that you're ending in one location on a night, and you're supposed to start on days somewhere else in the middle of the week, you may not have enough turnaround between days. In this case, you may have to insert a turnaround day – where the crew and cast take an entire day off – or create a short day that starts later and ends early enough to get you back on days.

Days of the Week

Ideally, you want your day(s) off to occur during the week. This way, you can make runs to/from your vendors, payroll company, SAG office, and/or other businesses that only keep normal business hours. It also gives you a little more schedule flexibility, as you'll see below.

Bars, event halls, restaurants, and clubs are easiest to shoot in during the day (you can black out the windows if you have a night scene; most clubs have no windows anyway), and especially between Monday and Thursday.

Houses and apartments are best shot in during weekdays (even if it's a night scene). Most people are at work during the day, so the noise level tends to be lower. Also, you run the risk of neighbor complaints if you shoot at night.

Exteriors vary tremendously. If you want some control over the crowd, then weekdays are best in residential neighborhoods; weekends are best in business districts. If you want a lot of background action, then reverse that.

Offices and most industrial areas are easiest to shoot on the weekends.

Crew Considerations

So at this point you've got your schedule grouped together by location, in a pretty decent order. You start out with your day exteriors, then move inside for a few days, gradually moving over to your nighttime scenes. At this point, it all looks great, except that you've scheduled a high-school graduation scene that requires a lot of art department work, right before a housewarming party in a location that has to be dressed from scratch. Congratulations, you've just thrown your art department staff under the bus. They will have to wrap out one set while preparing the next one, or sacrifice any decent turnaround. Or you'll have to hire some additional hands.

Likewise, if you have back-to-back costume-intensive scenes, the costume designer may not be able to get the wardrobe ready for the second scene.

Women take significantly longer to get through hair/makeup and wardrobe than men. If you have a lot of women in your cast, try to schedule scenes with men first thing each day and after lunch. The hair/makeup and wardrobe departments can get the women ready while you're shooting.

Your grip and electric budget is likely to be very small, and so you can't have all the lights you'll need throughout the entire shoot all on the truck. You'll have to "day play" packages, which means your key grip and gaffer will separate out equipment that is needed specifically for just one set of locations. So throughout the shoot you'll be swapping out one set of gear for another. It's best then to keep locations that require the same (or similar) packages together, to minimize the amount of swapping in/out.

You may also have some locations that require rigging and derigging (where the crew will set up lighting and grip ahead of time). Unless you can afford rigging crews, you'll need to keep big rigging sets separated by "lighter" days so that your grips and electrics don't have to be derigging in one location while picking up gear and rigging another.

Can you space out your art-department-intensive locations with some that don't require as much work (an exterior, or some interiors that you can shoot "as is")? If you can't, one alternative is to end the week at one location, then pick up the following week at the next big place. This gives the art department the "weekend" to wrap out and prep. Similarly, if you can separate costume- and lighting-intensive scenes with ones that don't require as much prep/wrap work, you'll experience fewer delays during the shoot.

You may not be able to do this and satisfy your other priorities. If you can't, make a note that you'll need to hire more art department staff, wardrobe assistants, grips, and/or electrics, or allow for more setup time on the first day at the second location.

Company Moves and Travel Days

Now you have a decent schedule that keeps all your locations together in a logical order, from day to night, exterior to interior. Your weeks are also taking shape. You probably have some locations that you're sitting at for several days, and others that you only spend some part of a day in. Now you have to start taking travel and company moves into account.

I hate company moves. They add nothing to the production, and cost time. Whether you're moving a mile down the road or twenty, it seems to take forever to pack up the gear and the cast and crew, get everyone pointed in the right direction, get to the next set, and set up again. Inevitably someone gets lost. Plus, with every location, you have to research and secure holding, food, services (such as hardware stores and copy shops), and parking.

There are three ways to deal with company moves:

1. Avoid them by keeping your locations geographically close together.
2. Keep them as short as possible.
3. Consider "distant" locations.

Avoidance. Perhaps you have one scene that takes place in a playground, and another that takes place in a deli. You can probably find a deli that's close to a playground, so it's reasonable to put these two scenes together on the same day (all other considerations being equal). You've successfully eliminated a company move.

On *Found In Time*, we had to shoot several interior scenes in the main character's apartment, featuring two of our leads, Chris and Jina. But we also needed to shoot an important exterior walk-and-talk scene between them. This walk-and-talk was short – about two pages long – so it wouldn't "fit" comfortably anywhere in the schedule. I didn't want to stick it at the end of the schedule, in case of rain. So I put it in the middle of my day of apartment interiors, and resolved to find a stretch of sidewalk a block or two away from wherever the apartment location would be.

Keep it short. If you can't avoid a company move, be sensible about how much time it will take away from shooting. Try to put locations together that are relatively close geographically – so that the company moves themselves are shorter. You might also have to move some of your scenes from the end of one day onto the next one.

Distant. If you have locations that you know are going to be more than one hour's drive away from your "home base," your cast and crew's travel time will end up being "on the meter." This could mean some large overtime bills, along with severe creeping crawl. You're better off considering these locations "distant" ones and figuring out how to house and feed people, rather than driving them back and forth every day. While the room and board can get expensive, your days will be more productive and you'll have less overtime. Even if you have to pay the cast and crew for the travel days, you'll be better off. If part of your shoot does end up as a "distant" location, you'll have to add two travel days (one to go there and one to come back).

Travel days. If you have a location that's more than a couple of hour's travel from your home base, you should either schedule very little shooting on the travel day, or none at all. It may not be worth it to travel three hours, check the crew and cast into their lodging, go to the location, set up, shoot for an hour or two, break for lunch, come back and shoot a little more, then break (at 12 hours).

Overall. I usually like to start the schedule with company moves, and end it in the main location of the story. It's better to get the moving out of the way when the crew and cast are a little fresher, and then reward them by keeping them in one spot at the end. Also, the main location usually takes more time for the art department and grip/electric crew to prepare, so anything you can schedule in front of it can help them. Finally, if you can leave your gear in the location overnight (safely), you can dump some of your equipment transportation during your stay.

I like to put distant locations either first or last. If it's first on the schedule I can use the equipment check-out day as my travel day. If it's last on the schedule then I can do some of the equipment returns (or shoot a short scene) on the travel day. Either way I can "absorb" part of the cost of the travel day by using it for other things.

Cast Considerations

So now that you have a schedule that's pretty well-organized, grouped logically by location and time of day, it's time to tear it apart for the cast members.

If you want a "name" actor for one of the roles, it's generally better to consolidate her days on set. It's easier to sell an actor on a low-budget film if the time commitment is concentrated, so it doesn't interfere with her other obligations. But even if you don't have any "names" it's usually easier on the actors and the costume designer (and possibly the hair/makeup team) if everyone's days are consolidated.

Another reason for consolidating cast days is to save money. If you're on a distant location shoot and you have an actor who's shooting on day 1, not needed for days 2–3, and then shoots again on day 4, you either have to shuttle them back and forth from your home town, or feed and house them for two days. Can you move their scenes on day 1 to day 3? That way you don't have to bring them up until day 2.

If you're working under the SAG modified-low-budget or low-budget agreements, you can convert actors from daily to weekly players and thus get a "discount" on their wages. This only makes sense, however, if your actor is scheduled for three or more days in a given week – if not, it's cheaper to keep him as a day player. So if you can get John's scenes shot on days 1–4 instead of 1, 4, 7, and 8, you can save some money. The exact savings will vary depending on overtime (we'll look at budgeting your cast in more detail in the next chapter).

It's not always possible to consolidate your cast days *and* your location days. It may also completely screw up the schedule that you've already put together. But you should at least try to get your leads' days consolidated, and whatever supporting roles you think will be played by "name" actors. While it could create a more inefficient schedule, if the "names" are getting you the financing and/or distribution, it's worth the extra effort.

Often, some kind of compromise between location and cast considerations is possible, especially if you're shooting in one place for an extended period of time.

Tricky Stuff

Okay, so you've moved your schedule around a bit to try and keep actor days together, but hopefully the shoot is still in some kind of location-based order. Now it's time to look through the schedule and identify problem areas. After all, not all scenes are equal. A 2/8th-page scene with a stabbing and fight could take a half-day to shoot (at least), whereas a 1-page walk-and-talk could take a couple of hours. (Figure 9.4 shows an example from *Found In Time*.)

FIGURE 9.4 This scene, which lasted less than two minutes onscreen, took eight hours to shoot. (Photo: Simeon Moore.)

Some examples of "tricky stuff":

1. **Fights/falls/stabbings/shootings/chases.** These take a long time to rehearse, tend to require a lot of setups, and shouldn't be rushed if you want them to look good.
2. **Animals.** These are somewhat unpredictable, even dogs and cats. They generally can't shoot for extended periods of time, so you have to work around them or take breaks while they're resting. Or use a second animal.
3. **Children.** Even if trained actors, children can't last as long at one stretch as adults. You also can't keep them on set for longer than a certain period of time, or you'll run afoul of child labor laws and SAG regulations. So if you've scheduled all your child actor's scenes on one day, you may have to break it into two days, or hire a body double and shoot all the kid's angles first, or move all the scenes that don't feature the child onto another day.
4. **Car shots.** Rigging cars takes forever. Budget some extra time for these scenes.
5. **Large crowd scenes.** Here you generally have the opposite problem. On a tight budget, you probably can't afford to pay much for extras, so if you have a huge crowd of them showing up, you're going to start losing them over the course of the day. Also, if you're counting on free extras, make it easier for them – don't schedule their scene for 4AM.
6. **Scenic/breakaway unit.** If you have some wide establishing shots, aerial setups, effects/CGI work – anything that doesn't involve cast members – it's best to schedule it for a separate day, maybe during the equipment returns, or in postproduction when you know exactly what you'll need.
7. **Restaurant/large group conversations.** These always take a while to set up, especially if you have more than two people in the conversation. As we discussed in Chapter 6, the number of camera setups you need to shoot a conversation goes up geometrically with the number of people in the scene. This is made more difficult by the layout of a typical restaurant booth or table – there will be a few places you literally can't put the camera, so you'll have to cheat people a bit.
8. **Night exteriors.** These require the most lighting, are the most subject to weather issues, and tend to take longer to get going, in part because most people would probably rather be sleeping.

How do you handle tricky scenes? Here are several ideas.

Break down these scenes into parts. For example, if you have a scene that starts with a conversation and ends with a fight, then you would want to create PT1 and PT2 strips, figure out the length of each one, and label them accordingly ("John and Josh Conversation," "John and Josh Engage in Fisticuffs"). If you have a scene involving a child, you may have to break out the strips even further so you can figure out what parts of the scene you need the kid for. You can then "block shoot" the scene – shoot all of the kid's angles out first, then proceed to shoot the other angles (so you can wrap the child out on time). You may not know the exact camera setups you'll need at this point. That's okay, just take a guess.

Schedule tricky scenes as early as possible in the day, but not first thing if you can help it. People seem to be at their best about an hour into the shoot. Then their focus tapers off after lunch and doesn't come back again for at least an hour. Consider the physical demands on your cast – if you have a lot of fighting/chasing/physical activity, then asking them to do anything really dramatic afterwards may not yield the best results. On *Found In Time*, I scheduled a chase scene in the morning, followed by a series of relatively uncomplicated shots in the afternoon, where the actors had little dialog and not much to do.

Add some rehearsal time to the production schedule, either on the same day as the scene to be shot or the day before.

All of these adjustments will probably make your schedule grow a bit in length. In the next step, we'll look at how to get it back down to within your budget range.

Adjusting Your Page Count

So you've made all these tweaks and additions to your budget. You probably started out thinking you could shoot your film in 12 days, and suddenly you're looking at a 21-day schedule. What the hell? At this point, you'll have to answer three difficult questions:

1. Can I get away with a longer shoot schedule on my budget?
2. Can I safely consolidate my days without sacrificing too much coverage?
3. Can I creatively consolidate my days?

The first question is related to budgeting, which we're going to tackle in more detail in the next chapter. Unless you really know what your per-day and fixed costs are, you won't be able to accurately assess whether your schedule fits within your budget. But to give you some idea of what you can probably afford, if your budget is less than $100,000 and you're shooting locally and cashing in some favors, you might be able to stretch your shoot to 14–15 days. If your budget is between $100K and $200K, you're looking at 18 days, tops. You can't really start affording a fourth week until you get to around $500K (and that's still assuming a fair number of favors).

If you find that you're spending a lot of time in one place – like three to four days – you can probably pack more scenes onto the second and third day and trim a little off the schedule. Part of what costs time in film is the load-in and load-out from a location, so if you can leave the set "hot" from day to day you can accomplish a little more. On *LL*, we shot for six days in one hotel room, and were able to leave everything in the room overnight. After the first day we were averaging about eight to nine pages of fairly intense dialog per day.

Similarly, on *Found In Time*, we spent the first week (five days) outside but were able to put our gear in a community center at the end of each day. After the first day we averaged about eight pages per day, and that included some very "tricky" scenes. At one point we had to break up one very long scene into three different chunks, spread out over two days, because of some actor availability and production issues. So we really shot closer to 10 pages on those two days when you factor in the overlapping coverage we had to pick up.

If you have some scenes that are truly minimal – day exteriors with one character, for example – you could consider creating a day of "scenic/second" unit material that you can shoot with a smaller crew. This might give you the "space" to put more complex scenes together.

Can you block-shoot some scenes? Suppose your script includes a series of dinner table scenes between John and Jane. If you're planning on shooting these scenes from the same set of camera setups (master and two singles, for example), try breaking up each of these dinner scenes into smaller strips. You can then schedule them in camera setup order instead of strict scene order. This will save you a *lot* of time in camera/lighting setups. We did this on *Found In Time* for a series of scenes that took place in the protagonist's living room and bathroom.

Can you shoot some scenes as "oners"? This is dangerous, but if you have a bunch of dead-simple 1/8th-page scenes, you don't necessarily have to plan extensive coverage.

Can you shoot multiple sets on one location? On *Found In Time*, I had written several scenes that take place in two shrinks' offices (Jina and Anthony). When trying to schedule it, though, it became apparent that treating them as separate locations would create problems – company moves, art department dressing concerns, etc. So I resolved to find an office that could double for both locations, by simply rearranging the furniture and some wall art, and varying the lighting slightly. We ultimately found one office that worked, and shot Jina's scenes against one wall that had a couch and a chair. We shot Anthony's scenes against the opposite wall, that had two chairs and a table. We took some artwork and diplomas off the wall and moved a bookcase around. While it's hard to know at this stage of the game if you can do the same thing, it's still worth looking at your script and asking the question.

Between these different tricks you may be able to compress the schedule somewhat. In the next chapter, we'll begin to go back and forth between the budget and schedule. It may be that, with a small enough cast and crew, the number of shooting days is less of a constraint. On the other hand, if you have to account for a lot of costumes, production design needs, special effects, etc., then you may need to trim days so you can afford a larger crew to deal with these things.

CONCLUSIONS

The breakdown and schedule are a first attempt to grasp the logistics of the film. They'll give you some perspective on your script, and reveal some unexpected details. When I read *The Toe Tactic*, I didn't realize that a good third of the film takes place outdoors. We were shooting in the middle of the winter, so this became a major scheduling consideration. The first and second AD on the project revised the schedule quite a bit to deal with weather issues, adjusting for the fact that people tend to move slower in cold and inclement weather.

But don't lose sight of the creative thread while trying to figure out these logistical issues. It's a strange business, when you think about it – in most art forms, the needs of the artist dictate the "order of assembly." Painters often work from the background to the foreground, starting with the canvas itself (stretching and priming it). Writers usually write from the beginning to the end. When they skip around, it's because they feel like it or haven't quite worked something out in the middle. Even music and theater production, which have periods where technical concerns take priority over creative ones, are more artist-friendly. But when you shoot a film, you have to dice up this (hopefully) organically conceived and written story into short segments, shoot multiple takes and angles to protect yourself from the inevitable mistakes, and hope you can put it all back together in the editing room. It's a miracle anything good gets made.

At the end of the day, the breakdown, schedule, and budget are tools, but they shouldn't be confused with the film itself. Don't ignore them, but don't become their slave either. In the next chapter, we'll talk in more detail about the budgeting process, and see how it loops back on the schedule and breakdown you've worked on here.

QUESTIONS

1. What are the "big" set pieces in your script?
2. How flexible is your script in terms of time of day? Location?
3. Do you have any scenes requiring a fair number of extras?
4. Can you spot the longer conversations in your script?
5. Can you identify, within a particularly long scene, where you could chop it up into smaller "sub-scenes" if necessary?

## Chapter 10

Budgeting

Continuation of Account 2620

Acct No	Line	Description	Amount	Units	X	Curr	Rate	Subtotal	Total
	3	WRAP		3 Days	12		12	$450	
	4	Total							$3,750
2630		Costume Purchase/Rental							
	1	New costumes, rentals, buy & ret		1 Allow	1		2,000	$2,000	
	2	Army Fatigues		Set			100	$500	
	3	Major Jean Uniform		1 Set			100	$100	
	4	Total							$2,600
2640		Cleaning							
	1	Dry and wet cleaning		19 Days	2		10	$380	
	2	Total							$380
2650		Alterations and Materials							
	1	Stitching, padding, etc.		1 Allow	1		0	$0	
	2	Total							$0
2670		Expendables							
	1	Thread, tape, photos, etc.		Allow	1		100	$100	
	2	Total							$100
2680		Kit Fees							
	1	Kit Fee For Costume Designer		19 Days	1		0	$0	
	2	Total							$0
2690		Breakage Fee							
	1	Damage to owner's clothing		1 Allow	1		0	$0	
	2	Total							$0
Account Total for 2600									$12,080
2700	CAMERA								
2710		Director of Photography					250		
	1	PREP		13 Days	1		250	$3,250	
	2	SCOUT		1 Days	1		250	$250	

FIGURE 10.1 Oh, the glory of numbers.

THE BUDGET FROM 30,000 FEET

This is *not* a step-by-step guide to budgeting your film. The topic is too broad to squeeze into one chapter. There are many worthy books and online resources that cover the details of budgeting (some of these are listed in Appendix A). What this chapter will give you is an aerial view of the budget and how it impacts the shoot. We'll also talk about how the budget structure of an indie feature like yours differs from that of a studio or "Indiewood" feature.

It's easy to get lost in the details of the budget and forget why you're building one in the first place. A budget is really a set of things:

1. **A list of spending priorities.** What you think is worth allocating money to in the film.
2. **A set of creative constraints.** You'll have to come up with less expensive ways of doing certain things, or get your point across indirectly. Even big directors have to work within

a budget. And all of them started out on smaller projects where they had to spend every penny wisely.

3. **A sales document.** When you're approaching investors asking for money, showing them how you intend to spend it can only help.
4. **An assessment of risks.** While a budget can never account for all the costs you're going to encounter, it can certainly give you some idea of what's going to be expensive.
5. **A table of organization (TO) for the film.** It shows you who's on the staff, and what each department head's area of responsibility covers.

The choice of software is secondary. I use Movie Magic Budgeting. If Excel is all you have, then use that; but be warned, some pain is up ahead.

THE STEPS TO BUDGETING

Budgeting is like the director's script analysis process. You'll start with some rough ideas of where you want to end up, then through research and analysis you'll come closer and closer to a concrete "truth." In this case, you'll start by making some key decisions (or assumptions), then punching in numbers, then revising your assumptions and possibly your schedule. You'll go through this cycle several times. Along the way you may find you need to tweak or rewrite the script, either for creative or budgetary reasons.

Let's first look at the budget structure.

THE STRUCTURE OF THE BUDGET

No two producers budget films in the same exact way, so what I will tell you is in part based on my opinion. But there is a generally accepted standard for budgeting features, shorts, and webisodic projects – anything that's narrative in nature. It's somewhat logical and well-understood by line producers and production managers.

To make the discussion more concrete, I've included the "final" topsheet from *Found In Time* (Table 10.1).

Sections

A budget is typically divided into six or seven sections:

Above the line. The "creative" people – directors, producers, writers, actors, casting directors; also expenses that are associated with these people (travel, lodging, development, assistants, copyright fees, clearance reports, etc.).

Below the line. The crew, equipment, food, transportation, fuel, locations, props, costumes, and other material needed to make the film.

Post. The editor, sound designer, composer, visual effects artists, colorist, and all their gear.

Overhead. Office space rental, legal fees, postage – all the expenses of running the business.

Promotion and distribution. Costs associated with marketing and distributing the film.

Contingency. Usually some percentage of the sum of the above. Some producers will exclude insurance and other fees from this amount, on the grounds that you don't need to have any "padding" on your insurance costs. I generally agree, except in cases where the budget is insanely low, and then you need all the "padding" you can get. A contingency is there to protect you from all the things that can go wrong that you *can't* plan for. Bad things that you *can count on* happening (like overtime, meal penalties, breakage) should be accounted for somewhere else in your budget, however.

Insurance. Some producers like to break insurance down into the various types, and put each in its proper place in the budget. Others like to come up with a percentage-based figure (like the contingency).

TABLE 10.1 The topsheet of *Found In Time*'s production-thru-distribution budget, with explanations of each category

#	Description	Total	Comments
	ABOVE THE LINE		
110–00	STORY & OTHER RIGHTS	0	The writer's fee and copyright fee
111–00	PRODUCER'S UNIT	0	The producer's fees and expenses
112–00	DIRECTOR'S UNIT	0	Director's fees
113–00	TALENT	13,098	Cast, casting director, casting expenses
114–00	ATL TRAVEL/HOUSING	0	Travel/house for cast/prod./writer/dir.
999–96	ATL FRINGE BENEFITS	4,813	Employer fringes, HP&W payments
	TOTAL ABOVE-THE-LINE COSTS	**$ 17,911**	
	BELOW THE LINE		
200–00	PRODUCTION STAFF	0	UPM, ADs, script supervisor, walkies
201–00	BACKGROUND	150	Extras, including their wardrobe and food
202–00	PRODUCTION DESIGN	0	Production design STAFF
203–00	PROPERTY	900	Propmaster and props
204–00	SET DRESSING	0	Set dressing and dressers
205–00	SET CONSTRUCTION	0	
206–00	SPECIAL EFFECTS	0	On-set special effects
207–00	CAMERA	5,050	DP, ACs, DIT and camera gear
208–00	ELECTRIC	1,820	Gaffer/electrics, generators, lights
209–00	GRIP	0	Key grip/grips, dolly, grip gear
210–00	PRODUCTION SOUND	5,603	Mixer, boom op, mics
211–00	SET OPERATIONS	6,112	Catering, crafty, garbage bags, etc.
212–00	COSTUME/WARDROBE	4,019	Costume designer, wardrobe
213–00	HAIR/MAKEUP	3,870	Hair and makeup artists, kit fees
214–00	LOCATIONS	7,125	Location manager, rental fees, stage
215–00	TRANSPORTATION	4,737	Fuel, tolls, vehicle rentals
216–00	PRODUCTION STOCK/ DIGITIZING	600	Hard drives, tapestock, DVDs
217–00	PRODUCTION PUBLICITY	0	Still photographer, EPK "preditor," gear
218–00	BTL TRAVEL/HOUSING	0	Crew housing/food for distant locations
219–00	PRODUCTION OVERHEAD	9,670	Office rental, legal fees, insurance
999–97	PRODUCTION FRINGE BENEFITS	0	Employer fringes, HP&W payments
	TOTAL BELOW-THE-LINE COSTS	**$ 49,656**	
	POST-PRODUCTION		
501–00	EDITING	14,610	Editor, assistant editor, drives, computer
502–00	DIGITAL CONFORM/FINISH	7,120	Colorist, output to tape master
503–00	POST-PRODUCTION SOUND	10,700	Sound design and mix

#	Description	Total	Comments
504–00	CGI/OPTICALS	2,000	Includes artist, materials & gear
505–00	MUSIC	4,150	Composer, studio fees, licensing
507–00	POSTPRODUCTION OVERHEAD	7,100	Office rental, working meals, postage
999–98	POSTPRODUCTION FRINGE BENEFITS	0	Employer fringes, HP&W payments
	TOTAL POSTPRODUCTION COSTS	**$ 45,680**	
	OVERHEAD		
601–00	PUBLICITY	0	This is covered under Distribution
602–00	GENERAL OVERHEAD	0	Office supplies, postage, etc.
603–00	DELIVERY	0	This is covered under Distribution
999–99	TOTAL OTHER FRINGES	0	Employer fringes, HP&W payments
	TOTAL OVERHEAD COSTS	**$ 0**	
	DISTRIBUTION/MARKETING		
701–00	GENERAL DISTRIBUTION LABOR/FEES	5,500	Producer's rep, consultants
702–00	DVD/BLU-RAY DISTRIBUTION	13,660	DVD duplication, fulfillment, postage
703–00	PUBLICITY	18,008	National/regional publicists, campaigns
705–00	CREATIVE MATERIALS	0	Graphic designer, key artwork, trailer
706–00	PRINTING MATERIALS	3,950	Posters, postcards, other promo materials
707–00	THEATRICAL PRINTS	6,350	HD, DCP, or 35mm prints
708–00	THEATER EXPENSES	2,500	Theater and projector rentals
709–00	DIRECT MEDIA	15,700	Advertising expenses (print/web/other)
710–00	TRAVEL	5,100	Travel to festivals
711–00	GENERAL OVERHEAD	2,000	Office supplies and postage
712–00	DELIVERY	650	Cost to deliver items to distributor that weren't completed during post
	TOTAL DISTRIBUTION/ MARKETING	**$ 73,418**	
800–00	CONTINGENCY: 10.0%	**$ 9,724**	Excludes overhead, insurance, and distribution/marketing
	GRAND TOTAL:	**$ 196,389**	

Note that on *Found In Time*, I didn't have a separate insurance section. I had purchased short-term production insurance (this was listed under 219–00, production overhead). When the film is acquired by a distributor, I will most likely have to purchase errors and omissions insurance.

Categories

Each section is further divided into categories. One category usually corresponds to a department. There are some exceptions to this, which we'll get into a little later on.

Above-the-line categories usually proceed in the order listed in Table 10.1 (writer, producer, director, actors, travel). Below-the-line categories usually start with the production staff and extras, but after that point I've seen them listed in a variety of orders. There are a few traditions. Art department-related categories (production design, set construction, props, set dressing) are usually listed sequentially. Likewise, hair/makeup and costume design, and camera, sound, electric, and grip, are listed together. At some point in my career I found an order that made sense to me, so I've stuck with it pretty much ever since (it also makes comparing budgets from different projects easier).

You'll see that there are a few categories that have nothing in them. If a budget category is empty, there should be a good reason. It's important to include categories and line items even if they're empty – this shows you what you *aren't* spending money on.

Line Items

Each category is further divided into line items (sometimes referred to as accounts). Table 10.2 shows the summary view of a few below-the-line departments from *Found In Time*.

TABLE 10.2 Selected summary budget for *Found In Time*

Item #	Item	Subtotal	Total
207–00	**CAMERA**		
207–01	Director of Photography	4,950	
207–02	Camera Operator	0	
207–03	1st AC	0	
207–04	2nd AC	0	
207–05	Red Tech	0	
207–06	B-Camera Crew	0	
207–07	Additional Red Tech	0	
207–08	Steadicam Operator	0	
207–10	VTR Assist	0	
207–12	Camera Package	0	
207–16	Additional Rentals	0	
207–17	Dolly – SEE GRIP	0	
207–30	Kit Fees	0	
207–31	Expendables	100	
			$5,050
208–00	**ELECTRIC**		
208–01	Gaffer	0	
208–02	Best Boy Electric	0	
208–03	Generator Operator	0	
208–04	Electrics	0	
208–05	Rigging Crew	0	
208–15	Lighting Package	1,300	
208–16	Day-Play Package	0	
208–17	Generator Rental	0	
208–30	Kit Fees	0	

Item #	Item	Subtotal	Total
208–31	Expendables	520	
208–32	Breakage	0	
			$1,820
209–00	**GRIP**		
209–01	Key Grip	0	
209–02	Best Boy Grip	0	
209–03	Dolly Grip	0	
209–04	Grips	0	
209–05	Rigging Crew	0	
209–15	Grip Package	0	
209–16	Day-Play Grip Package	0	
209–17	Dolly Rental	0	
209–18	Car Rigging	0	
209–30	Kit Fees	0	
209–31	Expendables	0	
209–32	Breakage	0	
			$0
210–00	**PRODUCTION SOUND**		
210–01	Production Mixer	2,275	
210–02	Boom Operator	0	
210–03	Playback Operator (Music)	0	
210–04	Sound Utility	0	
210–15	Sound Equipment	2,275	
210–16	Additional Rentals	600	
210–31	Expendables	453	
			$5,603
211–00	**SET OPERATIONS**		
211–01	Set Medic	0	
211–02	Craft Service	0	
211–03	Craft Services Utility	0	
211–15	Craft Service Package	650	
211–16	Unit Rentals/Expendables	650	
211–20	Meals	4,642	
211–21	Caterer	0	
211–25	Walkie-Talkie Rental	170	
211–30	Kit Fees	0	
211–31	Expendables (See 211–16)	0	
			$6,112

(Continued)

TABLE 10.2 (Continued)

Item #	Item	Subtotal	Total
212–00	**COSTUME/WARDROBE**		
212–01	Costume Designer	2,550	
212–02	Costume Assistant	0	
212–03	Wardrobe Supervisor	0	
212–04	First Set Costumer	0	
212–05	Costumer/Shopper	0	
212–06	Costume/Wardrobe PAs	0	
212–15	Purchases/Rentals	1,144	
212–16	Cleaning	195	
212–30	Kit Fees	0	
212–31	Expendables	130	
212–32	Damages	0	
			$4,019
213–00	**HAIR/MAKEUP**		
213–01	Key Makeup Artist	2,600	
213–02	Key Hair Artist	0	
213–03	Assistant H/MU Artists	0	
213–05	S/FX Makeup	0	
213–15	Hair/Makeup Expenses	520	
213–30	Kit Fees	650	
213–31	Expendables	100	
			$3,870
214–00	**LOCATIONS**		
214–01	Location Manager	0	
214–02	Assistant Location Manager	0	
214–03	Location PAs	0	
214–04	Location Scout	0	
214–06	Security	0	
214–10	Scouting Expenses	25	
214–15	Site Rentals	3,400	
214–16	Soundstage Rentals	3,200	
214–31	Expendables/Location Supplies	500	
			$7,125
215–00	**TRANSPORTATION**		
215–01	Transportation Captain	0	
215–02	Truck Drivers	0	
215–03	Non-Truck Drivers	0	
215–15	Production Vehicles	3,222	
215–16	Fuel	260	

Item #	Item	Subtotal	Total
215–17	Tolls	225	
215–18	Parking	630	
215–19	Parking Tickets	0	
215–20	Taxi/Subway/Bus	400	
215–32	Loss/Damage	0	
			$4,737
216–00	**PRODUCTION STOCK/ DIGITIZING**		
216–01	Production Drives	600	
216–02	Shipping	0	
216–05	Downconversion	0	
216–06	Deck Rental	0	
216–07	DVD Dailies	0	
216–09	Additional Fees/Tests	0	
			$600
217–00	**PRODUCTION PUBLICITY**		
217–01	Still Photographer	0	
217–02	EPK Camera Operator	0	
217–03	EPK Sound Mixer	0	
217–04	EPK Editor	0	
217–15	Rentals	0	
217–16	Still Photo Stock/Processing	0	
217–17	Making of Stock	0	
217–30	Kit Fees	0	
217–31	Expendables	0	
			$0
218–00	**BTL TRAVEL/HOUSING**		
218–01	Airfare	0	
218–02	Lodging	0	
218–03	Per Diems	0	
218–04	Additional Ground Travel	0	
			$0
219–00	**PRODUCTION OVERHEAD**		
219–01	Legal Fees	5,000	
219–02	Office Expenses	470	
219–03	Office Rent	0	
219–04	Production Insurance	3,300	
219–05	Worker's Compensation	0	
219–06	Incorporation	900	
			$9,670

Your head may start spinning – mine always does when I see all the items I have to budget for – but just stare at the table and some things will become apparent to you.

First, notice that each line item number uses an XXX–XX nomenclature. The first three digits indicate the department; the last two the line item. Each line item number should be unique. Further, it helps if you have "matching" line items across different departments. Note above that department heads are usually "XXX–01," your seconds are "XXX–02," major rentals (equipment or locations) start at "XXX–15," special rentals are "XXX–16," and so on. This makes it easy to compare different departments' budgets and also identify a line item just by looking at the number (handy when you're tallying up costs later).

Second, notice that there's a typical order of items within a department. It should ideally go something like this:

- **Department Head** – sometimes called the **Key**.
- **Second/Assistant** – sometimes called the **Best**.
- **Staff** – works under the second and department head. Sometimes called the **Third**.
- **Additional Special Crew** – day players (people who are only needed for specific days).
- **Main Equipment Rental/Purchase** – the main lighting package, camera package, mixer, etc.
- **Additional Equipment Rental** – for specific days or periods during the shoot.
- **Kit Fees** – a way of compensating crew for using their equipment and supplies.
- **Expendables** – items you have to buy such as tape, sash, gels, staples, etc.; anything that is used and then disposed of.
- **Breakage/Damage** – an estimate of gear that won't make it back, or damage to the owner's property.

This reflects the order in which you'll be dealing with each department's components. Usually I hire the keys first (who then bring on their staff), then figure out the gear they need, then figure out the expendables and kit fees, and at the end of the shoot pay out the missing/damaged charges.

Some producers prefer to put *all* the crew into one category. They then list all the equipment, location rentals, etc. in separate categories. The reasoning is that your crew is a labor expense, which should be kept separate from the equipment/location/other non-labor items. I don't recommend this. It may make some accounting sense, but it doesn't reflect the way the shoot works in real life. In actuality, each department head is responsible for his/her own budget and crew.

I recommend that you leave some gaps between numbers in case you have to insert a line item later.

Details

Finally, each line item consists of a set of detailed expenses. Table 10.3 shows the detail level for item #212–15, Costume Purchases/Rentals, and Table 10.4 shows the detail level for item #212–01, Costume Designer.

TABLE 10.3 Detail-level of line item #212–15, from *Found In Time*

Description	Amount	Unit Type	X	Rate	Total
All-In	1	ALLOW	1	350	350
Psych-Cops	4	Uniforms	1	100	400
Surgical Scrubs – Miners	8	Uniforms	1	13	104
Doctor Scrubs – Jina/Anthony	2	Coats/Pants	1	20	40
Jina	1	ALLOW	1	100	100
Seconds	1	ALLOW	1	100	100
Comfort Robes	2	Robes	1	25	50

TABLE 10.4 Detail-level of line item #212–01, from *Found In Time*

Description	Amount	Unit Type	X	Rate	Total
Prep	3	Days	1	150	450
Shoot	13	Days	1	150	1,950
Wrap	1	Day	1	150	150

You'll notice that some expenses are pretty specific – the day rate for the costume designer or the number of uniforms for the miners. Others are more general. If I don't know exactly how much money I'm going to need to spend on something, I write ALLOW under the unit type, and then throw in what I consider is a reasonable estimate.

Here is where your work on the breakdown and schedule pays off. Knowing what props, picture vehicles, locations, cast members, etc. are in your film and for roughly how long will help you figure out the details.

Labor Expenses and Terms

When you start budgeting for your crew and cast expenses, you shouldn't just consider the actual time spent during the shoot (or post). There are several other items that you should be aware of, even if the number you put down for them is a "0." These include scouting, prep, wrap, travel days, rehearsals, fittings, and the various flavors of overtime.

In the case of union crew and cast members, these additional expenses are *mandatory*. Non-union crew and non-guild actors are a different matter. According to labor laws, employees are entitled to overtime and compensation for travel. In reality, these are negotiable. I try to be fair to the crew and cast on a non-union shoot, because it's a good way to keep productions from becoming too crazy (endless days) and because it's the right thing to do.

Overtime. SAG cast members and union crew get overtime after 8 hours. Non-union cast and crew should be paid overtime of some kind – I usually start it after 12 hours. Overtime is typically calculated at *1.5 times the pro-rated hourly rate*. As you'll see below, I budget overtime for the cast as part of their base salary, since a typical film shoot day is 12 hours anyway. I usually put in an hour of extra overtime per *shoot* day per crewmember (union or non-union) as a buffer.

Doubletime. Union cast and crew get doubletime after 12 hours. I usually start doubletime for non-union folks at 14 hours. Doubletime is (you guessed it) paid at 2.0 times the pro-rated hourly rate.

2.5× time. Same principle as overtime and doubletime. Union: starts after 14 hours (depending on the contract). Non-union: starts after 16 hours.

Travel days. Union crew and cast get travel days paid for, though the rates are usually lower (on union crews a travel day can be a 4-hour day). I typically pay non-union/non-guild folks a half-day for travel unless it's a *really* distant location they're traveling to.

Meal penalties. You're supposed to break for meals every 6 hours. Anytime you violate this rule, you have to pay the actors (and crew) a penalty. This penalty varies (see below) and you get a "break" if you happen to be in the middle of a take when the 6 hours is up. It's a good idea to budget for at least one or two of these over the course of the shoot.

Prep, wrap, scout days, rehearsals. You may not be able to pay for all of these fully, but you should at least put them in the budget, even if you put a "0" next to them.

Independent vs. Studio Budgets

Sometimes I depart from some of the more "standardized" budgets I've seen in a number of key ways. Every producer has a slightly different way of grouping things. Here are the major discrepancies and why they matter.

Line producer. Some people categorize the line producer as a *producer*, whereas others put them at the top of the *production staff* department. I do the latter. In my experience, the line producer is mostly involved in the preproduction and production stages and gets a salary, whereas a true producer is involved from day one and often only gets a fee at the end.

Script supervisor. Some budgets have this person occupying their own department. I understand this because, technically, it's true – the script supervisor really is a department of one. But mostly just for convenience, I put them in with the production staff department.

Props vs. greens. Greenspeople are specialized props personnel who take care of plants, flowers, and other flora (either real or fake). In some budgets, you'll see greens listed as a separate department. I usually put them under the props department, because on low-budget shoots it's unlikely you're going to need a whole separate gang of greens people running around. On *I Am Legend*, the greens department was huge, because they had to put overgrowth *everywhere*. So they had their own trucks, generators, PAs, and most likely their own department listing in the budget.

Special effects. Some budgets break out the items listed below into other departments. However, on low-budget films these items are usually tied together in some way (you generally have a pyro and armorer together) and aren't necessarily the responsibility of the rest of the crew.

Animal handlers. While technically animal handlers could be considered their own department, functionally animals are usually treated as special effects.

Armorer/pyro/guns. Some people put the armorer, gun rentals, and pyrotechnics staff in the *props department*. On low-budget shoots, however, they belong together as part of the FX budget.

Greenscreen materials. I've seen greenscreen materials and visual effects supervisors listed in their own departments, or as part of the camera department. I keep them in the special effects category.

Set operations vs. grips. Grips are actually considered part of the set operations budget. This is because one of their primary roles is set safety. So on some budgets you'll see the grips listed in set operations (Set Ops), along with the craft services and set medics.

In actuality, the grips behave like and are paid as their own department. Their equipment needs are also very different from that of the rest of the Set Ops folk. For these reasons I list them separately.

Walkie-talkie rentals. On a lot of budgets, these are lumped in with the sound department, on the principle that they're often rented from the same place that you're getting your sound gear. The production department is usually responsible for distributing and caring for walkies. But since they're used on set, I feel that Set Ops is a good department to list them in.

Dolly rental. While technically the dolly is part of the camera department, it's handled by the grips and rented (most of the time) from the grip/electric equipment house. So unless it belongs to the DP I usually end up listing it in the grip department.

Grips, electrics, and grip/electric. On most shoots, you *want* to separate grips from electrics. They serve different functions that call for different skill sets. However, on *really* low-budget shoots ($50K–$100K), you will probably only be hiring a key grip and gaffer, in which case they'll be doing a little bit of each other's jobs and the equipment will be coming from the same rental house anyway. In those cases, I collapse the grip and electric departments into one.

Costume, wardrobe. You will sometimes see these listed as separate departments. Costume designers and their staff work on the creative end – figuring out the color schemes and dress style for each character, and working with the director to establish a look. The wardrobe supervisor is more practical – they fit the actors to the wardrobe, repair and take care of them, and keep continuity. There's some overlap between them. On low-budget shoots, however, I'm hiring one or two people to do everything wardrobe-related, so I usually collapse these into one department.

Hair/makeup. Some producers like to separate these into two departments, if there's a need to hire more of one than another – for example, if the script calls for a lot of wigs or "special" hairdos, you may need more hair stylists. I usually just list everyone in one department.

Still photographers, EPK crew. Still photographers and EPK camera operators are covered by the same union local as the DP, so they're often listed in the camera department. I prefer to keep all the publicity-related personnel in their own department, since that's how they actually function on set.

Overhead and insurance. Some producers like to keep all the overhead together at the end of the budget. I'd rather segregate production from post overhead because the needs are different, and the money is spent in different stages. The same is true of insurance. Insurance needs are very different at each stage of the project.

Digital conform and finish. Every film seems to have a slightly different post workflow and target projection format. On some you'll end up outputting to film, but for most films budgeted under $4M, you'll end up making a DCP (digital cinema projection) or HDCAM-SR master, plus several sub- and projection masters. There's no real standard here – I've included many different steps, but some may become obsolete (I hope we're not still making DigiBeta masters in a couple of years).

APPROACHING THE BUDGET

There are two general approaches to budgeting: the top-down and bottom-up. In the top-down approach, you start with a target number (say, "$500,000"), and then you try to fit the budget to the target. In the bottom-up approach, you figure out the details, then add them up – and that's your total.

The danger of the top-down approach is that it can often lead to wishful thinking – you start trimming costs unrealistically to meet the target. I strongly believe that, at least for the first draft of the budget, you should pessimistically cost out everything and then see where you are. You can always subtract in subsequent drafts.

On the other hand, having a target in mind will help you structure your thinking. If you're trying to make your film for $100K–$200K, you're going to aim for a certain shoot length, SAG agreement, and crew size.

KEY DECISIONS TO MAKE

There are really seven key strategic decisions that you have to make in order to do a budget. You should try to decide them before you get too deep into the process. You can change your mind about these things later, but they'll give you a good jumping-off point from which to actually start generating your first draft. So, ideally you should:

Decide on your target. What is it you have or think you can "realistically" raise? What number makes sense from a business perspective?

Figure out the cast salary structure. Are you going to use one of the SAG low-budget agreements? Are you going to try and "sweeten the pot" with a flat offer to a name actor? This will affect your crew salaries, the length of your shoot, and other variables.

Figure out the crew "gestalt." What kind of shoot do you need to support the script? What kind are you most comfortable leading as a producer and/or director? Will you be using a union crew? This will of course have a big impact on your budget.

Decide on the length of the shoot. Look at your breakdown and preliminary schedule. This will tell you how many shoot days you "ideally" need.

Decide on the length of post. This is determined by the complexity of the script, the speed of your editor and director, and of course your target. *Found In Time* was a complex script, with a lot of scenes (145) that go back and forth in time, following multiple storylines. Sound design was also very important to me. So I initially figured on at least 10 weeks of picture editing plus synching and logging, and 8–10 weeks of sound post.

Decide on a shooting format and camera. While the shooting format has become less and less relevant over the last few years (thankfully), your choice of camera and format can have a big impact on your budget. Shooting with an Epic at 5K means renting more support gear, hiring more staff, and buying more hard drives, than if you're shooting with a Canon 5D Mark III.

Figure out your running time. A 2-hour film is a different animal than a 90-minute film. The script will determine this to some extent, but the running time can be more compressed or more elliptical depending on taste.

These decisions impact on each other in various ways – if you need 21 days to shoot the film and you're going to be giving a "name" actor a good chunk of change, you may not have a lot left for crew salaries. Let's look at each of these decisions in a little more detail.

THE TARGET NUMBER

Most producers, whether they admit it or not, have a "target" number that they want to make the film for (hopefully, they're including distribution costs in this number). This could be how much they've got saved up, how much they think they can raise in a year, what the insurance payoff will be when they kill their rich uncle, or how much they can get from presales, tax incentives, and private equity.

You usually want to stick to a specific "sweet spot" for your target. Aiming between the sweet spots can sometimes *hurt* your budget. For example, if you make a film for $200K, you'll have to pay $100 plus overtime and fringes to your cast per day under the SAG ultra-low-budget agreement. However, if you raise $300K you'll have to shell out $268 per day plus overtime and fringes. Unless that higher salary will get you bigger "names," you're essentially paying more for salaries without getting a better or more marketable movie out of the deal. This is then taking money away from other things – like location fees, the DP's salary, a better sound mix, etc. – that *can* make your movie better.

Without going all the way up to *Avatar* territory, Table 10.5 shows the different target budget levels that you want to aim for. As you can see, going up in budget doesn't mean you get more movie for your money. Being more cold-blooded about it: at each level you end up having to spend more on salaries, which is a good thing but doesn't *necessarily* lead to more production value.

However, it does make it possible to get a name actor, which can interest other investors, distributors, and sales agents. Since getting distribution is what makes your investors whole again, this should be a serious consideration.

As you go up the budget ladder, however, the risk becomes greater that you won't make your money back. The basic rule of thumb is that the *gross revenues* have to be 3–4 times the budget of the film for you to be "in the black." This multiple accounts for the exhibitor/licensee fees, distributor and sales agent percentages, any deferments you've had to pay out, delivery expenses, fees due to SAG, interest payments on any loans you had to take out to make the film, and other assorted costs that whittle the money down from *gross* (what the audience pays) to *net* (what you get).

So it's possible to make a film for $200K and make your money back. But the quality of film that you're going to be able to make for $300K won't be significantly high enough to make it worth the additional $300K–$400K in revenue it'll have to bring in.

Since you're still in exploratory mode at this point, pick a number you think you can raise and see if it's supported by the budget. You can always change the target later.

TABLE 10.5 The different budget "sweet spots"

Budget	Description	Shoot Length (Days)	Picture Edit (Weeks)	Sound Edit (Weeks)	Crew Size	SAG	Other Unions
$50K	Your friends are working for free or next to nothing. You're editing it yourself or with a friend. Your sound mix is very basic. You have enough money for some festivals and may have to raise additional funds if a distribution deal comes through	10–12	6	2	0–10	N/A	N/A
$100K	You have some money for a more ambitious story. You may have enough to pay your crew and cast. Your post will be short. You'll have very little for promotion and distribution	12–14	8	4	10–20	Ultra low budget (maybe)	N/A
$200K	You have enough money for a small paid crew or a larger unpaid crew. Post is a little longer	12–18	10–12	8	10–20	Ultra low budget	N/A
$500K	You have enough money to think you have more money than you do. You should start looking for a "name" actor. You may have a couple of heavier-hitters on the crew. You can afford to move up the ladder in terms of shooting format. You have a larger distribution/promotion budget	18–21	12	8	20–30	Modified low budget	N/A
$1M	Ironically, you may have to scale down your story somewhat. Your cast salary takes up nearly half your film. You will need some presales money to help you out	25	12–15	10	40–50	Modified low or low budget	Teamsters? IA?
$2M	Same as $1M but union crew involvement is more likely	25–30?	12–15	10+	40–60	Low budget	IA Teamsters DGA?
$10M	Union crew all the way, two–three "names." Maybe a five- or six-week shoot and a decent post period	30+	16+	10+	60+	Basic	IA Teamsters DGA WGA

CAST SALARY STRUCTURE

This really comes down to two decisions: to sign up with SAG or not, and what guild agreement you'll enter into with them.

Unless you're shooting at the $50K–$100K budget level, you should seriously consider signing up with SAG. For one thing, casting directors don't generally want to work with non-SAG projects. It makes their job a lot harder because it limits who they can bring in to audition. Agents and managers also don't want to go near non-SAG projects because there's less of a percentage in it for them. You'll also be cutting yourself off from anyone with significant experience, and of course no "name" actor will take on the project.

However, there are some reasons to go non-SAG:

1. **Less paperwork.** While SAG has gotten better over the years (they're being dragged kicking and screaming into the electronic age), they still saddle producers with a lot of paperwork. And if you screw it up, you can be fined or they can hold onto your bond.
2. **No bond.** When you sign with SAG they'll expect you to pay a bond, which they hold onto until after the shoot is done and you've turned in all your paperwork. The bond is pretty hefty and it's due in cash (certified check or money order). So you have to fork over some post cash and not see it for a while.
3. **No oversight.** Depending on what agreement you sign with them, you will have to submit your cast list to SAG for them to check against their membership database. If they find out that one of your cast members is behind on their dues or isn't a member, you'll have to make a case for hiring them or risk paying a fine.
4. **No SAG reps.** I've had wonderful reps. I've also had reps who've screamed at me over the phone, lost my paperwork, and/or held onto the bond for months. If you're on your last nerve making your film, you don't need them getting on it.

I still think the pros outweigh the cons. So it's worth it, in most cases, to sign with SAG.

Now, for the second decision: what agreement do you sign with them? This depends on your *production* budget. What SAG means by the production budget is fairly vague, but a safe guess is anything related to prep, production, and post; excluding distribution, promotion, contingency, and overhead. There are five SAG agreements currently in place. By the time this book is published, the SAG/AFTRA merger may result in these being shifted or modified.

Your cast salary changes dramatically depending on what budget level you end up in. What's not included in Table 10.6 is all the overtime, payroll fringes, health and pension payments, and agency fees you'll be paying to your cast.

Figures 10.2 and 10.3 give you a visual idea of what you're going to pay per day or week per actor, depending on the agreement you end up signing. Keep in mind that these figures are inclusive of fringes, agency fees, and overtime (more on this below).

Note: the "no SAG" agreement still assumes that you're paying your actors as minimum wage employees. More on this below.

The first thing that probably stands out is how steeply the salaries climb from one agreement to another. The leap from the ULBA to the MLBA wage scale is pretty astonishing. This is another reason to stay in the sweet spot.

"Wait a minute," I hear you say. "I went to this seminar given by XXXX and was told by YYY that I can get a SAG actor for $100/day under the ultra-low-budget agreement." This is technically true. But whoever told you this was stretching the truth quite a bit.

TABLE 10.6 SAG agreements at a glance

Agreement	Budget	Terms	Base Daily Rate	Base Weekly Rate	SAG Actors Required	SAG BG Required
Short/student	$50K	No bond. Short films only; no commercial distribution	0	0	No	No
Ultra low budget (ULBA)	$200K	Can mix SAG and non-SAG actors	100	Daily rate × days/week	No	No
Modified low budget (MLBA)	$625K	SAG actors only. SAG background optional	268	933	Yes	No
MLBA background initiative	$725K	Same terms as MLBA. SAG actors only. Higher ceiling for MLBA if you hire a certain number of SAG background	268	933	Yes	3 per day averaged over shoot
MLBA diversity in casting	$937K	Same terms as MLBA. SAG actors only. Higher ceiling for MLBA if you hire over 50% of cast in one or more minority categories or women	268	933	Yes	No
Low budget (LBA)	$2.5M	More stringent requirements on extras	504	1,752	Yes	30/day in LA 85/day in NY Some exceptions
LBA diversity in casting	$3.75M	Same terms as LBA. Higher ceiling for LBA if you hire over 50% of cast in one or more minority categories or women	504	1,752	Yes	30/day in LA 85/day in NY Some exceptions
Basic	$2.5M+	The standard SAG contract	809	2,808	Yes	As above

The true wage calculation is more complicated. In fact, the numbers I outlined are simplifications that don't account for distant location shooting, six-day weeks, travel time, meal penalties, etc. Here's the basic formula:

Base Rate + Overtime + Agency Fee + Payroll Fringes + SAG HP&W Payment

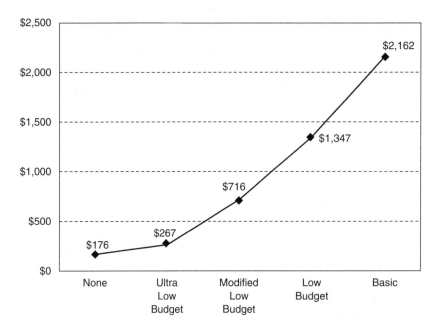

FIGURE 10.2 Comparison of SAG daily complete fees across various agreements.

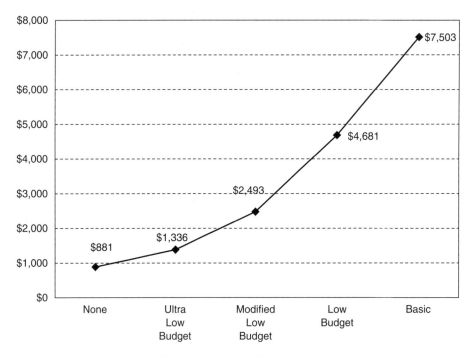

FIGURE 10.3 Comparison of SAG weekly complete fees across various agreements.

Base rate. This is the $100/day you've been hearing. However, this rate is for an *8-hour day.* You are *rarely* going to work an 8-hour day. Budget for a 12-hour day. Incidentally, lunch is off the clock.

Base Rate = $100

Overtime. This is 1.5 or 2.0 times the pro-rated hourly rate, times the number of overtime hours up to 12. There are overtime breaks and ceiling that apply to the basic agreement, and to the weekly contracts. For our typical 12-hour day, then, the overtime calculation is:

$$(\$100/8) \times 1.5 = \$18.75/\text{hour} \times 4 \text{ hours} = \$75$$

Agency fee. If your actor has an agent or manager, they're supposed to get 10 percent of their net salary. It's traditional for the producer to "bump" the salaries by the 10 percent rather than make the actors pay out of their already low wages. Some producers base the 10 percent on the base rate; I usually use the base + OT rate.

$$\text{Base Rate} + \text{OT} = (\$100 + \$75) \times 10\% = \$17.50$$

Payroll fringes. SAG actors are supposed to be paid as employees, as opposed to subcontractors. Exceptions apply for loan-out companies, but you won't know about which cast members are loan-outs at this stage of the game (more on loan-outs below). As the employer, you're responsible for paying a portion of the employee's medicare, state and federal unemployment insurance, social security, disability, and the payroll processing fee. Some of these fees, like the social security and medicare, are fixed. Others vary from state to state. I usually put in a guesstimate of 22 percent of the actors' gross wages. So:

$$\text{Base Rate} + \text{OT} + \text{Agency Fee} = \$192.50 \times 22\% = \$42.35$$

SAG health, pension, and welfare. One of the great things about guild membership (for members) is that they have healthcare and pension plans, which employers pay into. This is a fixed fee based on the gross income (not including fringes). Sometimes you can get away with excluding the agency fee from this, but I usually "bake" it in. So:

$$\text{Base Rate} + \text{OT} + \text{Agency Fee} = \$192.50 \times 16.8\% = 32.34$$

If you add all these figures together, you get (for an actor working for one day under the ultra-low-budget agreement):

$$\$100 + \$75 + \$17.50 + \$42.35 + \$32.34 = \$267.19$$

This doesn't include the various premiums you'll have to pay for meal penalties, overtime past 12 hours, travel time, or turnaround invasions (those are very expensive). Now you can see why it's a good idea to eliminate "one-line" actors where possible.

When budgeting cast salaries, I typically put in the full salary including overtime, etc. There are some exceptions:

- **Minors** can't work more than a certain number of hours per day (the exact number depends on their age) and under no circumstance should they go past eight.
- **Stunt coordinators** have *much* higher rates, even under the low-budget agreements, but they usually don't have agency fees. Most will also agree to work on a "flat" daily rate.
- **Stunt players/adjustments.** Stunt actors are usually paid the same as regular cast members but may get a "bump" for a specific stunt. Actors may also get a stunt adjustment.
- **Walk-on roles/bits.** If you have an actor who only appears in one scene and you have a reasonable hope of shooting it in less than 8 hours, then you can put this person down for the basic rate + fringes.
- **Non-SAG.** If an actor is a member of another guild (AFTRA or Actor's Equity), or has had professional training, you're still supposed to pay into the Health, Pension, and Welfare fund. If the actor is really a non-actor or just starting out, you can sometimes argue your way out of this.

umentogon,

Payroll Issues

You can't really pay SAG actors as subcontractors. SAG specifically disallows it in their agreements. Also, you're telling the actor where to go to work, when to be there, and for how long. The IRS considers those hallmarks of an employer–employee relationship. So you're stuck paying the 22 percent (roughly).

You can save a little money by doing the cast payroll yourself and not hiring a payroll company, but the amount of paperwork and check writing this entails is not really worthwhile, especially while you're in production. I've seen payroll companies charge between $15/check to 5 percent of gross wages. They usually want a deposit of at least one week's pay (by wire, money order, or certified check). You typically want to go with a payroll company that works with film and television companies, since they have the forms and systems customized for this kind of work.

Some actors form loan-out companies. These companies, like your production entity, were created to structure the actors' business. Instead of paying the actor directly, you pay the loan-out company – almost as you would a vendor – and the company "lends you" the services of the actor in return. This will save you the payroll fringes.

So, what do these fringes consist of, anyway? They're a combination of state, federal, and payroll-company-related charges that all employers are responsible for (Table 10.7).

On top of the 20–22 percent that you'll have to fork over for various payroll fringes, you have to also pay 16.8 percent of the gross wages (not including fringes) to SAG's health, pension, and welfare fund (HP&W).

TABLE 10.7 Payroll fringes by type

Type	Name	Percent of Salary	Explanation
Federal:	Social security (OSADI)	6.20	This is your half of the contribution to the social security fund; the other half comes out of the employee's wages
Federal	Medicare (MEDI)	1.45	This is your half of the contribution to the Medicare fund; the other half comes out of the employee's wages
Federal	Federal unemployment insurance (FUI/FUTA)	Min. 0.80 Max. 6.00	The federal portion of unemployment insurance. You only have to pay this on the first $7,000 of wages for each employee. Starts out at 6.0% but you get credited for your SUTA contributions, which brings it down to a minimum of 0.8%
State	State unemployment taxes (SUI/SUTA)	Varies (5.0)	Depends on the state – in NY State, the minimum is 1.5% and the maximum is 9%. The rate is only applied against the first $8,000 of wages for each employee
State	Worker's comp (WC)	Varies (3.5)	Depends on the state and the payroll company, but 3.5% is a good measurement
Payroll	Payroll company fee	Varies (3.0)	Can be either a flat fee per check (usually $15–20), or a percentage of gross payroll (between 3 and 5%). I usually write in 3%
	Total:	**19.95**	Because some states have higher fringes than others, I usually increase this to 22% to be on the safe side

Exceptions to the Rule

Some producers will pay actors a "co-producer fee" on top of their minimum salary, so as to avoid the SAG HP&W fee. While this can work, SAG certainly frowns on it.

If you've hired someone who is not legally allowed to work in the country (this happens for all sorts of reasons, such as improper immigration paperwork filing; visa overstays; or if you're making a really low-budget film and you cast an actor who's undocumented) you may have to figure out some kind of "alternative" arrangement. This could mean paying cash, or paying the person's best friend some kind of fee. If you're working on a non-SAG project or ultra-low-budget project, this is less of a problem – just be sure to keep the person out of any official paperwork. If you're working under the SAG MLB or LB agreements, however, you'll be under more scrutiny.

Other Things You Need to Consider

Rehearsals are paid. I budget rehearsal days at 8 hours (no overtime).

Fittings and makeup tests are also supposed to be on the clock. I typically budget 2 hours of fittings per actor on a pro-rated basis (divide the daily rate by 8 hours). More if it's a period or sci-fi/fantasy project. In reality, actors will donate fitting time if you can be flexible with their schedules – especially on low-budget films, it's better for them to have the designer come to them at their convenience.

Travel time is on the clock, if it's outside of a reasonable (usually 30–45 minute) travel distance from the home town/city of the actor.

Stunt coordinators get a basic rate even under the various low-budget agreements.

Meal penalties. This penalty *is* expensive – $25 per actor for the first half-hour, then $35/actor for the second half-hour, then $50 for each half-hour after that. Sometimes penalties are unavoidable. So I typically budget about one penalty per actor day. So if John has three days of shooting scheduled and Jane has two, that's five penalties total. That's not a huge amount of cushion but it does help prevent unpleasant surprises.

Paying a "Name" Actor

SAG has a standard "buy-out" salary, called a Schedule "F." As of this writing, the fee was $65,000 (plus fringes). Overtime and rehearsal time is negotiable under this schedule. In exchange for this salary, you "buy out" the actor's time – he/she can't make another commitment during your shoot.

In reality, everything is negotiable. Perhaps the actor would work for $20,000, or $200,000. You'll have to pay fringes and SAG HP&W on some portion of this money (depending on how the fees are paid out). Often an actor will get a "co-producer's fee" in addition to their salary.

How do you budget this fee? One rule of thumb says that in a $1M budget, no more than $500K total should go to above-the-line categories (including cast and fringes). This means that you might be able to swing two cast members at $100K each (plus fringes), or one actor for $200K and a couple of others for $25K–$50K. You don't have to pay all your "names" the same amount of money, but you do have to make sure each of them is treated equally – if one gets a private dressing room, so does everyone else.

On a $50K–$200K film, you might be able to get *one* name, for up to 25 percent of the budget. Anyone signing up for a film at this budget range is doing so primarily for non-monetary reasons – they like the story, they want to work with a particular director or actor, or they feel that the role will advance their career somehow.

You may have to pay for other perks – an assistant, a trailer, an international cellphone or broadband connection, etc. I usually have a line item called "Star Costs" that's part of the cast budget. It's a bit of a garbage-bag category to cover some of these items (a trailer is really part of transportation). It's very difficult to figure out what this number should be if you're trying to get a name.

If you decide to get a name actor (or two), you'll have to adjust your below-the-line salaries and gear rentals accordingly. You may have to compress the schedule so you can make up for the more expensive cast. You may also have to consolidate the schedule to favor that actor's role.

Casting Directors

A casting director is an absolute must on any film that has a budget over $100K. This is often a position that gets short shrift, but casting is a *huge* undertaking. Trying to do it yourself is not the best use of your time. A casting director, even one who's just starting out, will be able to reach more actors than you can, and can handle a lot of the logistical details that would otherwise completely swamp your prep time.

Salaries for casting directors range all over the map. Some favor a 2–5 percent structure for any films over $200K. Keep in mind that you also have to account for audition and rehearsal space rental, script copying, and possibly other office supply expenses. On films with budgets of $1M and above, you should *always* budget for a casting assistant.

DECIDING ON THE CREW STRUCTURE

This isn't just about filling in the crew salary rates, but also deciding on your crew structure, how much of the crew's responsibilities you can shoulder yourself, and whether there are special needs in the script that you'll need to consider.

Back in Chapter 4, we spoke about the different crew structures. To review, there's the:

- **Run-and-gun team:** A small cadre of 5–15 folks, who aren't overly specialized.
- **30-man team:** Emulates the larger shoot structure – more people, in more specialized positions.
- **"Real shoot":** Specific positions, larger departments.

Along with each of these structures comes a question of what the salaries should look like. There are several pay models out there, and each of them mesh more or less well with the structures I've outlined above.

Free. People *will* work for free, if the shoot is short enough, they love the script, they're trying to get a film credit, they think you'll reward their loyalty, or if they're related to/sleeping with/friends with you. The free model works if you're part of a collaborative team and work together all the time, and if you have the kind of flexibility that can deal with the side effects of "free" (like people having to take a paying job when it comes up).

When I first started I did a few jobs for free, to get a track record and learn. I got experience and credits I wouldn't have otherwise.

Deferred. This is where you pay nothing up front, but promise to make it up when money comes in down the road from the sale of the film. This is another way of saying "free." I did a number of "deferred" jobs at the beginning of my career, and haven't been paid for any of them. However, I did them because I wanted experience.

Flat/egalitarian. This model was popularized by NY-based production company InDigEnt in the early 2000s. Everyone is paid at $100 (or some other number) per day, with the rest deferred. This can be a great way to alleviate one of the problems on set – people feeling like they're "above" others because of their pay grade. But it may turn away more experienced people who feel they should get more for their work.

Tiered. This is the "standard" model – the keys get more per day than the seconds, and the seconds get more than the thirds. The thirds get more than the PAs. This rewards experience but penalizes people who are starting out, sometimes too much if the discrepancy between the tiers is too high.

Hybrid. This is where you adopt some version of all of the above models. Your DP may get a premium rate, but everyone else will be paid at the flat rate. Your PAs may end up working for free.

I usually start out with the tiered model, but then end up building a hybrid. On *Helena from the Wedding*, the DP and I took flat rates (different ones) because we liked the script and the producers. The other keys got a key day rate, and the seconds got $50–$100 less than the keys. We had two interns who worked for free – one in the wardrobe department, the other in production.

My opinion. I tend to value experience among the keys, and to favor smaller crews over larger ones. So if the budget allows, I aim for the tiered system, with some allowances for a slight premium for the DP, production designer, editor, and sound designer. If I'm asking one person to cover multiple positions, I'll also try to get them a "bump" in salary.

Table 10.8 shows what the different crew structures look like in terms of the budget. It represents a "somewhat" idealized version of the crew structure. Reality is of course a little more complicated (hence all the "depends" notes).

TABLE 10.8 Crew structures in detail

Department	Item #	Item	Run/Gun	30-Man	Full
Production	200–01	Line producer	X	X	X
	200–02	Unit production manager		?	X
	200–03	1st AD	Line prod.?	X	X
	200–04	2nd AD		X	X
	200–05	2nd 2nd AD		?	X
	200–06	Key PA	?	X	X
	200–07	Set PAs	Free	Free?	X
	200–08	Production coordinator		X	X
	200–09	Assistant production coordinator			X
	200–10	Office PAs		Interns?	X
	200–11	Production accountant		Part time	X
	200–12	Assistant accountant			X
	200–13	Script supervisor	?	X	X
Production design	202–01	Production designer	X	X	X
	202–02	Art director	?	X	X
	202–03	Art dept. coordinator		?	X
	202–04	Scenic		? (Part time)	X
	202–05	Camera scenic			X
	202–06	Scenics			X
	202–07	Graphic designer		(Part time)	(Part time)
	202–08	Storyboard artist	Free?	(Part time)	(Part time)
	202–11	Art PAs	?	Free	X

(Continued)

TABLE 10.8 (Continued)

Department	Item #	Item	Run/Gun	30-Man	Full
Props	203–01	Propmaster	?	X	X
	203–02	Best boy props		?	X
	203–03	3rd props		Free	X
	203–04	Key greens			? (Depends)
	203–05	Best boy greens			? (Depends)
	203–10	Props PA		Free	X
Set dressing	204–01	Set decorator	?	X	X
	204–02	Leadman		?	X
	204–03	Key off-set dresser		?	X
	204–04	Set dressers		? (Part time)	X
Construction	205–01	Construction coordinator		Depends on story	
	205–02	Key carpenter		Depends on story	
	205–03	Carpenters		Depends on story	
	205–04	Construction key grip		Depends on story	
	205–05	Construction grips		Depends on story	
	205–06	Construction electrics		Depends on story	
Special effects	206–01	On-set V/FX supervisor		Depends on story	
	206–02	Animals and wranglers		Depends on story	
	206–03	Armorer/pyrotechnic		Depends on story	
Camera	207–01	Director of photography	X	X	X
	207–02	Camera operator			X
	207–03	1st AC		X	X
	207–04	2nd AC		?	X
	207–05	DIT		?	X
	207–06	B-camera crew	?	?	?
	207–07	Additional DIT		?	?
	207–08	Steadicam operator		?	?
	207–10	VTR assistant			X
Electric	208–01	Gaffer	X	X	X
	208–02	Best boy electric	?	X	X
	208–03	Generator operator		?	?
	208–04	Electrics		?	X
	208–05	Rigging crew		?	?
Grip	209–01	Key grip	?	X	X
	209–02	Best boy grip		X	X
	209–03	Dolly grip		?	X

Department	Item #	Item	Run/Gun	30-Man	Full
	209–04	Grips		?	X
	209–05	Rigging crew		?	?
Sound	210–01	Production mixer	X	X	X
	210–02	Boom operator	? (Part time)	X	X
	210–03	Playback operator (music)		Depends	Depends
	210–04	Sound utility		?	Maybe
Set operations	211–01	Set medic			X
	211–02	Craft service		X	X
	211–03	Craft services utility		?	X
Costume/ wardrobe	212–01	Costume designer	X	X	X
	212–02	Costume assistant	?	X	X
	212–03	Wardrobe supervisor		?	X
	212–04	First set costumer		?	X
	212–05	Costumer/shopper		?	X
	212–06	Costume/wardrobe PAs		? (Free?)	X
Hair/makeup	213–01	Key makeup artist	X	X	X
	213–02	Key hair artist	Key MU may double	X	X
	213–03	Assistant H/MU artists		?	?
	213–05	S/FX makeup	Depends	Depends	Depends
Locations	214–01	Location manager		X	X
	214–02	Assistant location manager		?	X
	214–03	Location PAs		?	X
	214–04	Location scout		?	X
	214–06	Security	Depends	Depends	Depends
Transportation	215–01	Transportation captain			X
	215–02	Truck drivers	Set PAs double as drivers	Set PAs double as drivers	X
	215–03	Non-truck drivers			X
Production publicity	217–01	Still photographer		X (Part time)	X
	217–02	EPK camera operator		?	X
	217–03	EPK sound mixer		?	X
	217–04	EPK editor		?	X
Editing	501–01	Editor	X	X	X

(Continued)

TABLE 10.8 (Continued)

Department	Item #	Item	Run/Gun	30-Man	Full
	501–02	Assistant editor	? (Free)	X	X
	501–03	Apprentice editor		? (Free)	X
	501–04	Postproduction supervisor		?	X
Post Sound	503–01	Sound designer	X	X	X
	503–02	Additional sound editors	? (Part of package)	? (Part of package)	X
	503–03	Foley artists	? (Part of package)	? (Part of package)	X
	503–04	Additional services		Depends	Depends
CGI/opticals	504–01	CGI/opticals design (all in)	Depends Single VFX artist	Depends Single VFX artist	Depends (Post house?)
Music	505–01	Composer	X	X	X
	505–02	Music producer		?	X
	505–03	Music clearance supervisor		?	X
	505–04	Music editor			?
	505–05	Musicians			Depends
Titles	506–01	Opening/end credits	Above VFX artist	Above VFX artist	Title house?

Legend: X = definite hire. ? = possible hire.

Your target budget is a factor here. Generally, on $200K-or-under films, you may not be able to afford much more than a run-and-gun crew. On films in the $500K–$1M range, you'll have to decide between the 30-man and the full-size crew, but you're likely going to have to pay that crew a lower average wage, and possibly settle for somewhat less experienced people.

You can increase your crew size by lowering the pay scale either across the board or in certain departments. On *Rock the Paint*, the gaffer and key grip brought their seconds and thirds aboard for discounted rates, mostly because they had a relationship with them. On *Found In Time*, the gaffer was willing to work for less than his usual rate because we rented his gear, and he liked working with us.

In order to move forward, I recommend you start with a larger crew, then trim away positions in the second and third drafts of the budget.

A Further Note on Deferments

Deferments can come in one of four forms, and they impact the budget in different ways. Usually, everyone's deferment is the same, with no one person getting their money before anyone else.

- An **at-funding** deferment means that you'll pay salaries (or some part of them) as soon as you're fully funded. This is pretty rare – essentially you're just issuing an IOU and so you'll still need to include salaries in the budget.

- A **first-position** deferment means that you'll pay salaries from the first monies that come in from licensing the film. In this scenario, the deferred crew are basically treated the same as investors and bank lenders.
- A **second-position** deferment means that you'll pay salaries out once the investors receive their original money back plus some percentage. This puts the investors ahead of the crew but only slightly.
- A **third-position** deferment means that you'll pay salaries out once profits are declared, usually from the producer's share of said profits. For a crewperson, this is the worst place to be, since there are so many people in front of you.

The difference between second and third position is a little subtle, so an example may help.

You make your film for $200K and you have $50K in total deferments. You win the distribution lottery and receive $300K from all the distribution fees. In a second-position situation, the investors get their $200K plus, say, 25 percent back (= $50K). This leaves you with $50K, which would go to the crew.

In the third-position situation, the investors get their $200K plus 25 percent. The remaining $50K is now "profit." This is typically divided between the producer and investor 50/50. This gives you $25K to pay back the deferments with – which means the crew will never get back all their money.

You can arrange for a "modified" deferment where the crew's deferment is considered equal to the investor's money. So the crew's deferment is converted into points, essentially. In practice this is pretty rare – you want to hold onto your points because your cast and possibly some of your crew (editor, DP) may get a few.

Overtime-Eligible vs. Non-Eligible Crew

Traditionally, certain departments and positions get overtime, while others don't. This also applies to meal penalties. The breakdown is typically as shown in Table 10.9. Note that I'm discussing overtime rates for *non-union* crew. The DGA, IATSE, and teamsters have their own rules for overtime, which we'll touch on in Chapter 13.

TABLE 10.9 Overtime eligibility by department

Department	Overtime?
Production	No, except for script supervisor
Production design	No, except for scenics
Props	Yes
Set dressing	Yes
Set construction	Yes
Camera	Yes, except (sometimes) the DP
Electric	Yes
Grip	Yes
Sound	Yes
Set ops	No
Hair/makeup	Yes
Costume design	Yes, except for costume designer
Locations	No, except for parking PAs/security
Transportation	No
Production publicity	No
All post positions	No

The reasons for the discrepancy in overtime eligibility are many. It can be argued that the less "glorious" craftspeople – grips, electrics, props, sound, etc. – should be compensated monetarily for their work. Production designers and costume designers have traditionally been considered "on call" staffers – they don't have to stick to a set number of hours per day or week. Production staff have always had a bad deal in terms of overtime. These rules were inherited from the union world.

You don't have to follow this arrangement – you can give everyone overtime, or put everyone on a flat daily rate. Production assistants who worked past 16 hours, for example, sometimes get a "double-day" (instead of overtime, they get twice their daily rate, which is typically less than you'd have to spend in overtime anyway).

My opinion. On shoots budgeted up to $200K, I usually give all the departments overtime except for production staff. I will sometimes instead pay a premium to the UPM and 1st AD. For example, if the standard key rate is $150/day, I'll pay $200/day to the UPM and 1st AD. Since the costume designer and production designer are typically working more than one job, I'll give them overtime too.

On shoots budgeted from $500K upward, I start to follow the overtime model above. I budget one to two PA double-days (that could also be used for extra prep or wrap days if needed).

Crew and Gear

A DP bringing his own camera or a sound mixer lugging her own recorder should get *something* for that gear. I usually like to keep gear and personnel on separate line items, just in case we hire someone without gear and have to rent it separately.

Crew and Payroll

Do you pay the crew as subcontractors, give them cash under the table, or run everything through a payroll company (as you will the cast salaries)? If your budget is $500K or over, your crew is larger than run-and-gun-sized, and/or if you're hiring a union crew, you need to put them on the payroll. The IRS doesn't consider crewpeople contractors (since you're telling them where to go, and when). If you're shooting a *very* low-budget film and/or are working with a run-and-gun crew, you can usually get away with treating the crew as contractors.

If you do decide to treat your crew as employees, you'll have to add the 19–22 percent employer fringes mentioned above, plus applicable union fringes (see Chapter 13 for more on union fringes).

Overtime, Meals, Working Conditions

If you're not signing an IATSE union contract (which you probably won't be doing unless you're shooting a film in the $2M–$4M range), you have some freedom in how you deal with crew overtime, meal penalties, travel time, turnaround, and per diems. However, I've usually followed some version of the standard union contracts. This is good for everyone. It's good for the crew because they know that they won't have to work endless days without overtime or meal breaks. It's good for me because I don't have to spend time on set trying to figure these things out, or in a worst-case scenario, trying to replace someone who quits because they felt too exploited.

What follows are some guidelines for dealing with these issues on *non-union* shoots.

Overtime. When doing the budget, I usually add a "cushion" of one hour of overtime per *shoot* day for each eligible crew member. I don't budget overtime for prep, scout, wrap, and travel days.

Prep, wrap days. It's best if you can offer the crew at least something here. When I'm hired on as a line producer, I usually have to work at least one day of prep for every shoot day. Then I have to work for at least a week after the shoot to tidy up all the paperwork, pay all the vendors, return the gear, and get the post started.

On low-budget films, I don't expect to get paid for all of this time (though it's nice when it happens), but I do generally ask for something so I don't have to take on other work during prep just to pay the rent.

If you're shooting a $50K–$500K film, you probably can't afford to pay for all of the prep you'd like to get. When you approach the crew about this, you can usually find some flat rate that everyone can agree on, in exchange for a little time flexibility at the beginning.

Table 10.10 shows a quick summary of the number of prep and wrap days that you should budget for, by department. This is only a rough guide – every budget is different.

Travel days. On very low-budget shoots ($200K or under), I'll try to budget and negotiate a half-day for travel rather than a full day for each eligible crew person. On $500K-and-up films, the crew may ask for a full day's pay for travel.

Meal penalties. I usually stipulate 15- or 20-minute increments for each penalty. The penalty rate is smaller than that of SAG's standard:

- For the first hour, $7–$10 per penalty
- For the second hour, $8–$12 per penalty
- For the third hour, $9–$13 per penalty

Unlike overtime, meal penalties are somewhat less predictable. If the director, 1st AD, or DP are very green, or if we're shooting in very horrible weather, I'll put down a fixed number of meal penalties for the entire shoot, for each eligible crewmember.

TABLE 10.10 Prep/wrap days for each department

Department/Position	Prep Days	Wrap Days
Line producer/UPM	1–2 days per shoot day	1–2 weeks
1st AD	3–4 weeks	
2nd AD	2–3 weeks	
Script supervisor	3–4 days	1 day
PAs	1–2 days (equipment checkout)	1–2 days (return)
Production designers, costume designer	1–2 days per shoot day	1 week
Set construction	A LOT – depends on the size of set	A LOT
Props & set dressing	1 day per shoot day	3 days–1 week
DP	3–4 weeks, ideally	
1st AC/camera op.	1–2 days (equipment checkout and testing)	1 day (return)
Gaffer, key grip	1 week + scout days	1 day (returns)
Best boys (grip & electric)	1–2 days (scout plus pickup)	1 day (returns)
Sound	1 day (scout)	
Set ops	Craft services will need 2 shopping days plus days in between each week for replenishing	1 day
Hair/makeup	1 day? (If tests are needed)	
Special effects makeup	Depends on size/shape/complexity of prosthetics	
Locations	3–4 weeks or more (depends on number of locations)	1–2 weeks (depends on locations)

How the Crew Impacts the Rest of the Budget

Your crew size affects many other aspects of the budget, including:

Transportation. As your crew size grows, you'll need to budget more money for gas, passenger van rentals, tolls, and subways/buses/taxis. If anyone's working without pay, I generally try to budget subway cards or cash to cover their transportation to/from set. If your shoot calls for a number of company moves and/or different locations, you'll need to make sure you have enough "seats" available to transport everyone who can't walk, bike, or bus to set.

Meals and craft services. Once I've figured out my total headcount, I then budget a certain amount per head for breakfast and lunch for each shoot day, and lunch for each prep, wrap, scout, and travel day.

I've tried several formulae over the years to calculate the craft services snacks budget, but have yet to find something that's perfect. So I guesstimate a daily "rate" based on the total size of the crew. If you have a run-and-gun crew, you should budget between $50 and $100 per day for snacks. A 30-man crew could consume as much as $150–$200/day. A "full-size" crew can go through $300 or more of food per day.

Production department infrastructure. It's pretty common, especially on the 30-man crews, to end up with a lopsided structure where you've got two-to-five people in each department – but the line producer is still trying to do everything on his/her own, without an adequate office staff. If you end up with a 30-man crew, you really need at least a production manager, a part-time accountant, and an office intern. As your crew size grows, so should your production department.

Balance. If you have fully staffed grip, electric, and camera departments, but you only have one hair/makeup artist and a large cast, one part of your crew is always going to be waiting on another, which is bad. This is how 30-man crews eventually "creep" into full-size ones (and another reason I don't like the 30-man structures).

Locations. The larger the crew, the larger the "footprint." We'll talk about the footprint in more detail in Chapter 17. Just keep in mind that in addition to finding a set to shoot on, you'll also need to find rooms/spaces for wardrobe, hair/makeup, holding, catering, craft services, equipment/set staging, and storage. If this can't be accommodated at your locations (if you're shooting in the middle of the wilderness, for example), you may have to rent trailers, tents, and/or mobile homes.

Budgeting the Crew from the Script and Your Strengths

You should fit the crew to the story, schedule, and your own strengths and weaknesses, rather than the other way around. If your script is a period piece, you'll need to beef up your production and costume design departments. Even if many of the positions in these departments are unpaid, it's not a good idea to simply let them go unfilled.

If your script takes place largely indoors, you may need to beef up your grip and electric departments.

If you or your producing partner can take over a position, or if one of the people you've hired (or want to hire) can double up without it seriously affecting the performance of their primary job, you may be able to shrink the crew somewhat by combining positions.

On *LL* and *Helena from the Wedding*, I doubled as UPM and 1st AD. While this meant some longer days for me, it also got rid of an unnecessary layer of management. *Helena* took place largely in one location, with a small cast. *LL* was more ambitious, but the director and the DP were used to working in a barebones way, so it didn't make sense to bring aboard a separate AD. I simply had to do more work during prep.

On *Found In Time*, Ben Wolf (the DP) and I decided early on that we could function on a time-table effectively without a 1st AD. Even so, I had to delegate a lot of things to the PAs.

The lead actor/writer/director of *Disoriented*, Francisco Aliwalas, couldn't afford a makeup artist for the entire shoot, but did hire one to work with the cast for a day to create "looks" and give them each a set of foundations and blush. Many of the cast were used to working in off-off-Broadway theater, so doing their own makeup was nothing new.

Some directors I know love doing most of their own production design, and a few prefer to shoot and just hire a strong gaffer.

On *Helena from the Wedding*, we debated about having a script supervisor, but ultimately decided that we couldn't swing it. Instead everyone picked up the slack – the production designer and costume designer took extra photographs, I took some set photos, and the producers, DP, and sound mixer really read over each day's sides to make sure we were getting coverage.

On the other hand, we had one day on *LL* where the entire cast (which featured three women in the lead) plus over 25 extras showed up. We hired a day-player makeup artist to assist our key makeup/hair artist; if we hadn't, we wouldn't have made our day.

On *Rock the Paint*, we had a large cast, and needed two full-time hair/makeup artists. On *Racing Daylight*, we had a larger-than-the-budget-would-indicate production design team, because it was a period piece.

Sometimes I get the formula wrong. *LL* was a big challenge for the production designer, who was a one-person art department. She had to be in two places at once a lot of the time. I should have budgeted for an assistant. On *Company K* – a World War I film – we really needed at least a swing grip/electric to augment our small G&E departments.

What are your strengths? Are you (as producer or director or both) capable of doing certain jobs? Do you think you'll need more crew people on board for certain parts of the shoot? Are your keys more self-sufficient, or do they need strong bests?

THE LENGTH OF THE SHOOT

Now it's time to dig out the schedule you created in the previous chapter, and tally up the number of production days, and by extension the number of prep and wrap days.

Most of the departments need at least some prep and wrap days. This includes days for scouting, equipment checkout, returns, and discussing things at length with the director. You may have to modify some of those prep and wrap days to make your budget work (for example, taking the DP's number of paid prep days down from 20 to 18). Just don't strip all the days (even if unpaid) from the budget – you'll need to account for the ancillary costs of feeding and transporting people during prep and wrap.

This is where the budgeting and scheduling process start working in a nonlinear way. Perhaps your first schedule calls for a twenty-day shoot. But after tallying up your crew needs you realize you can't afford to pay your entire crew for twenty days and stick to your target budget. So you start to compress the schedule a little bit, and redistribute some smaller scenes. If you cut two days out of the budget, you may end up having to pay more in overtime. So you go back to the budget and strip out a couple of crew positions, to see if you can add at least one of your days back in.

This process can last for a while. It takes some patience and you may have to create several different schedules and budgets. This can actually be helpful for playing "what if" scenarios (what if we added one more day to the schedule?).

POST LENGTH AND WORKFLOW

Just as you determined your crew staffing according to the script and your strengths, so you need to also figure out the length of your post. Unlike production, where everyone is working at once, post is a more linear process. You can't start your sound post or finalizing your visual effects until you've locked your picture. In turn, in order to finish cutting your picture, you'll need to figure out the "ideal" length of your picture edit, and how long your synching/logging/prep period lasts.

If you're budgeting a $500K-and-up film, you should try to bring aboard the assistant editor and editor as soon as you start shooting, so they can start logging and synching while you're still shooting. This can help you get into post a little faster, but obviously you'll have to pay for this time (at least for the editor).

Sound post is harder to estimate, but to some extent it depends on your expectations and your production audio. If you want a layered, rich, complex soundtrack and your production sound is a bit messy, then you can expect it to take longer and cost more.

You also need to schedule some time between each phase of post. When you're done shooting, you need to schedule time to sync, transcode, and log your footage. When you've locked your picture, you need to prepare and deliver video and audio files to the sound designer. When you're ready to do your color correction and conform, visual effects, and titles, you'll usually have to spend some time exporting or preparing your final video files.

Each of these interstitial "steps" adds up and should be included in your post supervisor's or assistant editor's time. If your picture editor is shouldering a lot of these tasks, you should add this to their time.

You also need to figure out your basic post workflow. To do this, you need to answer the following questions:

1. What format are you shooting on?
2. What system do you want to edit on? (Final Cut Pro, Premiere, Avid, Vegas?)
3. What is the projection format you're aiming to end up on? (DCP, 35mm, HDCAM, DVD, Quicktime?)

The answers can change over the course of the production and post period, but for the purposes of putting a budget together, it's best to answer as firmly as possible. Once you do, you'll need to research the best post workflow for your film. This will influence your sound post length as well.

I usually budget no less than six-to-seven months for postproduction, broken down as follows:

- 2 weeks of transcoding/synching/logging
- 12 weeks of picture editing
- 2 weeks of sound prep
- 8 weeks of sound editing
- 1 week of mixing
- 1 week of color correction
- 1 week of prep for final output, sound checking, and final output to tape/disk

To stick to your budget, you may have to add more time to the schedule and do some of the tasks yourself. On *Found In Time*, I couldn't afford a paid assistant editor, so I transcoded and synched the footage after the end of the shoot. It took roughly one month. On the other hand, I couldn't do the special effects, so I hired someone to do them (and saved myself a good deal of agony).

DECIDE ON A SHOOTING FORMAT AND CAMERA

Your shooting format choice can influence the size of your crew, lighting package, and transportation. It can also influence how easy or difficult it is to get certain shots. The current crop of cameras and shooting formats boil down to five broad categories:

1. **Camcorders.** The Sony EX1, Panasonic P2, and older generation HDV cameras fall into this category. They're relatively lightweight and are a little more filmmaker-friendly out of the box. On the other hand, they do represent older technology, which can cost you more (with a tape-based camera, you'll need to transfer the footage to files). If you shoot to HDV, XDCAM EX, or another long-GOP (group of pictures) format, you'll need to transcode the material into something that's more edit-friendly (ProRes or DNxHD). These cameras generally perform well in low light.
2. **DSLRs.** These shoot full HD to some variant of H.264. They're small and light, take up very little space, and you can kit them out with various lenses and accessories. You don't need a lot of room in your equipment vehicle for the camera. You do need to transcode the footage to an edit-friendly format.

3. **Mid-level HD cameras.** The Canon C300, BlackMagic Designs, Sony F3, and Panasonic AF100 fall into this category. They're larger than the DSLRs but offer some advantages – like less compression, more cinema-friendly controls, the ability to capture your images at a higher bitrate/sampling rate, etc.
4. **Full-size 2K+ cameras.** The Red, Epic, Arri Alexa, and Sony F65 cameras. These cameras capture more data, with less compression, and feature more varied image controls, than their smaller brethren. You can also record the images to a variety of formats. This comes at the expense of size and complexity.
5. **Film cameras.** Super 16mm and 35mm cameras used to be very different beasts, but thanks to miniaturization, the latest crop of 16mm and 35mm cameras looks almost identical. Film of course is very expensive – you pay for negative and developing by the foot, and you have to digitize the footage to Quicktime in order to edit it.

The cameras in categories #3–5 take up progressively more space and require a larger camera crew. This of course affects your budget as well – shooting on film will require you to rent a separate truck for your gear. If you're shooting on a Canon 5D, you can fit the camera into the back of the equipment van.

As you go up in the camera/format category, you also need to consider the downstream budget effects. The less compressed formats take up more hard-drive space. While you can comfortably fit 10–12 hours of HD H.264 footage on one 500GB drive with room to spare, you'll need to budget up to 15GB of drive space *per minute* if you're shooting to the ArriRAW format.

Unless there's a format standardization among camera vendors (unlikely at best), you'll have to keep up with the constant stream of new cameras and formats. However, all of the options deliver good bang for the buck, and what you shot on is mattering less and less as long as you can project it on whatever format the distributor wants. If your film's target budget is $200K or less, consider one of the cameras/formats from categories #1–3. If your film's target budget is $1M or more, consider something from category #4. If your film is budgeted at $4M, film may make sense.

RUNNING TIME

Ideally your running time is reflected in your script – one page is supposed to equal one minute. But dialog-driven scripts tend to run longer. The length of action scenes depends a lot on the director's execution and intentions. Likewise films such as *Titus* and *Tree of Life* are very hard to estimate based on the screenplay.

If your running time is less than 80 minutes or longer than 2 hours, you're going to have some difficulties licensing the film down the road. If your script is on the long side, you may be saddling yourself with something that you can't shoot within your budget. In this case you may have to assume that you'll do a rewrite and trim a few pages out.

PUTTING IT ALL TOGETHER

Throughout most of this chapter we've discussed the assumptions that go into a budget. Once you've decided on some of these, plugging in the numbers becomes relatively easy. For example, I have a script that's 88 pages long but has a couple of phone calls (so it's really 92 pages' worth of strips).

Target budget. I think I can raise about $200K.

Cast salary. I don't think I can afford a "name," but I want to sign up with SAG. I go for the ultra-low-budget agreement. There are three leads, three supporting actors, and two day-players.

Crew structure. I can probably only afford a "run-and-gun" structure. There's nothing remarkable about the script in terms of props, costumes, etc. but I do have two female leads and they're in a lot of scenes together, so I may need to hire two people for hair/makeup. Also, I have two scenes that take place in a haunted house, so I'll need to beef up the art department on those days. I figure I can pay the keys $200/day, the bests $175, and the thirds $150. I can't afford for all the PAs to be paid, so I budget for one key PA who'll make $100/day, and the others will have to be interns.

Shoot length. The first draft of the schedule came in at 16 days, but I can probably squeeze that down to 15 without making the days longer. I redo the schedule based on 15 days.

Post length/workflow. If we shoot on the Canon 5D, I can transcode the footage to DNxHD for editing on the Avid. I can probably afford a ten-week picture edit, and then a six-to-eight week sound post. My goal is to output to DCP packages.

Shooting format. If I shoot on the Canon 5D I might be able to get by with just one equipment truck. This means more money for other things. On the other hand, if I upgrade to the Canon C300, I can take advantage of the higher ASA rating and better image stabilization. After running through the numbers, I decide on the C300. This means I have to add a 1st AC to the camera department, but I think I can make up for it by subtracting one person from the grip department (so there will only be one gaffer, one best boy electric who'll now have to swing, and one key grip).

Running time. Even after juggling the numbers, it looks like I'm still going to go over $200K. If I can trim four pages from the script and consolidate my locations I can safely shrink the shoot down to 14 days without risk of too much overtime. If that doesn't work, I'll go back to the script again and see what else I can cut.

WHAT TO DO NEXT: RESEARCH AND MATH

Now that you've made your initial decisions, you can build the framework. From this point, it's about doing research. If you want to know what the going labor rates are for non-union crew, call local producers and production companies. People are fairly generous when dealing with someone who has a genuine interest in learning and has done some homework ahead of time. Use the budget assumptions above as talking points. Talk to your war council – either they can help you directly or refer you to people who can.

A lot of information can be found online. You can check out the latest SAG rates online (by the time you read this, it'll be SAG/AFTRA). See Appendix C for more details.

Once you've amassed enough answers, start filling in the details for each line item, and work your way down from the top. Chances are the first draft of your budget will be higher than you expected. That's normal. It's always better to start with more and then peel expenses away. We'll talk about this in more detail in the next chapter.

You'll probably have to go through at least two drafts of the budget.

QUESTIONS

Try to answer the following questions about your film.

1. What is the target budget?
2. Will you go SAG or non-SAG?
3. What size crew do you envision leading?
4. Is there a department that might need some reinforcements? (For example, do you need to find a dedicated location manager because your script takes place in over 20 locations?)
5. How long would you like the shoot to be?
6. What is your end goal? What media do you want to deliver your film on?
7. What format would you want to shoot the film on?
8. Based on the script and your sense of timing, what is the running time?

## Chapter 11

Thinking Strategically

FIGURE 11.1 Look at the big picture for a second.

So at this point in your prep work, you have a pile of documents on your hard drive, (hopefully) including the script, a breakdown, a schedule, a budget, the business plan. In fact, you probably have more than a few drafts of these docs.

Now it's time to think strategically about how you're going to actually make the film. This parallels the director's prep outlined in Chapter 7. You'll also be gathering resources, but with a slightly different purpose. Your goals are to:

1. **Discover connections.** Who do you know who can help you?
2. **Trim the budget.** Do you know people that can get you goods/resources for free? Or, can you figure out what you can live without to shrink the budget down?
3. **Come up with a game plan.** Set a shoot date, and start working towards it. Everything and everyone will respond with more urgency when there's a start date.
4. **Start getting the team together.** With your connections, can you get to some talented, affordable crew and cast?

DISCOVER CONNECTIONS

If social media has taught us anything, it's that we're more connected than we ever believed possible (and, in some cases, ever wanted to be). What you need to do is to figure out, roughly, who among your circle of friends, acquaintances, bosses, roommates, teachers, boy/girlfriends, vendors, and other contacts you can go to for help of some kind. This doesn't mean that these people will necessarily come through. But you have to start somewhere.

Open up a spreadsheet or grab a notebook. List all the connections you think might be able to help you, including how you know them, and important info (birthdays, job changes, anniversaries, upcoming gigs). Keep this list organized and refreshed.

Start with your closest friends and family, and work outward. Include people you know through other people, and maybe even folks who are two degrees away. Don't restrict yourself to film people. Most of the interior locations on *Found In Time* came to me through non-film friends and friends-of-friends. You don't necessarily want to include your entire e-mail list in here either, though.

Once you've got your list, you should start prioritizing. The things you need right now are:

- Advice
- Financing
- Distribution
- Casting
- Locations
- Crew
- Equipment
- Other resources

Your priorities may be different, so reorder the list as you see fit. But advice should always stay on top. No matter how well off you are in terms of financing, crew, locations, etc. you'll always need someone to go to for some problem or another.

Once you've shuffled your list according to your priorities, make sure you have up-to-date contact information. Then start sending out emails and making calls. I recommend calling your closer contacts (unless they never answer calls) because it's more personal. On the flip side, I recommend emailing your "weaker" connections.

You don't necessarily want to get in touch with everyone right away. But you can send out a quick set of individualized emails asking them how they are, and mentioning you're making a film. If you have a specific request that's not urgent, put it in the first paragraph. Busy people appreciate direct requests more than indirect ones. If you're not personally acquainted with the person, make sure to mention who your mutual contact is.

Keep track of who gets back to you and who doesn't. Don't give up after one attempt. You never know when someone will turn out to be in a position to help you. Practice "good dharma" – be willing to help other people when they need it. I can't emphasize this enough – the independent film world runs on favors and cooperation. It will be your turn to help someone else out soon.

The first thing you're going to need your connections for is to tackle that horrible beast, the budget.

TRIMMING THAT BUDGET

The first drafts of the budget are likely to be horrifying. You trimmed out the fat, kept your crew size down, compressed the schedule until it hurts, and you're still 30 percent over budget. Or 300 percent. At this point, you have five steps to take:

1. **Give it another go.** You may have missed a few critical areas where you can save money.
2. **Consider your favors.** Who do you know who's got a house/camera/car available, who owes you one?
3. **Hire an expert.** If steps #1 and #2 don't work, find a line producer who can take what you've done and give you some feedback.

4. **Raise your target budget.** If you're still above your target budget, you may have to set your sights higher. The painful reality is that some scripts aren't cheap.
5. **Or, simplify the script.** There's usually a way to make the story cheaper to shoot, but it may require a real rewrite.

Revisiting the Budget

There are a number of "low-hanging fruit" items that I reach for first when trying to trim the budget (and a few that I keep on the tree no matter what):

Smaller salaries up top. The producers and director should be among the first to feel the pinch. This is a bit painful, but fair – you're going to be getting the most glory from the project, so you should drop your salary altogether or just put in some kind of subsistence (pay your rent) wage.

Add a second camera. If you add a second camera and operator, can you compress the number of shoot days to the point where you'll net a saving? Sometimes this is more trouble than it's worth (shooting with two cameras can complicate/compromise your lighting).

Day-playing. Perhaps you can shrink and add crew and equipment as you move from one location type (day exteriors) to another (night interiors). You can shrink your basic grip/electric package, transportation, and other logistical elements on the "light" days and beef them up on the "heavy" ones.

Putting your most stable location last. If your script is set primarily in a couple of locations – where you can stay for a significant chunk of time – try putting these locales at the end of the schedule. Once you're there you may be able to jettison any equipment you don't need, along with some of your equipment transportation (assuming you can keep things in the location overnight).

Ditch the dolly. Can you live without a dolly? Your shots will have a different feel to them but you'll be able to lose the dolly grip and a lot of space from your equipment truck.

Production staff. Can the production manager or line producer live without as much assistance? This is a hard question to answer, because it depends on how "big" the film is (how many cast members; the payroll size; how many locations; etc.). But you can usually trim the accountants out altogether or make them part-timers. I've often worked on films as a UPM or line producer where I just had a couple of interns under me.

The script supervisor. Some people would consider this an essential position, while others would not. I've worked on, and directed, films that had and didn't have them, and you *do* have to be more careful about continuity and coverage. But it *is* possible to work without a script supervisor.

Grips and electrics. When I first started working, film was the normal acquisition media, and you needed a *lot* of folks in these departments. While that can still be true, these days both the gear and the number of people needed to use it has shrunk dramatically. These days I start my budgets with three people in each department (commonly called a "3 and 3" setup), and maybe some additional monies for big days where I'll need to hire extra hands. But on *Helena from the Wedding*, we ended up having only a key grip and a gaffer. On *Exposed*, we had a "2 and 2" setup. On *Found In Time*, we had a gaffer, and the PAs helped out. This will limit the kinds of lighting setups you can do in a short period of time, especially if the DP is a "hands-off" guy who doesn't usually wade in there and start handling lights. But it's becoming increasingly common.

The DIT (digital image tech) or loader. If you are shooting on one of the larger cameras (the Alexa, Red, or a film camera), you really need someone in these positions. However, if you're working on one of the smaller cameras and exercise a little patience, you can get by without these positions. On *Helena from the Wedding*, the DP and one of the producers worked out a system for handing off the memory stick cards that the EX-1 used. The producer copied the card to an external drive, backed it up a second time, reformatted the card, and handed it back to the DP.

Assistant costume designer. Can your costume designer work by his/herself? If you have a small number of script days (say, less than 5) and/or a small number of cast members (less than 15), the answer is probably *yes*. Can you stagger the schedule so that you have as few scenes as possible with the entire cast?

Combining the hair stylist and key makeup positions. This is possible, but be warned – if you have more than one woman in a scene, it's going to take a while for the cast to get ready.

Minimize/skip the walkie-talkies. I have a love/hate relationship with walkies. They're very useful at times, but I can't help thinking that there must be better uses to put that walkie money towards. You can limit the number of walkies to the bare minimum, or try to shoot without them altogether. If you're shooting in a large outdoor space, it will help to have them. If you're primarily indoors, you may be five feet away from the people you'd be talking to, in which case you'll feel doubly dumb for wasting money.

Using interns instead of PAs. I really hate doing this. PAs are often the hardest-working people on the set. And trimming their pay seems absurd – how much can it really save? But sometimes you just have to do it.

Paying the crew as subcontractors. If you're working with a non-union crew, it's worth considering. It will save you payroll fringes (which are significant), but you'll be at risk of getting seriously fined if any of the crew decides to claim unemployment. I worked on a film where this resulted in the state tax department finding out about what we had done, and making the production company cough up the estimated fringes plus a fine.

Smaller cameras/fewer accessories. For *Found In Time*, we decided on a very stripped-down approach. We shot on the Canon 5D, had no external monitor, mattebox, or handheld rig, and only four lenses (the DP had one zoom, and we rented a telephoto and two primes). On other shoots I've worked on, we've tricked out the camera with everything, resulting in a rig weighing in at 50 pounds. There are good reasons to get all the gear, and to shoot with a more expensive camera. But sometimes it's worth it to go smaller.

You can even use this to your advantage. On *Found In Time* we were able to stick the camera right up against the wall in a really narrow hallway, and get a shot we wouldn't have been able to grab otherwise.

Smaller art departments. This is tricky. But if you don't have a particularly production-design-intensive shoot, you can have your propmaster double as your set decorator. You may have to boil the entire art staff down to two people who are jacks-of-all-trades.

Break up the shoot. The basic idea is to carve out two or more separate shoot periods (like shooting weekends). This is usually a miserable idea. It's hard enough to keep a crew and cast for a few weeks, never mind having to get them back together repeatedly. But it does have some advantages. It gives you time to think between each shoot. You can tailor the crew and equipment needed for each section. If you have a very modular script (discrete characters, time periods, and/or locations) it can work out quite well, both dramatically and logistically. *Blue Valentine* did this – the PA and NYC sections of the film were shot at different times. It can give you the chance to shoot some material and then raise money for the rest.

On the other hand, you'll have to spend more money on insurance and other overhead costs. The savings on equipment and crew may not amount to very much. SAG will hold onto your bond longer. Your post will drag on for longer. And you run the risk of losing key crew or cast members.

DIY EPK. If you decide to trim out your still photographer and/or EPK shooter, you *must* find a way to get good stills. You might be able to pull frame grabs, but the best option is to knock off some shots by yourself.

Consider the college intern crew. We'll cover this in more detail in the next section, but the basic idea is that you partner up with a local film school, and you'll get most of your crew and possibly resources and locations for free (or at low cost). You'll be able to bring one or two "ringers" (like your DP). The students get a credit and high-level experience on a real feature film, you get low-cost labor. You will probably have to extend the length of the shoot – these folks won't necessarily be able to work as fast as more seasoned pros. On *Racing Daylight*, a good chunk of the crew came from the North Carolina School of the Arts. They were among the best folks I've ever worked with. On *Favorite Son* (which I didn't work on), the entire project was coproduced by Fairleigh Dickinson University as part of an ongoing production program. Apart from the DP, the entire crew was composed of advanced students and recent graduates. They shot the film over the course of five weeks, and it looks amazing.

Side effects. Whenever you trim crew positions, shoot on a smaller-format camera, or trim shooting days, you'll also save on craft services, per diems, gas, tolls, vehicle and equipment rentals, and other per-day/per-head expenses. So don't forget to bring these down as well!

On the other hand, there are expenses that you *really* shouldn't trim, if you can help it.

Sound. You can't fix bad sound in post, no matter what you've been told. If your boom operator can't find the actors, or the rig is substandard, or the mixer doesn't know how to handle a noisy location, no amount of sweetening will save you. You'll have to employ ADR (additional dialog recording) on the scene, which is just terrible (it's expensive and you'll rarely get the performance levels back). A good sound mixer and boom op is a worthwhile expense.

Food. It should go without saying, but I've been on plenty of shoots where the producer's idea of craft services was some cookies. Your crew and cast need clean water (filtered or bottled), lots of coffee, and a mix of nutritious *and* junky snacks.

Locations. Don't assume that you can get any location completely for free, unless you own them.

Transportation. It would be really wonderful if you could just shove your entire crew, cast, and gear into a single van with a seat taken out. But I've yet to work on that shoot. Don't try to budget too small an equipment van, or you'll just end up needing to rent a bigger one come production time.

Call in Some Favors

Let's say you've gone after the low-hanging fruit. Now it's time to budget some favors. This is always a bit tricky, and as a line producer I really don't like doing it. A lot of favors tend to evaporate. People get very excited to hear you're making a movie, offer you help, and then retract the offer when it's time to put up or shut up.

Reach into your brimming list of contacts, and figure out who can help you get the "friend" or "free" rate on locations, gear, personnel, props, transportation, etc. If the favor looks unlikely, don't put it in the budget. If it looks solid, then figure out a fair "value" for the favor.

I usually indicate favors in the budget by adding a detail line to the location/equipment/crew position in question. I then put in a negative number that indicates how much the favor is going to *take away* from the original expense. Table 11.1 shows an example.

This way, I still have some idea of what the item will cost if the favor disappears. I also have a "favor reminder" right in the budget, which helps when it comes time to remember all the people you need to thank in the credits.

"Free" is of course rarely free. You'll either have to pay it back, or you may incur additional costs you weren't counting on. For example, if your friend offers his house for you to shoot in *but* needs to be put up at a hotel while you're shooting, you'll get the location for free but you'll have to pay

TABLE 11.1 Budgeting a favor

Description	Amount	Unit Type	X	Rate	Total
Bar Six	3	Days	1	1,000	3,000
Bartender Friend Discount	1	Allow	1	(2,000)	(2,000)
		TOTAL			1,000

for his room and probably his food. Do you still come out ahead? Likewise, a free crew member with less experience may create drag in the shoot, so you'll have to decide if this will cost you in additional shoot time.

Hire an Expert

If you've done what you can on your own and you're still over budget, it may be time to bring in another opinion. If someone on your war council or on your connection list has producing experience, then show the budget to them. You may also need to hire a line producer, production manager (UPM), or producer. A line producer or production manager will have experience with the nitty-gritty, day-to-day grind of running a film shoot. I've done a lot of budgets for hire over the years.

When you make the initial calls (try to get at least two or three names from your contacts), ask for resumes and references. Be upfront about your dilemma – the gap between your budget and the numbers you have so far. What you're looking for is an opinion about your budget and breakdown. The ideal line producer is someone with experience at the indie level who can still work for your fee. If you're not asking for a "from scratch" breakdown and budget, some kind of consultation fee can usually be arranged.

I usually ask to read the script and anything else the producer has ready for me before walking into the interview. This is when doing that prep work on the script pays off, by the way. Nothing screams "amateur" to me more than finding a dozen typos or breaks from the proper format within the first few pages.

No matter how fast I work, the process of reading the script and tweaking the budget and schedule never seems to go as quickly as I hope. Either it takes a few drafts to push the budget into the target range, or we have to build a new one practically from scratch, or I have to fill in the details in the breakdown. The whole process can easily take up to a month. So don't wait until the last minute (like the day before you meet a prospective investor) to hire someone!

Line producers can be cautious creatures, and some of us are used to budgeting things "a certain way." So please push back – ask for explanations for why things cost what they do. Ask to see if there's another way. Sometimes it's a question of learning the risks. All of the budget cuts I suggested above carry risks – but if you understand the implications of them, then you can make an informed decision as to whether to cut or not.

Take Another Look at the Script

It could be that the script really can't be made for what you want it to be made for. A couple of years ago I was hired to budget a film that looked simple enough, about a guy who's a bit adrift in New York, who eventually ends up confronting his arch-nemesis from high school at their reunion.

But it was a long script (about 110 pages). There were a *lot* of locations, about 48 speaking roles (most very minor), and some very big scenes – including a 12-page restaurant conversation with five or six people. There were some stunts, a couple of large set-pieces with a lot of extras, and two long night exterior scenes. The producer was hoping the budget would come in at $200K.

There are limits to how fast you can shoot stunts, and restaurant scenes require either a lot of coverage or some nifty camera work (or multiple cameras). It was the director's first feature, so I didn't want to pile up 10-page day after 10-page day. Eventually I was able to get the budget down to $275K, which I'm sure was more than they wanted, but I honestly couldn't bump it down to $200K. And that was stripping the budget to the bone – one mistake and they'd be dipping into their contingency. This also left next-to-nothing for promotion and distribution.

Sometimes you have to work in the other direction, and rework the script. Your script may need a tighter focus – fewer characters and a more contained story. This is the biggest problem with a lot of the scripts I've been hired to budget, and it's certainly a problem in every early draft of my own material. I want to cram too much into the script, but this often produces a strange effect of making the story too diffuse and, of course, expensive.

You may have to go back and watch the films of some directors that inspired you, particularly their early work. Note *what's not there*. Often, a lot of things are implied or barely shown onscreen, that suggest a bigger world. *Metropolitan* never actually features one of the balls that are the central obsession of the story. The namesake event of *The Unbelievable Truth* unfolds in a monologue that the main character tells another — there's no flashback. *Narc* tells a lot of its story through short flashbacks. There are also very few characters. *The Puffy Chair* is basically a three-person road movie. *Beasts of the Southern Wild* only features a few "big scenes" with a lot of people, and the storm that happens at the end of the first act is barely onscreen. Even *Blood Simple* is a four-person movie, that somehow feels a lot bigger. *Down By Law*, apart from some scenic footage of New Orleans, is shot in a series of small rooms. We don't even see the jail outside of the cell the characters share.

Somehow these films don't seem small to us. The screenwriter, director, actors, producers, and crew were able to convey a lot indirectly — sometimes through off-screen sound design, other times through dialog, other times through the clever insertion of some scenic shots. And indirect methods are cheap!

PUT THE PLAN TOGETHER

Okay, so you've got a budget that's solid, a script that's tighter than a drum, and a list of connections. Now it's time to start setting some dates.

The big date to set is the start of production. Even if you don't have all the money in the bank yet, you won't get much traction until you can tell people when you want to shoot. So how far into the future do you set this date? There's no set answer, but here are a few guidelines:

If your script is *really* ready, four to six months. If you have the money, the script is pretty simple, and you've done most of the steps outlined in this book up to this point, four months is not crazy. If you don't, six months is possible, though you'd better have some help.

This seems like a long time, but the months will fly by. You have to find locations, crew up, cast the film, negotiate equipment deals, sign up with SAG, find catering and holding, and make a million other decisions. If you have a day job, this may not even be enough time.

Adjustments. If you're doing more than one job on set (if you're the producer *and* director, for example), add a month. If you have some of the locations, cast, and crew already, subtract a month. You don't have to stick to your date religiously — productions get pushed all the time. If it looks like you need more time, push.

In January I formed the LLC for *Found In Time* and set an August 2nd production start date. I felt that I realistically needed seven months to raise money, rewrite the script at least one more time, do my script analysis, and accomplish the other tasks that I'm writing about in this book. We ultimately shot in September.

Daylight. If your script is season-dependent (you need it to be snowing outside) and/or takes place largely outdoors, consider the season and light quality in your calculations. One of the concerns on *Found In Time* was daylight. We were shooting very close to the Vernal Equinox, which meant we were just about getting 11–12 hours of usable light per day. Since most of the script takes place outdoors, if we'd had to push to October we would have needed additional days to shoot everything. I also didn't want to be shooting in the cold.

Day of week/holidays. Obviously, you should consider how the holidays will affect your start date. Starting in December is usually not a great idea, unless Christmas somehow plays into your script (hey, we don't have to decorate the lawns!). Whatever your start date is, you want to make sure that your *day(s) off are during the week*, as mentioned in Chapter 9.

Once you set this date, you can figure out your other milestones (Table 11.2). These are touchstones that you can organize all your other work around. Things will slide around quite a bit, and every situation is different. But now you have a game plan.

TABLE 11.2 Key dates

Finish financing:	Yesterday
Casting:	Right away
Interview crew:	2–3 months before shoot
Hire key crew:	6 weeks before shoot
Hire remaining crew:	2 weeks before shoot
Sign with SAG:	6 weeks before shoot
Location scouting:	Right away (this will take a while)
Lock locations:	1–2 weeks before shoot
Pick the camera, format, and workflow:	2 weeks before shoot
Start editing:	2–3+ weeks after shoot
Rough cut:	6+ weeks
Scoring:	4+ months
Sound post:	4+ months
End of sound post:	6–7+ months
Color/conform:	Simultaneous with sound post
Titles and final VFX:	Before end of color

TRACKING OTHER FILMS

You also want to pay some attention to other films that are either in post, in production, or recently released that are somewhere in your budget range and/or genre. If they're shooting in your area, they may be employing crew that would be willing to work on your film. If one of these films has done well in the marketplace, you can add their figures to your business plan.

If it hasn't done well, don't spend too much time trying to figure out why. Unless the script is a disaster (you should probably see the film yourself to judge), the reasons for failure are so varied and complex, and apply in any case to a marketplace that will be very different by the time your film enters it, that analysis is probably futile.

On the other hand, if three or four films have come out in the same genre, and *all* of them have suffered or done poorly (either critically or financially), that could mean the beginning of a cooling trend. Genres heat up and then get oversaturated. There's no telling when this will happen and how long it will take for the genre to heat up again. But it's worth noting. Perhaps there's a way to distance yourself from those films (without rewriting the script)? Perhaps you can reorient your marketing materials a little differently?

This is something that you'll have to come back to periodically during preproduction and post. Especially as your film nears completion, you'll want to see how other films are doing, and adjust your strategy accordingly.

PUT THE TEAM TOGETHER

Now it's time to start sending out feelers for crew and cast. Particularly, you're looking for a casting director, DP, production designer, editor, and sound editor; and also for some prospective leads.

It's never too early to start collecting resumes, reels, and headshots. It also gets the word out that you're shooting a film. About 80 percent of your ultimate hires will come from about 20 percent of your connections. Figuring out which of your connections constitute that 20 percent will take up a fair amount of time.

As all this material comes in (and believe me, it will be a lot), you'll want to separate people into various categories: A (first choice), B (second choice), C (third choice), X (no way). How do you decide what pile to put someone into?

1. The work itself (if you're watching a reel).
2. Experience.
3. Name value.
4. Fit. You probably won't know this until you meet the person.

Don't throw anything away yet. I usually set up baskets for each "pile" on my desk or a shelf, and keep track of who's in what pile (and whose work I still need to look at).

THINKING STRATEGICALLY

If you find yourself too worried about minutiae, like which brand of chocolate to buy for craft services, it helps to go back to your game plan and figure out whether you're neglecting more important duties.

Once more people get involved in the project, things take on a life of their own. I worked on a film where we had a night exterior walk-and-talk scene. It was decided early on between the DP and director that it should be a Steadicam "one-r" – a single setup that would last the entire scene. This shot ended up requiring us to rent additional lights and cable, an extra generator, an extra truck, some tents and heaters (we were shooting in the winter), and hiring additional electricians, grips, and a Steadicam operator. To do the light rigging, we had to do precalls and still went into overtime. Between all these costs and the overtime incurred, we spent about $10,000–$15,000 on one shot. Many of the crew were up for 24 hours. The shot made it into the film but only in a cut-down form.

None of the people involved – the director, producers, line producer, or myself (as production manager) – stopped and asked whether this made sense. In truth, it didn't. As the costs mounted, we should have said "let's do this some other way." You will probably find yourself in a similar situation, where something that looked fine initially turns out to be massively more difficult or expensive than you thought. If you can stop at least once a week, step back and review your major activities and how they're affecting your overall game plan, you'll (hopefully) be able to spot these problems before they snowball out of control.

QUESTIONS/EXERCISES

1. Do you have a "go-to" list of contacts that you can tap? If not, start making one right away.
2. What kind of favors can you count on – free locations, cheap crew, good cast?
3. Call some producers in your area (and/or your attorney), and ask for line producer referrals. Even if you don't want to hire someone just yet, it's good to have some names in your back pocket.
4. Can you set a shoot date?
5. Are there any films like yours that are shooting right now? Or that have just come out?
6. Do you have a pile of reels and resumes you can start looking through right away?

## Chapter 12

Vendors, Equipment, and Negotiations

FIGURE 12.1 The crane day, from the set of *Favorite Son*. Ben Wolf, who shot *Found In Time*, is somewhere up there. (Photo: Jay Scrimizzi.)

Armed with your budget, schedule, game plan, and contact list, you're now ready to start the fun of dealing with vendors and equipment. Why now? Why not wait until you have your crew onboard?

You can't really "seal any deals" until you've discussed things with your crew. But you can gather information and put together a shortlist of people and companies to call. Also, vendors can be surprisingly helpful when it comes to answering technical questions and even referring crew your way. Of course, they're doing this so that you'll rent or buy from them, but a good vendor is more concerned about the long-term relationship than the current sales opportunity.

In this chapter, we'll talk a bit about the different types of vendors and equipment, cover some basic rules for negotiating with salespeople, and how to feed vendor input back into your budget.

OVERVIEW OF VENDORS AND EQUIPMENT

Vendors fall into four broad categories, and the tactics for dealing with each are slightly different.

1. **Gear** – camera, sound, lighting and grip, set operations, walkies, special props, wardrobe; usually items you rent.
2. **Services** – post house, labs (if you're shooting on film), insurance, other production companies (if they're providing some kind of turnkey or consulting service).
3. **Non–film-specific** – vehicles, catering, hardware supplies. While there are caterers that specialize in film shoots, you should also look into other options.
4. **Expendables** – gels, sash, tape, hardware supplies, craft services, garbage bags – anything you'll have to buy in bulk.

Table 12.1 shows a preliminary list of the vendors that you're going to have to find and seal deals with, and what you're going to them for. In some cases, one vendor may serve more than one purpose. In other cases, you might have to go to several vendors to fulfill your order.

TABLE 12.1 Vendors, by type and department, cross-referenced with what you'll be purchasing/renting from them

Type/Departments	Rent/Buy	Stuff	Vendor Possibilities
Gear			
Camera	Rent	Camera package Lenses Camera support Camera accessories (filters, etc.) Monitor Handheld rigs	Camera rental house Owner/operator
Sound	Rent	DDR Mixer Microphones Boom/pole Lockit box Slate	Sound gear rental Sound mixer (own gear) Boom operator (own gear)
Grip/electric	Rent	Lights Stands Cables Small generators Flags, nets Ladders Scaffolding Rigging Hardware Safety gear	G&E house Theatrical lighting house Gaffer or grip with truck
Grip/electric	Rent	Larger generator	G&E house Specialty generator rental co. Gaffer or grip with truck

(Continued)

TABLE 12.1 (Continued)

Type/Departments	Rent/Buy	Stuff	Vendor Possibilities
Camera/grip	Rent	Dolly and track Camera crane Camera jib	G&E house Camera rental house Gaffer or grip with truck Jib/crane rental
Grip/electric	Rent	Lift Cherry picker or other large rig	G&E house Construction company
Wardrobe	Rent	Wardrobe racks Privacy screens Wardrobe mirrors	Unit supply house Wardrobe rental co.
Wardrobe	Buy/rent	Special costumes	Wardrobe rental co. Uniform supply co. Seamstress/designer
Hair/makeup	Rent	Makeup chairs Makeup mirrors	Unit supply house
Hair/makeup	Buy	SFX prosthetics	Special effects house S/FX prosthetics expert
Special effects	Rent	Animals	Animal rental house
Special effects	Rent (sometimes buy)	Greenscreen material	G&E house Camera rental house S/FX rental house
Props	Rent	Guns, knives, blanks Stunt weapons	Weapon rental house Armorer S/FX house S/FX specialist
Art/set dressing	Buy	Wallpaper Paint Hanging fabrics Rugs Props Furniture	Fabric house Unit supply house Hardware store Prop house Theater company
Location	Rent	Stage Greenscreen	Soundstage Location owner
Set operations	Rent	Coolers Heaters Tents, tarps, weather protection Tables, chairs Coffee urns	Unit supply house
Set operations	Rent	Walkie-talkies	Sound rental house Walkie rental Unit supply house

Type/Departments	Rent/Buy	Stuff	Vendor Possibilities
Services			
Lodging	Rent	Rooms/housing for cast/crew	Hotels Motels Renters/subrenters
Camera	Rent	Steadicam Glidecam	Steadicam operator Camera rental house
Production	Rent	Payroll (for cast and/or crew)	Payroll company Accountant
Editorial	Rent/buy	Main edit computer Support computer Editorial support	Post house Editor Computer dealer
Sound post	Rent	Foley studio ADR studio Design suite Dub stage or mix suite	Post house Sound designer Sound post specialty house
Online	Rent	Acquisition Color/DI suite	Post house Colorist Online specialty house
Overhead	Rent	Production insurance Worker's comp	Insurance company Worker's comp. company Payroll company Film insurance specialists Other prod. company
Non-Specific			
Transportation	Rent	Crew and cast vans Equipment trucks	Vehicle rental
Transportation	Rent	Taxi/car service	Car service company
Set operations	Buy	Craft services Locations supplies (bags, floor protection)	Costco/Sam's Club Unit rental house
Set operations	Buy	On-set catering	Caterer Restaurant Film catering company Parents
Expendables/Purchases			
Production stock Editorial Color/conform	Buy	Hard drives (for acquisition) Hard drives (for post) Tapestock (for post) Filmstock (for acquisition & post)	Videotape stock house Mail-order supplier Film vendor/reseller
All	Buy	Gels Beadboard Clothespins Tape Sash Cleaning supplies	Unit supply house G&E house Sam's Club/supermarket

At first, this list will seem overwhelming. But you'll usually only have to deal with a dozen different vendors (on *Found In Time* I used 12 vendors). Often you'll be constrained by what's available where you're shooting – there may only be a few places to go.

A note about unit supply houses. These are places that have a little bit of everything – tents, gels, sash, wardrobe mirrors, coolers, reflector boards, lumber, etc. Sometimes these are called expendables suppliers, because a lot of their business is renting/selling expendables. Some New York examples would include Kits and Expendables, Expendables Plus, Wits End, and Raygun. You can sometimes find better deals by figuring out exactly what you need and hitting up discount stores, hardware stores, camping suppliers, party supply rental dealers, sporting goods dealers, etc. If you're shooting in a place that doesn't have one of these houses, that may be your only option. But you also need to measure the convenience factor and hidden costs. The gas, tolls, and time spent picking up all these items from different places and then returning them may outweigh the savings.

Prix-Fixe vs. *à-la-Carte*

You'll notice that certain vendor choices come up over and over again – unit supply houses, grip/electric houses, etc. Many companies offer a wide variety of gear for rent and/or purchase. As gear has become smaller and cheaper over the years, and the obsolescence rate has sped up, vendors have diversified their offerings, hoping to become one-stop shops for small-to-midsize shoots. A good example is a company called Abel Cinetech. They have offices in New York and Los Angeles. They focus primarily on camera rentals, but they have a big camera sales unit, and also offer sound and small lighting/grip packages for rent or purchase.

There's a lot of appeal to going to one place for all your stuff, especially if you don't need a lot of it. But typically you'll end up having to use multiple sources. It's rare that one vendor can supply *all* your needs for the shoot, or if they do you'll pay a premium for the convenience.

Many crew people are also in the rental business. A lot of DPs own their own cameras and lights. Most of the gaffers I work with have small-to-medium grip/electric packages (some have entire trucks outfitted with pretty much everything I'd need on a typical shoot). And almost every sound mixer I've worked with owns their own rig (recorder, mixer, mics, boom, cables, power, cart, etc.). My opinion is that it's better to rent from your crewpeople (assuming they keep their equipment in good shape). You'll often get a better deal, you can always rent additional equipment if you need to, and it will lower the learning curve.

Owning vs. Renting Equipment

With the price of gear getting lower every year, it's tempting to just go buy your own camera, get a basic lighting kit, maybe a few mics and a boom, and call it a day. But you have to consider a few things first:

Will you use the equipment? If you're a shooter, then having your own camera makes sense – you can make money off it. Or if you're producing a documentary where you don't always know when you'll need to be ready to get out and shoot stuff, then an interview rig is a great idea. If you think your shoot is going to go on for a while or you have other projects lined up, then great. But in most cases that I've seen, the equipment spends 90 percent of its lifespan gathering dust and depreciating in value.

Will you sell it? Some filmmakers sell their gear after making the film. Given how fast cameras become outmoded, you may not get very much for it. This may still be worth it to you.

Can you rent it? Some of my friends have tried this, with mixed results. To successfully rent your gear, you usually have to have a complete kit (see below), and you have to organize a rental business. This can be a distraction. Also, what happens when the equipment breaks in the field? Do you have a spare you can send the crew? Or do you have to rent a replacement from somewhere else?

Can you afford all the accessories? A camera body or light by itself is not terribly useful. The light needs a stand, an extension cord, and some spare bulbs. A camera needs lenses, a tripod, some kind of onboard monitor, memory cards, etc. If you have to rent or buy all these items, are you coming out ahead at all?

Can you replace it? If you rent a camera and it breaks down, the rental company is responsible for replacing it. They have staff that maintain and check out their cameras. If it's your camera, any problems are on your head.

A lot of people I know buy from companies like Abel Cinetech, which also has a rental business, so they can rent stuff and send the camera in for maintenance periodically. If you live in an area with vendors you can hit on for replacements/tech support/accessories, then perhaps owning your own stuff makes sense. But I think that it's easier in most cases to rent. This is also why I don't rent from owner-operators unless I know them very well, and/or they're working on the shoot as crewmembers.

As always, there are exceptions. Over the years I've accumulated a variety of handy things – a cordless drill, a ton of hand tools, a flexfill, a handtruck, assorted video and audio cables, some folding tables and chairs, storage containers – that I schlep along to every shoot I go on. One of my producer friends has a four-unit walkie set that she bought cheap at Home Depot that's come in handy countless times. Owning these kinds of small-ticket items won't save you much money, but they can save you some hassle.

Local vs. Non-local

If I'm shooting in a major city (like New York) I usually have a good selection of options. If the shoot is somewhere outside of a major city, I'll have to weigh and measure the problems of transporting gear versus the availability of local resources. It depends on the type of equipment and how close the nearest replacement is (or if the local company even has a replacement).

When shooting *Racing Daylight*, the producers evaluated local equipment options. We were able to pull some favors – we got a free tent from one of the associate producers, and some lights from a local stage. A local jib operator donated his time, his crew, and his 40-foot jib arm to us (that was amazing). But we ended up bringing most of our gear and our truck from New York City. At the time there weren't enough local vendors. We found one guy with a grip/electric truck but he was fairly inflexible on his price and didn't have everything we needed. We would have had to go to Albany or New York to get everything else anyway.

On the other hand, when shooting an industrial on Rhode Island a few years ago we were able to grab almost everything we needed from nearby companies and people, with the exception of our camera (which came from New York). By going local we saved some transportation expenses and avoided the hassle of trying to close a deal with a vendor over a hundred miles away.

If you can rent locally, you'll go a long way to establishing goodwill in your community, not to mention boosting the economy. When shooting *Helena from the Wedding*, we spent almost half our budget in the town we were shooting in – between catering, lodging, props, craft services, picture vehicle rentals, expendables purchases, location rentals, and hiring one of the local crewmembers as our key grip. This helped us a lot when we needed the town's support to shoot on the main street, and got us some good press in the local newspaper. But we still had to truck a lot of our grip/electric equipment from New York.

FINDING AND COMPARING VENDORS

You've probably been staring at Table 12.1, wondering how the hell you're going to figure out all that. Fortunately, there are a number of ways to attack the problem.

Prioritize Your Search

First, let's focus on the equipment/services that are specific to your script. If your script has any of the following:

- Prosthetic effects
- Floor effects (fog machine, wire work, water or fire)
- Special photography (special lenses, miniature shots, infrared film)
- Stunt weapons (this could include chairs, rocks, and anything that, if thrown/wielded, could hurt someone)
- Soundstage
- Special camera support (jib, crane, cherry picker, Steadicam)
- Picture vehicle rental
- Special costumes
- Animals
- Greenscreen
- Lodging

… start researching vendors for these things *now*.

Second, let's look at things that you'll need no matter what:

- Insurance company
- Payroll company
- Car/van rental
- Camera provider
- Grip/electric provider
- Sound gear rental
- Unit supplies (and wardrobe, hair/makeup, specialty expendables)
- Prop rentals/purchases
- Hardware store
- Low-cost supermarket
- Caterer
- Tapestock/filmstock/hard-drive supplier
- Post house
- Sound post house

These two lists still seem pretty big but they're more manageable. Try to find at least two vendors for each of the items listed above, and see if you can get them to compete on bids.

Where to Look for Vendors

Start with your war council and your connections list (from the previous chapter). Ask them for referrals. Also, find your local and state film commission office. Local colleges/universities with film programs are another resource, though you may have to wade through the school bureaucracy to get to the right person. Gentle persistence pays off here.

What you want is to start the conversation, pick up an education, and maybe test your budget against reality a bit. Unless you already have your crew and locations locked in, you can't finalize any bids. But you can get equipment catalogs, fill out credit card/account papers, and get some preliminary bids.

Before you start making calls, it's good to have some information written down in a text file, so you can copy and paste it into your emails. This would include:

- Film title
- Production company
- Company EIN
- Producer name
- Address, phone, fax, email
- Shoot dates (as of your latest schedule)
- Equipment pickup date
- Equipment return date
- Shooting locations (what town/city/state)
- Insurance company policy number (if you have one)
- Headcount (for hotels and caterers)
- DP's name (for camera rental)
- Gaffer's and key grip's name (for grip/electric rental)
- Sound mixer's name (for sound rental)
- A one-to-two sentence description

You should also create a PDF by scanning in:

- The front and back of whatever credit card you're using
- Your driver's license
- Your tax resale certificate

Obviously, don't email this PDF to just anyone! You'll find it's a real time-saver to have this material close to hand when you're opening up accounts, though.

The best way to start a relationship is still over the phone, during business hours. It's good to hit up a vendor's website to download a catalog or a set of forms, but you should also call and talk to at least one person. If you're referred by someone else, mention that person.

Crew as Vendors

If you have a DP, mixer, or gaffer that you want to work with and she has an equipment package, get details. You may still have to fill in the gaps (like larger monitor or a hi-hat) by going to a vendor. She can probably recommend a vendor.

Most crew people have their favorite vendors. It's good to take their suggestions seriously – but as suggestions only. Get some other quotes.

A lot of grips and electrics have their own trucks with gear and sometimes crew. These are usually good value propositions, *if* you're working in their niche. On smaller-scale projects ($200K and under), you may not be able to justify the cost – and for the gear owner, it's hard to drop the price past a certain point.

Alternative Vendors

There's probably a public access TV studio, small production company, or theater nearby. Chances are they have some equipment that they'd be willing to rent out as long as you have insurance. Don't rule these places out. They can also be resources for finding local crewmembers, cast, and extras. The trick is to see if they have enough of what you need so that you don't have go somewhere else as well.

Starting the Negotiations

When you get on the phone or show up, you want to be nice to the folks at the desk (obviously) but you'll also want to talk to the middle managers. In a grip/electric house, that's usually the person in a small shabby office right next to the floor. In the hotel, they're hiding in the office next to the front desk.

These folks probably have the hardest job short of the janitors. They get problems from above (why are the rentals down this month?), from below (I'm sorry I'm three hours late for my shift and I didn't call), and from customers (the last three HMI lamps you rented me were strobing). So be nice to these guys at the outset. Try to get to know them a bit. If you talk to them like real human beings they'll appreciate it.

Mention your dates, the gist of what you need, and that you're an independent feature. Some vendors will care about the story, others won't. *Most* will be interested to know where you're shooting. *All* of them will want to know that you'll have insurance by the time you pick up your stuff.

Some vendors will ask you for your budget for their equipment: "What do you have in the budget for lights?" or "What's your budget range?" I usually give them vague answers up front. "You know, it's the usual low-budget stuff" or sometimes I'll say "Let's just see what the bid is and I'm sure we can make it work." A rule of thumb in negotiations is *whoever spells out a price first loses*. The idea is that once the price is mentioned, it becomes fixed in everyone's minds regardless of the actual value of the services/goods being rented or sold. It's better to keep things a little vague.

Note that this assumes that you and the vendor are locked into a zero-sum game. This is not always the case – many vendors would rather have their gear earning some money rather than taking up space, even if it's not the top rate. Also, customer loyalty is important. If they give you a break now, you'll be more likely to rent from them in the future.

So if you think you're being *too vague* and actually putting the vendor into a somewhat hostile position, then tell them what you have for their department's goods, minus a little bit. I usually understate my budget by 10 percent. This gives me a little wiggle room. The vendors know that producers rarely state the true figure, so of course they assume that a little wiggle exists. Just like in the crew negotiations, everyone assumes each party is stretching the truth a little bit. So you might as well go along with it.

How you carry yourself is important. Suit your dress to the vendor. Equipment rental houses are jeans-and-t-shirt places. Hotels and restaurants may be a little more upscale, but tie-and-formalwear is probably too much. You don't have to pretend you know everything about filmmaking. But you don't want to come off like a complete idiot. Do a little homework so you know something about the company before walking in. Owners, especially, are flattered that you took the time out to find out a little bit about them.

If you're part of a producing team, it may be good for both of you to go. This is especially true with your biggest vendors. If you're shooting in a distant location, your biggest expense will probably be food and lodging. On *Helena from the Wedding* the producers and director (and later myself) made several trips upstate to meet with the managers of various hotels. I think because we took the time out to meet them in person, we got better deals on both the rooms and the food.

If you don't have a real sense yet of what you'll need – this is usually the case with grip and electric gear – it's better to just make introductions and get a sense of what they have to offer and their basic rates.

Prices

Film vendors generally deal in day rates – they'll quote you a rental price for a single day's rental. The weekend, incidentally, counts as one day. Weeks are discounted to three days or less (on most items). That is, a one-week rental will be treated as three days. This is also called the "three-day week." If you can, push for a "two-day week." Or a discount on the day rate. Or, preferably, both. If you're willing to go with an older, heavier model light, or if you can drop some of the "nice to have but not essential" stuff, you can save some money.

Some vendors will only take checks. Others have various deposit arrangements. Find these things out now. Most will give you some kind of discount for cash or checks; others will charge you a 3.5 percent credit card fee to cover their transaction costs.

If you're dealing with an out-of-state vendor, you may have to pay sales tax – since your resale certificate is only good for things purchased within the state.

CATERING

Food is the most treacherous thing on a film shoot. You have to take into account vegans, vegetarians (of different types), lactose- and gluten-tolerant folks, carnivores, and people with various food allergies and/or prohibitions (such as Kosher or Halal). You won't know yet who these folks are, but it's critical when talking to caterers that you get it across to them that you're going to need some special treatment. If it's obvious that they don't get it, move on quickly.

I usually switch caterers at least once during the course of the shoot if I have the option, just to keep people from getting bored. Most caterers do a few dishes very well, and they'll fall back on those given your price. On *Found In Time*, I went to local restaurants near wherever we were shooting. It required more setup time but it worked out well, both for us and for the local community.

Caterers work on a per-head basis. You want to overestimate here, because you may find yourself having to accommodate the location owner, or a special guest on set (like the actor's agent). Some caterers may also charge for gas, tolls, and labor, if they're delivering to your set. If you're shooting in the countryside and there aren't a whole lot of options, it's probably worth it to pay for this.

For breakfast, you're looking for hot protein and "good" carbs. Bagels, egg sandwiches, French toast, bacon, fruit. In the last few years I've tried to vary the liquids to include almond or soy milk, and for the vegans I usually get some vegan sandwiches, granola, or cereal.

For lunch, you want one meat dish, one veggie *protein* dish (this could mean tofu, seitan, or something nut-based), a salad, and maybe a side dish. I usually don't ask for desserts except on special occasions (like the end of the shoot week or someone's birthday) because they're overpriced. Everything should be hot. I can't emphasize this enough.

Another option is to plunk everyone down at a restaurant and offer them the menu. On *Helena from the Wedding* we did both – the restaurant/hotel was also our caterer. We ate breakfast at the restaurant (they usually prepared dishes for us), then picked up food from their kitchen for folks who were on-set. Anyone who wasn't working that day (or had a late call) could walk into the restaurant and order off the menu at a special price.

Avoid pizza, Chinese food, and fast food (especially the latter). While fast food has improved over the last few years, it sends out a bad signal to the crew and cast. Second meal is the exception – you have to go with whatever is the fastest and most convenient option. Try to aim a little higher if you can.

Always have a few emergency menus on hand. This will be handy in case someone can't deal with the food.

TRANSPORTATION

This is also a real headache on indie films. You want to find a rental company that doesn't charge crazy commercial rates and that has a 24-hour (or close to it) lot, so you can pick up and drop off your vehicles whenever you want. Make sure to get the collision damage waiver if it's offered. This will lower your deductible on any collisions, usually from $1500 to about $500.

The most common vehicles you'll need are:

- 7-passenger mini-vans – mostly for the cast (if you end up driving them separately to set). Also good for scouting.
- 15-passenger vans – for crew transport.
- Cargo vans – this is what you hope you can fit all your equipment, props, craft services, etc. in.
- 14-foot cube truck – this is what you'll probably need.
- 18-foot cube truck – this is only if you have a larger grip and electric package.

How many vehicles you'll need depends on your budget (Table 12.2).

TABLE 12.2 Transportation needs

Budget	Vehicle		Carries
$200K or less	(1)	15-passenger van[a]	Crew/cast
	(1)	Cargo van	All the equipment
$500K	(1+)	15-passenger van	Crew/cast
	(1)	Cube truck	All the equipment
$1M	(1)	7-passenger van	Cast
	(2–3)	15-passenger vans	Crew
	(1)	18-ft grip/electric cube	Grip/electric vehicles
	(1)	Camera/sound/wardrobe cube	Camera, sound, wardrobe
	(1)	Production cube	Craft services, production stuff, tables
	(1)	"Slop" cube	Everything that won't fit elsewhere
$2M	(1+)	7-passenger van	Cast
	(2–3)	15-passenger vans	Crew
	(1)	18-ft or larger grip/electric cube	Grip/electric vehicles
	(1)	Camera/sound cube	Camera, sound
	(1)	Production cube	Craft services, production stuff, tables
	(1)	Wardrobe/HMU cube	Wardrobe, HMU
	(1)	Additional G&E cube	Everything that won't fit elsewhere

[a] You may have to add additional passenger vans if you're shooting at a distant location.

Special Vehicles

In addition to these "normal vehicle rentals," you'll have to think about whether you'll need a trailer of some kind. Trailers come in a number of different sizes, and they serve multiple purposes. If you don't have a holding area on your location (say if you're setting up in the middle of the forest), you'll need somewhere for the actors to change and get made up, somewhere for people to go to the bathroom, and at least a desk and some electricity for the production "office."

On *Company K*, a film that was shot in upstate New York and in Pennsylvania, we rented camper vans through various connections. Our costume designer knew a woman in upstate NY who had her own van. One of the people who managed the location in Pennsylvania (a World War I reenactment site) had a friend with a similar-size camper.

When shooting in New York City, I've sometimes had to rent a camper because there was no place cheap enough within walking distance of the set.

Shelving and Liftgates

If you need one or more cube trucks, consider shelving them. Your gaffer or key grip will most likely know a carpenter who will work for a reasonable day rate plus materials (cheap lumber). Just pick up the truck a day early or have the carpenter come to the equipment checkout. A few of the truck rental companies I've rented from actually had an informal arrangement with local carpenters.

Especially if you're moving to a different location every day, this can prevent gear from getting destroyed or damaged. It can also prevent injuries – I've opened a few unshelved trucks and nearly gotten brained by falling loose gear.

If, on the other hand, you're staying in one location for most of the shoot, this may not make much difference. On some shoots, we simply didn't have the $200 to $300 to spend, so we took our chances, with mixed results.

If you end up renting cube trucks, spend the extra money and get ones with liftgates as opposed to ramps. Liftgates are safer and easier to work with, especially when you have to haul hampers and heavy lights on and off the truck.

INSURANCE

Insurance is a big pain in the butt, but there's no getting around it. SAG and your payroll company will *not* deal with you unless you have production insurance. Most equipment vendors and property owners won't want to rent to you. And also, you expose yourself to tremendous liability without it. There are a *huge* number of insurance options out there, but we're going to focus on just the ones that are relevant to independent film.

First off, you'll want to decide whether you want a long-term vs. short-term policy. A long-term policy will cost more up-front, and it will be renewable every year. A short-term policy spans a very specific time period (usually the production period plus a few days on either side so you're covered during equipment pickups/returns and if you go over). If you think you'll be making a string of projects in the next year, then long-term insurance makes sense. Otherwise, however, you're better off sticking to a short-term policy.

Second, find a broker that specializes in film/entertainment insurance. They understand the business and price their policies accordingly, whereas a standard broker may not be able to get as good a set of rates. Brokers don't have to be located in your city.

Last, you'll want to consider the different types of insurance that will become part of the policy.

Liability. This is the basic policy. If something happens on the set – someone is hurt, a light falls down – your company is covered from any injuries and/or damages that result. The policy has very specific limits, however.

Equipment. You're covered from damage to or theft of any equipment that you rent. You'll have to guesstimate the replacement value of the props, wardrobe, and all the rented gear you'll need. For the initial quote I usually specify a low amount (about $100K).

Third-party property damage. This is an addition to the equipment policy. If the wall or furniture belonging to one of your locations gets damaged, this policy will cover the claim.

Auto. This is sometimes required by SAG and by your payroll company. This covers liability and (sometimes) theft. It's a good idea to get this from the broker unless your car rental company can offer an identical policy for less.

Worker's compensation. This covers anyone (cast, crew, extras) who gets injured while working for you, except for executive members of the production company. This includes subcontractors. Worker's compensation is *mandatory* in most states and in most employment situations. Your payroll company usually includes worker's compensation as part of its services (for which it charges a per-check or percentage premium). If you're paying your crew separately, though, you'll have to get a compensation package for them.

In some states, worker's compensation can be obtained from a non-profit, state-run company (like the New York State Insurance Fund in NY). These companies sometimes charge less than their private insurance counterparts.

There are other types of insurance that are less useful to independent filmmakers, but which your broker might try to sell you anyway.

Negative insurance. This covers the replacement cost of filmstock or tapestock in the event that an incident happens that ruins the day's work (for example, if all the filmstock is prematurely exposed). **Pickup insurance** is even more complete, covering all the expenses relating to the work lost. So if you lost an entire day's worth of work due to faulty equipment, pickup insurance would cover all the costs (crew, cast, location, etc.) associated with that day. This sounds wonderful, but it's very expensive, doesn't pay out quickly enough so you can actually just add the day back to your schedule, and may not pay out at all if the insurance company determines that the incident isn't covered.

Terrorism coverage. They will try to stick this to you on every policy you get. It's not expensive ($30 or so per policy), but it is ridiculous. Most brokers will drop the fee if you sign a waiver saying that you won't seek a claim in the event of a terrorist attack.

Errors and omissions. Important to consider, but not during preproduction. This type of policy protects you and the company from accidental trademark/copyright infringement, libel/slander, invasion of privacy, plagiarism, and other intellectual property disputes. For example, in your script you have a character named Ned Stewart from Newark, NJ, who goes crazy by the end of your film and commits some crimes. A real man named Ned Stewart, living in Newark, NJ, decides that you've slandered him in your film. Or that your story rips off his life. Or that he wrote a script just like yours years ago. When he sues you, your production company, and the distributor for one (or all) of these issues, your errors and omissions policy will (theoretically) protect you and your company.

You shouldn't really buy this type of policy until your film is done and you have a distribution deal on the table. Why pay for something you may not use?

Completion bond. This is something you'll rarely see on low-budget films, but it's not unheard of. The completion bond company watches over the schedule and budget of the film as it's progressing. If the film goes over budget past a certain percentage, the bond company fires the director (and possibly the producer as well), takes over control of the film, and either completes it (by shooting just basic coverage and editing) or shelves it. This makes investors feel comfortable – they'll know that their investment won't get diluted and that the film will at least be finished. Completion bond companies usually charge a percentage of the budget. They don't usually like to bond smaller films (under $4M) since the risk of going over budget is higher.

I've seen a couple of films made in the $1M–$2M range that had a completion bond attached, at the behest of the investors. In both cases, the producer and his attorney successfully argued that the investor should cough up the bond (or that the cost should be added to the budget rather than carved out from it). The completion bond is usually *not* considered part of the "production budget" for the purposes of determining what SAG (or union) agreement you'll fall under.

The Awful Cost of Insurance

There is no getting around it, insurance is *hugely expensive.* It becomes more expensive if you have stunts, animals, gunplay, or rap music (I'm not kidding). I've noticed that insurance company rates for short-term policies have gone up quite a bit in the last ten years.

There's also not a whole lot of wiggle room in the price. You can sometimes get the broker to come down on his commission, or you can shave a day off your policy (policies for 14 days or less are cheaper than ones for one month). Your best option is to get quotes from a couple of vendors. Be very clear with each broker that you're obtaining multiple quotes. Chances are that any two or three of the brokers you're talking to are working with the same underwriters. The underwriters will alert them if they see multiple requests coming in for what looks like the same project. It's better that they find out from you.

Initially, what you want is a quote on a $1M/$1M policy. That's a $1M liability policy, with a $1M *per incident* limit. So you can have several insurance incidents or one big one, but no single incident will be covered past $1M in costs. This is the baseline policy and is usually good enough for most locations, for SAG, and for your payroll company.

However, some states have higher insurance requirements if you want to shoot on their land. New York State, for example, has a $2M policy minimum requirement. This means that if you want to shoot on a SUNY campus, state park, or state trooper office, you'll have to get the bigger policy, which of course will be more expensive. Check with your state and city/county office to see if they have an insurance minimum requirement.

You usually want your insurance policy to start when you begin rehearsals and equipment pickups, and end after you've returned all your gear. Most policies get more expensive at the 15-day, 30-day, and 60-day mark. Worker's compensation policies are usually set either for a three-month or year-long period. Some people will argue that you should continue your policy during postproduction. Unless you end up doing an extensive reshoot, I don't think this is necessary. If you think your editing staff or post intern won't be comfortable without worker's comp, then you can consider extending it.

Deductibles

Just because you have an insurance policy doesn't mean you won't have to pay for problems that come up. Each policy type has a per incident deductible. This means that if you have one car break-in and one case of a light falling and getting smashed, each incident will count separately. There's no "banking towards" your deductible. Chances are you'll have to pay for this.

If your film's budget is $500K or above, try to put some money in the missing and damaged line items. This keeps the deductible from coming out of the contingency.

Alternatives to Insurance

You can try to get another company to pick up the tab for your insurance. There are a few ways to do this. One is to contact a *production services company*. These are companies that work as producers-for-hire on various projects. They charge a fee above-and-beyond the costs. They typically have ongoing insurance policies (though not all do). If you have the budget for this, it may be worthwhile. They can handle many of the production chores. But for most projects budgeted at $2M and under, unless you have a personal connection it's probably not worth it for them to work on your film and tie up their resources.

You can ask if your film can be attached to another company's existing policy, as a rider. In theory, the company has to be involved in your film in some way, shape, or form (though this could be just giving them some kind of symbolic "producer" title). You would pay some pro-rated percentage of their policy premium. These arrangements have become rarer over the years. Most of the companies I've worked for as a production manager weren't willing to do it for me on my own film, because it would expose them to too much liability. If the insurance company determines that the relationship between the two companies is mostly bogus, it can refuse the claim. Whoever's making the claim can then go after both companies.

I'd advise against either of the above arrangements unless you have a personal relationship and/or if these companies are really making the film with you.

SPECIAL EQUIPMENT/SERVICES

If you have a prosthetic effect (like a two-headed beast), animal, or picture vehicle (like cop cars) in your film, start your research early. Also, don't rule out local resources that are somewhere "in the ballpark." Local manufacturers, farms, and car dealers have helped me out on many occasions when I couldn't rent from a "film" vendor.

On *Helena from the Wedding*, we contacted an auto repairman named Todd Possemato. He was referred to us by several local folks. He turned out to be terrific. First, we needed a jeep. He had a friend who had a World War II-era jeep that he serviced every winter (Figure 12.2). We were able to rent the jeep pretty inexpensively. He also towed it for us when it broke down.

We also needed a police car. The local police chief couldn't spare any of his vehicles (to be fair, he had a very limited force and had to cover a lot of territory). Todd had a spare emergency roof rack with halogens, and we rigged them to the top of the art director's own car. He also knew a guy nearby who did auto decaling. The production designer sent him a design for a police logo and stripes, and he produced a washable decal.

The producers made the deal with Todd after having already talked to a number of people and companies in the area; I remember even calling a few NYC-based picture vehicle rental companies. We were still scrambling to get the police car, but because we'd already established the relationship with Todd he was able to come through for us in time.

Prosthetics experts need a lot of creative prep time. One film I worked on, *The Reawakening*, called for a character to appear as a Dark Spirit Being from the Onondaga (Native American) religious system. I knew an effects artist, Josh Turi, who'd been working for several years and thought he'd be a good fit for the project. It took over a month for the director, Diane Fraher, and Josh to hammer out the details of what the spirit should look like. It took another few weeks for Josh to

FIGURE 12.2 Our "jeep."

create a full-body prosthesis from the head and chest of the actor, then let it dry, sculpt it into the right shape, and texture and paint it.

On *Found In Time*, Weapons Specialists needed about two weeks to create a prosthetic rock that I could have the actors throw at each other. They needed that much time to make the mold, mix and pour the latex, let it cool, then sculpt and texture it properly.

In all these cases, starting ahead of time saved our bacon, especially since we didn't have a lot of dough.

PRODUCTION/SET GEAR

What's *always* in the classic picture of a film set? Cameras, dollies, lights, grip equipment. What's almost *never* in these pictures? All the *other* stuff you need: garbage cans, brooms, tents, chairs, tables, etc.

But don't give these items short shrift. You have to think about them and how much space they will take up in your production vehicles. Each department has its own needs for these "smaller-ticket" goods. Table 12.3 shows a *somewhat* complete list.

You probably don't need *all* these items. Some of them are weather- and location-dependent. If your film takes place entirely indoors, you don't need umbrellas or tents, and you can probably get by without handwarmers (unless it's cold inside). If you can find a holding area with private rooms, you can cut down on or eliminate the need for privacy screens.

Just start thinking about where you can get these items from. If you live in a city with some of the aforementioned expendables/production supply houses, get some quotes and find out what they have or don't have. If you're working in an area without a lot of film resources nearby, take a trip to the hardware store. You may have to mail-order certain items (gaffer's tape and gels are hard to find), but almost everything else you can get from a hardware store, CostCo, party supply house, supermarket, etc. On *Racing Daylight* the producer, director, and associate producer all pitched in with things they had at home (tents, coolers, garbage bags) and we also bought a lot of things from the local supermarket and hardware stores. So we didn't have to rent as much gear from New York.

TABLE 12.3 Production/set gear

Department	Needs
Wardrobe	Long mirrors Clothing racks (foldable) Steamer – to dry-clean clothes Hangers Privacy screens Wardrobe bags Tags Printer and ink (can share with HMU)
Hair/makeup	Director's chairs – short and tall Square mirrors Clip-lights Tables Extension cords for their blowdryers Rubbing alcohol Sponges Q-tips Paper towels
Production	Printer and ink (can share with wardrobe and HMU if necessary) Copier Table and chairs Paper (lots of it) Pens Stapler/staples Three-hole punch – a really good one
Set operations	First aid kit Craft services table Crafty supplies (paper towels, plates, plasticware, cutting board, etc.) Chairs and tables for eating meals Coolers Heaters (in winter) Handwarmers (in winter) Coffee urn Pop-tents Umbrellas for nasty weather (preferably big ones) Tarps or Visqueen (waterproof plastic) Cots (for actors)
Locations	Garbage bags Recycling bags (please) Cleaning supplies Brooms – street for exteriors, push for interiors Mops and buckets Toilet paper Soap Floor and wall protectors – cardboard, blankets Construction (blue) tape Caution tape (maybe)
Art/props/set dressing	Paint, tape, paper of various types

(Continued)

TABLE 12.3 (Continued)

Department	Needs
Sound	Sound blankets
	Batteries
Camera	Lens pens
	Lens cleaner
	Markers
	Camera tape
	Chart tape (for follow-focus)
Electric, grip	Gaffer's tape
	Paper tape
	Sash
	Clothespins
	Gels
	Lumber
	Dulling spray
	Pledge (for oiling dolly tracks)

GETTING TECHNICAL

Technology changes very quickly in some areas of filmmaking – cameras, lighting, and sound rigs – and less so in others. It's close to impossible to keep up with everything that comes down the pike, but establishing vendor relationships early can be a good way of learning new things. The larger rental houses will send people to trade shows such as the NAB (National Association of Broadcasters), or will have booths of their own. I heard about the Red camera two years before it came out from a company I'd rented from that saw the prototype at the NAB.

Knowing some basic lighting techniques and the uses of the different grip and electric gear will help enormously as well. Everything has a name, though some of them are regional and others are just downright confusing. When I talk to the rental manager at a grip/electric house about Kinoflos (fluorescent lighting units), there's always some confusion about what we each mean by a 4 × 2 (is that a fixture with two four-foot bulbs, or four two-foot bulbs?). Since your grip and electric package is probably the most specialized, expensive, and space-consuming of all the equipment you're going to rent or buy, it's prudent to know what you're paying for. It will also help you talk to the grip/electric crew intelligently.

EXERCISES

1. Look up the nearest film commission office. It may be in your state or county if you don't have one in your city/town. Call the office up and see if they have a resource directory they can email or snail-mail you.
2. Pick out at least two grip/electric houses and email or call them, asking for a catalog and a rate sheet.
3. Ask any contacts you have about local production companies and theaters.
4. Start making a list of items you and your friends can bring to the table for free or low cost.

## Chapter 13

Unions, Guilds, and States

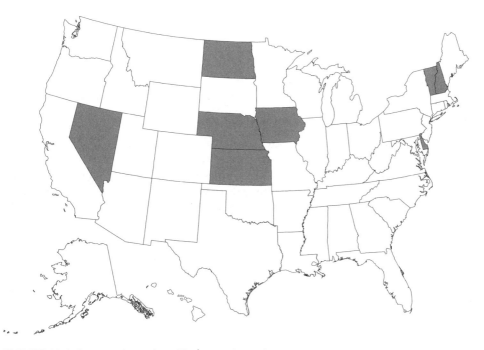

FIGURE 13.1 State tax incentives. Dark = no incentive.

In the wonderful book *The Macintosh Way*, Guy Kawasaki talks about "working with the mothership." In his case, he was talking about how, as a third-party software developer, you deal with a company like Apple that's so damn big you can't get away from it. That's why I lumped the guilds, unions, and states together in this chapter. They're too big to ignore, and you can't treat them in the same way as you can the other entities that you'll be doing business with.

Let's get some terminology out of the way. The Screen Actors Guild, Writers Guild of America, and Directors Guild of America are actually *unions*. The chief difference between a guild and a union is that a union is empowered by its members (and recognized by law) to negotiate collective bargaining agreements. They adopted the moniker "guild" for various reasons. There *are* some technical differences between the DGA, WGA, and SAG and the below-the-line unions (IATSE and BC), but they're minor. So just for convenience, I'm going to call all these organizations unions from this point on.

Low-budget independent films and unions have always had a very uneasy relationship. On the one hand, the unions do have various "low-budget" agreements that offer discounts on member rates and benefits. And at least in New York, there's a tacit understanding that if your profile isn't too big, the unions aren't going to hassle you. But the truth is a little more complicated than that.

First, there isn't one "union" but several. The "guilds" are organized by discipline: the WGA represents writers, the DGA reps directors, ADs, and UPMs. The below-the-line locals are part of either IATSE (International Association of Theatrical Stage Employees, Moving Picture Technicians, Artists and Allied Crafts – IA for short), or BC (Basic Crafts). These large unions set national wage, pension, and work condition standards.

The locals within IATSE and BC are organized either around disciplines or regions, or both. For example, Local 52 in New York and Local 476 in Chicago both represent the same group (see below for details on Local 52). On the other hand, Locals 600 (Camera) and 892 (Costume and Production Design) have national jurisdiction. Some locals participate in a national benefits/pension plan, while others have their own. Each has a certain degree of freedom to negotiate one-off contracts. Regional associations between locals in IATSE and BC, such as the East Coast Council, also put together special contracts.

Appendix C details the various unions, the professions they represent, and their low-budget agreements. The IA locals referenced are either national or New York-based. In LA, there are more locals, each even more specialized than the ones in New York. In smaller cities and rural regions, there are fewer locals that cover more employees.

Producers, line producers, post supervisors, production assistants, and certain other positions (craft services inside New York, for example) aren't included in this list. As a producer, you're "management."

The second thing you'll see is that while some of the divisions within the unions make sense – like grouping hair stylists and makeup artists together – others don't (why is wardrobe in a separate local than costume design? Why do the teamsters represent casting directors as well?). Suffice it to say that the history of film unions is full of twists, turns, and setbacks, and the result is the quiltwork you see today. When casting directors were looking to organize, the teamsters gave them a great offer. Why start a new local if you can join one of the most powerful ones already in existence?

All of the unions support their members, offer employer-paid healthcare to members who work over a certain number of hours or dollars per period, and fight for their rights. They differ in how their pension, health, and welfare plans are set up, their dues amounts, and in how active and well-run they are.

I have a disclaimer. For a few years I was a member of Local 161 as a payroll accountant. I joined when I became the payroll accountant for two seasons of *The Naked Brothers Band*, a short-lived kids' TV show that aired on Nickelodeon. My grandfather and stepfather also belonged to unions. So I'm probably a bit partial to them.

THE UNION CATCH

The union low-budget agreements look very reasonable on paper – and they are, compared to the basic rates. Even when you factor in the overtime, meal penalties, travel allowances, and so on, you're not in bad shape. However, the fringes, specifically the health, pension, and welfare (HP&W) payments you'll have to make on behalf of each member, can really break the bank if you're not at a certain budget threshold.

In Chapter 10 we spoke a bit about SAG's HP&W rate – 16.8 percent of the gross salary. The DGA's is 14.5 percent, and the WGA's is 14 percent. The teamster's HP&W payments are 28 percent (though there are breaks)! The below-the-line unions' HP&W schemes are more varied depending on the local and the agreement. A good rule of thumb is that you can expect to pay somewhere around $100 per day per union member (which, if you're just at the budgeting stage, should include everyone in your crew). These percentages and figures do not include the normal employer fringes.

So if you're making a $200K movie with a crew of 10 people (not including PAs), you can't afford to pay out $1000 per day for 13 days of shooting, 5 days of prep, and maybe a day of paid wrap (that's nearly 10 percent of your budget), even if the unions agree to a "one-off contract" wherein their salary is pretty negligible.

On the other hand, if you're making a $2M–$3M movie, going union may make sense. Union crewmembers have experience.

HOW DOES THIS AFFECT ME?

If you're trying to make a film for less than $1M, you're probably only going to be dealing with SAG/AFTRA. However, there are significant exceptions that you should pay attention to:

1. If you're shooting during a slow season.
2. If your director is a DGA member.
3. If your writer is a WGA member.
4. If one of your key crew members (say, your DP) is a union member and wants you to sign up with their local.
5. If you need to rent a truck larger than a 14-foot cube – this increases your profile.
6. If you're renting a lot of grip/electric or camera gear, and/or renting from a union-affiliated equipment house.
7. You're shooting on 35mm.

Unions have many ways of finding out about your film. In New York, they check the local production list that the Mayor's Office keeps of all active permits. Some of the rental houses are either union-affiliated or are part of union-signatory soundstages, so they'll hear about equipment orders going out. The teamsters pay attention to what's on the street while they drive by, and most film crews stand out.

If your shoot includes any of the risk factors above, then you have a few strategies.

DGA. If your director is in the DGA, you're in a bit of a tight spot. You can negotiate his salary and perks. But you may have to bring aboard a DGA UPM and 1st and 2nd AD, which will saddle you with salaries and fringes that will be hard to support, even if you're at the upper end of the $1M range.

On the other hand, if your UPM or 1st AD is in the DGA, they may not in fact want the union to know about the shoot. What they may ask you to do is to keep their names off the crew lists and callsheets, and/or pay them in cash.

WGA. The WGA agreement for films with $500K and lower budgets isn't that bad. As stated above, you can defer *most* of the salary requirements, but you have to cough up a $10,000 writing fee plus a $5000 publication fee. These are due on the first day of principal photography. Now, if you're the writer-director, you can "invest" that money back into the production as soon as the check is cashed. However, you'll have to pay payroll taxes and the WGA's 14 percent HP&W fringes on the amount. This can be a big hit if you're shooting a $100K-or-under film.

Teamsters. These guys have a reputation as *people you don't mess with*. The truth is that I've found them individually very friendly, and most aren't out to "get" anyone. The best thing is to be straight with them. Tell them your budget. If it's less than $500K, they'll probably wish you good luck. If it's $1M, they might ask you to throw one of their guys on board. This will cost a pretty penny, but they do know their job – it's always a little scary to me to see these 19-year-old PAs driving trucks (I was that 19-year-old once, and did crack a few mirrors in my day).

What you don't want to have happen – especially if you're in the $1M end of the spectrum – is to have them *find you* during production. That's where the "don't mess with us" thing comes up. They'll drive by your set and honk their horns in the middle of a take, or try to intimidate your PAs, or park their trucks in your spots. They also won't be disposed to be benevolent with the rates either.

IA. First of all, be honest when interviewing your crew about whether it's a union gig or not. If a union crewmember wants to work on your shoot, they'll be doing so knowing that you don't intend to sign up. In New York at any rate, a cordial "understanding" exists wherein union crewmembers will do non-union jobs periodically. I think (though I'll never know for sure) that the union doesn't crack down on this behavior because they feel it's better that their members are working, and there's not always enough union jobs to go around.

You can't really carve out a deal with a single local without getting the others involved. In theory it's possible, but in practice the local reps talk to each other, so they'll want you to sign a blanket agreement of some kind. For a $1M-or-below film, the members will be working so they can bank hours towards their healthcare and pension benefits. So they'll usually agree to not-such-great wages. You'll still have the aforementioned HP&W fringes to add to the budget.

If you find yourself in the position of having to go union for one reason or another, you can usually get a one-off deal. *Henry May Long*, a film that some of my friends worked on a few years ago, started out as a $1M non-union film. However, the project was scheduled for what turned out to be one of the quietest winters in recent history in New York, and they were shooting on 35mm. About a month before the shoot, someone from one of the union offices called the production company and "invited" them to become a union signatory. The crew worked for a very low rate – less than what I paid for a $200K film that shot earlier that year – but in exchange the production company agreed to hire on a minimum number of union crewmembers, and to pay out a flat HP&W payment per day per member. Even with the discounted rate, approximately $40K came out of the budget. This impacted the rest of the schedule and budget, of course. But the film still got made and it came out well.

$2M AND UP: GENERAL GUIDELINES

You don't have to sign up with *all* the guilds and unions at once. If you're shooting a SAG film, you don't have to also bring aboard the WGA, DGA, IA, and teamsters.

Most films in the $2M to $4M range sign with SAG. And, once the budgets get up around $3M, they go with IA and teamster crews. Most, however, don't sign with the DGA or WGA until the budgets get up around $4M or if the director or writer is a member.

This is understandable. The WGA agreement is pretty steep – you're looking at paying out $40K plus additional fees plus fringes, for any film made between $1M and $5M. This isn't a big chunk of change on a $4M picture, but it is on a $2M film. The DGA agreements have more granular "tiers." But you're still looking at paying fairly hefty rates for a DGA production manager, plus completion fees, studio fees, and fringes.

Refer to Table C.1 in Appendix C for more general guidelines on what union you're likely to sign up with and at what level.

THE STRUCTURE OF THE LOW-BUDGET AGREEMENTS

All of the low-budget agreements are actually "tiered" – each one has a rate structure designed for films that fall within a specific budget range. For example, the DGA defines a "Level 1A" tier for films budgeted at $500K and below, "Level 1B" tier for films budgeted from $500K to $1.1M, "Level 2" from $1.1M to $2.6M, and so on. Not only are the salaries higher at each tier, but so are the side benefits.

This same hierarchical structure is in place in the SAG, WGA, IATSE, and BC agreements. The HP&W provisions of the IATSE agreements also vary depending on the film's tier and location.

These agreement specifics change every year (either the tier limits, rates, benefits, or all three go up). Further, the contracts are renegotiated periodically (usually every three years). The rates and other data for all the contracts in this book are from the 2012–2013 period, except as noted.

In Appendix C, you'll find a condensed breakdown of each union low-budget agreement. The contracts are somewhat intricate and their effects on your film vary. This is one reason why it's hard to a make a $3M movie – by the time you get to $3M, you'll probably be a full-union shoot, which will push all your costs up. This in turn will make it more imperative to find name leads and supporting roles to justify the expense, so before you know it you've hit $4M.

All of the tier ceilings exclude the contingency, insurance, and financing fees (loan interest and legal fees). This gives you some cushion – so if your film's total budget is $2.7M, you'll probably still qualify for the DGA Level 2 rates.

Keep in mind too that the salary guidelines are minimums, and some are not spelled out completely (the "STN" rates for the IA contracts). You may not be able to get everyone to work for the minimum rates. Other issues to consider are:

Turnaround. The DGA and IA agreements have specific turnaround rules.

Overtime. The weekly DGA rates assume a 12–14 hour day (depending on the level). Overtime after that gets pretty expensive. IA crew overtime starts after 8 hours, and doubletime starts after 12.

Minimum call. This is the "shortest" workday allowed. If you send someone home after 4 hours, you still owe them the minimum call's worth of pay. Most agreements stipulate an 8-hour call. SAG will let you pro-rate wardrobe fittings if they're less than 2 hours.

Meal penalties. IA, SAG, and the teamsters have "escalating" meal penalties, but each has a slightly different interval (usually either ¼ or ½ hour).

Per diems/mileage. When shooting on distant locations, you have to pay for room and board for all crew – IA, DGA, and teamsters. Any travel that crewmembers do outside a 30-mile radius of either the production company office or certain LA/NYC landmarks is reimbursable and on the clock.

Distant location pay. Union crew and cast who aren't working during the weekend but who can't go home are paid for the days off, at a reduced rate.

Bond. IA may ask you to deposit two weeks' worth of the total payroll for your union crew with the payroll company, or with the union's escrow account.

Holidays, bereavement leave, week length. The agreements are for five-day weeks. It doesn't matter when your week starts. There's a premium for working a sixth day. Holidays and bereavement leave are paid for depending on the tier.

Daily DGA rates. The DGA agreements include partial week rates and daily rates (if you have to day-play an additional 2nd AD).

THE SIGNATORY PROCESS

When your film becomes a "union" shoot, what that really means is that the production entity becomes a *signatory* to an agreement between it and that union. This binds your company to certain obligations, for the lifetime of the company – one reason you don't want to sign personally or use your ongoing development company. Once your company is a signatory, it can't produce non-union projects.

However, signing with one union doesn't obligate you to sign with another. The only significant exception is that if you sign with IA, you're *probably* going to sign with the teamsters as well. But if you sign with SAG, you don't have to sign with the DGA, WGA, IA, or teamsters.

Becoming a signatory means filling out an application, and sending it into the union office along with your budget, schedule, payroll company info, insurance certificate (if you have it), the state filing certificate and operating agreement for your company, and other paperwork as requested. Once they approve the application, they'll send you a thick set of documents to sign, and you may have to put down a deposit.

Since the agreement is between the union and the company, your crew or cast don't have to fill much out. SAG has a one-page form that each cast member signs that affirms that they understand the rate and what agreement the production is working under. The guild also has a daily "sign-in" sheet (called the Exhibit G) that each actor has to sign, listing their time in, time out, lunch hour, time entering/leaving set, etc. SAG will insist that you send the cast payroll checks to their offices first along with a special report (which your payroll company can usually provide). They will then distribute the checks to the actors.

The WGA has a reporting requirement, but the other locals, by and large, don't have much paperwork to fill out. At the end of the shoot or post, all will send you a few forms to fill out to "close out the agreement." You'll have to list your actual costs. You'll also get a "logo bug" graphic that you'll have to put in your end credits, indicating that your film was produced in cooperation with one of the unions.

RIGHT-TO-WORK STATES

About 22 states have right-to-work laws. This *doesn't* mean that there are no unions in those states, or that the unions won't want you to sign up with them if your film's budget is past a certain level. It merely means that you can hire non-union personnel, even if you enter an agreement with the union.

In right-to-work (RTW) states that don't have a strong union presence, this *could* mean that you can shoot films in the $2M+ range without signing up with the union, assuming that you can find enough non-union workers. In other cases, you'll end up mixing and matching.

Officially, you can't discriminate in hiring based on someone's union membership. Unofficially, that's often what happens. Also unofficially, the unions can certainly make their feelings of displeasure known (honking their horns, picketing your location, etc.) if you elect not to sign up with them or mix-and-match membership in too-disproportionate a number. The situation also depends on where the shoot takes place – Arizona is a huge state, so conditions are different in Tuscon versus St. Michaels.

The best thing is to contact some other producers who've worked in the area you're interested in, and see what their *recent* experience was.

DOES ANY OF THIS MAKE SENSE ON MY FILM?

SAG is pretty much a constant on feature films made in major metropolitan areas, for all the reasons discussed in previous chapters. Don't sign up with the WGA unless your screenwriter is already a member. IA and the teamsters make sense if your budget is hovering in the $4M range. There won't be much difference in salaries, and you can shift costs around a bit to cover the fringes. The DGA doesn't make sense unless your director is already a member or unless you don't have much choice in non-union UPMs and ADs where you're shooting.

STATES, CITIES, AND GOVERNMENT OFFICES

You'll be interacting with the government in four ways: first, when you're setting up and maintaining your business (which we mostly covered in Chapter 3). Second, when you're applying for a state tax incentive program (if you decide to). Third, you'll have to receive a minor's work permit (if you have minors in your cast). Finally, you'll probably be working with local permit offices wherever you happen to be shooting.

As you can imagine, working with the government – at whatever level – entails a certain amount of red tape, patience, and planning. So start your research on your state's program *now*, before you lock in your locations. The state next door might have a better tax incentive program, and the town down the road might have a more cooperative police department.

INCENTIVE PROGRAMS: THE POWER AND THE GLORY

Many countries heavily subsidize their film industry through direct grants, tax breaks, and various incentive programs (free or low-cost government offices, national parks, discounts on travel, etc.). The recent film *Coriolanus*, based on the Shakespeare play and directed by Ralph Fiennes, was shot in Macedonia and Bosnia. The Macedonian government allowed the filmmakers to shoot some critical scenes in the national Senate chambers.

Governments are generous because film production is an economic "multiplier." Production companies spend money on food, gas, tolls, equipment rentals, material, and labor. All of these things are taxed in some way, shape, or form – employees pay taxes on their wages, gas prices include tax, tolls are a tax of a sort, and all the equipment houses and vendors are taxed on their income. So even if the government gives the production company some kind of break, they get it back – and boost the local economy in the process. When a lot of film work went overseas or north of the border – pursuing cheap goods and labor – state governments began thinking of ways to lure production companies back. Thus the production incentives were born.

Some economic studies have backed up the "multiplier" effect claim, and others have refuted it. Since the recession began, some states shut down, curtailed, or temporarily shelved their incentive programs. Other states, however, expanded their programs and appear to be doing well.

Each state has a different program, but they all fall into one (or more) categories:

1. **Sales tax exemptions.** The production company is exempt from sales tax, even (in some cases) on items like hotel rentals that are normally taxed even if you have a resale certificate.
2. **Free locations.** State property (parks, prisons, hospitals, government buildings, state trooper offices, etc.) is free or cheap to shoot in.
3. **Tax credits.** The state tax department gives the production company or the investors a credit against any taxes you owe now or in the future. In some cases this credit can be sold to another company for cash.
4. **Refunds/cash rebates.** The state tax department gives the production company or the investors cash back.
5. **Grants.** The state awards a grant to the production company. Pretty rare.

Some programs combine these offers. In some cases, a credit can be transferred to another company in exchange for cash.

Media Services and Entertainment Partners, two of the larger film payroll companies, have state-by-state incentive breakdowns on their websites: www.entertainmentpartners.com and www.media-services.com. (Disclaimer here: I've worked on films that they've done the payroll for.) Most of the states also have websites that discuss the details of their programs as well.

If you plan it out properly, *you can finance part of your film or at least recoup some of the costs.* This is amazing. However, there are some catches, and there's a process for qualifying your film.

Incentive Catches

Apart from the dough that you can get, the programs are a great way to attract local film production and keep people employed. However, they come with a few requirements that you need to pay attention to before your start signing up for "easy money." I've summarized the most common ones here. Also, just so I can stop saying "credit or refund" in this section, I'm going to refer to both types of incentives as "credits."

Local hiring. Some states give you a higher credit if you hire from the local talent pool. Louisiana's default credit is 30 percent, but they'll give you an extra 5 percent. In a few cases (such as Montana), you'll *only* get credit for local hires.

Caps. Most states have some kind of cap on the amount they'll credit, though it tends to be so large that it won't usually be a problem on your film. Wisconsin has a $100K per project cap – meaning that they won't write a credit out for more than $100K.

Exclusions. Some states will exclude non-local hires; others have certain spending categories that they don't count. New York State doesn't count above-the-line spending, insurance, legal fees, and some other expenses. Almost all states exclude promotional expenses. So on *Found In Time*, only $100K of the budget was eligible for their 30 percent refund.

Partial credits. You may qualify for a partial credit – a lower percentage for doing some part of your work (like post) in the state. New York State has a 10 percent post incentive.

Minimum spend. Some states require you to spend a minimum amount in their jurisdiction before your film becomes eligible. Louisiana has a $300K minimum spend. Pennsylvania's minimum is 60 percent of the total budget.

Non-transferability. Some credits are non-transferable – you can't sell them to another company.

Incorporation/registration. Some states require that your production company be incorporated in that state, but most only require that your company do business in the state. Some are even more liberal, allowing you to work through a loan-out company that's incorporated or registered in that state.

Special requirements. These can add costs that you weren't counting on. New York State requires that you shoot at least one day on a qualified soundstage, and that you build a set on that stage.

Pool/sunset. Many states set aside a fixed pool of money to be allocated to their incentive program. Once the money is gone, so is the program, until it's resurrected. Other states have specific sunset clauses built into their programs – after a certain date, the program will cease (until it's resurrected).

Politics/economics. When a new governor or legislature comes into office, or when a state is broke, the incentive program can be cancelled, or downsized.

Calculating the Incentive

First, make sure you actually hit the minimum spend requirement. If you don't, see if the state next to yours (assuming it's within a reasonable distance) offers an incentive, and what the minimum is there.

Second, pay attention to the exclusions. In most budgeting programs, you can create groups so you can play "what-if" games, turning on and off certain groups. Create a group called "Excluded" and assign it to any line item that looks like it's excluded according to the incentive program. If you have doubts about whether something will be excluded or not, play it safe. Then exclude the group from the grand total.

Third, add in any additional fees you'll have to cough up to qualify (higher insurance, soundstage shooting, etc.). Assign these items to another group, called "Included." Your new grand total is what the percentage refund/credit will be based on. Turn "off" the "Excluded" group and you'll see how much your eligible costs add up to. Knowing the credit percentage, you can then calculate the credit amount you can expect. Does the credit offset the additional costs you'll have to incur?

Does It Make Sense?

While the programs look good, they may not make sense. Refunds are typically better than credits. And transferable credits are better than non-transferable ones (since those can result in cash).

If you're shooting a $150K film in Louisiana, it *doesn't* make sense to artificially double your budget so you can get 30 percent back. If your state is going through some political turmoil and it looks like the incentive program is going to be cancelled, don't count on it being there for you.

On *Found In Time*, I had to spend an additional $4000 in soundstage costs and another $200 in set construction to qualify. But I reasoned that I would have had to shoot those scenes on a practical location in any case, so I really only had to stretch the budget by about $2000–$2500. In return, I got back $26K – but not until a year later when I finally closed the books and finalized the application.

Helena from the Wedding, on the other hand, was shot a year earlier, during a period when the state pool had run out. So it wasn't clear whether any new films would qualify or be swept aside once the pool was renewed (if it would be). So we would have had to spend the $3K–$4K without knowing if we would still be in line for any money back. It didn't make sense given that the budget for the film was tight already.

I've sometimes played "what-if" games with producers, trying to figure out what the costs would be of shooting in another state versus what we could get back. Sometimes the room-and-board costs, even after the refund, are too high to justify the extra 5–10 percent. In other cases, where the cast was pretty small or the travel time was nominal, it made more sense to shoot in another state.

Applying for the Incentive Program

Each state has its own process, but there's a general pattern that goes something like this.

First, you fill out the initial application and submit it to the state film commission along with your bio, budget (formatted according to their specs), schedule, script, and any other information they ask for. States that don't have a commission have some other office that takes care of these matters.

Then they get back to you (usually via email) with questions, requests for further clarification, and sometimes more forms to fill out.

You may have to take an in-person meeting with the commission office. In New York, they recommend that you bring the producer, line producer, production manager, and accountant. I showed up by myself, which they said was becoming more common.

They then outline the way the program works, give you back an initial estimate of how much the refund/credit will be for, and, if all goes well, make it official that you're in the applicant "pool."

Some states require paperwork be submitted during production (I had to send in my callsheets and final schedule).

At the end of post, when you're ready to collect, you'll have to fill out a final budget, along with other data (typically a hiring report of some kind).

Assuming this passes muster with the commission, they'll issue you a certificate and pass their recommendation on to the tax office for that state. The tax office will then audit the paperwork and issue the refund or credit.

This sounds like it will take a lot of time. And it does. I recommend getting your paperwork together no less than 3 months before you start shooting. Pay special attention to their budgeting framework – chances are their accounts don't line up with yours, so you'll have to do a fair amount of addition/subtraction to make it work. For *Found In Time*, I put together a quick database that mapped my budget line items to the state's official budget form.

If this isn't your thing, find a production accountant or line producer who can help you with it. Some payroll companies also have incentive consulting services, though you'll probably have to pay more for them than if you hire a part-time accountant.

I've found, by and large, that the folks working in the commissions were genuinely helpful, and didn't mind answering questions.

Local Incentives

Some cities provide some form of incentive as well. New York City used to have a 5 percent refund, but now only offers specific services – some discount cards on local museums and other entertainment, and free advertising on billboards and posters.

On *The Reawakening* (shot on the Onondaga Nation and in Syracuse), the county sheriff provided us with a jail, an armorer for some gunfights, and himself and his deputies as extras. It was a somewhat informal "incentive" but it worked out very well.

CHILD WORK PERMITS AND LABOR LAWS

If you employ minors on your shoot, you have to abide by the child labor laws of whatever state you're shooting in. That means obtaining a child labor work permit – this entitles you to hire minors. This is usually a straightforward-enough process. Most states have a form online you can either fill out electronically, or download, fill out, and print out. The fee varies between $400 and $700 per state. In most cases you only have to answer a few questions. You'll get an official work permit in the mail, which you'll copy and forward on to your payroll company and SAG (if they ask for it).

Your payroll company will require a copy of this permit in order to be able to pay the child. In addition, the child's parents will have to supply a work permit specifically for their kid – basically, the child *also* has to be authorized to work (this is the parents' responsibility). Also, parents have to supply trust fund account information (this is commonly called a Coogan account) and specify an allocation percentage. The payroll company diverts the specified percentage of the child's pay to the trust fund, and the parents can't touch it. The kid can't touch it until s/he turns 21.

If your shoot is during the school year, and your actor will miss more than 2 days of school, you'll have to provide a private tutor (at the production company's expense) and a private classroom. This can be any decent-sized room, but it has to be separate from the other production areas. The child has to be in "school" for three hours for every day missed. The school time can be interrupted by work, but in order for the time to count each tutoring session has to be at least twenty minutes long. You can bank hours – so if your actor got four hours of tutoring in on one day, they would only be owed two hours the next.

Finally, you can't keep kids up past 10PM or midnight, without the parents' permission.

LOCAL PERMITS

Every state, city, county, parks department, and town has a permit requirement for shooting on its property. Some of these are of great value – New York City gives you free police, free parking in most spots, and a towing service if other cars have violated the permit regulations. Others are horrible – I've been to a few towns that didn't want production "in their backyard" and so had permit application fees of $500–$1500. Which didn't get us anything except cold stares.

In smaller towns, the permit process tends to be less formalized – an email to or a sit-down with the town clerk is all that's required, sometimes along with a fee. In New York, the Mayor's Office of Film, Theater and Broadcasting handles permits for stills, trailers, film, and television shoots.

If you're shooting in a locale that doesn't get a lot of production and therefore doesn't have an official film commission office, prepare a written pitch. The pitch should be one or two pages long, and include a brief synopsis, a list of the locations you want to shoot in, your shoot dates, and a rough estimate of how much money you'll be spending while you're in town. This last item is very important. I've gotten a lot of leeway from town boards once they saw that the cast and crew would be spending a good chunk of money on food, gas, hardware, location rentals, paint, and props.

PERMIT GOTCHAS

There are some "gotchas" with these permits. Read the fine print before you apply!

Permit fee. New York City permits used to be free. Starting in 2010, they added a $300 fee, which can be waived if you plead extreme poverty. The trend seems to be to charge for permits.

Personnel fee. In New York, the police are free – and required if you have a scene taking place outdoors that involves crime, gunplay, actors dressed as police, stunts, any kind of car chases or dangerous work, etc. You have to make arrangements through the permit office. In Newark, we had to pay the police. Likewise, some cities will charge for "renting" their bus drivers, fire department staff, police, medics, and other civil service staff, whereas others won't.

Location fee. Just because you have a permit doesn't mean you can shoot on a given government location for free.

Jurisdiction. In New York City, shooting in a park requires that you get in touch with the New York City Department of Parks and Recreation. You have to speak to the actual manager of that park and get his/her okay *before* the permit office will give you a permit. Sometimes, it's not clear who you have to ask. On a film I worked on a long time ago (as an electrician), we were shooting in the Staten Island borough president's office, which is technically NYC property. The location manager had gotten a permit to shoot there, but hadn't checked in with one of the borough president's staff, who promptly kicked us all out. The production lost almost a whole day of shooting and a lot of money. The location manager lost his job.

Parking. You can usually get parking, but in most cases that just means they give you the permit signs. It's up to you to go to the location, tape them up, and shoo off people who want to park there. On larger films ($1M and over) you'll probably have a small staff of parking PAs, armed with tape, cars, and cones, who plant themselves the night before your shoot and "cone out" the space. On smaller shoots, you'll have to fend for yourself.

Insurance. This is the big one. New York City only requires a $1M policy. But New York *State* requires a $2M policy. This is obviously a lot more expensive. Sometimes it's not always clear who owns a given building, park, or area, so find out during or right after the location scout.

LET'S STEAL THE SHOT

Sometimes this is unavoidable. The NY MTA charges an arm and a leg for shooting on the subways – or refuses outright – so I've always stolen these. On the other hand, some cities and towns don't even require a permit to shoot on the street as long as you're not blocking traffic or asking for special parking. If you have a small footprint – one or two vehicles, small crew, small camera – you can often get away with just running and gunning.

Other times, you can reach an informal accommodation with the local police or town. On *Racing Daylight*, we needed to post people on the road near one of our locations so they could see what was coming. If it was something really noisy, we would wait until the all clear to start (especially since the scenes we were shooting were set in the 1860s). The county sheriff told us to wear safety vests so they knew who we were. And that was about all we needed to do.

You have to weigh the risks. Sometimes, getting caught by the police and having your shoot shut down or delayed while you "work it out" could cost you more than the permit fee.

DEALING WITH THE CIVIL SERVICE

Government workers get a bad rap for being bureaucratic, bitter, and/or apathetic. My experience (both in and out of the film industry) is that government service has no higher or lower a percentage of "clock-watchers" than the private sector. Ask other producers who their favorite person is in the permit office. There's always at least one person who's excited by filmmaking. If it's a small town and there's a scene that you need extras for, offer to make them one. Invite them to the set. This doesn't always work but it's worth a try.

Be organized. If you show up with your paperwork in order (don't color outside the lines), then you'll have gone 75 percent of the way towards making them happy with you. The other 25 percent is in treating their office as important, no matter how high or low on the totem pole it is. While this sounds obvious, there's a terrible urgency about film shoots that can blind you to the fact that the rest of the world just doesn't care. Even if that guy wrecks your shoot because he doesn't sign the form that he lost on the bottom of his desk (always bring extra copies), it doesn't affect his job or his life one way or the other. But *the surest* way to delay that form getting signed is to start harassing or blaming the person on the other side of the desk, or threatening to go over his head.

Avoid false flattery or outright bribery. Unless you know from previous experience or a trusted source that these tactics will work, more likely than not they'll backfire on you. A "donation" to the local Policeman's Retirement Fund is one thing, but making the check out to the sheriff is probably not a good idea.

START EARLY

When dealing with these large organizations, you don't have as much wiggle room as you would with a vendor or crewmember. This can be very frustrating, especially when their approval can make or break your shoot. Just start your research early. If you're a little hesitant to talk to the unions at this stage (they do track projects) you can always say that you're doing a budget for another film (and use a false title).

QUESTIONS/EXERCISES

1. Create a new draft of your budget by duplicating your existing one. Using the rate table in Appendix C, figure out how much the budget would change if the film was an IA Tier 1 project.
2. If this pushes your budget past one of the SAG low-budget agreement "ceilings," make adjustments to the cast salary.
3. Does your film have a state film production incentive? What are the constraints? What's covered and what's excluded?
4. Call up the local film commission or town clerk (if there is no commission) and find out what the permit process is (if there is one).
5. If you're in a small town, find out what the adjacent town's film permit process is. Is the fee structure better or worse? Do they charge for locations? What are the insurance requirements?

## Chapter 14

Rights and Contracts

FIGURE 14.1 Rights.

Disclaimer: I am not a lawyer. What's in this chapter – in this book, for that matter – shouldn't be construed as professional legal advice.

The above is an example of how carefully you have to tread in the film world. We live in a litigious society. That's unlikely to change. A film project can be seen as a series of contracts that ensure that all the parties stay on the same page, everyone gets paid, and everyone's rights are respected.

There are several basic contracts that you'll need for your film shoot, and most cover some rights issue or another. Table 14.1 goes into more detail. This is not an exhaustive list. I'm not including whatever rental agreements you may have to sign with the equipment or vehicle rental companies. You can see why you'll need at least a small filing cabinet and some binders to hold all the paperwork.

TABLE 14.1 Contracts and rights

Agreement	Usually Dealt with During	Applies to	Description
Joint venture	Development	Producer & director	Specifies the nature of the relationship, salary, profit participation
Operating agreement/ subscription agreement	Development	Investors	Outlines the operation of the production company, the investors' role, the cost of the subscription, profit participation
Option agreement	Development	Writer	What the terms of the screenplay option and purchase are; order of payments
Life rights agreement	Development	Subject	If you're writing a biopic or something fictional that's based on a true story, you'll probably need permission from the real-life people involved
Legal services agreement	Development	Attorney	What the services of the attorney are; how much they'll cost; when payments are due
Assignment of copyright	Development	Writer	Assigns copyright to the production company
Casting agreement	Preproduction	Casting director	Spells out the term of the casting period, the fee, how assistants are paid (if at all), what the casting director's credit should be, and what happens if additional casting is needed
SAG contract	Preproduction	SAG	Contract between SAG and the production company; spells out the specific agreement, the actor's salary, work conditions, and residuals payments
IA/DGA/WGA/Teamster contracts	Preproduction	IA/DGA/ WGA/ Teamsters	(If you sign with these unions.) Same as per SAG – spells out work conditions, salaries, profit participation
Crew deal memo	Preproduction/ production	Crew	Assigns salary, title, position of credits, work conditions, profit participation. All work by the crew is the intellectual property of the production company
Cast deal memo	Preproduction/ production	Cast	Assigns salary, role, position of credits, perks
Location agreement	Preproduction/ production	Location	Specifies payment for shooting/ holding/rigging on location
Appearance release form	Production	Extras/cast	Allows you to use someone's likeness on film; used for extras (and for cast if there's no SAG agreement)
Product placement deal	Preproduction/ production	Ad agency or advertiser	Allows you to depict a product or a company's trademark onscreen, either for money or some other consideration (free publicity, free copies of the product, etc.)

Agreement	Usually Dealt with During	Applies to	Description
Vendor services agreement	Production/ post	Vendor (or crew member if acting as vendor)	Describes the services being rendered, when they'll be delivered, how much, and when payment is due. You might enter into one of these with a post house, or your sound designer
Payroll company agreement	Preproduction	Payroll company	A boilerplate contract that the payroll company will give you when you sign up with them (if you use a payroll company)
Composer agreement	Post	Composer	Broad outlines of what the composer will be providing; the delivery schedule, payments, and what rights the production company is getting vs. what rights the composer retains
Musician agreement	Post	Musicians	All work by a musician working in the service of the composer would be considered as work-for-hire
Media rights license	Post	Owner of clips	Gives the producer the right to include a video or sound clip from another source in the film (for example, a clip from a TV show that's on in the background)
Sync rights agreement	Post	Owner of sheet music	Gives the producer the right to use the lyrics and music from a particular musical piece in the film
Master rights agreement	Post	Owner of master recording	Gives the producer the right to use a particular recording of a musical piece in the film
Distribution agreement(s)	Post/delivery	Distributor or sales agent	A set of contracts between the producer and the distributor, licensing certain rights (either worldwide or within specific territories) to the distributor, spelling out what the deliverables are, giving the distributor/agent access to the lab (if any)
Distribution assumption agreement	Post/delivery	Distributor	Distributor assumes the responsibility for paying out deferments and other obligations (like residuals)

Your attorney will have some version of these contracts readily available in his bag of tricks, and can customize them to suit your film. There are a few online and printed boilerplate contracts that aren't too bad, but they rarely get specific enough to cover all the nitty-gritty situations that can land you in trouble later. But if you're really in a position where you can't afford an attorney, then definitely pick up one of the more recent editions of the film contract books (don't get a used edition, because contract laws change over time).

WHY BOTHER?

If you're trying to make your film, contracts just seem like another dish in the sink. And it's true – it's not a lot of fun to modify a location agreement, then chase after the location owner so s/he signs it. But contracts help strengthen relationships, by showing that you take them seriously. They spell out the perks – the credit, pay, on-set niceties, profit participation, and so on. And they (hopefully) provide a protocol for settling messes so you don't have to deal with them on set (what's a meal penalty?).

Friendships are stronger than contracts, but sometimes they don't last as long or they get frayed during the shoot. Also, people who are cool when there's no money involved can sometimes act very greedy when there's a hint of some. Contracts are a hedge against both these problems.

Contracts are also part of your deliverables. Prospective distributors and sales agents want to know that they're not walking into a potential legal minefield by getting involved with your film. They may go as far as to ask for copies of your contracts. So while they're just a pain now, they have a big payoff later on. I've seen a few distribution deals go south because the music licenses weren't in order, or the rights to underlying source material for the script hadn't been completely secured.

Let's delve into a little more detail on these contracts, why they're important to have, and what should be in each one. We won't be able to cover them in much detail, but you'll get the gist of what you'll need to know.

WHAT ALL THE CONTRACTS SHOULD HAVE

All good film contracts should establish the following sets of principles or answer the following questions.

- **Rights.** Who owns what? In most cases, the production company owns whatever the crew and cast make, and the underlying intellectual property rights to the film and script. In other cases, the person is licensing a particular right (like their likeness rights, in the case of extras) to the production company.
- **Service/role.** Who's doing what for whom? The producer agrees to option the script from the writer. John agrees to work for the production company as the gaffer.
- **Deliverables.** What does the person or party have to deliver to each other? The sound designer usually has to deliver the stems (bounce files) and ProTools sessions.
- **Period.** How long is the agreement good for? When are payments or deliverables due?
- **Credit/titles.** Who's getting credit? How is that reflected in the title sequences and in advertising?
- **Up-front money.** How much is getting paid out and on what timetable?
- **Downstream money.** Deferment of fees and profit participation.
- **Overtime, meal penalties, kit fees, other up-front money.** How are these calculated?
- **Acts of God.** Who gets blamed for "stuff happens" (earthquakes, unforeseen circumstances, etc.)?
- **Dispute resolution.** How do you deal with things when they get messy? Who pays for what?
- **Termination/exit.** How do the parties gracefully (or otherwise) exit?

Beware a contract that doesn't spell these things out. In general, the more vague the contract, the more it tends to favor the more powerful party. This may sound great when you're sticking it to the cast and crew, but when the distributor hands you a two-page "basic deal" you can bet they've deliberately left things out or "fuzzied" them to the point where they're essentially meaningless.

EARLY AGREEMENTS

When you're first getting started, the world of the film consists mostly of you, the screenwriter, the director, your partner, and your investors. You may be all these people, in which case hopefully you don't need too many agreements with yourself. But hopefully, you have at least one other person involved in your film. Getting these contracts out of the way early on will prevent misunderstandings from happening down the road.

Joint Venture Agreement

This is a common story: two friends (Christine and Norman) get together to write a screenplay and make a movie. Christine will direct, Norman will produce. They get along well and the work goes smoothly. Then Norman goes to Germany for a few months on a job. Christine goes on to make the film. Which is fine, until it's time to figure out who should get the producer and screenwriter credits. Should Norman have his own producer card, even though he was only on board at the beginning? How much of the final shooting script is his? Maybe Christine feels like he shouldn't get equal credit, so she bumps him to a "story by Christine and Norman" card and they share the producer credit. Or he becomes the "co-producer."

Then a distributor comes knocking. Suddenly Norman's ears perk up. And he's not happy – with his credit, the deal, and the fact that his contribution is not being respected. Who's right?

Well, if they didn't sign a joint venture agreement – and why would they, they're friends, right? – then it's a crisis. The reader might agree with Christine's position: "Hey, I did the heavy lifting, I should get the lion's share of the credit and the profits." But what if key elements of the Norman/Christine script survived? What if Norman, prior to decamping to Germany, introduced them to their biggest investor? What if he fronted most of the development money? In theory, that money should be worth more.

I've seen this scenario play out in real life a few times. It's a mess. Usually the project implodes before it gets financed, but in a couple of cases the "invisible co-writer" showed up when there was money in the offing, and caused problems.

The remedy is to put together a joint venture agreement, that covers you and however many partners you have. You want this agreement to answer all the questions above, but also:

- **Credits.** Who gets what title card, in what position?
- **Screenwriter.** Who gets the screenwriting credit(s) and it what order?
- **Ownership.** Who owns the underlying film and/or the production company, and in what proportion?
- **Exit.** What happens to the company and/or film when one or more people exit the joint venture? Can the partners "fire" each other? In the *Caleb's Door* joint venture agreement, I believe my producer, Marilyn Horowitz, could fire me as the director under extraordinary circumstances, even though we were married at the time.

Subscription/Operating Agreements

We covered these in more detail in Chapter 3. But as soon as there's a hint of investment money coming into the project, you'll want to have these ready to go.

Screenplay Option/Purchase Agreement

If you want to produce someone else's script (written on spec, for example), you'll want to set up a writer's agreement (sometimes called a screenplay option or screenplay purchase agreement). The agreement sets up the writer's credit, title card position, the length of the option, the total option amount, the option period, the renewal process, and the ultimate purchase price.

So what is an option? Essentially, it's a method of "renting" the screenplay. Say you want to film a screenplay written by your friend Jeff named *Dangerous Indie Movie*. Jeff has no interest in or ability to help you produce the film version of his script; he'd like to get paid $10K for the script. You can't fork over $10K right now, since you have to go raise the money for the film first.

So you pay a certain amount (say $1000) *against* the ultimate purchase price of $10,000. In exchange, he takes the script off the marketplace for a specified period of time (say, 18 months).

You then scramble to raise the money for the film before the clock runs out. If you succeed, you owe him the remaining $9,000, plus whatever profit participation you've agreed to. If you fail, you (usually) can offer to renew the option for another period of time, in exchange for more money.

Once you've *purchased* the script, it belongs to the production company. Until then, you don't really own it, but you can, depending on the agreement, make changes or ask the writer to make changes.

So, a good option agreement spells out:

- **The property.** What is it you're optioning?
- **The period and price.** How long are you optioning it for, and for how much?
- **The renewal.** When can you renew, for how long, and for how much?
- **The purchase.** What is the ultimate purchase price of the script, and when is it due (first day of principal photography? In payments?)?
- **Rewrites/other writers.** Can you request changes? How about bringing in other writers? How does this affect the copyright?
- **Cancellation/extraction.** How do the parties get out of the option, and does the writer get back their original draft or the modified ones? This is stickier than it sounds.

What you're looking for as a producer is the longest option period for the lowest price. Of course, the writer is looking for the opposite. A happy medium is about 18 months – you can't realistically get a feature off the ground in less time than that unless you've got the money in hand.

Life Rights

If you're writing a true crime script or a biopic based on a public figure, you are, technically, allowed to write about anything that's in the public record (i.e. published in a court transcript, newspaper, broadcast on the news, etc.), without getting permission from the person(s) involved. Other cases are sketchier. Sometimes an heir or spouse can claim that they own the "life rights" even if the legal basis is somewhat tenuous. The truth is that if someone feels like their privacy has been violated, or that they've been made fun of or cast in a bad light, they may sue you even if they don't have a real case.

So it's usually prudent to get the cooperation of whoever you're writing about. If you're telling a story from multiple viewpoints, then you may need to contact everyone involved. Typically, "life rights" agreements work in the same way as options – you "rent" the rights for a period of time. If you don't make the film, the rights revert back to their "owner."

Hopefully, you figured this out *before* you wrote the script; but if not, now's the time to get those agreements signed, before the financing comes in.

Legal Services Agreement

Your attorney will present this to you. Essentially, it outlines what she's going to do for you, what her credit should be, and when you should pay her. Most of this you've already agreed to, hopefully. But pay attention to the scope of the work involved. If the attorney won't be coming aboard for distribution talks, now's a good time to know.

Casting Agreement

This is a type of services agreement. Essentially it spells out how long the casting period should be for, when it should start, how expenses are reimbursed, the fee, onscreen and advertisement credit, and payment schedule. One point that should be included is what happens when more casting is needed, for whatever reason, beyond the original period in the agreement. Does the casting director get more money? Is it decided on a case-by-case basis?

Assignment of Copyright

This is usually rolled into the joint venture or option agreement. It states that the writer will transfer the copyright to the production company. The production company then becomes the owner of the script.

Union Contracts

These are what the union(s) hand you to sign. They will spell out in somewhat agonizing detail what the rates are for their members under your agreement, how much the fringes should be, what paperwork is due at what point in the process, what the other charges are (meal penalties, overtime, turnaround invasion, per diems, etc.), and the residual percentages, if any.

There's not a lot of wiggle room with these contracts. About the only thing you can ask to change is the size of the bond, if one is required.

SAG will also give you a one-page blank memo to fill out and hand out to each actor. The memo, called a "Screen Actors Guild Employment of XX Performer" Contract (XX = Day or Week), specifies the production company, actor, the SAG agreement, the start date for that actor, and his/her role in the film. You'll want to print out three copies of this contract per actor, sign them, and have the actor sign them. One copy stays with the actor, one stays with you, and the last one goes back to SAG. Copies go to the actor's agent and the payroll company.

Payroll Services Agreement

As with the union contract, this is something that the payroll company will give you to fill out and sign. It specifies how much their fees are and what the deposit arrangement is (do you have to put in the entire payroll up-front, or just a portion of it, or do you wire money every week?). You may have to provide some personal information on the managing members of the LLC (your addresses and contact information) – this is so the company can come after you if you default or bounce a check on the payroll.

PRODUCTION CONTRACTS

These you'll want to have ready before the first day of production, if possible. You don't want to be in the awkward position of chasing people down after the shoot.

Product Placement Agreement

Product placement is a way for studio films to make money. Characters walk into FedEx, drink Coke or Red Bull, wolf down McBurgers … you get the idea. These companies have legions of lawyers waiting to pounce on a film that depicts their products in a bad light, or in some cases that didn't seek their permission before using the product onscreen so blatantly. Disney is known for being very protective of depictions of Mickey and other characters in non-Disney films.

If you're shooting a scene outdoors, where there are advertisements and brand logos every-where, you don't need to go chasing after each company as long as your two characters don't start a knife fight in front of a giant McDonald's logo. If you're shooting a scene in a bar, chances are that you'll be fine unless you focus specifically on a particular bottle (or the bartender throws said bottle at someone).

On the other hand, you may *want* to seek out a product placement or similar agreement if your story specifically calls for it. A typical example is if your hero works at a fast-food restaurant. Sometimes you can get McDonald's to let you shoot in their restaurants and feature their logo, but it can take a while.

Usually, the big companies will be the ones presenting *you* with a contract. Make sure your attorney looks at it, because these can be a bit difficult to read. What you want to know is whether they want some editorial say in the final product (often they don't care).

Typically these companies aren't really looking to pay much for product placement in indie features, but they may give you coupons or discounts, or promise to promote the film in some way. One thing you *don't want* to do is approach a company after the film has been shot.

Crew Deal Memos

If your film is an IA, DGA, and/or SAG shoot, this should be a fairly short contract, since most of the terms are covered in the contract (see above) between you and the union. On the other hand, if your film is a non-union shoot, you'll have four versions of this contract. Each one should specify:

Day rate. What is the person being paid per day?

Deferments. If you're deferring the crewperson's salary, when is the deferment payable? From first monies in, or when the investors are paid back their initial money, or out of the producer's share of the profits?

Work for hire. This is *very important*. This clause states that anything that the crewperson does is considered the intellectual and/or physical property of the production company. Otherwise, the costume designer, production designer, and DP could all claim that anything they made or shot on the film was their own work, merely loaned to the production. This doesn't come up often but it can be an occasional sticking point.

You can carve out exceptions. If the costume designer makes a dress or the production designer a prop that they could use on another shoot (or would like to keep as a showpiece) which would only go into storage otherwise, you could specify that they can keep the item, as long as the production company can use it for reshoots. If it's a very specific item (like a monster prosthetic), you can have them keep it but promise not to use it on another film for a period of time.

Credit. What is the person's role, and where in the (front or end) credits will it appear?

Cancelled call. If the crewperson is given less than 24 hours' notice that they're not required the next day, or are asked to "hold" certain days in their schedule, are they owed a salary? This is sometimes called the "hold/blackout" clause.

Minimum call. What is the shortest "day," and are half-days allowed?

Turnaround. What is the turnaround between days?

Travel time. Is it on the clock, does it count towards turnaround, and/or where does the "clock" start (usually a 30-mile radius from a central point)? If you're shooting in a distant location and everyone's staying in a hotel, does the travel time from the hotel to set count as "on the clock" or not?

Meal breaks. This defines what a meal is. We'll talk about this in more detail below.

Petty cash/reimbursements. How are these handled? Who authorizes the crewperson to spend money?

Termination. Under what circumstances would the crewperson be terminated (alcohol/drug use on set, sexual harassment, etc.)? What is the procedure for termination?

Disputes. What is the recourse for the two parties in case of a problem?

Copy. Each person who works on your film should get a copy of it. This clause defines when that happens and in what format. You generally don't want to hand out copies of the film until it's commercially available. If someone wants scenes for their reel, however, you should make those available as soon as you can.

On top of these clauses, each of the four subtypes will have additional information:

1. The **OT contract** will define overtime and meal penalties. Most of your crew will fall under this contract.
2. The **non-OT contract** will leave these items out. Your PAs, production staff, editor, sound designer/editor, still photographer, EPK crew, post visual effects folks, colorist/conformist, and location staff will fall under this contract. Some people give these to the production

designer and costume designer as well, but I usually give them the OT contract since they're doing so many jobs.

3. The **deluxe contract** is a customized variant of either the OT or non-OT contract, that includes tickets to a premiere, profit participation (in the form of points, usually), what formats are acceptable for the crew copy, and/or whether the credits appear in paid advertising. Certain key crewmembers will get one of these. The DP will usually want the best copy possible of the film for making her reel (ProRes or DNxHD files are acceptable, with Blu-Ray or DigiBeta a second choice). The costume designer, editor, sound designer, production designer, DP, composer, and special effects artist will usually get a credit in the "billing block" section of the poster, one-sheet, or other advertisement.

4. The **union contract** is a variant of the OT or deluxe contract, that basically says "refer to the IA or DGA contract" for just about everything except for the credit.

It *is* possible that you'll have a mixed crew – you could have an IA crew but a non-DGA production staff, or (less commonly) vice versa. In those cases you'll need all four types of contracts.

Meals Defined

I've probably spent at least as much time on this part of the deal memo as I have on the entire rest of it. In your crew contract you have to distinguish between several different types of meals, and how they impact the schedule.

Breakfast is usually considered a courtesy. I try to leave a little leeway when it comes to what should be *for* breakfast – for example, if we're shooting nights, the crew may not want a hot "breakfast" but would be just as happy with sandwiches. Breakfast is commonly served at or before the call time, and is served without a formal line or sit-down. If you're on a distant location, breakfast is often somewhere else (like at the hotel).

First meal or lunch falls into two broad categories: walkaway and catered. First meal should always be called no earlier than three but no later than six hours after the call time. Typically, you take breaks every six hours.

A **walkaway lunch** is where the crew is given a set amount of money and literally "walks away" to wherever they want to eat. They're given 60 to 70 minutes to eat and come back. The first hour of a walkaway is off the clock.

A **catered lunch** is where the crew stays put and the lunch comes to them. This type of lunch follows the "last-man-through rule." Once lunch is called, the cast and crew lines up to eat. Once the last OT-eligible employee gets her food and sits down, whoever's watching the line calls "last man" and the clock stops for 30 minutes. After 30 minutes, the crew is "back in" (back on the clock).

If I'm driving the crew to a restaurant, I usually consider that a walkaway. If the restaurant is more than a few minutes away, then I usually call the crew back on the clock after one hour, so part of their lunch break is paid for.

Second meal is called six hours after the crew is back in from first meal. Second meal is usually on the clock, since at this point you're in overtime. Each crewmember gets 15 minutes to stop work and eat. There's no last-man-through rule, but each person's 15-minute break may begin at a slightly different time.

Meal penalties apply to first and second meal, but not breakfast. So if breakfast is late, the crew can't claim to "be in penalty."

Grace is a mechanism whereby meal penalties can be waived for fifteen minutes, if you're in the middle of a camera setup or trying to wrap up for the day. You *have* to ask for grace before the meal is due, and the crew has to agree (more on this below). If you go past fifteen minutes, meal penalties start retroactively. The deal memo usually specifies how many times grace can be called during a work week, and for which meals (usually you get two graces for first meal and two for second). Graces can't be planned.

Per diems/dinner. If you're shooting on a distant location, you either have to feed the crew or give them a set amount of money to buy dinner with. If you're providing them with dinner you *don't* have to give them their per diem. Dinner is off the clock.

No fast food. Sometimes, the crew will ask for specific provisions in the meal section – such as a "no pizza/fast food/Chinese" clause. I'll usually agree to this for first meal, but not for second.

Cast Deal Memo

If you've signed up with SAG for your shoot, they'll give you the aforementioned one-page "Agreement" between you and the individual cast members. You *must* collect this from each of your cast members, ideally before the end of the first week of payroll.

What's left out of that agreement is a whole host of issues that you, the actor, and the actor's manager/agent will want to iron out before the shoot starts. So you'll usually end up typing up a separate "Cast Deal Memo" that refers back to the SAG agreement, but will also include:

Start date. This is specified in the SAG agreement but I usually put it in here as well, prefaced by "on or about," which gives me 24 hours of flexibility in either direction.

Minimum guarantee. Agents will usually want you to put in the minimum number of shooting days and the shooting period you'll need their client for. Always underestimate the guarantee (unless it's one day, obviously).

Pay rate. This is usually the SAG minimum, but if you're going non-SAG or intend to pay above the scale rate, you'd indicate this.

Credit order. Where does their name appear in the cast "billing"? You'll want a little flexibility here – you can specify "no later than X position" – but generally there's a definite order, at least for the leads.

Title card. The leads will want their own title card. You'll usually have to specify that the font, duration, and visibility of their credit will be no different from anyone else in the cast who's getting a single title card. Supporting actors who are getting a front cast credit will prefer that you don't jam it in with twenty other cast members.

Travel/hotel arrangements. If you're bringing in someone from out of town, the agent may want you to put them up at a certain "class" of hotel, with their own room, internet access, and phone. They may also want you to state in the contract what class of flight they'll be taking. Often, they'll also state that if one of the cast is flying first class, everyone else gets to as well.

Favored nations. This basically states that all the actors are being treated equally – not that everyone is paid the same amount, but that no one actor's trailer, dressing room, travel/hotel, or any other conditions will be better or worse than any other.

Profit participation. This can range all over the map. The agent will want a percentage based on the gross reported earnings. Do *not* agree to this. You have no control over what's reported, and by the time the "gross" earnings get back to you (i.e. the exhibitor, distributor, sales agent, and whoever else gets their cut) you could end up owing the actor more than you're receiving. A better solution is to offer some of your producer's points.

Sensitive/nude scenes. If you're asking the actor to take their clothes off, you'll need to specify whether there will be a closed set, what the conditions of the nudity are (how much do we see?), whether a nude (body) double will be used, and also whether the actor can use a covering of some kind (a nude suit, sheet, mini-panties, and/or sock to cover certain areas).

Checks. Who should the check go out to? The agent will usually request that checks be sent to them, so they can deduct their 10 percent before passing it to the actor. In some cases, I've been asked to write in the escrow account name and bank.

Looping. I usually ask for a day of ADR/looping from the leads, if needed. If I can get away with it, I'll ask that it be for free if it's four hours or less.

If you're a non-SAG shoot, you may have to spell out the overtime and meal penalty provisions as well; you can usually borrow the applicable sections from the non-union OT crew contracts for this.

Note: if yours is a SAG shoot, your cast is not obligated to sign anything except for the one-page SAG cast agreement. But I've only witnessed one case where an actor refused to sign their deal memo, since it spelled out all the other things that were missing from the cast agreement.

Location Agreement

This you should get from your location owner by the time you hand over the deposit check. It should state, in as plain language as possible, how many days you're renting the location for (including prep and wrap days), for how much money, and how the location and/or the owner should be credited in the film.

Some owners will want you to add a clause wherein the location name will *not* appear in the film. For example, if you're shooting a scene in a hospital wherein one of the characters dies, the administration of the real hospital you're shooting in will probably want to keep their name from appearing anywhere on the screen.

Some owners will also want you to indicate the production company's level of liability in case of damage to the property – that you'll at least cover the insurance minimums if something breaks.

Last, you'll want to make sure that if things go awry – if the owner changes his mind – that you're not still on the hook for the rest of the fee.

Keep the location agreement short. I can't emphasize this enough. Most owners are busy people, who are doing you a service. If they see an agreement longer than two pages they're going to get scared or annoyed: scared because they'll think you have something to hide, or that the shoot will be bigger than you'd told them; annoyed because you're making them read something long, boring, and written in legalese.

Appearance Release Form

This is for extras. This gives the production company the right to use someone's likeness in the film. This could apply to someone who's featured only in a still photograph or poster within the film, as well as someone who walked by the camera. Usually there's no fee involved, but if there is, that will be indicated in the release form as well.

Ideally, anyone who shows up on camera (apart from the cast) should sign one of these. This protects you down the road from a possible lawsuit. If you use your crew as extras, you will also want to either incorporate some kind of likeness rights release into their deal memo, or get them to sign one of these.

In *theory*, if someone isn't identifiable – if they're out of focus in the deep background, or just passing by with their head away from the camera – then you don't need a release form from them. If you're shooting in a private space, then you should get a signed release from anyone who passes by the camera or at least whose face is in focus. If you're shooting in a public space, then the rules get a little muddier. Generally, the presumption of privacy in public spaces is more circumscribed, so you may not need to get a release form.

You can also make up sandwich-board-style signs and post them in front of the area that's on camera. Make sure that the sign says, in big, readable type, that there's a film being shot on this stretch of road/sidewalk/area of the buildings, and that anyone who passes by the sign is agreeing to be photographed. Whether this sign has any real legal standing is up for debate, but at least you've warned people.

Make the release short, never more than one page long. And make a version for minors. This version will read just like the regular one, but it will include a signature line for the parent or guardian.

Vendor Services Agreement

This covers a broad spectrum of contracts between the production company and a vendor. Most equipment rental houses have a one-page short-form that you'll sign when you check out the gear, basically holding your company liable for missing and damaged goods, and authorizing them to extract payment by credit card. You may, however, want to write up a more complete contract if you're dealing with a post house, sound designer, music studio, or special effects house that's not just renting you gear, but providing a special service for the film. This agreement should include:

- **Delivery.** What is the vendor delivering? For a sound designer, this could be the ProTools session files or just the audio track files. What format (tape, file, DVD) will the final product be delivered on?
- **Services provided.** What is in the scope of the agreement? For the sound designer, this could include audio editing and a "temp" mix, or a full design, mix, and printmaster.
- **Expenses.** Who approves expenses and what's covered?
- **Out-of-scope work.** What happens when you need them to do something that isn't in the original agreement? How are any additional fees calculated?
- **Dates.** This is a rough estimate of when the work will start, and when certain milestones are due.

POST CONTRACTS

While ideally you'd like to get these squared away before you start shooting, the truth is that you may have so much on your plate that you can't get to them until post. I'll be going over music and media licenses in more detail, because this causes a *lot* of confusion among independent filmmakers.

Media Rights in General

There are basically two types of media in the world of your film: media that you've created or own (because it was created for hire); and media that you're licensing from another entity. Media in this broad sense includes music, still photographs, artwork, clips from other films/TV episodes/news pieces/stock archives, and your film itself.

Anytime you include a piece of media in your film that your company doesn't own, you have to *demonstrate that you have the right to use it.* This is the case no matter how briefly the media is onscreen (or heard), even if the media item is free, in the public domain, or falls under the fair use doctrine (where you're using the video/audio/still/text to make a rhetorical point).

If you have something in your film that you don't own, *and* you can't prove that you have the right to use it, no distributor will touch your film. They don't want to expose themselves to a potential lawsuit.

So, first you should make sure that any media that the crew, cast, vendors, etc. produced for the film belongs to the production company. Your crew, cast, and vendor deal memos, and whatever agreements exist between the company and the screenwriter, should accomplish this.

Your EPK's behind-the-scenes footage, whatever your DP shoots or your production mixer records, any signs or graphics your production designer creates, or effects work your VFX artist produces – all of it should belong to the company outright. In addition, the composer and musician agreements should include a "work-for-hire" provision.

It gets a little trickier with the composer agreement, however, because there are actually two sets of rights: synchronization and master rights.

Music Rights – in More Detail

Music is actually two separate things: the composition (think of sheet music), and the recording (the track on the CD).

The *synchronization rights* apply to the underlying composition. The *master rights* apply to a specific *recording* of that composition. You need to secure both sets of rights in order to use a piece of music in your film. And finding out who owns which rights is more complicated than it first appears.

Most musicians are broke, particularly at the beginning of their careers, so they sign away their compositions for an upfront fee, plus the promise of some royalties, to a publishing company. The record label that's putting out their songs usually owns the recordings. However, sometimes the label owns both; sometimes the artist owns both; sometimes the artist's heirs own one or the other; sometimes – if there are multiple writers on a song – you have to track down multiple owners. If the music was created for another film, it's possible that the record label owns the synchronization rights, but the production company for that film owns the master rights.

This is why a musician is often the last person you want to ask for permission to use a song in your film. Even if they like you or the script and want to help, the best they can often do is point you in the direction of who they sold the rights to. And those catalogs are tradable commodities – the small label that used to own his recording of "My Great Song" was bought by Sony, so now you have to deal with Sony. And the publishing company that he sold the synch rights to went bankrupt a few years ago. During the resulting auction, the company's song catalog was sold off piecemeal to a bunch of companies … good luck finding that.

Generally, the synch license and master license will cost the same amount of money. More popular tunes are more expensive. There's no real standard rate. That's why producers hire a rights clearance supervisor, whose sole job is to figure out who owns what, and license it from them.

What about classical music or early twentieth-century scores that are in the public domain (John Philip Sousa, anyone)? Well, the synchronization rights won't cost you anything, but if you want to use a particular recording of Bach's "Unaccompanied Cello Suite No. 1" – say, Yo Yo Ma's awesome version – you'll have to pay the master rights.

On the other hand, you could license the synch rights to a song (such as Led Zeppelin's "Rain Song") but then hire a bunch of starving musicians to record it. Part of your agreement with the musicians is that you own the recording. This is legitimate as well.

Composer Agreement

This is basically a lot like a vendor services agreement, except that you're contracting a composer to create a score for your film. Typically, the production company owns the master recording (and consequently the master rights), while the composer owns the compositions, and thus the synch rights. Usually, the composer is restricted from re-recording the score for another project in any way without permission, for a period of three to five years. The composer also gets royalties for any soundtrack album or single that may come out down the road.

Typically, the composer agreement will include a clause that specifies that any musicians he hires to complete the score will be working on a for-hire basis. However, it's sometimes necessary (as in the Led Zeppelin example above) to contract out the musicians individually.

Musician Agreement

This functions in much the same way as a standard crew deal memo. The musicians are working for a fee (or free or deferred pay), and are producing a work that you own the master recording to. This is different from the composer agreement in that the musicians are only playing music, not composing it. The minute they start making up tunes, they become composers. The composer often handles these contracts on his/her own, but you may be involved as well.

"Royalty-Free" Music

Some musicians put together libraries of basic tracks, loops, or complete songs, and license them for a one-time fee. Essentially, this is the same thing as licensing the synch and master rights for any other song, except you're dealing with the artist herself.

More Fun with Licenses: Step Deals

When you actually get a license agreement from a record label or publishing company, or the artist (if he still owns his own material), you should expect what's called a "step deal." The idea is that, rather than expect payment for the rights up front, you'll be allowed to pay smaller fees in exchange for limited use of the material. So the ultimate fee depends on what "step" up the commercial ladder you end up. For example, to play in a festival you'll be expected to pay $2000 for a song ($1K for the synch and $1K for the recording), but if you get a theatrical distribution deal you'll have to fork over another $10,000. Perhaps if you only release on DVD you'll have to pay $7,000.

Beware these deals, and beware a company that doesn't want to spell out what the "steps" are and the corresponding fees. Labels love putting filmmakers over a barrel because they figure that at the point you're ready to release the film, you'll pay just about whatever they ask – if you don't you have to yank the music out, put new tracks in, remix, and do all that in time for the delivery deadline

Other Types of Media Rights

If you needed a shot of an airplane taking off but didn't get one, you can approach an online company (such as FootageFirm.com) that specializes in fixed-fee footage, where you put down a one-time payment in exchange for the right to use that wonderful airplane shot they have in your film.

On the other hand, you may need to use a clip from another film or TV show. You'll have to track down who owns the media. This can be tricky. The producer of the film or show may have been working for hire for a distributor or network. Or the producers sold the intellectual property rights to another company years ago. Typically, you'll be dealing with a distributor or network first, and the producers second. Expect a long wait. With enough persistence they may eventually give you a contract giving you permission to use the clip in your film, for a fee. You may encounter the step-fee situation that I mentioned earlier.

Believe it or not, you may even have to get permission to display a painting, photo, or sculpture prominently in your film. Tracking down who owns the painting (if the artist isn't alive any more) can also be a bit of a pain.

Some artwork and clips are available through the public domain or under creative commons licenses. The alternative is to shoot the clip footage or create the artwork as part of the production.

Fair Use

Fair use doctrine is woefully misunderstood by many filmmakers. Technically, it's an exception to copyright law, which allows you to use media you don't own in your film, for the purposes of commentary, criticism, teaching, research, and/or news reporting. A specific example is if a piece of music is playing in the background while a reporter is recording a story for television. Or if you're shooting a review show and you want to use clips of the film as part of the review. Or if you're trying to incorporate other clips into your documentary's story.

The truth is that copyright owners, particularly big companies, will find any chink in your armor that they can get at to avoid "giving away" their media. The application of the law is a mess. Most works of fiction won't pass the above tests, and even documentaries run into trouble sometimes. So be careful about falling back on the fair use doctrine.

Proceed with Caution

Sita Sings the Blues is a wonderful film that was written, directed, and animated by Nina Paley single-handedly over a period of years. I saw it at Tribeca Film Festival in 2008. The multi-level plot cuts between a retelling of the story of Rama and Sita from the Indian epic *Ramayana* using the music of Annette Hanshaw (a jazz singer from the 1920s–30s); a running commentary on the story by several Indians; and Nina's own experience of heartbreak. It's a labor of love. It's everything that independent film should be – genre-defying, personal yet universal, unique. And it almost got killed.

The music *recordings* of Annette Hanshaw that constitute the heart of the film were in the public domain, but the underlying *compositions* were owned by a number of companies and individuals, who first charged her about $500 per song just for a festival deal, and then collectively wanted to rake her over the coals for upwards of $220K for a commercial distribution deal. That was more than the budget of the film! And replacing the music would not only have been expensive, but wouldn't have worked creatively at all. Nina ended up having to take out a loan for $50K for a step deal, so she could distribute the film for free or on DVD. She has since figured out how to make some money on the film through donations, merchandising, and alternative distribution. But she can't distribute the film in certain commercial venues or on television except under specific conditions. Nina Paley is a talented, intelligent person, and has been an animator and director for many years. And she still got snagged in the quagmire of music rights.

An alternate story is the equally wonderful (but very different) horror movie *Bubba Ho-tep* directed by Don Coscarelli. The main character is Elvis Presley. Yes, that's right. The story is about how many years ago, sick of the pressures of stardom, he switched places with one of his own impersonators. Then he fell on stage during one of his "impersonation" acts, and is now stuck in a rest home that's being terrorized by an evil deity from ancient Egypt.

Throughout this film, you will not hear a single piece of Elvis music. The director got the composer to score the film, and particularly the "impersonation" scenes, in an "Elvis style." The director was very forthright on the DVD commentary – he couldn't afford the fees. So he came up with a creative alternative. No one I've spoken to about the film (which is more than you'd think) have ever noticed the lack of Elvis music, until I pointed it up to them.

DISTRIBUTION AGREEMENTS

I actually won't be talking much about these. First, unless you're lucky enough to get a true pre-sales agreement, you're probably going into production without distribution in place. Second, explaining the ins and outs of distribution would take up its own book.

Typically, the distributor comes to you with the distribution agreement, which your attorney will (hopefully) vet and request changes to. This agreement is really a rights licensing contract, except that your production company is licensing certain rights under certain conditions (medium, territory, and/or timeframe) to the distributor, in exchange for some kind of fee (typically paid out of profits but sometimes upfront).

The first thing you'll want to check is the *time period* of the contract. You don't want to sign away your rights forever.

What rights are you licensing? If the distributor is a DVD company, you want to hold onto your streaming and theatrical rights. If the distributor is a TV network, do you license away your VOD rights as well (it *might* make sense, or not)?

What territories are covered by the agreement: worldwide, a particular country or region?

What is the timeframe for each right being licensed? Some producers feel that a film should be available in all media on the same day ("day and date"). Distributors often object to this, since it makes their distribution channel less "special" and possibly costs them money. This is a key reason why studio films are still usually available in theaters first.

What is the delivery schedule and deliverables list? Do you have to make copies of the film in several formats (Blu-Ray masters, DVD masters, DigiBeta, 35mm)? Do you have to cut a trailer? Do they expect the ProTools sound sessions? Do you have to re-edit the credits for their logo? Hopefully, you budgeted for most of these deliverables items before you shot the film.

What is the payment schedule? Is there an up-front advance or fee on the table?

Distributors will ideally want a vague contract that gives them many rights, for as long as possible, throughout the world, for low to no cost. You, on the other hand, will be looking for a specific agreement, will want to hold onto as many rights as possible, and will want some kind of money up front. Whether you can get this or not is difficult to say, but don't expect a lot of wiggle room.

Assumption Agreement

When you sign up with SAG, you'll get a huge packet of forms, including the assumption agreement. The distributor is supposed to sign this, stating that they will assume the responsibility for adhering to the royalty terms in the agreement that you signed with SAG. SAG can then chase after the distributor rather than you for royalty payments or other monies owed them.

Many distributors don't want to sign the agreement. SAG stresses that you *can't* sign a distribution agreement without the distributor signing the assumption agreement. You, the producer, are at the bottom of this particular pile, caught between a rock and a hard place.

What do you do? Sign the distribution agreement. SAG can still try to go after the distributor, and will not be likely to penalize you, because they know that you're in a tight situation.

CONCLUSIONS

Your head is probably swimming. You now know more about contracts than you ever wanted to. What sucks is that, most of the time, the contracts are unnecessary, like insurance. They add no production value to the film directly, and burn a lot of brain power.

But if you don't deal with them now, during preproduction, you could end up with a film that can't be distributed at all. And while I've presented these contracts to you all at once, you don't have to deal with them all at once. Many of them may not be relevant – if you're a solo writer/producer/director, then you don't need a joint venture or option agreement. If you're hiring a composer to write all your music, you can avoid the music licensing search. And so on.

QUESTIONS/EXERCISES

1. Who wrote the script for the film? Did you? Or did you option it from someone else?
2. Who else is involved in your film at a "top level" (producer, executive producer, or director)? Do you have a joint venture agreement with them?
3. Do you have any nude scenes in your film? Talk to the director about how much/how little should be onscreen.
4. Are there specific musical cues referenced in the script? Do you have any scenes where the television is on in the background?
5. Do you have any big crowd scenes in your film?

## Chapter 15

Casting

FIGURE 15.1 Casting.

If the script is the blueprint for a film, then the cast are the support beams. A good cast can't save a bad script, but they can smooth over the rough patches on a good but imperfect one. They can strengthen and focus the subtext, and reveal layers in the story that the screenwriter probably wasn't aware of. A good performance can rip you out of yourself and make you forget you're watching a movie. Bad casting, however, points up the flaws in the script. Weak performances remind the audience that they're watching a film.

It's easy to blame actors – and in Hollywood, A-list actors can sometimes make rather bad choices that they only have themselves (and their management) to blame for. However, the bulk of the "credit" for bad casting has to go to the director and producer, especially at the independent film level. Either the director didn't communicate what she was looking for in the role, or the producer pushed too hard for a minor "name" that wasn't right, or both.

It doesn't have to be this way. In Chapter 8, we went over the director's side of the casting process, and touched on the budgeting aspects of casting in Chapter 10. Now it's time to look at the process from both perspectives.

THE CASTING PROCESS

Casting is a series of steps taken over the course of a few months which sometimes repeat and loop back on each other. I've summarized the process in a flowchart (Figure 15.2).

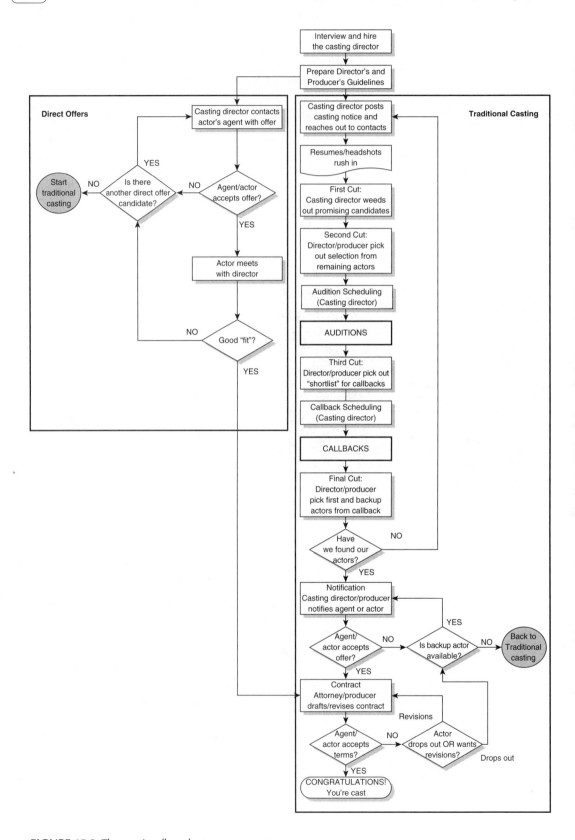

FIGURE 15.2 The casting flowchart.

As you can see, there's more going on than just what happens in the casting sessions – in fact, the majority of your time will be spent preparing documents, reviewing work, and waiting for agents and actors. What's less obvious is how long this can take. Unless you already have your actors picked out, this process can take several months. On *Found In Time*, I started the casting process in April (when I first met the casting director), and we finished casting a week before the shoot in September. This was in part due to some circumstances outside our control – we had to switch out a lead actor due to a scheduling conflict – but this is not an atypical amount of time to spend on the process.

Let's go through the "big" steps as outlined above.

Finding Casting Directors

Do you want to cast the film yourself, or hire a casting director? I would argue strongly in favor of hiring a casting director. If you're on a low budget, you can often get someone who's been a casting assistant for a long time, but who's looking to move up the ladder. Artistic directors for theater companies, theater and comedy troupe directors, and even other film directors are possibilities as well.

Doing the casting yourself will just about double your workload. Between sifting through the thousands (I'm not kidding) of resumes and headshots you'll get, to scheduling all the actors and then reworking the schedule as they cancel or want a different timeslot, calling them back in, and dealing with the hundreds if not thousands of emails, texts, and phone calls you're going to get, will put you very far behind on the rest of your work. I've helped out with the casting on *Windows* and on several short films, and it just about killed me.

Beyond the work, though, what you really need is another *perspective*. Especially if you're the writer/producer/director, you may have a very strong idea of who you want. But your ideas may not ultimately be grounded in reality, or they may be a bit ossified from having been in your brain too long (you've probably been working on your film for a couple of years at this point). A good casting director is both well-organized *and* creative.

So assuming that I've convinced you that you need a casting director, where do you find one? This is where your connections list (see Chapter 11) and your war council (Chapter 3) will come in handy. You want to generate two lists: casting directors you can get to through connections, and those whose work you admire but may have no "in" with. This second list should be populated with people who you've seen on IMDbPro attached to films that are similar to yours in terms of budget and genre. Or perhaps you've noticed that they keep casting a particular actor that you would like to get on board.

Do some research before you make contact. I recommend starting up a spreadsheet or to-do list that looks something like Table 15.1.

Look for patterns in their credits. Do they each work with a particular set of actors? Who seems to like films in your genre? Do they have a history of working with first-time directors and producers? If you have *any* information on the budgets of other films they've worked on, this could also give you a sense of their price range.

TABLE 15.1 Casting directors

Name	Credits	Producer	Director	Cast	Was Assistant to?	Recommended by	Contact Info	Status

Also, see if they've worked as an assistant for someone else on your list. This would imply that they may still talk to each other. Also, look at addresses (if available) – if two people on your list share the same address, they may actually work for the same office. In these situations, carefully pick out which person you want to call during your first round. You're trying to make the casting director feel that you want him or her, not just anyone. If they hear that you're calling a lot of other people, they won't feel so special, will they?

Then start working your way down both lists. Limit yourself to a few people at a time (somewhere between five and six). I recommend calling instead of emailing because unless you already know the person, your email could end up in their spam folder. In your call, you want to pitch the project, discuss your background a bit, and tell the casting director *why* you're calling her instead of a million other people – was she recommended to you or do you admire the casting on a particular film or show? This is a lot of information to convey in a short amount of time.

Your main limitations at this point are your shoot dates, your script, your budget, and how much of it you've raised to date. The script may not appeal to all of your candidates. You may not be able to afford everyone on your list. And your dates may conflict with other projects that the casting director has going on.

Most casting directors will want to know what your budget is, whether you've raised the funds or not, and what your plans are for the film. Be honest. If you're hoping that you can raise most of the money by casting a "name," say so. If they have any level of experience at all they've seen this kind of situation before. However, you do need to reassure them that you have enough money to at least pay a retainer. At this point, a few casting directors will drop out. Send the script to whoever's left, along with your bios. If you've already prepared a director's cast breakdown and/or producer's cast list and schedule, mention that fact but don't send them automatically. You may just be giving them more work to do. On the other hand, some casting directors may want to see what the director or producer has in mind.

So out of a list of about 10 casting directors, you can expect possibly half will pass. Out of the remaining five, you'll have to negotiate the main points:

1. Their fee
2. The casting schedule (how long, how many parts)
3. The "name" game

The fee. There's no set fee for casting directors, even among union films. Some will want a percentage of the budget. Others will want a weekly or monthly rate. Some will be willing to work on a deferment, in exchange for a credit. During the budgeting phase, I typically put in a percentage of the budget, anywhere from 2 to 5 percent.

Also, what does the fee cover? The casting space? An assistant? Copies/DVDs/taping the auditions? Make sure to bring these points up early on, so that there are no misunderstandings. On an indie film, I typically budget the casting space rental, copies, audition tapes, and sides copying separately from the casting director's fee. You probably can't afford to pay a casting assistant on a film with a budget of $500K or less, but you should at least consider hiring an intern. Depending on the size of your cast, it may be too much for one person to coordinate everything.

The schedule. I'd say that casting takes a *minimum* of six weeks. That's if you get lucky and there are no snafus, the agents don't screw up, and you find everyone you want in the first round. I'd budget for more time if possible, understanding that the casting director won't be needed every day of that period.

The "name" game. If you're looking to snag a "name" for your film, you'll need to either extend the casting period out to allow for the agent/manager grind, or take a "join or die" approach. I'll illustrate both methods later on in this chapter. Extending the casting period may mean offering a larger retainer (or multiple retainers, if the process stretches on for a long time). The "join or die" approach will probably save you some aggravation and money but you may have to settle for a "non-name" actor, so you'll have to go through the traditional casting steps. Also, your casting director may want some additional consideration for opening up her rolodex – an associate producer credit, or a bonus if the actor accepts the part. These are fair requests and should be taken seriously, especially if the actor is the key to your financing.

One thing to remember about the "name" game is that you can't put it all on the casting director. If you're a first-time writer/director/producer with a limited track record, unless you already have an "in" with a "name" actor, your casting director will have very limited pull. Even if your script has gotten some real attention (if it's been to the Sundance Screenwriter's Lab, for example), or you have some actual money in the bank ($1M or so), the likelihood of someone attaching themselves to your project is very low. Your casting director will not necessarily be able to change that.

Interview with a Casting Director

At this point, you're probably down to about 20–30 percent of the names you started out with. The next step is to meet them and see if you get along. During this interview, listen as much as possible instead of speaking. Find out how they feel about the story, and the characters. Does it ring true? Do they have some ideas for who might be a good fit for some of the parts? You might want to ask them about the supporting roles – what do they think of the characters? A good casting director takes all the roles seriously, because even a small part, if badly cast, can bring the whole film to a stop.

Once you've nailed down the details and assuming everyone still likes each other, you'll want to hit up your attorney for the casting director agreement (see Chapter 14 for more details on this). Congratulations! You've hired your casting director.

At this point, your next decision is to either go after "name" actors, or go through the traditional casting method. We'll cover the "name" actor (offer-only) approach later on.

What Are You Looking For?

The first thing you'll want to do is give your casting director a "day-out-of-days" (a list of who's working on what days, and for how many, in total, according to your idealized schedule), a preliminary cast breakdown, and a "dream cast list." You'll also want to separate out your leads from your supporting and day-player roles, and decide how to handle the latter.

On *Found In Time*, I had a total of 17 speaking roles. Of these, eight were leads, two were supporting children, and the rest were supporting adults. We decided to focus on the eight leads and the two kids, and cast the remaining adult roles from among the close contestants for the leads. If your cast is smaller and/or you only have a few supporting players, you may decide that you should audition everyone.

During the *first-cut* phase, the casting director does most of the legwork – getting headshots and resumes, throwing out the ones that don't match what you've specified (you'd be surprised at how a lot of people *don't read* the breakdowns, and just apply for everything), and organizing the remainder for you to look at. Depending on the arrangements you've made, the casting director may handle all the first-round auditions, or the director, producer, and casting director may do them together.

When you're looking at the first-cut choices, you of course want to see if the person fits your "vision" as the director. But you need to look at the actor from a producer's perspective as well. Specifically, what you're hoping to find is someone who fits into one or more of these categories:

1. **The rising star** – someone who's been in a few things who might break out. Consider that by the time your film is done, you will hopefully be in a position to ride that name recognition. On *Rock the Paint*, the lead actor, Doug Smith, had just wrapped the first season of HBO's *Big Love* series. By the time *Rock* was ready for distribution, the *Big Love* gig was "big enough" so that a few distributors took notice.

2. **The fan fave** – someone who might have a built-in following – he's been in a bunch of indie films or shows up in genre films a lot. Or she did something early in her career that people still remember. Some actors build their entire careers out of being "scream queens" in horror films, or "second stringers" on dramas. These folks may not have enough "name" juice to ring out to financiers or distributors, but they can help you connect to a new audience.

3. **The steady workhorse** – someone who works a lot, and preferably for the same group of people. This is an indicator that they're reliable and won't flake if they commit to your project.

You may have to do a little digging – IMDb doesn't always tell the whole story. You may have to hit up the websites of the official films, or ask the casting director if they've heard about the actor in question. This can be a huge amount of work, so prioritize – start with the director's "A" choices and work your way down.

Scheduling Auditions

Once you've picked out your audition candidates, it's time to start scheduling them. I recommend putting together a mix of audition "blocks" – some evening, weekend, and maybe a weekday session. This gives everyone a chance to come in (a lot of actors have odd jobs, so a weekday slot may be easier for them than a weekend or evening).

How much time should you set aside for the total audition process? That's mostly a matter of math. Auditions are typically 10 minutes long each. You will probably end up seeing an average of five people per hour. Either someone will run over or cancel, or you'll need to take a short break. If you already know how many candidates you're looking at across all the roles, you can arrive at the total audition schedule:

$$(\text{Total candidates} \times 10 \text{ minutes})/(60 \text{ minutes}) = \text{Total hours of auditions}$$
$$+ 10 \text{ percent "break time"} = \text{Total hours to be scheduled}$$

Table 15.2 will make this more concrete. These are generic figures, and you may not have to deal with this many, candidates to begin with, especially for the supporting roles. But this gives you some idea of what kind of time commitment you're looking at.

I recommend that you *don't* schedule back-to-back 8-hour casting sessions unless you have no alternative. By the end of the second day your eyeballs and ears will be bleeding and you will have absolutely no way to judge any of the auditions. Space them out a little bit. If you do have to do non-stop auditions, take a longer lunch break.

TABLE 15.2 Calculating hours needed for auditioning

Type	Characters	Candidates Per Role	Total Candidates	Total Hours (@ 10 Minutes Each)[a]
"Heroine"	1	50	50	8.50
Leading roles	5	30	150	25.00
Supporting roles	4	20	80	13.50
10% for breaks				4.75
Total				51.75

[a] Totals have been rounded to the nearest quarter-hour.

The Audition Space

According to SAG, you *can't* have auditions in your house or in a hotel room. This rule was probably instituted because of the practices of … unscrupulous producers. If the casting director doesn't have a casting space at his disposal, you'll have to rent one or use a connection to get access to one. The ideal casting space is a private room that's at least 10 feet across on each side (15 is better), has enough light for the video recorder, and has a waiting/reception area outside. When I'm casting out of New York I call around to a number of places and try to get deals. When you're in a smaller town, you may have to look for a dance/yoga studio, theater, or conference center. If you book a non-film space, be sure to talk to the receptionist or security guard to let them know what's going on – otherwise they may turn people away or bug you in the middle of auditions. Once you've booked the space, the casting director will put the actual schedule together. If you're going to be there for the first round, she'll send you a list of who's coming and at what times.

What/Who to Bring

Apart from the obvious (pen, paper, sides), you'll also want to bring along your director's scene-by-scene breakdown, just to refresh yourself, and your list of adjustments. Some waters and snacks are good. Either you or the casting director should bring along a video camera (I don't recommend an iPhone because I find it jitters just a little too much), a tripod, and either tapes or cards. Ideally, the camera has a decent built-in mic so you can hear the audition.

You should also bring a reader in, preferably an actor, to read opposite the candidate. You don't want to read yourself – you should be listening and making notes. Likewise, it's better if the casting director doesn't read either (he may be operating the camera anyway). If your budget is too tight for a paid reader, you can usually entice actors who want more reading experience to come in and promise them an audition, or at least some food and transportation money.

Apart from the reader, the casting director, and the producer and director, who else should be there? At most, the casting assistant. The DP and costume designer may come in for callbacks (particularly for period pieces), but I prefer a smaller crowd. The audition process is nerve-wracking enough for everyone, so the fewer people involved the better. The exception to this is if a major investor wants to come by. It's her money, so it's her call. Just go over the etiquette with her ahead of time.

During the Audition and After

During the audition, you want to watch the performance live. Avoid the temptation to look through the camera or at the monitor (if there is one). This is the only time you'll get to see the actual performance as it's happening.

The reader should read the lines as written, without injecting too much into it. When a non-actor does this, it comes out terribly; somehow, actors can walk this fine line between being out of the scene completely and jumping into it as full scene partners (you don't want either one of these extremes).

During the audition, the actor will come in and read the sides: first, without any direction. Then possibly a second time, after the director or casting director has given an adjustment. I prefer to give the adjustments if I'm directing, but I'm not as supple as the casting director, or she may come up with something better than I could have.

When the actor first comes in, be warm but not too personal. Try to put them at ease if they're nervous. Don't answer questions about the script beyond the obvious (as in, what time of day is it?). Don't get into long conversations. There simply isn't time. If the actor hasn't read the entire script, they may be a bit confused. If you sense that they're really going to give a sub-par audition as a result, you can give a thumbnail plot sketch, but not much more than that. The first read will tell you what the actor has prepared; the adjustment read shows you what they can do with some direction.

Make sure that the actor *slates* the camera before the reading – as soon as the camera rolls, have the actor state his name and what role he's reading for. If he doesn't do this or the camera isn't rolling, you're going to have a hard time matching up the audition to a name later on.

What you're mostly looking for during the audition is fit, surprise, adaptability, and inquisitiveness. You want the actor to *fit* the part, emotionally and physically. You want to be *surprised* by his take on the character, make sure he can take direction (*adaptability*), and see what kind of questions he asks (*inquisitiveness*). Fit is almost impossible to define, but if you feel that the actor really inhabits the role, then that's a good sign.

Surprise is rare, but when it happens, you should note it. Even a completely *wrong* take, if outrageous and energetic enough, is worth noting. You want actors to make bold choices – you can always dial it back, but it's much harder to push the energy up.

If someone gives you exactly the same performance on both reads, you're either not giving clear enough directions, or the actor isn't very good with adjustments. If you get the same lack-of-response from a couple of actors, you should confer with the casting director and change the adjustment. If it's just the one person, it's probably a limitation on his/her part.

Even a badly worded adjustment, however, should produce *some* change. Actors often have to deal with directors who don't speak their language. So if someone gives you the same reading both times, you need to consider whether the fit is good enough to deal with the lack of adaptability.

You may find that someone you thought was right for one role could actually work better for another. If you and the actor have time, ask them to read for the other character. If not, try to schedule another audition. Sometimes these surprises are the best thing that can happen.

At the end of each audition, if someone blows you away, mention it to the casting director. If you're lucky, this will happen two or three times a day. But don't be too eager – review the tapes every night or other night. If you're doing back-to-back sessions, wait until you've had at least one day off before reviewing everything.

Keep in mind that reviewing the auditions takes time – you're probably only going to record the actual "takes," so out of every ten-minute audition you're probably only looking at five-to-seven minutes of footage. But multiply that by everyone who showed up, and you can see how this adds up.

When you're watching the tapes, try not to look for a polished performance. We are so used to watching films that this is hard to do. You want to make sure that what you saw in the audition was really there. You also want to see how the person translates onscreen. Do they have presence? Do they still fit the character? The camera distorts figures (which is one reason why actors diet so much). Can you see the actor in a scene with one of the other candidates?

If you're working with a producer, watch the auditions together if you can. You'll both be looking at the same thing at the same time. It will save time later on when you're trying to argue over who to call back.

I usually keep a spreadsheet of audition notes (big surprise), something that looks like Table 15.3.

Having the date and audition order helps me remember who was who (sometimes the slate isn't perfect). The "Possible" followed by a percentage indicates what bracket they're in. If I'm pretty sure I want to see someone again, I put an "X" down in the "For Callbacks." If I think they were terrible, I put a "No" in the Eval column.

I fill this out while I'm watching the tapes, then email it back to the casting director with my thoughts. Ideally, you should be able to winnow out 90–95 percent of the candidates during the first round of auditions, and end up with 2–5 people per role for callbacks.

TABLE 15.3 *Found In Time* audition notes

Date	Order	Name[a]	Role	Evaluation	For Callbacks	Note
Sun 07/18	1	XXXXXX	Chris	No		
Sun 07/18	2	XXXXXX	Chris	Possible 50%		
Sun 07/18	3	XXXXXX	Chris	Possible 40%		
Sun 07/18	4	XXXXXX	Chris	Possible 50%		
Sun 07/18	5	XXXXXX	Chris	Possible 50%		
Sun 07/18	6	XXXXXX	Jina	Possible 50%		Reads "heavy"
Sun 07/18	7	XXXXXX	Chris	Possible 50%		Watch reel
Sun 07/18	8	XXXXXX	Jess	Possible 50%		
Sun 07/18	9	XXXXXX	Chris	No		
Sun 07/18	10	XXXXXX	Jina	Possible 50%		
Sun 07/18	11	XXXXXX	Anthony	No		
Sun 07/18	12	XXXXXX	Chris	Possible 40%		Soap opera
Sun 07/18	13	XXXXXX	Chris	No		
Sun 07/18	14	XXXXXX	Chris	No		
Sun 07/18	15	XXXXXX	Chris	Yes	X	
Sun 07/18	16	XXXXXX	Jina	Possible 50%		

[a] Names have been masked.

Going Again?

What happens if you go through the process and you're not "wowed" by anyone? First, you may need some perspective. It's hard to be wowed by anything after hearing the same set of lines spoken 20–50 times. You may need some "ear cleaning" (this happens during sound post as well). Listen to some non-vocal music and/or do something non-film related, even if it's for a few hours.

Second, it's possible that the casting director has a very different idea of the characters than you do. Try to be more specific about what you're looking for. Third, it's also possible that the first "pool" just didn't really contain any standouts. If yours is a non-SAG film, it could be that you have to bite the bullet and consider signing up.

In these last three cases, you'll have to hold a second round of auditions. If necessary, broaden your geographic search a bit, but keep in mind your budget constraints. Anyone who's not local will have to be fed and housed for their entire stay. On *Rock the Paint*, the producers ended up casting the lead out of Los Angeles, which put a crimp in the budget (travel, per diem, and hotel accommodation added up to quite a chunk).

Hopefully, however, you'll end up with a shortlist of people to call back.

Callbacks

Callbacks work in the same way as auditions, except that the structure is more open ended, as we discussed in Chapter 8. This makes calculating the time commitment difficult at best. For some roles, you'll only have two or three people you'll want to see; for others, as many as five. Some characters only interact with one other person in the script; others have scenes with just about everyone. You should, however, budget more time (20–30 minutes) for each callback session. Also, you may want to cast the "hero/heroine" of the film first, then the second lead, and then progress outward from the leads to the supporting characters.

During the callback, pay attention to chemistry, and again to adaptability. How much do the actors change their performance when paired up with different partners? How well do they respond to your new adjustments? Watch out for *indications*. For whatever reason, these come up more during callbacks than during the first round of auditions. An "indication" is when an actor indicates a truth through action rather than experiencing it, like making a frowny face or wiping away non-existent tears to indicate sadness. You can try this at home in the mirror. First, make a sad face. Second, think of something that made you sad. If you're paying attention, you'll notice that your first expression was less convincing than the second. Indications are attempts to show off. Don't buy them.

Other things I find distracting is when actors try to get too physical too soon, without understanding *why* the character is moving around. I'd rather they stay seated and listening to each other than try to impress me with their blocking choices. Any movement should come from a real feeling, rather than because they *think* they have to. Both indications and bad physicality are a way of *playing the result* – like trying to "act sad" instead of experiencing sadness. Acting is ideally about working the process, and the result will come out naturally.

When watching the tapes, do you see a fit? Do you see something unexpected going on? As a producer, can you see these actors together on set? In a poster? On a DVD cover?

You also need to pay attention to inadvertent race/gender issues. Is your only black actor the antagonist? Is the protagonist the only white person in the cast? Visuals matter. You may be sending out a message that you don't intend to. On the other hand, if you're not careful, you could be diluting part of your message as well. This is not, by itself, a reason to deny a job to a good actor. But you have to be aware of how some people might take it.

On *Found In Time* I had two excellent foreign candidates for the two shrinks in the film, who may or may not be hiding an agenda. However, since everyone else in the callbacks was American, the accents stood out – almost as though I was typecasting. After much discussion with the casting director, I ended up deciding against casting them. This was a difficult decision to make, but was ultimately the right one.

Finally, if you have an iconic figure in your script – say, Jesus, like I did in my first film, *Caleb's Door* – you'd better cast someone *who looks the part*. During the casting for *Caleb's Door*, I auditioned several Jesuses, some of whom were quite good, but only one of whom looked the part. You don't want to confuse your audience unintentionally. Intentional confusion (such as casting Alanis Morissette as God in *Dogma*) is just funny.

Ideally, at the end of this process, you'll have your first choice for each actor, and a backup in case the first one doesn't work out. Less than ideally, you'll at least have one person per role. If you're really not happy with anyone, you'll have to think about what to do next – review the tapes again, start over from scratch, or maybe look at some of the people you passed on the first time.

Casting is, in many ways, *the* make-or-break part of your job as director. Do it right and you won't even feel like you're breaking sweat on set. A casting misfire, however, can mean you'll be spending your time pounding the actor into the performance – or changing your conception of the role to fit the actor, which may not be something you want. So while everyone will want you to make up your mind, don't be too quick about it. If you really feel, after ruling out your own perspective (or lack of it), that you haven't found your "guy" yet, say something now.

But let's assume that everything goes peachy, and you've got your "A" choices lined up. Now comes the not-so-fun part: wrangling with the agent. The casting director will call the actors' agents/managers with the good news, and then pass along any personal information you need for the cast deal memo. In some films, the casting director will take care of the majority of the paperwork. But in case you get stuck with it, here's an overview of what to expect.

Negotiations with Agents and Actors

In an ideal world, the agent loves your script, the actor loves their part, everyone's happy with the salary and credits, and the deal memo is signed and returned to you right away. And in my experience, that is actually what happens most of the time. You may have to move some dates around to accommodate another commitment, or make sure there's vegan catering on set. But those are relatively minor issues. It's not uncommon for a deal memo to require a few rounds of minor revisions until everyone's happy.

Sometimes, however, the agent or manager stalls. It looks like a "yes," but you don't have the contract back. Or you're finding it next to impossible to schedule time to meet the actor. Or the agent keeps telling you that he's "checking with" his client, but the actor's in the middle of a shoot… Or the agent wants to "think about a formula" for profit participation, but doesn't seem to get around to spelling out the formula until late in the game.

While all of this sounds rather sinister, it's not (or usually not, anyway). You have to consider the actor's and agent's perspective. While your film may be the most important thing in your universe, to them it may be one of a dozen projects that they're considering or in the middle of. Also, the economics are not in your favor, unless you're working at a higher budget level ($2M or more). The agent works for a 10 percent commission, for a client who may work all the time or only once a month. If you're shooting a SAG ultra-low-budget film, and your actor is going to be getting $100/day + overtime + 10 percent for five days … well, that's somewhere between $50 and $87.50 in the agent's pocket. That's almost the same amount of money that he's going to get for booking the actor on an under-five role on a half-hour TV show – a one-day commitment. And which role will push the actor's career further along – a short bit that will be seen in a few months by millions of viewers, or a bigger role in an indie film that may never see the light of day or only be released on Amazon in two years?

Also, actors who work regularly may be getting other offers. Technically, under all of the low-budget SAG agreements, you can't "lock out" an actor from taking another gig if it pays more. On the other hand, it's pretty bad form if the agent's already accepted your offer, and the actor ditches it in favor of something else. Or calls and says that he'll do your job but can you move your entire shoot forward a few weeks. Some agents maneuver around this by letting your deal memo "age" on their desk while they try to lock down a better job. Your film then becomes the "backup plan" in case the bigger gig doesn't pan out.

Alternately, the agent may be playing it straight but the actor is having doubts. This is not uncommon, because *actors always have to be somewhere else.* If they're at their day job, they want to be auditioning. If they're auditioning, they have to leave early to get to their class. If they're in class, they need to get out early so they can do an off-Broadway play. If they're in the play they can't come to the early rehearsal because they're shooting your film. And so on. It's an unfortunate side effect of the freelance nature of their work. No actor wants to pass up an opportunity, because they never know if *that* gig will be the one that takes them to the next level. Signing up as the lead on your three-week shoot means potentially turning down a lot of work.

You'll probably never know what's going on exactly between the agent and the actor. If the actor has a manager as well as an agent, the two may even be in conflict with each other. The only thing you can do is make it easier for them to say *yes.* As soon as the casting director calls the agent with the good news, have the first draft of the cast deal memo ready to go. If there's a nude scene, stunt, or something a bit out of the ordinary (sports, war, gunplay) be up-front about it. Also, be as firm as possible about the start dates for each actor. Agents respect organization.

You can sweeten the pot by promising some points, reassuring the agent that you know what you're doing, and talking about who else is in the cast. *Don't automatically offer more money up front,* however. Unless the actor is a name, the fee will not "buy" you anything, and may get you in trouble with the other actors and their agents if they find out.

The other technique you can do is use the *join or die* approach. Tell the agent that they have a deadline – if you don't hear a "yes" by a certain date then you're moving on. Once you go down this path, however, there's no wiggle room. Be prepared to start casting (hopefully with your "B" choice). If you waver on the "join or die" strategy, it will weaken your bargaining power later.

If worse comes to terrible – if someone drops out – then don't stress out about it too much. If a relationship starts out with this much trouble, then it may be best that it doesn't continue. Check your backup actor's availability. Hopefully, you won't have to repeat the casting cycle again. If you do, at least the prep you've done to this point – and the auditions themselves – will have sharpened you a bit and you'll be able to plow through the auditions faster.

OFFER-ONLY/"NAME" CASTING

You may want to try and go after a "name" actor, either for the lead or one of the supporting characters. Having a name in your cast will often attract more attention from distributors, sales agents, and (yes) film festivals. You may also have more luck raising money, and getting other cast and crew to sign up. And you'll know that you're getting a professional with a track record. However, there are a few pitfalls that you need to consider before going down this path.

Is it a Fit with the Rest of Your Film?

This goes beyond the economics. If you're trying to get a name for a walk-on part but the rest of your cast is unknowns, will this work or will it take the audience out of the movie? Are you better off trying to find a name actor for a larger role, even if it costs you more money? Also, the agents of these actors usually will not agree to auditions – hence the term "offer-only" (in my experience, actors are more willing to audition than their agents). Finally, you may not be able to get the actor in for any kind of rehearsal, and may even have to rearrange the schedule significantly for him. This, however, may be completely worthwhile, and even necessary if your financing is cast-contingent.

Can You Afford a Name?

If you're working on a film with a budget of less than $500K, you can't afford to pay much more than scale or double-scale for an actor. If you have a small cast, you may be able to goose this number up, but you still need to have enough funds to finish and promote the film. You might be tempted to short the post or distribution/promotion categories, but this could bite you later on; you don't want to be raising money for post.

If you're looking to raise $1M or more for your film, you *should* have a name in your cast, even if it's in a supporting role. It's not a guarantee of anything, but it will put investors at rest. Again, depending on the script, you may not have a lot of wiggle room in terms of salary – and keep in mind that once you cross the $2M threshold, the chances of it becoming an IA shoot become higher, so the pot of money for a "name" doesn't grow in a linear fashion.

What Is a Name Anyway?

A "name" is someone who can either (a) excite an investor, (b) excite a sales agent/distributor, or (c) both. If you have to pick, go with (b). Sales agents and distributors ultimately control the fate of your film as much as, if not more than, investors. Keep in mind, however, that a "name" to you may mean nothing to a sales agent. A "name" to a sales agent is someone that has a record of attracting distributors. A "name" to a distributor is someone with some face recognition in that distributor's marketplace. There's no magic list on the internet anywhere of who's hot and who's not. You can try to go by the IMDbPro actor's rating system, but your best bet is to look at who's working a lot at your budget level or in your genre. If you've been doing your marketing homework, you probably have some idea of other films that are in your wheelhouse, and who was in them. Some of these actors have their own production companies, which means that they may partner with a producer on the right project. On the one hand, that makes them harder to get – their production companies will prefer to work with more established producers. But it may also mean that they're actively looking for good material.

Attracting a Name and Making Contact

A good payday in exchange for a small-time commitment is attractive to almost any actor, but you stand an even better chance if you can offer her something different from the roles she's been getting up to this point. Actors do like to stretch themselves periodically, to keep from getting pigeonholed or bored (or both).

The first step, then, is to figure out the pitch – the salary, time commitment, and character. How is your bad guy different from the 300 other bad guys the actor has played before? Do you want to cast him against type? What makes him or her special to you? And is there something special about *where* you'll be shooting? Some actors like to travel (it's one of the perks of the job).

The second step is to have you or the casting director contact the agent or, preferably, the actor. Even if the actor refers you back to her agent or manager, you're on her radar. There's a better chance of your script not ending up at the bottom of the pile on the agent's desk if the actor says "What happened to those guys who called me who I sent your way?"

For each role, you'll have to decide whether to go after everyone on your "name wish list" or make one-at-a-time offers. If you have two or more actors on your list that are repped by the same agency or management company (even if by different people), you're better off making one-at-a-time offers for these folks. You're trying to make the actor feel special, so you're working against yourself if you're also approaching his agent's other clients.

This process takes a lot of time. The agent and the actor both have a pile of DVDs, scripts, novels, and other materials to sift through on their desks (and probably another one by their beds). If you don't know the actor or the agent very well, it's hard to expect them to prioritize your low-budget film over their other projects. The one thing you can do is be firm about your dates, and hope that the agent believes you. If your financing is cast-contingent (meaning the investors won't write checks until they see a name attached), then you really *can't* stick to your intended dates. The agent may assume that to be the case even if it isn't.

The Negotiation

Your goal is to get the agent to issue a letter of intent (LOI) stating that the actor would like to appear in your film in the specific role, barring certain circumstances (schedule conflicts or illness). You can take this LOI back to your investors, and to sales agents to see if you can get some pre-sales (unfortunately, that's when you may find out that the "name" won't get the film as much traction as you'd hoped).

Assuming you can get over the hurdle of hearing back, you'll have to negotiate the contract points as you would any other. Name actors may have special needs:

1. You may have to carry their assistant.
2. They may have a preferred makeup artist or hair stylist.
3. You may have to hire their preferred stand-in.
4. If they're working away from their home base you may have to provide additional tickets for back-and-forth travel.
5. They may have special dietary needs or requests.
6. If they're traveling from another country, you may have to give them a US phone.
7. You may have to put up their families.

This is not an exhaustive list, but it gives you some idea of what you may have to work through. Hopefully you have a little money in the "Star Costs" line item to cover these expenses, or you can push back against some of them. It's important that the agent understands what your situation is – if you don't have money for trailers, or if you're shooting on a DSLR as opposed to a 35mm rig, you should mention this now so you're not misrepresenting yourself.

The last step is the meeting with the director and producer – especially the director. This meeting can be a series of phone conversations or an in-person meeting over coffee. This meeting will, hopefully, determine the "fit" between the actor and director. What you should mostly do at this meeting is *listen* to what the concerns of the actor are and respond appropriately. Does she want to talk about the film? Great. Is she into politics? Cool. To some extent, this is a dress rehearsal for the relationship. She may have some totally off-the-wall ideas about the film, things that you know in your heart won't work. Go with it – see where it takes you. You don't have to say "yes" to every idea, but you don't want to say "no" right away. For starters, no one likes hearing "no," especially if they've taken the time to come up with ideas in the first place. Second, what seems like a bananas idea may have some real merit to it, or lead to something that does. We'll talk about this more in Chapter 20, but the main point is to try and be nonjudgmental, and encouraging.

THE TENSION BETWEEN PRODUCER AND DIRECTOR

Directors and producers can sometimes be at odds over casting. It could be part of the normal tension between creative and business concerns, or a difference of artistic opinion (yes, producers have artistic opinions). Or both sides have lost perspective and are clinging to their defenses long past where it's necessary.

Even if you're both the director and the producer, you will sometimes face this problem. On *Found In Time*, I had the good fortune of meeting a terrific actor, who I'd admired for a while. We got along really well. I'm not sure if he was a "name" but he had been in some high-visibility work. The agent said that it was an offer-only situation. There was just one problem – he didn't really fit the role. I would have had to have rewritten the part. My producer side kept telling me that the rewrite might actually make the script better. I did actually start working on a tweak, but it caused too many other problems in the script and the "tweak" started snowballing into a rewrite. I was in danger of slipping my dates, which would mean putting the whole machine back to together again (it was early August at this point, and my shoot was only a month away). At the end of the day, I had to pass.

Was this the right call? I'm not sure. You may find yourself arguing in the mirror, which is difficult enough. But if there's two or more of you, the arguments can get even more fun. The best thing to do is to try and separate out the issues. Are they:

- Economic?
- Artistic?
- Schedule-based?

Economic arguments can go either way. The director may want to fly in an actor from out of town who fits the role better, but it could put too much of a strain on the production. In this situation, the economics wins out *unless* you can find a way to make it work within the existing budget. If you have to raise more money it's probably not worth it unless the actor really is the only person who can play the role, and/or brings some "name" recognition to the table.

What if the producer is pushing for a "name" but the director prefers a relatively unknown actor that did a good job during the auditions? In this case, you may have to "wait and see." You can't hire the unknown actor and then dump her when the "name" becomes available. But you can try to wait it out for a little bit, depending on how much time you have left. This can backfire – the unknown actor may take another gig rather than wait around, and then when the "name" actor says no, you're left with no one. Don't play the waiting game for longer than a couple of weeks.

Artistic disputes are harder to deal with, in a sense, because passions run high in casting. The producer may feel that the director is taken with the "look" of the actor but is blind to the performance. The director may feel that the producer hasn't given the actor a chance to really shine – that the performance is there. Here, I'm tempted to side with the director. If he's done his homework, he really does know more about what he's looking for, so you should give him some slack. If, however, the director has a close relationship with the actor in question, his loyalty may be blinding him to the truth. In this case, I'd side with the producer. There's no easy way to settle this dispute, except to use whatever leverage you have as a producer to get the director to keep looking at other alternatives.

Schedule issues can usually be worked through, unless they will throw the entire project into chaos. On *Found In Time*, another really good actor auditioned for one of the roles, but was going to be out of the country during the first week of the shoot. When I started looking at the logistics of pushing the shoot or swapping the first- and second-week schedules, it became too difficult to make it work.

Seeing a few more people is always a tie-breaking option. Or the two of you may have to sit down with the casting director and get a third opinion. This is fine as long as you don't thrust the ultimate decisions on him/her. That's on you both.

SIDE BENEFITS OF CASTING

During the casting process, you're going to hear the same set of scenes over and over again. You will probably get some ideas for script tweaks from this process. Pay particular attention to redundant dialog – can you trim it or get rid of it altogether? Also, see if the scene structure is tight or if it needs some trimming. Perhaps the climax of a scene comes too soon, or the transitions are awkward.

Sometimes an actor who isn't right for the part otherwise will make a great interpretive choice. Make a note of it – this could become part of your direction to the actor you do hire.

You'll also get to practice your directing skills (another reason why I prefer giving the adjustments rather than having the casting director do it). You may find that what you thought were a set of clear, concise adjustments are in fact too verbose and confusing. Or alternately, you find a handful of adjustments that work like a knife through butter.

As you get down to your callback candidates, you may want to start (discreetly) showing headshots to your DP, costume, and/or production designer. They may be inspired, or suddenly see your vision of the film in a more concrete way.

CASTING CAN BE FUN

What I've just described sounds a bit fraught with peril – there are so many things that can lead you astray on that flowchart that it's almost like playing a boardgame. But after sitting with the script in your head and on paper for months, it's a great feeling to watch it come to life in front of you. Cherish these moments.

Also, the audition process can be a bonding experience between the director and producer (or both sides of your head). You're going through a dry run of production, in a sense – balancing artistic and financial needs, making decisions in the face of large uncertainties while sticking to a schedule, and trying to keep the big picture in focus at all times despite the wealth of little details. So use this time to really hone the relationship.

QUESTIONS/EXERCISES

1. See if you can sit in at an audition for another project, where you can watch and observe what's going on.
2. See if you can hold a mock audition with a couple of friends. You'll be the director, your friends will read the scene, and then you'll give an adjustment and have them read it again.
3. If you're thinking of a particular "name" for your film, go through their IMDb listing. Is there a common thread to their work? How would working on your film be different? Or, how would it fit? Are they in a number of projects listed as "in development"?
4. See what would happen to your budget if you had to pay double SAG scale for a couple of roles, or a buyout. How big a bump does it create? Is it fixable by trimming elsewhere, or do you have to bring the cast salary down a bit?
5. Research the costs of renting a Winnebago or similar mobile home unit for a week. Keep in mind that under the "favored nations" clause (depending on the wording) you may have to upgrade your other actors' dressing rooms to match.

## Chapter 16

Hiring the Crew

FIGURE 16.1 Hiring the crew. From the set of *Helena from the Wedding*. (Photo: Brendan Mason.)

Films are very much handmade creations. Even when the computer is doing a lot of the "fabrication" of the image, that machine is being guided by a ton of programmers, compositors, artists, IT managers, and all the people who support them. On an indie film, resources are stretched even more thinly, the crew works even harder with less sleep, and yet the results can be magnificent. So what makes a "good" crew? How do you pick the best people you can afford? How do you deal with the different minds, each with a slightly different perspective and skillset?

In many ways, the crew hiring process is a bit like casting – and some folks even use the term "casting your crew." There's some merit in this idea, but the processes are different enough that I don't think the term applies. During the crew interviews, you are auditioning for them just as much as they are for you. Also, a crew that doesn't have great chemistry with each other or you can still create a good film; the same can't be said of the cast. However, the sentiment rings true: you don't just want to hire a group of mercenary professionals, but a family that works together and looks out for each other.

WHO TO HIRE

In the "good old days," the producer and director sat down and made a list of who they had to bring aboard. It usually looked like this – in descending order of immediacy:

- Line producer
- Director of photography (DP)
- Production designer
- Costume designer
- Editor
- First assistant director (1st AD)
- Production sound mixer
- Hair/makeup key
- Script supervisor
- Sound editor
- Visual effects (VFX) artist

The DP usually brought aboard her camera crew and called in the gaffer and key grip. The other department heads also pretty much staffed their own departments. However, over the past few years or so I've had to directly hire all the way down to the PA level. This is partly due to the fact that experienced crews move on from independent work at some point, so the folks you're likely to hire have fewer connections/favors that they can call in. It's also a sign of how shoots across the industry are operating now – the crews are getting smaller and the schedules shorter, so it's become even harder to keep your "gang" together. And the apprentice-ship period – where you work as a third, then a best, in a department – has gotten shorter, for a number of reasons.

In any case, I still start with the above list, but now I add:

- Art director
- Propmaster
- Gaffer
- Key grip
- First assistant camera (1st AC)
- Digital image tech (DIT)
- Production assistants (PAs)
- Colorist/conformist

If I'm building a "run-and-gun" crew (see Chapter 11), the gaffer and key grip positions may get condensed into one person, the script supervisor and camera crew are dropped, and the PAs become interns. Sometimes the 1st AD position goes away as well, and the production manager takes up the position.

Start by assuming that you're going to have to hire the entire crew directly. You'll need somewhere between two to three months for this. You don't want to start too early, because no one will want to commit to a start date that's too far in the future and is likely to change. But you don't want to wait until the last minute, because prep time is vital.

Crew Motivations

I see ads like this on mandy.com (one of the larger online film job posting services) all the time:

> Experienced DP wanted to partner on low-budget film directed by first-time award-winning feature director. Must have own camera and lighting package. Five-week shoot. Meals, transportation, copy of film provided.

So, you want experience and equipment, but don't want to pay for either? What, exactly, is the incentive for an *experienced* DP? She doesn't need another credit – she's got experience. And she's not getting paid. The director won an award, which sounds great, except that unless it's worth listing in the ad (like a Sundance win for his short), she's not going to care. And meals and transportation – that's a given. I'm still waiting for copies of some films that I worked on eight years ago (at this point, I don't really care if I get a copy).

As a line producer, I've had to write up mandy.com ads for low-budget shoots, so I sympathize. You want to put something in there that sounds good, hence "award-winning." But ads like these are written from the perspective of the director and producer, who are getting something very different out of the experience. So before you look for crew, you have to understand what would motivate them to take your job.

Some crew members are motivated by *career* interests: connections, better credits, visibility (if their work is onscreen). Others will come aboard for the *money* (and even a crummy rate is better than nothing). Still others care about the *personal* experience (travel, friends, loyalty to people they know). And finally, a lot of folks are in this business for *artistic* reasons, even if they don't want to admit it (they want to work on good scripts, or exciting opportunities to stretch their craft).

These motivations both overlap and conflict with each other. When I had cash in the bank I was less motivated by money and choosier about what I signed up for. When I had bills to pay I took whatever came my way. A good script is usually important, but so is the prospect of working for the same group of people again. In general, the less visible your job and the more experienced you are, the less motivated you'll be by intangibles, and the more you'll want to focus on cash and perks (such as travel).

Expectations of Crew

If you look again through the mandy ad, you'll see that there isn't much on there that would attract someone to respond, unless they're just starting out (which is specifically *not* what the ad requested). So you have to prioritize *experience*, *cash*, or *time*. If you don't have much cash, you can't expect an experienced person to commit so much time. If you want an experienced person, you'll probably have to throw some money their way, which will also mean shortening the shoot to compensate. But their experience will then help you achieve your shorter schedule, so it may even out.

You will probably have to set different priorities for each crew position. On *Racing Daylight*, the DP was very experienced, whereas most of the crew were just starting out. Having a "ringer" in your crew in a key position can help raise the bar for everyone else. On the other hand, I don't *expect* my PAs to have a lot of experience – that's part of why they're there.

If you can afford more than one ringer, spring for a more experienced DP, 1st AD, editor, production sound mixer, and/or sound designer. If you can only afford one, make it the production sound mixer. You can muddle through the shoot with a green crew as long as you get enough coverage. But if the sound is really bad you'll have to ADR the film or put it in a drawer. Audiences will not put up with unclear dialog.

So, for each major crew position listed above, figure out what you're willing to work with. This, in turn, should be based on a good understanding of your script and your available resources. If you're shooting a gory horror movie that takes place in one location (that you own), you might have to spring more for an experienced prosthetic artist and shrink the art department a little bit. If you (the producer) are experienced enough, perhaps you can get by with a "step-up" line producer.

A few other things to consider, especially once you start gathering resumes:

There's experience and then there's aptitude. It's a cliché at this point (I think I first read it in Edward DeBono's wonderful *Textbook of Wisdom*), but 20 years of experience could just be one year of experience repeated 20 times. I've often run into this problem myself – I will sometimes approach the budget for each project in a characteristic, cookie-cutter way. I have to stop and remind myself that each script really demands a fresh approach. Every time I turn around there's a new camera and workflow out. So an aptitude to learn new things, coupled with real wisdom gleaned from experience, is the ideal you're looking for.

Don't rule out non-film experience. Don't rule someone out because they don't have a lot of *film* credits. Sometimes you can get someone who's very experienced in the corporate or commercial world, who desperately wants to do something more interesting than shoot tuna cans. Stephen Harris, the DP on *Racing Daylight*, came aboard because it was different from his commercial work. The assistant production office coordinator on the film, Kathe Sweeney, had worked in non-film offices for many years, so the producers knew that she could handle organizing a production office.

Don't trust IMDb. I've had to chase after a few producers to add me to the credits. At least I'm the only Arthur Vincie – my friend is one of a few Ben Wolfs, and producers regularly screw up his credits.

Questioning doesn't mean hostility. Someone who pushes back against your ideas or asks you a lot of questions may just be expressing legitimate concerns, or requesting clarification. Or s/he has a lot of hostility, or a vastly different conception of the film than you do. How do you tell the difference? If you feel that the drift of the conversation is moving further away from your vision of the film, then that's a sign that you may not have the right fit.

Having the gear isn't everything. A person who owns a camera can call themselves a DP, but does he know how to light anything? While you can sometimes get a better deal by hiring someone who has his/her own gear, you're better off spending a few extra bucks and getting the person who knows how to *use* the gear better.

WHERE TO GET CREW

There are five channels you can get crew people from, and you'll probably use some combination of all of them:

- Personal connections
- Recommendations
- Want ads
- Production service deals
- Film schools/training programs

Personal connections and recommendations are awesome, of course. But want ads can yield some really surprising results. Just be clear in your ad what your rate of pay is, the dates, and any perks you can think of (a beach location in summertime might qualify as a perk, unless it's next to the sewer treatment plant). Use the logline in the ad as well.

The last two options should be weighed carefully, but can also be terrific under the right conditions. Let's go over these in more detail.

Production Service Deals

You may find a production company, line producer, DP, or other crewmember who can act as a turnkey operation – they show up with crew, gear, and/or facilities. This is a common situation on reality shows and industrials, where the client just hires the production company. The production company then uses its in-house staff and hires freelancers only as needed.

Depending on the size of your film and your relationship to the production company, this option may make a lot of sense. There has to be a good match between the size of the company and your budget as well. I worked on two films for a company called Gigantic Pictures. In both cases, the director and one of the producers came to Gigantic, who actually took on the tasks of getting the crew, locations, equipment, etc. together, and managed post.

However, both of those films (and most of the ones they take on) were big enough to justify the resources they were bringing to bear. If the margin on a job became too low they turned it down. So it didn't make sense for them to get involved in that way on *Found In Time*. On the other hand, I could have approached a small reality show or EPK production company, who often field smaller crews, and see if they wanted to take on something that *to them* would have been bigger or at least different than what they usually do. For a small company, the chance to get more feature credits and experience may be worth the low margin.

The production services situation doesn't have to be for the entire crew. On a few occasions, I've worked with gaffers or DPs who brought their regular crew plus a decent-sized lighting package on a truck. For a *prix-fixe* rate, I get a great deal – manpower, equipment, and a truck I'd otherwise have to rent. Some post houses offer everything-under-one-roof solutions – space rental, color correction, conforming, tape output, sound design and mixing.

The upside of this approach is that you have fewer things to worry about. The minus is that you give up some control, and potentially put a layer between you and the crew. In reality, this is less of a problem than you'd think. As the client, if you're having a problem with someone on the crew, you may find it easier to have the supervisor yell at him than doing it yourself. If you already have people you want to work with in certain positions, a mix-and-match accommodation can usually be reached.

If you're shooting a $200K-or-under film, talk to the local equipment rental houses, and see who's been renting small packages. They might be interested in working with you on your film.

Film Schools/Training Programs

The New York City Film Commission office, working with the DGA, put together a non-profit called the MadeInNY PA Training Program. They put prospective PAs through their paces, and then make them available via a hotline you can call 24/7. I got most of the PAs on *Found In Time* through this program, and they were terrific. On other shoots I've worked on, nearly the entire crew came from the local film school. If you don't have a local film school, you may still have some kind of communications/broadcasting/television production program – even at a nearby community college or public access station (almost all public access stations require training in order to use their equipment). I've worked with folks who've come from these programs, and they're often very eager to work on indie features. Especially if you have a "ringer" or two on your crew to provide some guidance, recruiting from a school or program can be a great way to pick up a crew for relatively little money.

Of course, unless you were in the program that you're now recruiting people from, it's hard to know what the quality of the training is. You're also usually asking people to "step up" in rank, and some folks handle this better than others. You can get some teacher references, and maybe adjust the schedule so you have a little more "slack."

THE HUNT

No matter what your budget level, you will probably get a heap of resumes. I use email folders and a spreadsheet (like the one for casting in Chapter 15) to keep track of the prospects. You may even want to get a separate email account just for this purpose. Sift through the resumes and separate them into three piles: "A" pile, "B" pile, and discards. What are you looking for though? How do you tell just from a resume or even a clip reel how good someone is? In this sense, hiring your crew can be harder than casting.

I usually start backwards, by putting people into the discard pile. This isn't as hard to do as it seems. If someone's resume is incomprehensible – very badly written, with a lot of typos or grammatical mistakes – they go into the discard pile. That sounds harsh, but job applications are serious, and if you can't take the time to correct your work, what does that say about how seriously you're going to take the job? One or two typos doesn't kill me, however.

Anyone who emails me their resume looking for a job other than what I've posted (unless they have amazing credits, in which case I might save the email for the next film) goes into the trash. I also get resumes from people in different industries, folks who think I want to read their screenplays, and some occasional crazies. Gone. Last but not least are the people who obviously didn't read the ad, and are based way out of town. Just by doing this, I can usually shrink the pile by about 20–30 percent. It looks a lot less scary at this point.

The next step is to read the resumes and compare the types of experience. For a key position, anyone with at least two features of experience in the same position (or one feature, if they're through a referral) will be a candidate for the "A" pile. I do check IMDb (though I don't swear by it) because there's an off-chance that someone I know worked on the same film. I can then call him/her and find out what the candidate was like.

I also look at reels and sample photos (in the case of prosthetic effects, costume designers, production designers, or makeup artists). However, I will sometimes turn the sound off when watching clips. Music has a big emotional pull – it's hard for me to evaluate the work. If I really respond to someone's work, they'll go into the "A" pile regardless of experience.

Who goes into the "B" pile? Folks who have a good chunk of experience but not at the same level.

If I'm working with someone else, we'll pass the two piles back and forth, debate about who should go in which one, throw a few people out, add a few people who responded later, and so on. Ideally I want to have somewhere between two and five candidates per key position to consider. Even if I'm pretty sure I'm going to staff the whole shoot from personal connections, it's good to have a backup plan in case someone can't commit to the dates. I list the "A" candidates first, followed by the "B"s.

If you have any doubts about someone, see if any of your connections or your war council knows them or their work. Even New York and LA are small towns. While there are many different production "circuits," you can usually find someone who's heard something about the person. Whether you can trust this information is another matter.

Then the fun begins. Call the candidates, explain the film in more detail, ask them questions about anything that struck you about their credits, and "take their temperature." Do you get along with the person right away? Do they sound genuinely enthusiastic about the script? Are they more wary? What's the first question they ask – is it "what's the rate?" (not necessarily a bad sign, by the way) or are they more interested in the story? Do they sound crazy (hard to tell over the phone)? Go into some detail about how they're going to get paid – through a payroll company, or as subcontractors – and when. I advocate paying at the beginning of the following week rather than on the last day of the current week – it gives you time to make out the checks and verify the overtime and other charges. More on that later. Getting this discussion out of the way early saves a lot of grief later on.

Usually, I lose about 10 percent of the candidates during the phone calls. Some of them have booked other jobs, or they thought I was kidding about the rates. Or they're not as grabbed by the story. After one round of telephoning, sometimes a few "A"s and "B"s switch places. If we're both still happy with each other by the end of the phone call, I schedule an interview, and email the script, the latest shooting schedule, and some version of the director's look-book or vision statement. If I'm interviewing the key, I'll also send along a summary of the budget for their department (usually minus a few dollars).

Some producers are very leery about sending scripts out. It's understandable, but you can't really have an intelligent interview as a crewperson without reading the script (I can't, anyway). And by sending out the schedule and budget, you'll be giving the person a chance to assess what they're getting themselves into.

The Interview

You want to start interviewing the keys first, and see if they can bring their own seconds and thirds aboard. If they're not in a position to do so (the rates are too low for their regular crew, or everyone's booked), then you'll have to coordinate the job search for their department with them.

You can interview crew in your home if you need to watch clips together, but the local coffee shop has become the default destination. I usually book 30-minute interviews for the keys, 20 minutes for the seconds and thirds, and 15 for PAs.

Who should come to the interview? That depends. If you're a two-person team, then both the director and producer. If the line producer is aboard already, then the line producer. If you're interviewing someone in the camera, grip, or electric departments, the DP. If you're interviewing a second, third, or PA, then whoever the key is for that department should be there.

The director should bring the look-book, vision statement, and some reference materials (visuals especially). Bring the budget so you can discuss it. You probably shouldn't show it to the interviewees. But you should be able to talk intelligently about the details ("What do I have for expendables?").

If you're having trouble breaking the ice, here are some questions to try out:

1. Tell me a little bit about (a film on their resume). A variant is "What was it like to shoot on that camera/in that environment/for that long/etc.?"
2. Do you have a look that you see for this film?
3. Was there anything that wasn't clear in the script?
4. Is there a scene or sequence that you think could require something special in terms of equipment or personnel?

Hopefully, the interviewee will be asking you a lot of questions as well. Pay attention to the tone as much as the text of the interview. Does the person sound excited to be in the room with you? Are they relentlessly negative (questioning is one thing, negative is another)? Can you see yourself working with this person for several weeks, in close proximity? Don't be too concerned with how nervous or shy the person is – some people interview better than others. If someone keeps trying to impress you with their weighty knowledge, don't be taken in too much. People who are blustery can cause trouble on set. On the other hand, someone who asks a lot of questions, or may even have ideas that contradict yours, could be very valuable.

Unless someone blows you away and you're afraid of losing him/her, don't hire the person right away. Give it a day. At least see the other candidates for the job. Almost anyone can wait a day – you can always ask if they're waiting on anything else. I usually go through the whole list before making a final decision, and then start calling people back. I start with the "winners," but I'll also call the people who didn't make the final cut. This keeps the relationships intact and lets them know that we liked the work. By going the extra distance, I'm also more likely to get a call back if, in an emergency (my first choice bails on me), the "loser" suddenly becomes my first choice.

When interviewing the PAs, it's good to talk a bit about what they want to do next. It may reveal a little bit about what they hope to gain on your shoot, and how committed they are to film in general.

Sometimes, instead of interviewing a second or third directly, I'll make the phone call, then pass their info on to the department head, and let her do the meet and greet. This saves me a lot of work, and also gives the department head the say she deserves.

If Things Aren't Working …

You may start prepping with someone and it becomes clear that it's not going to work out. They're overcommitted, unavailable to talk to you, and/or go from being excited to being negative and touchy now that they have the job … if this happens, don't just let it slide. This is the beginning of the relationship, when you're both supposed to be happy about each other. *It won't get better.* Talk to the person and find out what's going on. If they came to you through a referral, call the referrer and see if they have some insight. But if you're not getting anywhere, you're better off firing the person and bringing your second choice aboard. Similarly, if you've made an offer to someone and they're taking forever to get back to you, move on.

THE GESTALT OF THE SHOOT

In an ideal world, everyone gets along with everyone else, there's very little friction on set, and they turn in outstanding work. This rarely happens – but it's a worthwhile goal, and one that you have some control over. The crew will be taking their cues from you (and your partner, if there's more than one of you). Present a united, organized front from the very beginning, during the interview stage. This will help set the "gestalt" of the shoot. People respond to sincerity – if you like their work, share their tastes in films or books, or like to "geek out," show them that side of you. Note that I said "sincerity," however. If you are merely affecting an interest for someone or their work, they'll sense it and it may actually backfire. If you don't have strong feelings or you're just not a "warm and fuzzy" person it's better not to pretend to be.

Be open to feedback on the script. Some of the people you're interviewing will have worked on a lot more projects than you have. They may point out (hopefully tactfully) a problem or have a suggestion that you can incorporate through a tweak. It's usually a good sign if someone has suggestions – it means she's paying attention.

Think about the long haul. Some of the people who work for you may call you in on jobs down the road. My DP and I have worked together on a number of jobs – sometimes he recommended me as a line producer, sometimes I've recommended him as a DP. A few times he was my boss. Other times we were "fellow keys." You won't have this kind of relationship with everyone, but it's something to strive for. Who would you want to work with on the *next* film?

QUESTIONS/EXERCISES

1. Based on your budget, who are the keys, and how many of them have you already promised to friends/personal connections?
2. List the vacant crew positions out. For the seconds and thirds, contact your keys and see if they have a lead on people to fill these positions.
3. From the connections list you've been maintaining, identify prospective crewmembers and figure out if any might be right for your shoot.
4. Practice your interview technique with a friend. If you tend to be very soft-spoken, you may have to raise your voice a little bit. If you talk too much, try to hold back and listen to answers. Make eye contact but don't get into staring contests.
5. Call up a producer or line producer you know and see if they'll tell you their worst and best interview stories.

## Chapter 17

Scouting

FIGURE 17.1 The *Windows* location scout. (*Left to right*) Shahram Karimi (production designer), Shoja Azari (director), and John Bonafede (art director).

Scouting! The word alone fills me with joy. It's one of my favorite activities. There's nothing more fun than walking or driving around, looking at cool places, taking photos, and jotting down notes. Before reality comes swooping in and hits you in the head, you can think about blocking, color, light, and sound without having to worry about the craft services running out or the follow focus jamming.

It can also be a tremendous waste of time, though. If you're not thinking "outside the set" you will miss telltales that will bite you later on. You may love the quietness of the location in the morning, but by the afternoon when you're scheduled to be there it's a mess of pedestrians and street vendors. The apartment with the great view of the city at night is next door to a couple that loves to have really loud sex, or watch action films at full volume. The wiring in the church is from the dawn of the electric age and will fry as soon as your hairstylist plugs in her blowdryer. And the store owner who loves you now will hate you after you've disrupted his routine for four hours.

In Ye Olde Film Shoot days, you had tech scouts, which would typically happen after the preliminary scouting. The department heads would walk around the set and surrounding area, and figure out how to make a location work (or determine if they could make it work at all). With tech scouts becoming scarce due to budget pressures, it's up to you to analyze the location in the cold light of crew concerns.

WHAT DO YOU NEED, REALLY?

Print out your schedule and breakdown sheets. Print out a location and set report, or type it up manually (if you did your schedule by hand or in Excel). You'll have a lot of sets, but fewer locations. Figure 17.2 shows an example, from *Found In Time*.

What you'll be looking for are:

- Locations that can "double" for specific sets
- Locations that are physically close together in real life (or could be)
- Locations that are nonspecific enough so you can push them around in the schedule

On *Found In Time* I needed two psychiatrists' offices, but I realized I could probably just redress one a little bit and shoot from different angles. On *The Reawakening*, we used different rooms in the same house for very different locales (a law office, a living room, the bedroom of one of the main characters). On *Racing Daylight*, the same locations were supposed to double anyway, representing the same places in different eras. On *Helena from the Wedding*, all the exteriors except for one were about a quarter-mile away from our main set. You'll end up with an idealized list of locations that can shoot all your sets on, while minimizing company moves, lighting changes, and/or art direction changes.

Scheduled				
	8:15 AM CALL			
	LOCATION: PSYCHIATRISTS' OFFICES			
	MOVE OUTSIDE			
142	EXT STREET Ayana meets them at the edge of the park, they walk out together	Day	4/8 pgs. Day 7	CAST: 1, 2, 4 BG:
144	EXT STREET RJ, Chris and Ayana walk down the street together	Day	3/8 pgs. Day 7	CAST: 1, 2, 4 BG:
39	EXT ANOTHER STREET Chris walks down the block, picks up stuff	Day	2/8 pgs. Day 3	CAST: 1 BG: 3
41	EXT ANOTHER STREET Chris continues to pick up junk	Day	3/8 pgs. Day 3	CAST: 1 BG:
	JINA'S OFFICE			
32	INT JINA'S OFFICE Jina and Anthony discuss "the case"	Day	2/8 pgs. Day 102	CAST: 3, 5 BG:
51	INT JINA'S OFFICE Jina and Ayana have a therapy session	Day	3 pgs. Day 4	CAST: 2, 3 BG:
57	INT JINA'S OFFICE Ayana finishes her therapy session with Jina	Day	2/8 pgs. Day 4	CAST: 2, 3 BG:
111	INT JINA'S OFFICE Ayana tells Jina about Anansi	Day	3/8 pgs. Day 7	CAST: 2, 3 BG:
115	INT JINA'S OFFICE Jina and Ayana conclude their session, Ayana offers to take Jina to	Day	7/8 pgs. Day 7	CAST: 2, 3 BG:
105	INT JINA'S OFFICE Jina and Anthony look at the display on the screen again	Day	1 pgs. Day 102	CAST: 3, 5 BG:
107	INT JINA'S OFFICE Jina wonders whether the vendors should stay vendors	Day	5/8 pgs. Day 102	CAST: 3, 5 BG:
141	INT JINA'S OFFICE Jina realizes that Chris will leave her	Day	4/8 pgs. Day 102	CAST: 3, 5 BG:
	End Day # 12 Saturday, September 24, 2011 -- Total Pages: 8 3/8			
	8:30 AM CALL			
	ANTHONY'S OFFICE			
47	INT ANTHONY'S OFFICE Anthony has an initial session with Chris	Day	1 3/8 pgs. Day 4	CAST: 1, 5 BG:
49	INT ANTHONY'S OFFICE Chris and Anthony talk about Chris's "condition," take some tests	Day	1 5/8 pgs. Day 4	CAST: 1, 5 BG:
74	INT ANTHONY'S OFFICE Anthony tells Chris he's already in the mines	Day	1 pgs. Day 100	CAST: 1, 5 BG:
85	INT ANTHONY'S OFFICE Anthony tells Chris Jina fell in love with him	Day	2/8 pgs. Day 100	CAST: 1, 5 BG:
87	INT ANTHONY'S OFFICE Chris and Anthony argue over his time "slippage" and Jina's role	Day	1 4/8 pgs. Day 100	CAST: 1, 5 BG:
	ROOM MOVE			
50	INT WAITING ROOM Chris meets Ayana in the waiting room, Jina comes out	Day	1 7/8 pgs. Day 4	CAST: 1, 2, 3, 5 BG:
	MOVE OUTSIDE			
133	EXT ANOTHER STREET Chris walks up to Anthony, gives him a stone	Day	4/8 pgs. Day 7	CAST: 1, 5 BG:
52	EXT STREET Ayana walks down the street, picks up an apple, the apple bleeds	Day	4/8 pgs. Day 4	CAST: 2 BG:
109	EXT STREET Ayana walks down the street, shopping cart in tow	Day	1/8 pgs. Day 7	CAST: 2 BG:
	JINA'S OFFICE (PU from Day 12)			
48	INT JINA'S OFFICE Anthony and Jina continue to discuss Chris's "case"	Day	4/8 pgs. Day 102	CAST: 3, 5 BG:
63	INT JINA'S OFFICE Jina and Anthony try to figure out why Chris gets them so mad	Day	4/8 pgs. Day 102	CAST: 3, 5 BG:
	End Day # 13 Sunday, September 25, 2011 -- Total Pages: 9 6/8			

FIGURE 17.2 Sets and locations.

You did some of this work during Chapter 9, but the goals here are somewhat different. The list you're creating now will likely change, as you go to various locations and see which ones will work for which scenes (or won't work at all).

GATHERING YOUR LIST OF RESOURCES

Go back to the connection list you created in Chapter 11. See if any of the people on your list has a location that you can rent for low to no cost. These calls and emails will generate more than a few "no"s — but will also get you a few referrals. This is a good way of getting apartments, houses, and family-run businesses.

If you're trying to shoot in a big chain store, unless you have an "in" already, you'll have to contact the corporate communications department of the chain. If you can get away with leaving the name offscreen, sometimes you can just make nice with the manager of the local branch/restaurant/store. Some local film commission offices have people who can actually point you to great locations. The New Jersey film commission office has been terrific. They have a huge database of locations, including pictures and contact information, and they've helped me find everything from a hospital to a bar to a private house.

Your film commission office or town clerk may also be able to help you find government offices to shoot in. These are usually empty on the weekends and, with a little fixing, may also work as private/corporate office spaces. Parks and community centers can also be good resources, but some parks are actually under environmental protection, so the park rangers are more picky about letting crews shoot there.

Once you've got a few resources to hit up, schedule some scouts. Grab some gear: a video or still camera (a smartphone isn't bad, but a "real" camera can sometimes get you better results), a tape measure, a notepad, your script and schedule. Ideally, your partner (if you have one), the DP, production sound mixer, 1st AD, production designer, and/or line producer should go with you. But if you're flying solo for some reason, then bring a fresh pair of eyes and ears.

THE SET VS. THE SITE VS. FOOTPRINT

The set is just what will be in front of or immediately behind the camera. The *site* is the whole area, house, apartment, building, or street (and sometimes all of these) that the set is a part of. It's easy to find a really great-looking (and even sounding) set sitting on a lousy site.

One of the big things that non-film people don't understand is how much space even a small shoot takes up (the "footprint"). So a location owner agrees to let you use his shop, thinking it'll just be a few people and a camera, and then suddenly five trucks and a fleet of vans show up in front of his door, disgorge all this gear, run cables up the block to the generator, and take over the sidewalk with the crafty tents and video village. The shop owner is a bit frustrated, since he had it in the back of his head that maybe he could've stayed open while you were shooting.

The shop owner isn't the only one who doesn't get it. Producers aren't so great at it either. We constantly underestimate how much space, stuff, and manpower a shoot takes up. The problem is even more acute on really low-budget films because the thinking is: why do I need all this space?

A good rule of thumb is to figure that any shoot needs one room for hair/makeup (HMU), one room for wardrobe, one bathroom, one area for video village and the mixer, one desk for the DIT/video tech, one table for crafty, 0–3 rooms for all the stuff that has to get moved out of the location, and one-to-many rooms for all the grip/electric gear (nothing is worse than staging C-stands in the hall where the neighbors can trip over them and sue you). You also need holding areas for the cast. Depending on your SAG rep and your actors, you may be able to get away with dividing a large space up with privacy screens. You also need a place to feed everyone, preferably with tables and chairs provided (a restaurant will work). And somewhere for your 2nd AD, line producer, and other office staff to make calls and set up the next day's work.

There are ways around this. It's not uncommon for HMU and wardrobe to share a space, and for video village to be a single monitor right next to the camera. The DIT can go sit with the production staff as long as the latter aren't too loud. I've been able to set up in very tight spots by just economizing on space as much as possible.

What to Look for When Scouting the Set

You'll usually start your scout on the set and then work your way outward from there. Keeping that in mind, let's start by looking at the set:

Stuff. What's there that you can use? What will be getting in your way? Is there somewhere close by where you can stow the junk you don't need? What about set dressing changes – is the owner cool with these?

Set dimensions. Bring your script, a measuring tape, and a notepad. I jot down a quick set of measurements and sketch a floor plan. Later on at home I turn it into a set of scale drawings (using Visio or one of its open-source alternatives). If you have time, do some blocking, in your head or using whoever's available. The dimensions will change the character of the scene. This is a point where some directors go a little nuts, because a location didn't exactly fit their idea of what the set should look like. They had a perfect shot in their heads. You have to decide whether to sculpt the space to the scene, or tweak the scene. If the space is too divergent from what you had in mind, then it's probably not a good fit and you should move on. If it's in the ballpark or offers some possibilities you hadn't even considered (hey, a kitchen with an island separator – now I can put all the kitchen and living room scenes together) it might be worth holding onto.

Think about the size of the camera itself. If you're shooting on a Canon 5D, you can always strip it down to the bare body and lens, shove it against a wall, and still get a shot from a few feet away. But if you're shooting on a larger camera (such as the Epic or a 35mm rig), you'll need more space behind the lens. *The Toe Tactic* was shot a few years ago on the then-hot Sony F950, an HDCAM-SR camera that output to a separate recorder through dual-link HD-SDI cables. By the time we added the battery, handheld rigging, cinestyle lenses, mattebox, and onboard monitor, there wasn't enough space to fit the camera into one of the locations – a tiny cramped elevator – so we had to rent a separate remote rig for the day.

Production value. Does the location feature a balcony with a beautiful view of the city? Is the basement full of dark corners and sinister, rusting farm equipment? The right location can make a film seem much bigger than it is. *Next Stop Wonderland* (Brad Anderson) was shot in and around Boston, and really used every bit of the city – the aquarium, the beach, various bars and restaurants, hospitals. Robert Clem, the writer/director of *Company K*, was very good at picking spots that lent the tiny-budget World War I story a bigger, more "epic" feel.

Character. Does the location feel like the character lives or spends time there? If you're scouting for a corner office for a law-firm partner, you don't want to wind up in a tiny, dingy space. A biker is probably *not* going to hang out in your friend's swanky bar that you can get for free, but in a grungy dive, some dark spot that may cost you a few bucks. Even exteriors can be representative of a person's state of mind – dark woods are very different in character from a well-kept garden.

Color. If the space is good but you think you'll need to repaint or otherwise change the color scheme quite a bit (furniture covers), note this down. If that's the case then you want to move these scenes to the day *after* some simple exteriors, or after a weekend. This way your art department has some prayer of finishing the painting before you show up.

Light. Do you get good exposure from the rooflight or windows? Is it outside? If you're inside, what are the built-in lights like (CFL, old-school fluorescents, office halogens, etc.)? How does the light change over the course of the day? You may have to come back a couple of times to figure this out.

Sound. On *Windows* we scouted for an apartment and thought we'd found a perfect one – a second-story loft in Brooklyn, with a really nice view of the street outside, and only a few blocks away from the subway. However, the guy living there seemed to be hustling us out the door after we'd only been there a few minutes. We figured out why when we went downstairs – and the printing press on the first floor started up. Suddenly the perfect apartment wasn't so perfect anymore.

Some sound problems are fixable – leaky faucets, refrigerators, air conditioners, humming lights. Others are more problematic, like the highway or elevated train. It's Murphy's Law that the most interesting-looking locations will play havoc with any attempt to record clean dialog. Sometimes, however, there's a partwise-solution. Can you move up one block further away from the noise? Can you put some closed doors between you and one of the sources of noise? Can you shoot when the office downstairs is closed, or the loud-sex neighbors are away during the day?

Electricity. Consider not just the juice you'll need on the set, but also what you'll need in the holding area, to charge batteries, run the DIT's laptop, wardrobe's steamer, and the aforementioned hairdryer. How accessible is the circuit-breaker box? Do you know what circuits are tied to what rooms? If I get the chance on a scout I find the nearest breaker box, and throw switches (or at least write down the labels if there are any). You want to avoid having to either tie in or run a generator (the latter is noisy and expensive; the former somewhat risky if the gaffer and/or best boy are green).

There are times when renting a generator is unavoidable – if you have a lot of scenes that will be lit by daylight, you'll usually want at least one larger HMI lamp so you have a prayer of matching the daylight should it get cloudy or the sun goes down while you're still shooting. In these cases, you'll need to find a spot nearby where the cable run isn't too long (voltage drops over distance and cable can be expensive to rent), but where there's a nice big pile of dirt or a building between the set and the generator. If you can, use the tape measure and guesstimate the cable run – that will tell you how much cable you'll need to rent.

Video village. If you're shooting on a DSLR, have no script supervisor, and are trucking around a small monitor on a stand (or just using whatever onboard/handheld monitor the DP has), then this is not a huge consideration. On many shoots, though, you'll need to set up a separate tent/room/area for the director, producer, and set crew to look at the monitors. This should be as close to set as possible.

What to Look for When Scouting the Site

Stepping off the set now, let's look at what's in the immediate vicinity that you'll need:

Bathroom. Sounds obvious, until you're shooting in the woods. If the nearest bathroom is a mile down the road, you may need to find a local port-a-potty rental house. Phone any nearby construction company or parks department for a referral. These units tend to be reasonably priced, delivered, and picked up, and tend to be pretty clean (just remember to buy soap and extra toilet paper). You'll have to supply a lock and key, however, if you're worried about folks other than your crew/cast using them.

HMU/wardrobe/holding. This is where the cast changes, and HMU and wardrobe gets them ready. You want a few rooms if possible or one that can be subdivided by privacy screens. Access to electricity is critical, because the costume designer needs to plug in the steamer, and the hairstylist needs to run her blowdryer, and both need lights and a printer. I try to keep these areas as close to the set as possible.

Grip/electric staging. You don't want to have to go back to the truck every time you need to grab another C-stand or sandbag. Typically, the grips and electrics will try and stage anything they think they'll need close to set. This gear takes up a lot of space (even in hampers), and tends to trip up other people, so see if there's a room or hallway they can have to themselves. If your lighting/grip gear is small this may not be a major factor.

Art staging (related to **stuff**; see above). Is there somewhere you can put the props you'll need during the next scene? What about the couch that you need to remove, where should it go?

Sound cart. The sound department doesn't take up much space. Usually they lug everything around on a sound cart. So at least it's mobile.

Equipment station/printer/desk. The enormous pile of battery chargers has to go somewhere (cameras, walkies, sound system, onboard monitors, still cameras, phones … it gets bigger every year). Also, I like to have a printer that everyone can access (though this often gets commandeered by HMU/wardrobe). And enough of a horizontal surface to put a laptop.

Overnight storage. Is there a secure place at the location where you can put your camera, sound, grip, electric, and other gear? This can make a huge difference if you're going to be at the same spot for more than a day – you don't have to do a complete load-in/load-out, and can get straight to work.

Classroom. If you have minors in your film, they're supposed to be in a classroom during the school year. See the rules for classrooms and tutoring in Chapter 13 for more details.

Parking. You'll need to park the vehicles nearby, if at all possible. If your shooting permit entitles you to parking in designated areas, that's great. You do want to park somewhere that's actually secure, so things don't walk out the back of the trucks. You also want to be able to swing by and load-in/load-out gear (hooray for loading docks). Write down the traffic/parking regulation signs on the block where you're shooting. Also, look for 24/7 garages nearby. If you can leave the equipment van/truck overnight close by, you've just saved extra trips every day – which equals gas and toll savings as well.

Catering/eating. Ideally, you'll get your food locally, and eat it next to set. If it's catered, you'll need somewhere for everyone to sit down, and a table to put the buffet.

Access. How much of a hump is it from the passenger drop-off point to the set? Are you hiking through the woods? Are you going from floor to floor in a hospital? Make a quick map or grab one if it's available. Is there a subway/bus stop nearby? Also, find out the name of a local, reliable car service.

Security. Is there a security guard? Do you have to pay them as part of your location fee?

Garbage. Oh boy, this is a big problem on film sets. We generate a *ton* of garbage (and don't recycle as much of it as we should, though we're getting better). If you're shooting in a building, do they have the capacity to handle the extra load? If you're shooting in a park, you may have to take things out with you. Is there a nice dumpster somewhere nearby? Or will you have to legitimately hire a cartage service? Any business nearby can tell you about the local commercial trash companies. Just don't pile it all on the sidewalk and leave – that's a great way to burn your bridges so you won't be able to come back for the reshoot.

Access to services. Walk around the neighborhood. Look for, and jot down, the addresses of the closest:

- Hardware store
- Office supplies place
- Dry cleaner/laundromat
- Grocery/supermarket
- Pharmacy
- Internet café (with fax)
- Gas station
- Towing service/repair garage
- Snow plow service (if you're shooting in the winter)
- Hospital
- Firehouse
- Police precinct/state trooper barracks/sheriff's office
- Restaurants that deliver
- All-night dining options

Grab menus, write down addresses. Starbucks does *not* count as an essential service, though the cast and crew may beg to differ. How far away are these places – down the block, up the road, or in a mall fifteen miles away?

Neighbors. Listen and watch the neighborhood, preferably at different times of the day. Does the location owner have any insight – do people get rowdy on Friday nights, or is it quiet? Is every shot going to be ruined by ice cream trucks going by, or car radios blasting? Are you in a flight path? On the other hand, does it seem like a neighborhood where people are curious about the shoot, maybe even friendly or helpful? Is it a residential or retail neighborhood?

Other nearby locations. How close is the location to others in your script? Are there any spots nearby that could serve as locations?

Internet/cellphone/landline service. Oh, how everyone loves the cloud – until it's not there. Believe it or not, there are plenty of spots where you'll be without cellphone service, broadband access, and/or a landline. Figure out where the nearest landline is, so that in case of emergency you can get in touch with someone.

Opportunities for goodwill. Film crews can be like locusts – they come in and eat everything in sight, make a mess, and then leave. But sometimes you can make that work for you. If you can promise a local community leader that your crew and cast will spend money nearby, he may be more willing to make a deal. Or perhaps you have to do some community service ahead of the shoot to establish some goodwill (and a lower fee).

Short case study #1. *LL* was shot entirely in Manhattan, in some pretty busy areas, so we rarely had problems finding things. The shoot was very small, so we were able to go downstairs from wherever we were shooting, find a nice city shot, and steal an insert or two (or in a couple of cases, an entire scene) outside. The director walked around with a small 9-inch monitor, and we had no script supervisor.

Short case study #2. *Rock the Paint* was shot largely in and around Newark, and in upstate New York (near Kingston). In both areas, finding places open late at night for gas, second meal, and groceries was difficult. Many of the locations we shot in were too small to have their own holding areas, so we had to set up next door. And trash disposal was a constant problem – we usually snuck it into a nearby dumpster (this is illegal, by the way). We *were* able to park overnight in several locations and leave our gear on set (which was great).

Short case study #3. On *Helena from the Wedding* we found a cartage service that rented us a dumpster. The cabin we were shooting in had two rooms upstairs which were offscreen, so we used one for wardrobe/changing and the other for hair/makeup. We had to move the craft services around to wherever we *weren't* looking, and eventually put most of it upstairs between the two top rooms. Equipment went into another empty bedroom on the first floor. We ate downstairs in the basement garage. We had a larger HD monitor on a stand, using a wireless transmitter system so we didn't have to chain it to the camera, and we moved it around a lot. The producers also rented a house next to the cabin, where one of them processed the shot cards, and actors could go to chill out. We parked in the hotel every night.

Finding Things Nearby and Making Do

You'll rarely find a "perfect location" outside of a soundstage. But you can always rent a separate holding space for your bathroom, staging, eating, and HMU/wardrobe needs. Community centers, schools, and churches/temples/mosques are a great resource, and are usually willing to negotiate fees, especially if you're shooting during a period when they don't need those facilities.

If you're shooting in the woods or somewhere pretty remote, you may have to rent a mobile home or camper to serve as a holding/bathroom area, or have a car on standby to take people back and forth to the hotel or other nearby space. You'll also want to rent additional pop-tents and a small generator so that you can set up a "base camp." If you're shooting in the winter, you'll need to add some heaters in as well.

Considering the Season and Time of Day

The length of the day and angle of the sun changes over the course of the year, as does plant cover, snow levels, rainfall, and temperature. If you're scouting too far out from your projected shooting dates, you may be in for a nasty surprise when you show up. Keep in mind how much things may change between the scout and the shoot.

THE TECH SCOUT

The number of things to pay attention to during a scout is a bit overwhelming. That's one reason to do a separate tech scout – you can circle back and make sure that the location will serve your needs. So who should go? Essentially, most of the department heads (you can leave out the key HMU, costume designer, editor, script supervisor).

The tech scout requires some time, as the crew looks at, analyzes, and discusses the location's merits and issues, and starts jotting down notes for gear lists. The director can start working out blocking with the DP. The production and location staff can figure out holding, parking, and other logistical issues.

If you can't take everyone on the tech scout (or if you don't end up having one), bring back material – pictures, video, diagrams, your own description of the environment, and lists of nearby resources. Grab contact information. On *Found In Time*, I did one scout with Ben (the DP), and then came back a month later on my own. But I later emailed everyone videos, pictures, and diagrams and spoke with Anthony Viera, the sound mixer, about the issues with the different locations.

STAYING ORGANIZED WITH LOCATIONS

As you can imagine, location scouting produces a great deal of paperwork. I recommend that you create a location subfolder inside the project folder on your hard drive. In this folder you'll want to place:

- Signed location agreements
- Insurance certificates
- Local service lists (where the police, fire, hardware stores, etc. are)
- Maps
- Menus
- Location brochures
- Top-down diagrams
- Scouting photos (put these in a separate subfolder, for each location)
- Scouting videos (same as for scouting photos)

At this point I usually start walking around with a portable file box with hardcopies of the paperwork, and blanks of the location agreements (more on the portable file box in the next chapter).

Some producers put this material online so everyone in the crew can download it. I've done this off and on over the years and think it's a good idea overall, but make sure that you pick a secure service and keep backup copies on your local drive. The latest round of cloud storage services are a big step up (the offerings from DropBox, Google, Amazon, and Apple) from what came before.

WARNINGS

If you can at all avoid it, *don't shoot in your apartment/house.* You need a space where you can get away from the shoot, be a mess, and store your stuff.

Be honest with the location owner about how many people you'll be bringing, how much space the shoot will take up, and how long the days are. You will scare off some owners, but it's better that they freak out now than later, when you're shooting.

Be careful about announcing to the neighbors that you're scouting for a film shoot. Some people get dollar signs in their eyes when they hear that, and may try to hijack you for "quiet" fees. One of the neighbors living next door to our big location on *Caleb's Door* cranked his car radio up every time he drove by, until we gave him a parking spot. By the end of the shoot he wanted cash.

Don't be optimistic in your space estimates. If you're shooting in an apartment building and you have to pile equipment in the hallway, the neighbors may get very upset about it and complain. Or they'll walk by while you're shooting and say loudly "are you shooting a movie?" You're better off figuring out how to store the extra gear in the truck or rent another room or space in the basement, and stay less visible.

Be nice to the location staff. This should go without saying. These are the folks with the keys to everything. They can help you in all sorts of wonderful ways ("here's a closet you can store things in" or "here's a parking space you can use"). They can also make your life difficult if you or your crew give them a hard time. Spend some time with the security staff at the location when you're tech scouting.

THE END RESULT OF SCOUTING

In an ideal world, you'll now have a set of locations that work for you creatively, logistically, and budget-wise. If you have to pump a little bit more money into the locations budget, it's probably worthwhile. Locations add directly to production value.

You may have to make some small script tweaks to explain an unusual location feature, or fix a disconnect between the character and the space. And your schedule will probably need to be reshuffled, as your 1st AD starts figuring out how long it will take to load in the equipment and get ready for the first scene.

At the end of this process, you'll have a pretty clear idea of where you'll be shooting, what kind of basic equipment you'll need, and if you'll need to "day-play" people and/or gear for specific locations. You can now start to effectively previsualize your shoot.

QUESTIONS/EXERCISES

1. Walk around your neighborhood, taking pictures of different locations that might be of interest. Stop and listen to the sounds in the area, see how busy it gets, and note how the quality of the light changes over the course of the day.
2. Pretend that you're shooting in one room in your apartment or house. Where would you put the hair/makeup folks, the wardrobe rack, the grip/electric gear, craft services, etc.? How friendly are you with your neighbor? Do you have access to a larger room in your building that can be divided up?
3. Where are the nearest services to your apartment? Where's the nearest office supply store?
4. Just as an exercise – if you were going to use your space to shoot in, how much work would it take to turn it into the character's apartment? Is it just a matter of rearranging some furniture? Do you need to repaint? Or do you need to put in flywalls and make much bigger changes?

## Chapter 18

Staying Organized

FIGURE 18.1 Staying organized.

You've got your crew, cast, and locations together, and your equipment and vendor paperwork is starting to accumulate. You're probably on the tenth draft of your schedule and budget, and you lost count of how many script revisions you've done. Now that you're working with other people and are generating material for them, you have to stay on top of communications, paperwork, and money. In this chapter we'll look at some (hopefully) easy techniques for staying organized that will carry you throughout the shoot.

You can't do much about other people – some will be on top of things more than others – but you can make sure that you don't lose things or forget tasks. This is especially important as you get closer to production, and start losing more and more sleep. Because no two people organize their lives in exactly the same way, I can't really tell you how to keep yours together. But I'll tell you what's worked for me over the years, and you can take or leave aspects of it as you see fit.

THE "SYSTEM"

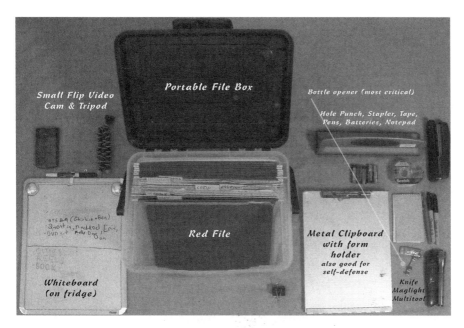

FIGURE 18.2 Components of the system. Very exciting.

I'm embarrassed to call it a system because I'm not a naturally organized person. I have a tendency to overbook my time, get behind on small tasks until they snowball, and often feel like I'm a step behind in my personal life. But during preproduction I become a different animal, mostly because other people are depending on me. Essentially, here are the components of my "system," for what it's worth (Figure 18.2):

1. A portable file box, into which goes:
   a. blank copies of timecards, contracts, location agreements, petty cash/expense sheets, and release forms
   b. schedules, callsheets, equipment lists, contact lists, location directions, insurance certificates
   c. filled-in contracts that I get back from the cast/crew/locations/vendors/extras that I haven't filed yet
   d. receipts and expense sheets that came back from the crew that I need to tally up
   e. the production sides for today
   f. a copy or two of the script
   g. envelopes, pens, and papers
   h. a *red folder* containing urgent stuff I need to hand out or take care of.
2. A project folder on the hard drive, which is organized something like Table 18.1 (most of my projects follow the same pattern). Whatever folder structure you decide on, make sure you can find files in it later.
3. A set of binders by my desk for things I don't need every day, but may need to get to later – signed deal memos, bank and credit card statements, callsheets from a few days ago, etc.
4. An inbox for stuff to be filed.
5. A small whiteboard on my fridge for writing down longer-term problems that need to be solved.

TABLE 18.1 Sample project folder

Folder/Subfolder	Purpose
Budget	The budget
OlderDrafts	Older drafts of the budget, and practice worksheets I used
Business	The business plan and associated charts and spreadsheets
Callsheets	All the callsheets
Cast	Headshots and resumes of the cast
Casting	Casting schedules, my notes on the sessions, reel clips
Sides	PDFs of the sides for casting
Crew	Prospective crew resumes
Distribution	Cover letters to distributors and sales agents, contracts from same
Expenses	Receipts, invoices, petty cash, hotcost spreadsheets
Festivals	Cover letters and applications to festivals, spreadsheets detailing what I've applied to
Fundraising	The business plan for the film, cover letters to investors, materials for crowdfunding platforms
Graphics	The stills and graphics files for the shoot
ConceptArt	Artwork/photos for the vision plan/look-book
Credits	Photoshop and TIFFs of the credits
DVD_and_Print	Artwork for the DVD, sleeve, poster, and postcard
EPK	A copy of the EPK that I can drop onto a CD (contains stills, the press kit)
Photos	Misc. photos of the shoot or other
Props	Pictures of props
ScoutPhotos	Scouting photos and videos
Signage_and_Graphics	Photoshop, Illustrator, etc. files for signs, and any kind of graphics, paperwork, logos, etc. seen onscreen
WebsiteGraphics	Graphics for the website
Insurance	Insurance quotes and certificates
Legal	Cast deal memos, crew deal memos, location agreements, etc. – any legal document
OlderDrafts	Older "redlined" drafts of legal docs
Locations	Location menus, maps, top-down diagrams, spreadsheet with information
NYState	Everything related to the tax incentive program
Payroll	Payroll agreement, weekly worksheet to them, check stubs and reports from them
Permits	All the copies of the Mayor's office permits
Post	Post documents (visual effects punchlist, music cuesheet, etc.)
Promo	Press kit, any other promotional/marketing material (bios, cover letters, etc.)
PRs	Production Reports
SAG	All the SAG-related paperwork (agreement, Exhibit Gs, report)
Schedule	All the copies of the schedule
Script	All the drafts of the script
Sides	PDFs of the production sides

Folder/Subfolder	Purpose
Sound	Production sound reports
Trailer	Trailer and associated files
Vendors	Vendor lists, equipment lists, quotes
Wardrobe	Info from me to the costume designer on wardrobe; photos for me to look at; continuity photos
Website	Files for the website (either code or content)
Rollbacks	Backups of the website
[Project main directory]	Latest contact lists, connection/resources spreadsheet, various notes, scans of my ID and credit card, anything I need to get to right away

6. A piece of paper that I write on with a sharpie or fat pen every night before I go to bed, of all the things I need to do *first thing in the morning.*
7. A big metal clipboard (see below) into which I put the stuff I need to get to right away – my checkbook, petty cash, a copy of the schedule, my copy of the sides and callsheet, and contact lists. I walk around on set with this.
8. I load all the cast, crew, vendor, location, and other contacts onto my phone and email client. I also define email groups on the client and smartphone so I can send group emails without having to type each name in.
9. A soft binder with my heavily marked-up script, scene analysis notes, and visual guides/ photos/artwork. I usually put plastic holders in the binder for storing anything that grabs my eye – a photo in a magazine or a CD. I used to carry around a look-book but more recently I've been keeping all of that material on my laptop, and emailing it to everyone else.

Along with this equipment I've developed some routines for staying sane (especially during prep).

Everything that needs real attention gets dumped into the red file, and processed when I get home at night or the next morning. Anything that I can file I pop into the inbox and deal with it whenever.

I tally up and check receipts every few days, and reconcile the petty cash and checks once a week. If I'm working for someone else as a line producer, I do this once every day or two (if the production is rich enough to afford a production accountant, then I look at her hotcost report every other day). The hotcost report lists all the expenses by line item, and compares them to the budget. This is probably the most crucial report you'll prepare during production. We'll discuss hotcost reports in more detail in Chapter 21.

I put the crew, location, and vendor contact information in one PDF, then email them off to everyone whenever they change. I do the same with location diagrams, scripts, schedules, scout photos – almost everything gets emailed to everyone. I only hold back on the cast contact list, releasing it selectively to people who need to contact them. Agents usually don't want their client information to be shared with the crew unless they (the actors) give explicit permission to do so.

COMMUNICATING WITH OTHERS

Despite the proliferation of online collaboration tools, I still find email to be the most efficient way to communicate with everyone.

You'll want to email your cast, crew, location owners, agents, investors, and your war council with weekly updates. During post and after, you can stretch this out to bi-weekly or monthly, but don't disappear. You want to keep people involved. These emails should include news by members of the team as well as info about the film, and they should go out ahead of any public e-blasts.

Subscribe this same group (ask first) to your monthly e-blast list, and invite them to your film's Facebook/Tumblr/Twitter/Pinterest/other social media pages. Some may say no thanks. Respect their wishes.

You should make sure to check your cellphone plan, and up your minutes, data, and text limit if necessary. A few years ago I was burning through 3000 peak minutes per month during a production. Now I can get away with 1400 to 2000 on a feature. But my text usage has tripled in that time, and everyone sends emails where they used to call.

Grab a few thumb drives from wherever you can get them super-cheap. You will want one to be your immediate backup/transfer drive for critical documents, and the others you can exchange with the cast/crew on an as-needed basis. For exchanging larger files, get a LaCie Rugged or similar triple interface drive. You want something that can get dropped and still work. A couple of years ago I bought a multi-card reader (it reads SD, micro-SD, CF, memory stick, and a few other card types) that plugs into a USB socket. If someone wants to give me something on a card-based medium, I can transfer it without heading to Radio Shack.

When someone does something really wonderful – goes the extra mile, saves you from a crisis, keeps their cool under difficult circumstances, etc. – give them a call, send them an email, or somehow otherwise acknowledge that you appreciate their work. You don't have to be gushing or do it every day, but it's always nice to get some well-deserved praise, especially from the boss.

Meetings

I really dislike meetings. After an hour my mind wanders, or I begin ticking off all the things I could have gotten done. Nonetheless, they're sometimes essential. It's important that you have regular in-person contact with your production designer, costume designer, DP, and visual effects supervisor (not to mention your partner). It's important that you keep meetings department-specific – i.e. don't have a meeting where half the participants are waiting for the other half to get their business done. Even if you have a decision that affects everyone ("there will be no color green in the movie, until the end"), you'll often make better use of everyone's time by meeting them individually and going into more depth about how it will affect them.

Encourage your crew to talk to each other and just keep you informed. More lateral communication means less work on your part and more relationship-building on theirs. If you feel like people are veering too far away from what you want, you can always get them back on track.

A week or so before the shoot, you'll want to have a production meeting with as many of the crew as you can. You can combine this with an all-cast reading (see Chapter 20). During the meeting, you want to do some very specific things:

1. Make introductions.
2. Hand out deal memos, contact lists, scripts, and schedules to anyone who doesn't have them.
3. Hand out insurance certificates to anyone who's renting equipment to you.
4. Note any significant script changes.
5. Go through the schedule, day by day, scene by scene. This will take up the bulk of the meeting. Your 1st AD (or whoever's filling this position) should lead this part of the discussion.
6. Discuss how payroll is handled.
7. Talk about transportation and/or hotel accommodation.
8. Take questions.
9. Break into smaller working groups if necessary.

I recommend that you *not* have a meal break in the middle, but either start or end with food. Ordering in the middle will just slow everything down, and people will focus on what they're eating rather than on what they're saying.

Last, you'll also want to schedule a meeting between your PAs and either you, your UPM, or your 1st or 2nd AD. This meeting is an "orientation" session – you want to get a sense of how much experience the PAs have, talk a bit about how sets work, go over walkie-talkie etiquette, the good way to do a lockup, and how *not* to hide parking or traffic tickets (just hand them in). You'll also want to distribute the contact sheets, scripts and deal memos, and some petty cash if they're doing pickups the next day.

I've found that having the PA meeting has helped enormously. When I was very green I got dumped into the deep end, no one explained anything to me, and I made a few screw-ups (like locking out the producer from his own set, or talking too much over the walkie). This way, the newer folks come to set knowing something about what they're getting into, and everyone has their paperwork.

That's about all the formal meetings you really need. You can always put together a Skype or conference call. Frankly these days I feel that the number of ways for keeping in touch with everyone has actually exceeded the *need* to do so. Instead I have to remind myself to unplug so I can get some think-work done.

SCRIPT REVISIONS AND LOCKING THE SCRIPT

At some point after you finish your casting, you should do your last "pre-shoot" tweak and lock the script. All the major screenwriting programs have a "lock script" feature. Any changes you make after this point will produce revision marks and "A" pages. To keep the existing page numbering scheme of the locked script, any revisions that spill over a page are put on their own, lettered page (so the revisions will flow from page 86 to 86A, 86B, and so on). Whenever you finish a revision, you'll want to print out just the revised pages, with the revision number indicated in some way.

Traditionally, each draft's pages were printed out on color paper, with the color matching the revision number. Your locked script becomes the "white" draft. The WGA West defines the standards shown in Table 18.2, but I've seen variations used from time to time.

TABLE 18.2 Drafts and revision colors

Revision	Color
	Unrevised draft production white
1	Blue
2	Pink
3	Yellow
4	Green
5	Goldenrod
6	Buff
7	Salmon
8	Cherry
9	Second blue
10	Second yellow
11	Second green
12	Second goldenrod
13	Second buff
14	Second salmon
15	Second cherry

Sometimes "Second" is called "Double." I worked on a film that went to Double Salmon drafts. At that point, everyone's script binder looked like a kindergarten construction paper project.

This system sucks for several reasons. First, unless you're really familiar with the color scheme, you're going to get lost (what revision is Pink again? Is it 2nd or 3rd?). I still have to look it up. Second, it gives you no written indication of the revision. So if the crew and cast are printing the script out at home (on white paper), it's useless. Third, color paper is expensive and of limited use; so you either have to be friendly with a production company and grab their stacks, or buy one ream of each color and hope you don't need more.

The method I prefer is to add the revision number and (manual) date to the top of each page, just to the left of the page number. Then I put the date and time printed in the footer. I email revised pages to everyone as PDFs, saving the PDF as XXXX_Rev01.pdf, XXXX_Rev02.pdf, where XXXX = the name of the script. This makes it pretty clear what people are getting. I'll usually print the revised pages out on white paper, and warn people that they're not going to get colored drafts.

Other Revisions

Whenever I revise a contact list, schedule, budget, or other non-legal document, I save the revised file as XXXX_revYY, where XXXX is the filename (hopefully indicating what the file contains) and YY is the revision number. Contracts I tend to save using the date, using the format: contractor-contracttype-yyyy-mm-dd. Contractor is the name of the person/entity the contract is for, contracttype is the type of deal memo (location agreement, crew agreement, etc.), and yyyy-mm-dd is the date in year, month, date format. Whatever system you use is fine, just try to be consistent.

CONCLUSIONS

However you organize things is really up to you. Keep in mind, however, that you may have to share your system with other people – the UPM, production coordinator, office intern, and/or accountant – so make sure it's something that others can get used to with minimal training.

Don't put a system together that's too rigid to maintain when you start running out of time. Instead of focusing on a "perfect" system, I try to focus on an "adequate" one that requires less time.

QUESTIONS/EXERCISES

1. Do you have a system for how you organize your life? Do you think it would be adaptable to film production?
2. Start organizing bits of your project.
3. Hit up the Staples website and browse. You don't have to buy anything, but start thinking about what you can carry with you that's lightweight but practical – some people like files, others like binders, still others like everything on the computer.
4. Do you have a scanner (or access to one)? A scanner can be a great way to cut down on clutter. Scan in paperwork, back up the files, and put the originals in deep storage.

## Chapter 19

Previsualization

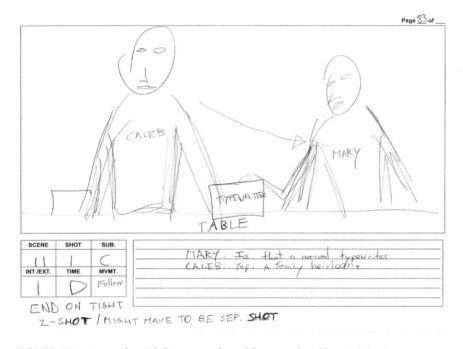

FIGURE 19.1 A sample stick figure storyboard from my first film, *Caleb's Door*.

Once you have your locations, and you have some idea of what camera you're shooting on and who's on your crew, you can create your previsualization ("previz"). I'm using this broad term to encompass several methods/tools – top-down diagrams, storyboards, "action-figure" mapping, special software, and straight-up shotlisting. This chapter isn't going to get into a detailed analysis of composition and camera movement. What you really need to know is *how* previz can help your film. So we'll focus on how to approach previz from different points of view, highlight the strengths and weaknesses of the different methods available (in a broad sense), and tie your efforts back to the script.

THE GOALS OF PREVIZ

Unless you have James Cameron's budget, your previz is likely only going to bear a passing rela-tionship to what you'll actually shoot and edit. Life, actors, time, money, the weather, and a host of other factors are going to get in the way of reproducing the sketches, diagrams, and other aids you've created.

But that's not a bad thing, necessarily. Part of filmmaking is collaborating with others. There's a good chance that your DP and you can come up with something more dynamic and interesting than either of you would be able to on your own. Or perhaps the actor decides to walk off in a different direction – or alternately, just stays and fumes at the end of an argument. While that may not be what you boarded, it might make a better shot. Independent filmmaking is sometimes all about embracing what's possible, spontaneous, or even problematic, and making it work for you.

There are five goals to previz:

1. To get you thinking about the film in three dimensions
2. To get some blocking ideas together
3. To communicate to the crew what you're after
4. To figure out your setups so you can schedule more efficiently
5. To analyze the script through other means

There are several different techniques you can use, and some directors like to combine them, depending on the scene and their personal tastes. If you're a good freehand artist, then perhaps storyboarding is your thing. Like maps? Use floor plans. Some directors use action figures or even chess-pieces to show everything (they either demonstrate the setups on set or videotape them). Other folks swear by their storyboard software, or put together simple computer animations. Whatever tools you use, try not to spend a huge amount of money on them. The results are just a means to an end – like pencil sketches are to an oil painter.

You'll probably be in a bit of a time crunch by the time you're really ready to do your pre-viz. Even if you've hired a storyboard artist or your DP is helping you, you're going to have to really fight for time to do this work. Don't leave it to the last minute. In any given scene you'll have between one and twenty setups; seven or eight is probably an average if most of your scenes take place between two people (2 moving masters from different angles, 2 close-ups, 2 cutaways, and 1–2 two-shots perhaps, depending on the blocking). Multiply this average by the number of scenes and you'll have some idea of how many camera setups you'll have to plot out or diagram.

If you have time, start on page 1 and work your way linearly through the script. If you're pressed, work in schedule order. Not all scenes deserve equal consideration, and some scenes can probably be shot with identical setups, so focus on the unique/important cases.

Before we get into the choice of tools, you may want to figure out the approach you want to take towards your previsualization.

TEXT VS. PICTURE FIRST

Comics creators know this situation intimately. Do you create the images first and then write text to fill the story, or vice-versa? In your case, you already have the script. But do you conceive the shots first, then work the script in; or do you use your script analysis as your guidepost for creating your shots? Music videos are where you see these different styles at their most pronounced. Do you cut on the beat, or follow the story being told by the lyrics? This is not just an academic debate. How do you shoot, light, and cut a film together that's both visually striking *and* compelling, story-wise?

On *Exposed*, the director, Burke Heffner, had the idea that as the story progressed, the shots should become less static, less centered on the characters, and a *little* more chaotic (I say a little because he didn't want the whole film to devolve into Michael Bay-ness, but did want the audience to be a little more jarred). As a still photographer, he thought in tableaus first, and fit the coverage around them. This was reflected in his shotlists and sketches. Stephen Leeds, the director of *The Magnificent Cooly-T*, had a strong sense of visual comedy, so he often started his scenes on a "joke" or "punchline" shot. *Garden State* (2004) featured a lot of static shots, where the composition and the set design featured some great visual jokes.

Nicole Quinn, the director of *Racing Daylight*, started with the characters first. Each of the three acts of the film is narrated by a different character. So she developed a distinct editing style, color scheme, and pace for each one, reflecting their distinct personalities.

Thinking image first can produce some amazing-looking imagery; but it can distance the viewer from the story and characters. When I saw Yimou Zhang's *Hero*, I found myself pulling away from the material, because every shot was *too perfectly composed*. On the other hand, paying too much attention to the story can lead to really meat-and-potatoes visuals. As a director (and producer), you don't want that either. Mike Nichols' *The Graduate* (1967) is a good marriage of visuals (camera composition is very important in the film) and story. There's no right answer, but it's something to think about as you build your world through previz.

WHAT DO YOU WANT TO SEE?

In a sense, previz is a way of not only *shooting* the film before production, but *cutting* the film as well. Do you have a style of editing in mind? Do you like long takes? Do you like to keep the cutting brisk? Do you favor camera movement or do you like still shots? Horror film "scares" often work by moving the camera *in the wrong direction*, away from the scary thing, then moving it back. Do you like shots that are carefully composed, or do you like things to look a little "untidy," almost like you "caught" the moment on camera? Todd Solondz seems to prefer a very composed frame. *Blue Valentine*, which goes between handheld work and very long, static takes, somehow feels more immediate.

You don't have to decide on your style now, in part that's what you're doing this work for. But it helps to ask the question periodically so you don't get lost in the details.

TOOLS OF THE TRADE

There are five broad categories of previz tools, and in the next sections we'll delve briefly into how to best use each one. In no particular order:

1. Storyboarding (either by hand or using software)
2. Top-down floor planning/mapping
3. "Action figure"/tabletop blocking
4. Machinima/CGI/"real" previz software
5. "Direct" shotlisting – which is also the end result of all the previous methods

You may find it takes you a while to find the tool that best suits you; or you may use more than one. This is the time to experiment, try different techniques, go on tangents … do it now before the shoot starts.

You'll want to have both your producer's script breakdown and schedule and director's scene-by-scene analysis sitting next to you. These can give you a sense of what the most critical scenes are, which will most likely take up the most time, and what's important to you dramatically.

DIY VS. HIRING

I'm a strong believer in doing your own previz work in conjunction with the DP, 1st AD, editor, and producer (or any combination of the above who're available). When you hand off the work to a professional storyboard/previz artist, you'll end up being almost as involved (at least mentally) as if you were doing it yourself. On the other hand, it may make sense to hire an artist if you're trying to use the previz to raise money, if you can't really devote as much time to it as you'd like, or if you need a fresh perspective.

STORYBOARDING

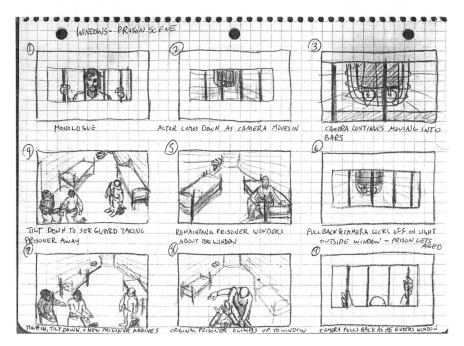

FIGURE 19.2 A first draft storyboard, from a real artist, John Bonafede.

Storyboards (Figure 19.2) are probably the most popular way of previsualizing your film, and they have a distinct advantage over other methods: just about anyone can grasp, by looking at a sequence of boards, how you intend to build a scene. We're trained from childhood to look at images in sequence and create narratives from them. If you can draw, that's great; if you can't, don't worry. There are a plethora of options out there.

The two downsides are that it can be harder to convey movement (arrows do the job but they're not perfect and are subject to some interpretation), and it can take quite a while to generate a full set of boards for a film. To give you some idea of the scale of the work: an "average" independent film has somewhere between 1500 and 2500 shots or what I'll call "significant camera movements" where the frame changes radically from the start of the cut to the finish. So if you're looking at drawing/making one frame per shot or camera movement … you'd better take some time to do this. The good news is that many of these shots are simply continuations of the same underlying camera setup, so you can write "Same as 89-A" instead of having to draw the same talking head over and over again.

I've seen storyboards put together using still photos, stick-figure drawings, watercolors by professional artists, software programs such as Storyboard Quick and FrameForge … and in pretty much every style (three on a page, one on a page, etc.). I recommend that you choose a form that gives you space to write the matching dialog or action underneath or next to the shot. You'll also want to write in the following:

1. Approximate shot type ("Long Shot," "CU," "ECU")
2. Camera movement (pan, truck, tilt, crane)
3. Lighting or visual effects

If you have a long, complicated shot, it's best to break it up into several sketches, connecting each one through arrows.

By Hand or Using Software

I used to think doing things by hand was a more effective way of learning, but the truth is that it takes too long unless you're a skilled artist. So if you want to do anything more than stick figures, I recommend looking into one of the software programs available. These programs also solve the common problems of hand-drawn boards: incorrect frame size/ratio, no indication of lens type, and no sense of perspective.

TOP-DOWN DIAGRAMS

I'm a huge fan of these (see Figure 19.3). Not only do they make up for my lack of drawing ability, but pretty much everyone can understand by looking at them where the characters, props, camera, and lights are in relation to each other.

I usually create a blank template of the top-down location diagram in Visio (some people I know use Illustrator or PhotoShop), and print out a bunch of them. I prefer Visio because you can create scale drawings, but Dia (open source, all platforms) and a few other less expensive programs work just as well.

At the top of the page, put in the scene number – if you're shooting multiple scenes with the same setup, write these in as well. Place your characters in their starting positions, and use arrows tied to the characters to indicate blocking changes. I usually use a box with a little lens or matte box to indicate the camera position for a given setup, and attach arrows to it to denote camera movement. A number or letter next to the camera denotes the setup.

Start with the master shot and work your way inward towards close-ups. I list cutaways separately because the diagram will get too cluttered otherwise. If the diagram starts looking impenetrable, I'll continue onto another blank form.

I've found that, compared to storyboarding, top-down mapping is a little more abstract, but takes less time, since you're focusing on setups instead of shots. It suffers from some of the same problems as storyboarding, in that your ability to convey movement is limited. Also, because everything is mapped on a two-dimensional plane, there's no sense of the lens height or angle. I'll sometimes write "Up-Angle" or "Zoom" next to the camera icon.

SOFTWARE OPTIONS

There are various inexpensive "Home Architect" solutions that let you build home blueprints, decorate them, then do limited 3D animatics. If you have some very production-design-specific needs this can be a good alternative to the more vanilla floor plan method I've described. The one thing that most of them suffer from is that, once you've created the space, you still have to indicate blocking and camera movement.

"ACTION FIGURE"/TABLETOP BLOCKING

As children, we did a lot of playacting with action figures, dolls, toy houses. In a sense, that's what you're doing when you use what I'll call the "action figure" or tabletop technique (Figure 19.4). Instead of drawing things inside of frames, or atop floor plans, you'll be using props (action figures, dolls, chess pieces, cars, toy houses, Lego bricks, or models) to indicate the characters, props, and sets. You create your set, put the characters and props in their first positions, and then push them around using your hands (or puppet sticks, if you're more sophisticated). You can either do this live in front of the cast and crew, or shoot it with your phone or a still camera.

The big advantage of this technique is that it's easier to see spatial relationships and character movement. Since you're executing everything "live" you can give some sense of pacing, narrate the story if you want, or alternately stop and explain something. One downside is that you have to be more explicit about where the camera is. You can indicate the camera position using another prop or assume that the camera you're using *is* the camera perspective. The other problem is that, as you

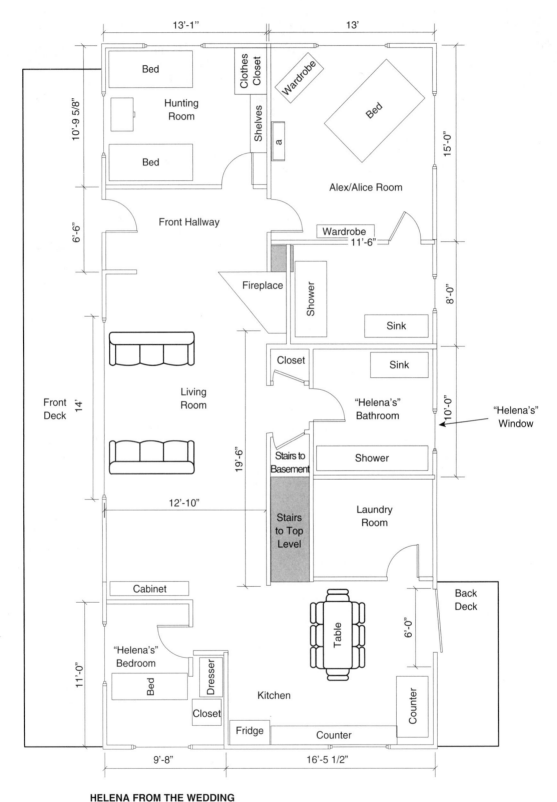

**HELENA FROM THE WEDDING
HOUSE INTERIOR**

FIGURE 19.3 An example of a top-down diagram.

FIGURE 19.4 Blocking a scene, using the tabletop technique.

can imagine, it can take a while to build and set up your tabletop universe. If you only have a few locations, this may not be much of a problem. You can also use top-down maps instead of building your sets in 3D. This is what old-school role-playing gamers do – they put miniatures down on top of flat maps.

Even if you don't use it as your primary previz technique, it's a great way of showing complicated sequences to the crew and cast on the day. If you want to see a good practical example of this, watch some episodes of the new *Battlestar Galactica*, where they run simulations by moving models on a big board.

COMPUTER-BASED PREVIZ

I'm actually lumping a lot of disparate tools and techniques into this one category, because they all involve using the computer as the *primary* means of not just diagramming, but animating your previz. In that sense, they're what a Hollywood visual effects company would consider "previz" tools. The main difference between these and the other techniques is that you're actually creating an animated version of the film. Consequently, they can be harder to master, more time-consuming, and potentially more expensive. But it's still cheaper than shooting, which is why visual-effects-driven films use it so heavily.

Computer-based tools come in several flavors, the main difference being in the degree of control you have over the environment, models, and other attributes of the world.

Machinima is really a specific type of animation produced by using a 3D game engine. It was made popular in the mid-to-late nineties when id Software's "Quake" came out. A lot of filmmakers saw the potential in using the included relatively-easy-to-use 3D modeling tools to create movies. You could build sets, use stock game characters or skin your own, set up the lighting, and then start the built-in-camera recording (previously used to record the game player's progress). Depending on the software, you either had to script character movements or actually have real players moving them around. Voice acting was added at the time or later on. Compared to both traditional 3D animation work and filmmaking, it was a very cheap way for people to put films together.

Entry-level programs such as Poser or ZBrush are a step up from machinima in the level of control, but are still *relatively* easy to use. They focus on the hardest part of 3D animation, which is creating and moving objects (such as people).

FrameForge deserves its own category. While it's not quite an animation program, it offers a *lot* more features than storyboarding software. The focus is on building individual frames, but it models lights, dollies, and lenses used in real life, so DPs generally like it.

CGI suites such as Strata 3D, Rhino, Maya, 3DStudio Max, and others vary considerably and would require an entire book to compare and contrast. You can't download these programs and expect to start working right away – it takes a few months to get proficient enough to do more than simple sketching.

All of these different applications will export individual frames or the entire film you create to a variety of video formats. You can then compress the video for web-friendly viewing, bring it into your editing system and further refine it, or break it down into scenes and play them back on set.

STRAIGHT-AHEAD SHOTLISTING

Some folks can size up a scene and start writing shotlists directly from their head. If you can do this, then that's awesome. And for some scenes, perhaps there's really no need to previsualize – there are only so many places you can put the camera in the shower or bathroom, for example.

TRANSLATING PREVIZ INTO A SHOTLIST

A shotlist (Table 19.1) is a powerful tool for the DP, director, and 1st AD, and is in some ways the ultimate goal of all these previz techniques. While it's good to have storyboards, diagrams, and the like on set – it can help remind everyone of what they're after – the shotlist turns this into a linear "execution order" which the crew can follow. Some ADs like to break strips down into individual setups.

You'll want to sit with the script and whatever previz you've done, and for each scene, translate the previz work into individual camera setups, preferably listed in order from widest to tightest.

TABLE 19.1 Sample preliminary shotlist

Sc. 34	A	Moving MASTER – End on Chris
[All handheld]	B	Moving MASTER #2 – End on Ayana
	C	WIDE Reverse Master (across street) – may be on tripod
	D	2-SHOT Follow Jess/Morton as they enter, open to OTS Jess/Morton on Chris/Ayana/RJ
	E	2-SHOT Leading Jess/Morton, open to OTS Chris/Ayana/RJ on Jess/Morton
	F	Tighter CUs Morton, Up-Angle
	G	Tighter CU Chris, Up-Angle
	H	Special on Ayana at end of Scene (may be tight 2-shot)
	J	Reactions RJ (single or dirty single with Chris), Up-Angle
	K	"Swinging singles"
	?	Cutaways – papers
TIME PERMIT	?	Exit Morton/Jess
TIME PERMIT	?	WIDER reaction shot Chris/RJ/Ayana

If you've been making top-down diagrams, you just have to copy the camera setups onto a new piece of paper or into a new file. If you've used any of the other techniques, you may have to look carefully through your shots and deduce the common setups. You're just translating from one medium to another. As you're transcribing the notes, look for setups that can be combined, opportunities for cutaways, and shots that are "nice to have" but not essential (time permitting).

The shotlist should be short – if you find yourself typing up more than one page per scene, you're not really getting the hang of it. Use common terminology whenever possible.

From the shotlist, the DP can figure out, to some extent, how many lighting changes each scene will require. Lighting setups and camera setups don't always match up (a move from a master to a close-up looking in the same direction will require tweaking, but turning around and looking in the other direction may require a very different lighting scheme). Your script supervisor and editor can also use the shotlist during the shoot as a guide, to make sure you're getting all the coverage you want/need. Finally, by looking at the list, the DP can figure out what special camera gear you might need.

Here is where the true complexity of the scenes is revealed. Once you start adding up camera setups, you'll have some idea of how big each day is regardless of the page count. This may prompt you to start moving scenes around in the schedule, or throw out unnecessary setups.

On *Found In Time* I tried to limit myself to five-to-eight setups per scene. Given how small the crew was and the time limits we were under, this was the only way to get through the shoot. To make up for the smaller number of setups, we tried to make the individual shots more dynamic. Often the DP combined setups during the shoot.

GETTING BEYOND PREVIZ

Previz is fun. You're building a "miniature" version of the film. If it starts to get boring or difficult in a way that turns you off, then switch gears and use another technique. Also, the shotlist is important, but it's *not the Bible*, despite what some ADs will tell you. I've worked (and been the AD) on several films where we didn't have a shotlist, but it was always pretty clear what the director wanted, and the crew knew how to get there. At the end of the day, good communication between the DP, 1st AD, and director is more important.

Don't get too hung up on the results of your work. No one besides you has to see your stick-figure storyboards or chicken-scrawled diagrams. You will have still accomplished a lot by going through the process – you'll know your visual strategy for executing the script in a way you couldn't have before.

Going Back to the Script

Some people advocate going back to the script and inserting at least some of the edits and camera work. I'm not so sure. These directions take away from the narrative flow of the script. But if it helps you then go ahead. I *definitely* tweak the script after going through this process, however. Most of the time I find that a reaction shot can effectively replace a line or two of dialog – the framing of the shot and the actor's expression will say the same thing, only better. Sometimes I make the blocking of action scenes a little more specific. These little things can add up in a big way, making your film more visual.

Composition vs. Performance

You can have the most intricate storyboards, script notes, and shotlists in your hands, and the actors will decide to do something different on the set. Or the location changes just before the shot, ruining your plans – the place at the bar where that conversation was supposed to take place is now occupied by a loud pinball machine. How you react depends in part on how you want to shape the film from this point onwards. Do you revise the storyboards and incorporate the changes, or rework the space and the performances around the boards? Both are equally good options.

Some directors favor telling the story through *composition*. Directors such as Tarsem Singh (*The Fall*, *The Cell*) and Darren Aronofsky (*Black Swan*, *Pi*) may be extreme examples. They get good performances from their actors most of the time, but they tell the story through imagery rather than text. Kevin Smith (*Clerks*, *Dogma*) may be an opposite example: the expression of the text through *performance* is everything. His shot choices tend to highlight and follow the actors. Some directors do both. The early Coen Brothers movies, *Blood Simple*, *Raising Arizona*, and *Miller's Crossing*, exemplify this earlier approach (their DP for most of these early films was Barry Sonnenfeld), whereas their films from *The Big Lebowski* onward focus on performers (Roger Deakins shot *The Big Lebowski*). The Coen Brothers haven't sacrificed anything in terms of style by changing direction, but I would say that their emphasis as filmmakers has changed in favor of performance, at least slightly.

How much emphasis you place on your shotlist is in part determined by your preference for composition or performance. You don't have to make this a universal choice for your entire project – some scenes will require stricter adherence to the shotlist than others anyway. On *Found In Time* there were a few scenes where I made specific blocking demands of the actors, so we could get the shots lined up right for post compositing. In other scenes we had a shotlist but threw it out and let the on-set rehearsal guide our choices.

QUESTIONS/EXERCISES

1. Take one scene from your script and try storyboarding it by hand. Use whatever template you find convenient. Stick figures are fine.
2. Previz the same scene using a top-down floor plan.
3. Compare the two methods – which one did you find easier? Which conveyed what you were after more effectively?
4. Translate these two efforts into a shotlist.
5. Do you have any shots you can get rid of or combine with others?

## Chapter 20

Rehearsals/Working with Actors

FIGURE 20.1 Rehearsal in action. Director Shoja Azari (*left*) steps Martin Bough through the scene before a take on *Windows*.

Don't be afraid of rehearsal. Often it seems to make the performances worse. But ultimately, I believe if you do it right, it can only deepen and strengthen the performances, and give the actors more confidence in the material. While there's definitely something to be said for off-the-cuff, spontaneous work, it takes a special breed of actor, combined with the right kind of director, to pull this off. More often, you're better served by doing some rehearsals ahead of time. But it's important to structure them correctly, and focus on what's achievable, given the time and budget constraints. Assuming you don't have Stanley Kubrick's money – he rehearsed and shot *Eyes Wide Shut* for over a year – you'll have to make every minute count.

DIFFERENT TYPES OF REHEARSAL

A rehearsal doesn't have to mean having all the actors "on their feet" and acting out the scenes from start to finish. In fact, that's best left to when you're on the actual set you're going to shoot. I'm going to be somewhat (okay, very) liberal with the definition of rehearsal, to include any *significant director/actor interaction that involves preparation.* That could include:

1. Meeting actors over coffee or lunch, and talking about the film
2. Working back and forth over the phone and through emails and texts
3. Table reads
4. Traditional "rehearsals"
5. Full-cast readings
6. Research/training

We'll talk about each of these types and how to adapt a strategy that uses all of them, but let's discuss the framework for rehearsals first.

THE OBJECTIVE

The objective behind all rehearsals is to increase the actors' and director's understanding of the characters, so as to strengthen the choices they make on set. In other words, you're not looking for a performance. Sometimes you'll have to ask the actors specifically to scale it back, hold in the intensity a bit. You don't want them to get too locked in their heads.

This is another point about rehearsals. Whatever you do should get you and them *out of your heads* and focused on concrete problems. When we intellectualize, we freeze and make "artificial" choices in our actions and intonations. But film demands action that seems natural, even if it's in fact highly stylized. Bergman, Tarkovsky, and Kubrick – very intellectual filmmakers – were able to get extremely warm, almost primal performances from their actors. So you want your actors to always have their thoughts directed on something outside themselves – preferably on the other characters in the scene, or if not, a threat, task, or physical object that has to be dealt with. So the objective of rehearsal is to get your actors centered on *their objectives.*

BUDGETING FOR REHEARSAL TIME

According to SAG, actors have to be paid for any formalized rehearsal (with the possible exception of the full-cast reading), at the standard day rate of the agreement you've signed up for. But it's a good idea to offer something even if you haven't signed with SAG, because it will make it a lot easier for the cast to set the time aside for you. Other expenses you should budget for are food, transportation (if you're rehearsing somewhere very far away), and script copies.

WHO SHOULD BE INVOLVED

You may want to have the DP and/or producer around, but I find that it's best if the director and actors are the only ones in the room. It's harder to maintain a focused, secure "zone" the more people are around. Also, once you start bringing the crew in, it starts feeling more like a shoot, which is the opposite of what you want.

RULES OF THE ROAD

Try to keep your rehearsals relatively brief, and take breaks. The breaks are important not only for your bladder, but for everyone's brain as well – all of you will need time to absorb and integrate the information. Keep the actors from directing each other (that's your job). Otherwise, be encouraging of pretty much anything they come up with, even if you initially disagree with it. Bring all your prep materials, but be ready to move in another direction. And be on time. I can't stress this enough. As a chronically "time-challenged" person, I had to make extra effort to get to rehearsals on time. Actors have difficult schedules, so being later than, say, 5 minutes sends the message that you don't value their time.

LISTENING AND PROBING

The quickest way to get actors to dig into a performance is to ask them questions, and then follow up on them with more questions. It makes them dig deeper into their characters. You can answer questions from time to time – but stick to the facts of the story whenever possible, and try not to psychologize or intellectualize. If one of your actors is having a hard time with a story point, you may have to step back and do some plot summary work, but it's important to stay away from over-explanations. Perhaps the confusion is useful – how often are we confused in our lives? Do we have all the answers? No, but we keep asking questions.

A good question to ask is "What is your character's last name?" Or "What does s/he do for fun?" A good question to answer is "How old was the character when his parents left?" Keep your answers to the point, and then turn them back into questions, like "What do you think it was like for him after his parents split up?"

A question you don't want to answer directly would be "Why does my character have an affair with his boss in scene 87?" In those situations, it's better to ask the question back. "How are things going with his wife in scenes 70–85?" Or "Have you ever felt tempted by someone at work, even just a little bit?" When the actors work for answers, they start owning their characters. Your job then becomes coaching them towards the choices you'd prefer.

When an actor gives you a vague answer, ask them to be more specific. For example, you ask the actor playing John "What are you trying to do in this section of the scene?" John says "I'm just trying to make breakfast." Perhaps that's a perfectly good objective – sometimes simpler is better. But what if you want John to be more engaged in the other big event in the scene – an argument between his wife, Mary, and his daughter Nell? If so, you can follow this up with "What about the argument going on behind you?" Or, perhaps Mary and John had a fight the night before – about Nell. This could have been offscreen, or in the previous scene. You could ask "Are you still feeling something about that argument you both had last night?" Or "Did you ever cook while you were angry? Did it help?" The questions you'll ask will be based partly on your prep work, partly on your chemistry with the actors, and partly on what they come to you with.

One exception to the question/answer ratio is production concerns. If an actor needs to know concrete details like "what are you shooting on?" or "what will you do if it rains?" you should have answers pretty close to hand, and be as specific as possible. If you don't know the answer, find out and get back to her. Production questions tend to have one of two subtexts: curiosity or fear. A lot of actors are curious about the other side of the camera and many work on both – a number of the actors in *Found In Time* teach, direct, or have crewed on other films. The fears can come from a variety of places, and most are well-founded. If they've been on other independent films or worked with first-timers before, they know how chaotic it can get and they want to know that you have a handle on it. In either case, you can expand on these questions a bit, unless you feel it's taking too much time away from the character discussions.

AVOIDING VALUE JUDGMENTS

Try and avoid using value judgments in your conversations. The moment you call a character a "dick" or a "bitch" you've collapsed the complexity of their character, which is the opposite of what you want to do. The actors may feel that way about their own characters, but encourage them to think of their characters as heroes.

Case in point: Darth Vader, one of the most badass villains in all movie-dom. To get inside his skin, James Earl Jones (who voiced the character) and David Prowse (who physically played the part) had to construct a narrative that made him interesting and gave his scene partners something to work against. This is even more difficult when you consider that he wore a mask for 99 percent of the film. How would an actor do this?

One approach would be to look at the rebels as Vader might: outlaws, perhaps even terrorists. Vader fights for an empire – but empires can be sources of order and relative stability, even technological progress. He serves the Emperor, who is a kind of father-figure, and tries to get his son to join him. Going back to the "love in the scene" argument in Chapter 6, perhaps he loves and craves the Emperor's approval, and also wants to reconnect with his son, who he's been separated from for years. Even his killing of Obi-Wan in the first film seems more justified now – Obi-Wan is getting in the way, taking his son away from him, posing a threat to the order.

Whatever the point of view of the screenwriter or the audience, the actors have to inhabit the characters, and they can only do so when they see them as fully human, in all their complexity.

INFORMAL REHEARSALS

You should make an effort to meet *all* of your actors, or at least talk to them, before the shoot. This could be very difficult if you've got a big cast or they're scattered geographically, but it's worthwhile anyway. Not only will it help you establish a rapport, it's also a sign (hopefully a genuine one) that you value their contribution to the film.

I aim for one-on-one lunch or coffee meetings, and keep things pretty informal. I may start by talking a bit about the actor's background, what kinds of movies he likes. I usually bring copies of my materials (see Chapter 7) – burned CDs, printouts of paintings or photos, books or articles, whatever I think the actor might find exciting. If the character specializes in something (a cell biologist, piano tuner, etc.) I'll see if I can find an interesting article that she can read. It's hard to know what will ignite someone's curiosity, especially after you've just met, so it's good to show up with a variety of tools.

When actors tell you about their lives, pay attention – not just because it's common courtesy, but because you may be able to draw some connections between them and the characters they're playing. If an actor wants to chat at length about their lives, I'm all ears. I'll ask questions, and sometimes bring the topic back to the script, but let her tell her story. Storytelling is a natural part of building a relationship, after all.

You also want to find out something about their training. There are a wide variety of acting methods, and each actor has a different interpretation of them. A lot of actors start out as adherents to one method, then pick up and incorporate others as time goes on. Their training will of course influence how they interpret your material, and how you'll communicate with each other.

Eventually, the discussion will get back to the script. Much of the work will be about filling in the gaps left by the writer, and making decisions about the character's story that are outside the script altogether. What happened over the weekend between scenes 23 and 24? Why is she rushing to work at the top of her scene? Remember the "moment before" tool from Chapter 6. You can also impart secret information – things you don't want the other actors to overhear during the normal rehearsals. These meetings will often generate new questions, which you can follow up on through emails and phone calls.

FORMAL REHEARSALS

I usually aim to get at least three days of actual, honest-to-goodness rehearsal in. I try to budget for as many days of rehearsal as I can get away with, but usually end up trimming some due to budget or actor schedule conflicts. Unless you can really swing a longer time period, where you can go through the whole script, you'll have to pick out the scenes that you feel are the most critical, and just schedule time for those.

On *Found In Time* I started by checking for cast schedule conflicts, and cross-referencing them with scenes that I wanted to rehearse. Then I came up with a schedule:

Tuesday 9/7

9:15a–10:45a:	Sc. 12 – Chris, RJ, Morton, Jess
11:00a–12:30p:	Sc. 31, 34, 36, 38 – Chris, RJ, Ayana, Morton, Jess
1:15p–2:45p:	Sc. 99–100, 104 – Jina, Chris, RJ

| 3:00p–4:30p: | Sc. 51, 57 (including v.o. under 52/53/54/55/57) – Jina, Ayana |
| 4:45p–5:30p: | Other scenes w/RJ, Chris, Jina, Ayana as time permits |

Wednesday 9/8

9:15a–10:45a:	Sc. 47 – Anthony & Chris
11:00a–12:30p:	Sc. 85, 87 – Anthony & Chris
1:15p–2:45p:	Sc. 22, 24–26 – Chris & Jina
3:00p–4:30p:	Sc. 17 – Chris & Jina
4:45p–5:30p:	Sc. 131 – Chris & Jina

I work in 90-minute to 2-hour blocks, and schedule breaks for lunch. The focus during the rehearsals is on building relationships and scene work, so I tend to spend less time on background material. I rented a rehearsal space – just a bare room with a table and chairs – and brought some snacks, plenty of pens and paper, and a couple of extra script and schedule copies. The costume designer may want to glom onto your rehearsal schedule so s/he can fit your actors. This is fine but only if it's not going to impact on the actual rehearsal time itself.

Here's where the scene-by-scene analysis you did earlier on will come into play again. You want to focus on working out playable, specific objectives for each character, and building subtext. Blocking is of secondary importance, unless you're rehearsing in the actual space – even then, it can be too much of a distraction. If the actors really feel like they need to get physical, that's fine, but the table is always there for them to come back to.

During the rehearsal period, keep the chit-chat to a minimum, and get right to it. I usually start with a brief read-through of the entire scene. Then we go through the scene, beat by beat, and work out the objectives for each person, answer questions that come up along the way, and then put the scene back together again.

Some actors prefer that this method be mapped out explicitly – "let's look at the second beat here" – and others come at the scene from a very different angle, and find this approach too mechanical. You don't have to discuss beats as "beats," but as *changes* in the scene – as in look at what's *changing* here at this point, why did this happen? You'll have to tailor your approach to each actor. Some actors need to make physical choices first, some need to work out their motivation, others need to work within the arc of the whole story, and others would rather know less than more.

Pay special attention as to whether the actors are listening to each other. If you hear an actor saying the lines over and over again in the same way regardless of what his scene partner is doing, then you need to figure out what's going on. You may have to say "I want you to throw your focus onto the other person" or even "listen to each other a little more, let the scene breathe." Again, the exact words you choose will depend on the actor's training and how far/close you think they are to what you want.

Dragging

If the scene feels like it's dragging, it could be because everyone's a little tired, but often it's because the stakes aren't high enough or the actors are playing the text rather than the subtext. You can raise the stakes by invoking arguments based on the script, or by coming up with something that makes the objectives within the scene more urgent.

For example, you have a scene where Jane is trying to convince her ex-husband John to give her $200. John doesn't want to give it up. The scene could easily descend into a silly screaming match, where you're watching two cardboard people beat each other up verbally. What is the $200 for? If it's in the script that she needs the money for a new dress for a job interview, remind her of that. Maybe what's not in the script is that it's the first interview she's had in months – she's been living hand to mouth since John left. Maybe she still loves him, and it's painful for her to even be there and ask? Or perhaps she thinks they can get back together. Okay, so what about John? Why would he refuse? Well, what if he was planning to surprise her with a gift of some kind to try and win her back, so he doesn't have the money? Alternately, what if he still loves her but he needs the $200 for his parents? Now, it could be that absolutely *none* of these ideas works, but they're worth trying, and they force the actors to raise the stakes and work from a subtext.

Have You Ever …

One great technique is the "have you ever …" question. If an actor is having trouble connecting to a character's motivations, you can find a "way in" by asking "have you ever … ."

On *Found In Time*, I used this a lot. Presumably none of my actors is a psychic, so there were times when they found the characters' behavior a little strange. But the psychics are very understandable, if you consider their situation – they're isolated, lonely, shunned somewhat by society. They have a talent that's seen as spooky but useful. They get harassed by the police and live in fear of psychiatric treatment. Most people in the arts have felt isolated in their lives – perhaps they were bullied at school for being into theater instead of cheerleading or football. Perhaps their parents still want them to get "real jobs." Perhaps they grew up as immigrants, or were recent transplants to New York, which is certainly an odd place if you've never lived in a city. So sometimes all it took was "Have you ever been bullied at school?"

Note that I'm not asking for a *narrative response*, just a yes or no. It's not necessarily important that actors dive into their memories and bring back a full-blown recollection of the event in question. Sometimes that can be counterproductive. It's just good that they know that it's there.

Daring Choices

Rehearsal is the time to try out gonzo things. Encourage your actors to do the same. There are no wrong answers, no bad performances in rehearsal. Everything is useful. You may have to stop something if it's going in an unproductive direction (usually you can tell when this is happening because the performances are getting stiffer). But even knowing where *not* to go is important data. So don't be afraid to be bold.

One way to be bold is to play opposites. Find the humor in the drama, and the drama in the humor. For almost any situation, you can construct an alternate, opposite interpretation. What if John just murdered someone? In the scene immediately following, he may be confessing his crime to Jane. If there's no conflict in the scene – if it comes off like a flat "look what I did/you shouldn't have done that" – then maybe it's time to turn things around. The victim could have been John's nemesis for years. Perhaps the murder, while tragic, was a moment of triumph? Perhaps it actually felt good to do something for once? Or perhaps Jane is happy that John finally did something instead of bitching all the time? Is there a way to make the subtext positive? While you may not keep this adjustment, or it may go too far, sometimes the "play the opposite" card can juice up a scene that's not flowing well.

REVISING THE SCRIPT

Some writer-directors are very specific about the dialog, and they don't want the actors to deviate from what they've written. I personally am not interested in absolute fidelity, except in specific cases, as long as the actors get the *intention* right. Either way, there may be some lines that an actor just can't seem to get a hold of. You'll have to decide whether to tweak the script or spend more time on the line.

If an actor can't say a line it could be because it's awkwardly written. We touched on this in Chapter 6. When you're writing, everything sounds great in your head. When it's uttered by a real human being, it may turn out to just suck. If that's the case, you're better off doing a quick rewrite.

Another possibility is that the actor isn't used to the diction of the character. Think of the characters in *Firefly/Serenity*. Joss Whedon wrote a science fiction show (and follow-up movie) where characters speak in a mix of nineteenth-century Western American English, twenty-third-century "sci-fi talk," and Chinese profanity. Their particular dialect depends heavily on their social standing and education. The actors probably had to really spend some time figuring this out. If you have a character who's a specialist – a scientist, shrink, or a computer programmer – you may know how these folks talk, but that doesn't mean the actors do. Sometimes giving them a little primer is all you need.

The last possibility is that the actor doesn't understand the subtext beneath the line. The best way to deal with this is to go at it "sideways." See if the actor is having issues with any other part of the scene. If he is, then go back a step and try making some adjustments from your script analysis. Or make the objective more specific. The line may just "snap" into place at that point. It could be some combination of all these factors, so be ready to try a little of everything.

REHEARSAL FEARS AND DON'TS

One of the fears that people have of rehearsal is that it'll make things worse – that you'll ruin a perfectly good performance because you're adding too much new information during the rehearsal. And there's some truth to that. When you learn new things, often your work suffers. But then it gets even better, as you integrate the new knowledge. Do you have enough time for this learning curve before the shoot? Usually, yes.

The rehearsal process I've outlined above doesn't really go deep enough for this fear to matter. You're not asking the actors to deconstruct and then rebuild their conception of the character, or live together for weeks or years on end. If you have the time and budget for this kind of work, though, it can only help.

There are two big things to avoid, if you can: line readings and "fixing things in place." I try to avoid saying the actor's lines altogether, because they're not mine to say. This sounds silly, but hear me out. The actors are looking to you for guidance, so you don't want to influence the delivery of the line. So try to avoid directions like "I want you to say it like this: … ."

The other thing to avoid is to try and "fix" the performance in the rehearsal, as in "great, now do it just like that when we shoot." This is impossible to do. The truth is that by the time you shoot, everyone's understanding of the characters and story will have evolved. And everyone will be slightly different by the time you shoot – a little sleepier, older, happier, whatever. Between these two factors, there's no way that an actor can deliver exactly the same performance twice, even within the same day. If you try to constrain the performance by referencing the rehearsal as a "gold standard," you'll be in trouble. You can, of course, remind the actor of some of the work that you did together during the rehearsal, to get them back off a tangent or juice up their performance. But at no point is there really a "perfect performance" that you should judge the others against; each is different, with some better or worse for your purposes.

FULL-CAST READING

I recommend you invite the crew, investors, and anyone else involved in the project. It's the only time everyone will hear the entire film all the way through, until the finished product is screened in a year or so.

If a supporting cast member can't make it due to scheduling reasons, you may want to hold it anyway, but fight hard to have everyone there. Don't forget to give someone (the line producer, AD, producer, anyone with a good voice) the narrator's job, or you'll be doing it yourself.

I usually make a bit of an event out of the reading, and bring some food and wine. It's a small expense but I think it helps people feel like they're part of something real. At the opening of the reading I hand out any contracts that people haven't gotten yet (again, this is a rare opportunity to get all the cast and crew together under one roof), introduce everyone to each other, and then dive right in without breaking. Before you start, you may want to just tell the actors to relax and pace themselves, and that you're not looking for a performance. This way there's a little less pressure on them.

The main goal is so that everyone can see the full work. While some directors feel that it's better that actors only see their roles in the piece, I think that they will get more insight into their characters if they have a sense of the "big picture." For you, this is your last chance to see any "bumps" in the script that may need fixing, or any lapses in the drama that you need to work on with the cast. You'll also be able to see who's gelling with who in the cast, where there may be some trouble spots, and if anyone seems like they've checked out a bit.

Once the reading is over, make sure everyone is clear on the schedule, hand out any other paperwork, and get some food.

RESEARCH/TRAINING

For the *Battlestar Galactica* series, the pilot director, Michael Rymer, asked for – and got – some money to send his lead actors to a version of boot camp. This was important, since they were supposed to play military "grunts" and officers. On *Blue Valentine*, the director Derek Cianfrance asked the actors Michelle Williams and Ryan Gosling to live in "their" house for the present-day material, for about a month before shooting. If you have a character playing a cop, can she spend some time with some policemen?

Some actors train with their bodies – losing or gaining weight for a role, practicing martial arts techniques, playing a musical instrument. Perhaps you can get them to hit the library, or visit a place like the one their characters work in. This doesn't have to be expensive or even that organized. Derek Morgan, one of the leads on *Found In Time* (he plays a psychic vendor), walked around 125th street and watched the street vendors, even approaching some of them and asking them about their work.

For *Rock the Paint* the lead actors knew how to play basketball well enough, but the director, Phil Bertelsen, asked for an extra rehearsal day before the shoot so they could get more time on the court. Sometimes it's just about giving the actors a prop to work with – a snapshot from the character's life, or a talisman of some kind. Any opportunity you can give them to know more about their "real life" counterparts is a good thing.

PRODUCER'S ROLE DURING REHEARSAL

The producer's role in the rehearsal process depends heavily on the producer/director relationship. If you're taking on both roles, obviously the producer is always going to be there, somewhere. Then it will mostly be a matter of reducing the producer's role to that of a timekeeper. Try to keep the logistical concerns of the shoot out of your head while you're rehearsing.

On the other hand, if the producer wrote the script, the director can lean on her for the tweaks that come out of the rehearsal, or have her attend one of the sessions so she can provide some feedback. If the producer is more of a logistics person, then her role should be more of a "guard" or "defender" – keeping the production world at bay while the director works.

It's very hard *not* to dive into production-land as the days tick off until the shoot starts. There's always a lot to do, never enough time to do it in, and directing can be really hard work with less tangible rewards. But if you don't invest the time now, you won't get it back on set.

QUESTIONS/EXERCISES

1. Go through your script. If you only had two or three days (8 hours each) of rehearsal, which scenes would you choose to rehearse?
2. If you can, get some friends together and do a formal rehearsal of a few scenes from your script.
3. Have lunch with an actor who's read your script and chat a bit about it, focusing on the character they'd most like to play. See how far you can get in terms of building the character.
4. Can you think of a "training exercise" for any of your actors? If one of your actors is in prison, can you arrange for a tour of a local sheriff's holding cells? If your character works in medicine, do you have a doctor friend who can spend dinner with the actor, or take her to his office? Do you have a family member who's like one of your characters, who he can visit?
5. Go back and refresh yourself with the notes and prep materials you created in Chapters 6 and 7. Do you want to add to those materials?

## Chapter 21

Routines for Success in Production

FIGURE 21.1 Production, at last! (Photo: Brendan Mason.)

Day one! We're in production, at last! After who knows how many weeks, months, and/or years of dreaming, dealing, prepping, and falling out of and back in love again with your film, you're here, producing and/or directing it. Congratulations. You are already one of the few and the proud. Many people talk about making a movie, and a few people actually get started down the path, but the number who get to the first day of production is few indeed.

So at this point, the focus of "prep" changes, since technically you're past preproduction. Instead, you're going to be using the time between each day or week of shooting to prepare for the next. The tension between being in the moment (as a director) and looking ahead to the next one (as the producer) will never be more acute, so we'll also look at how to keep these two outlooks at least somewhat separated. So this chapter will focus on some routines and tools you can use to keep yourself on track during the shoot, without losing your mind (too much).

If you have the budget to hire a production staff – a line producer, production manager, 1st AD, production coordinator, or any combination of these you can afford – then you should do so. You need to keep your eyes on either the big picture (as producer) or the scene right in front of you (as director), and all the middle-ground detail stuff (catering, light replacements, hiring extra PAs) can really get in the way of both of these things. However, if you're stuck doing everything yourself (or selves), then the next best thing is to "segment" your day.

THE TIME HORIZON

Throughout the day, your time horizon as producer and/or director will change drastically. It will probably go something like this:

1. **Coffee.** The first thing you need to do when you get to set, ahead of calltime, is to make sure the coffee and breakfast is ready.
2. **First shot.** As soon as the calltime hits, you want to be thinking about the first shot.
3. **Lunch.** Make sure it's ordered, retrieved/delivered, set up, and ready to eat *before* you call lunch.
4. **Tomorrow.** Once you're past the first shot and things are humming along, you need to start thinking about tomorrow. If you're the producer/director, this should happen at lunchtime. Get the callsheet ready for tomorrow. Start making calls to set up tomorrow's schedule.
5. **Coffee (again).** Right after lunch, you need to make caffeine or some other legal stimulant available to the crew and cast so they don't fall asleep.
6. **Later today.** How are you doing? Do you think you'll make your day? Do you have to cut out setups? Move something to tomorrow? Do you need to order second meal? Don't wait until the last minute to pull the trigger on this.
7. **Tonight.** Wrap out, make sure the day's work is safely copied, labeled, and backed up, equipment is back on the truck or in its spot in the holding area, and that everyone gets out at a reasonable time. Write up the production report.
8. **Tomorrow (again).** Email everyone tomorrow's callsheets and sides, process receipts, write the checks you'll need tomorrow, call the caterer with tomorrow's food order.

To keep this gear-switching from messing up your head, you should make it clear to the crew and cast that you can only deal with certain issues at certain times of the day – usually between scene changes, during meals, and at wrap. I also recommend delegating some control to your crew. Give your PAs more petty cash and make them responsible for doling it out. Have them make the calls to the caterer. If you have *any* money at all, get a paid craft services PA. That person will be worth their salary many times over in all the things you won't have to deal with – shopping, replenishing the coffee, keeping the set neat, and handing out waters. Find the person or people on the crew who don't mind working outside their departments a bit, and ask them for help if you need it. On *Found In Time* I was particularly lucky. Just about everyone in the crew had worked in multiple departments over the years, so they each knew enough about each other's work to pitch in when there was a shortfall. They also cut me a lot of slack.

For your part, you have to be honest about what you can and can't do during the shoot, if you're going to be doing multiple jobs at once. People who are used to bigger-budget films may be a bit taken aback at the "thin" or non-existent management tier, but sometimes this can be an advantage. Fewer layers of management also means fewer people who have to approve decisions, less bureaucracy, and less infrastructure to carry around from place to place.

PAPERWORK FLOW

A shoot runs on paperwork, for better or worse. If you have a line producer, UPM, and/or 2nd AD, at least some of this work will be taken care of for you, but if you don't, you'll be doing this yourself. Table 21.1 shows a somewhat "idealized" flow for the daily and weekly paperwork you'll be dealing with during the shoot.

TABLE 21.1 Paperwork flow on set

Timing/Paperwork	Method	Goes to/ Comes from	Explanation
As soon as you hire production designer/costume designer:			
Blank expense sheets	Hand out	Producer/ costume designer	Hand these out to costume/production designer, so they can track expenses
Blank resale certificates	Hand out	Producer/ costume designer	So they can get the sales tax knocked off purchases
Insurance certificates	Hand out	Producer/ costume designer	For any vendors they need to rent from that require it
Petty cash or check & credit card imprint	Hand out	Producer/ costume designer	So they can start buying materials and expendables
When you sign up vendors:			
Vendor packets	Email	Vendor	Insurance, tax, credit card forms to set up vendor account with
Equipment pick-up day:			
Run lists and petty cash	Hand out	PAs	To PAs so they know where to go to pick stuff up
When you get up in the morning:			
Preliminary callsheet for following day	Email	Cast/crew	Email this to everyone, making sure to note that it's preliminary
At call time:			
Callsheets for current day	Hand out	Cast/crew	Paper copies of the callsheet for the current day
Sides for current day	Hand out	Cast/key crew	The scenes you're going to shoot today
Petty cash	Hand out	Crew	Give these plus slips to anyone who needs their petty cash replenished
Petty cash/out-of-pocket receipts	Receive	Crew	Get these from people who need their petty cash replenished or out-of-pocket expenses reimbursed
Run lists, insurance, equipment lists	Hand out	PAs	Give to your PAs who are doing runs or equipment pickups/returns
Release forms	Hand out	PAs or extras	Give these to 2nd AD to distribute or directly to extras, to fill out and sign
"Start" paperwork	Hand out	Cast/crew	Give these to anyone (cast or crew) starting today, who didn't get a copy (or lost it)

(Continued)

TABLE 21.1 (Continued)

Timing/Paperwork	Method	Goes to/ Comes from	Explanation
Arriving at a new location:			
Location insurance certificate and check	Hand out	Location	Hand out the insurance certificate and check
Location agreement	Receive	Location	Receive the location agreement
Lunchtime:			
Reimbursements for previous day's out-of-pocket receipts	Hand out	Crew	Checks for out-of-pocket reimbursements turned in yesterday
End of the day:			
Final callsheets for next day	Hand out	Cast/crew	Callsheets for the following day
Exhibit G	Receive	Cast	Get all actors to sign the Exhibit G for SAG
Start paperwork	Receive	Crew/cast	Collect start paperwork for anyone not coming back tomorrow
Crew paychecks for day-players	Hand out	Crew	Try to pay anyone showing up for just one day, on the same day
Camera reports	Receive	1st AC	The 1st or 2nd AC gives you the camera report for the day
Sound reports	Receive	Sound mixer	Sound mixer gives you the sound report for the day
Script supervisor notes	Receive	Script supervisor	Script supervisor gives you script notes
Filled-in release form	Receive	Extras	Signed release forms from the extras
At editor's place:			
Script/sound/camera notes	Hand out (copies)	Editor/ass't editor	Hand out copies of camera, sound, and script supervisor's notes, along with the day's work on drives
That night, at home:			
Sides for next day	Email	Cast/crew	Email the next day's sides
Final callsheets	Email	Cast/crew	Email the next day's callsheets
Production report	Write up	Producer	Write up the production report for that day's work
Preliminary callsheet for the day after the next day	Write up	Cast/crew	Get the preliminary callsheet ready for the day after tomorrow
Exhibit G	Write up	Producer	Fill in the names of who's showing up tomorrow on the Exhibit G
Pre-fill start paperwork	Write up	Producer	Get the start paperwork ready for anyone starting tomorrow
Reconcile receipts	Write up	Producer	Enter any money paid out that day or due into your accounting system
Reimbursement checks	Write up	Producer	Write up checks to anyone who's due for reimbursement

Timing/Paperwork	Method	Goes to/ Comes from	Explanation
Insurance certificates	Write up	Vendors, locations	Fill these out for tomorrow's new location or vendors
Location agreement	Write up	Locations	Fill these out for tomorrow's new location
Location travel directions	Email	Cast/crew	Email public/private transportation directions to the location (if not included on callsheet)
Every 2–3 days:			
Hotcost report	Write up	Producer/ LP	Based on the reconciled expenses, figure out where you are relative to the film's budget
End of each week:			
Crew timecards/invoices	Receive	Crew	Get the week's timecards and invoices from the crew (timecards if they're employees, invoices if they're subcontractors)
During days off:			
SAG paperwork	Send in	SAG	Deliver to SAG copies of the Exhibit Gs and the cast SAG agreements for whoever worked that week
Cast timecards	Write up	Payroll company	Usually someone in production, working off the Exhibit Gs and production reports, types up the cast timecards
Cast payroll paperwork	Send in	Payroll company	You'll be emailing or handing in copies of the cast timecards, Exhibit Gs, payroll start forms, and your own payroll worksheets
Crew payroll checks[a]	Write up	Producer	Compare the crew timecards with the production reports, write up payroll checks
Final callsheet for first day back	Email	Cast/crew	Email everyone finalized callsheets for the first day back in the week
Revised shooting schedule	Email	Cast/crew	Updated schedule for the remainder of the shoot (based on progress to date)
Cast payroll reports	Email	Payroll company	The payroll company will email you estimates based on your filled-in timecards and the going rates; once you approve they'll cut and mail checks to SAG
At call time, 2nd day of the week:			
Crew paychecks (if not thru payroll company)	Hand out	Crew	Paychecks for the crew for previous week

(Continued)

TABLE 21.1 (Continued)

Timing/Paperwork	Method	Goes to/ Comes from	Explanation
During wrap:			
Return run list	Hand out	PAs	So they can return the gear
Final SAG paperwork	Hand out	SAG	Deliver the final week's Exhibit Gs and agreements, plus the casting data reports and final cast lists
Wrap binders	Bind	Producer	These binders contain copies of all the relevant paperwork generated (deal memos, release forms, location agreements, insurance certificates, etc.)
Vendor checks	Write up	Vendors	Last checks to go to vendors, including (possibly) missing and damaged
Reconcile remaining receipts	Write up	Producer	Reconcile any outstanding receipts, "check in" petty cash, and pay out any remaining out-of-pocket expenses
Final production hotcost report	Write up	Producer	Final tally of money spent during the shoot, broken down by line item
Logs[b]	Write up	Editor/ass't editor	You or the assistant editor prepares a log of the footage (detailed notes on the scenes/shots/takes, plus evaluations and comments)
Lined script[b]	Write up	Editor/ass't editor	You or the assistant editor prepares a "lined" version of the script so that the editor can see what the coverage was, and what lines/scenes were omitted

[a] Assumes you're not going through a payroll company for the crew.
[b] These often take a while to prepare.

This seems like a lot, but it's really a cycle of handing out and receiving the same forms and papers over and over again. If you can develop a routine for handling these things – as per the table above – you can keep the time you spend actually shooting relatively trouble-free. You should try to get a running start before the shoot starts, and line up your basic forms. Many of these forms are available in Appendix B.

Also, on super-low-budget films ($500K and under), I've noticed that camera reports and sound reports are becoming less common. Script supervisors are also becoming scarce on these films. Producers are either dumping the work on the editor without much documentation, or "lining" script after the fact (see Chapter 22 for more details on this).

Distribution List

On a big enough shoot – a 30-man or full-size crew – you should create a *distribution list*. This is a chart that tells you who gets what paperwork at the end of each day. Your hair/makeup artists, for example, don't need a copy of the production report, but your ADs, UPM, and line producer do. Your costume and production designers definitely need a copy of the shooting schedule (especially revisions), but they may not need script supervisor's notes. With a distribution list in hand, you can figure out who gets what, and only make the copies you need to make. This will save you a little money, but more importantly will save you time.

Recycling

If you can help it, hold onto all your paperwork during the shoot, including things that are discarded, and then recycle it at the end of the shoot. Not only is it more ecologically friendly, but you'll minimize the chances of accidentally throwing out something you really needed (like some petty cash receipts).

Dealing with Callsheets

Callsheets are a vital part of the production, because they tell everyone at a glance the day's shooting schedule, the locations, the actors in the scenes, the crew on set, any special effects/stunts/vehicles/props, and the advance schedule. Weather, emergency services (EMS, fire, police), production company phone numbers, and other helpful details are also on the callsheet.

Preparing callsheets can suck up so much time. The "official" legal-size, double-sided ones can take all day to get ready and print out – and then reprint or mark up if they need corrections. I'm a big advocate of letter-sized, single-sided callsheets. They can be printed anywhere, on scrap paper if necessary (since you only need one side), and it's easier to read on a computer monitor or smartphone (which more and more of them are being read on anyway).

Anyway, a callsheet should look something like Figure 21.2.

You can, believe it or not, make a film without a callsheet (despite what my DGA-trained friends will tell you), but you'd better have something that conveys the same information. What you end up with will probably look a whole lot like … a callsheet.

If you're stuck doing them, the best thing to do is to create a template (in Excel, Word, or whatever program you're using) and put in the basic information. Then you can base each day's callsheets on the template. Pre-fill out the timesheets as much as you can for the first few days, out to one week. You'll have to make adjustments, but most of your work will be done, barring significant schedule/personnel changes.

From day one onwards, you want to be fixing up the callsheets two days ahead (so the night after day one of the shoot, you'll want to fix up the callsheet for day three). During lunch, you'll be looking over the next day's callsheet and making adjustments based on how well you're doing up to then. By close to the end of the day, you should finalize the callsheet and hand it out. Even if you have to use a sharpie (always use a *red* sharpie, by the way) to mark up the copies after you've printed them, it's always better to hand out *something* to the cast and crew by the end of the day. Then when you get home, you can send the completely finalized version via email.

Sides

Sides also annoy the hell out of me. Production sides are a collection of the scenes (or sections of scenes) that are to be shot that day, either in scene or schedule order. It sounds simple except that you need to cross out scenes that *aren't* going to be shot in order to avoid confusion. And to save paper, you're supposed to print them at half-size double-sided – and that's when the trouble starts. Unless you have a good PA who really knows how to create half-size sides, just bite the bullet and print them full-size, double-sided. Yes, you'll be killing more trees, but you're also gaining at least a half-hour of sleep every night.

One way to conserve paper is to limit the number of sides you print out. Limit the sides to the cast, department heads, and a couple of extra copies. By lunchtime, you'll see sides in the garbage or left behind somewhere, and you'll be annoyed a couple of hours later at the person who asks "Who has the sides?" because it's probably the same guy who left their sides sitting around. This is normal.

"FOUND IN TIME"

FOUND IN TIME LLC 2611 28th St., #1, Astoria, NY 11102 XX-XXX-XXX DIRECTOR: Arthur Vincie XX-XXX-XXX SUNRISE: 6:40AM SUNSET: 6:58PM WEATHER: Sunny, some clouds in late PM HIGH: 80 / LOW 61	**REVISED CALLSHEET** **VAN P/U: 7:30AM ON W. 34th St. & 7th Ave.** **PRODUCTION CALL: 7:30am @ Location** **CREW CALL:8:00am @ Location** BREAKFAST: 7:45am @ Location LUNCH: 2:00 pm @ Location (catered)	DATE: Sunday, September 19, XXXX **SHOOT DAY: 08 of 13**
		HOSP. SUNY Downstate Medical Ctr 450 Clarkson Ave 11203 XX-XXX-XXX
		POLICE 79th Precinct 263 Tompkins Ave. 11221 XX-XXX-XXX
		FIRE NYFD: 911 XX-XXX-XXX

TIME	SCENE #	SET	D/N	SCENE DESCRIPTION	CAST	PAGES	LOCATION
7:30A				CARGO VAN REPORT TO SET			
7:30A				PASS VAN PICKUP @ W.34th St. & 7th Ave.			216 Macon Ave., #16
8:00A		REPORT TO SET		IN AT 8:00 AM			Btw. Thompkins &
	14	INT. CHRIS' APT.	N1	Chris walks in, puts away his stuff	1	3/8	Throop Ave.
	23	CHRIS' BATHROOM	N2	Chris and Jina prepare to go out for the night	1, 3	1 pg.	XX-XXX-XXX
	25	INT. CHRIS' APT.	N2	Chris/Jina proposal scene – she accepts	1, 3	7/8	Brooklyn, NY 11216
	80	INT. CHRIS' APT.	N2	Chris/Jina proposal scene – she declines	1, 3	6/8	Contact:
	61	INT. CHRIS' APT.	N5	Chris empties his pockets into the junk drawers	1, 3	2/8	
	82, 83	INT. CHRIS' APT.	N6	Chris looks for medication, confronts Jina	1, 3	2 5/8	
2:00p				LUNCH			
2:45p	17	CHRIS' BEDROOM	N1	Chris and Jina, in bed, talk about her new patient	1, 3	1 1/8	
	27	CHRIS' BEDROOM	N2	Chris and Jina continue their sc. 26 argument	1, 3	5/8	
				MOVE DOWNSTAIRS			
	24, 26	EXT. STREET	N2	Chris and Jina walk, argue over his time slippage	1, 3	1 3/8 pg.	
				MOVE BACK			
6:00p	44, 46	CHRIS' BEDROOM	N3	Chris and Jina argue, he agrees to see Anthony	1, 3	7/8	
	62, 64, 67	CHRIS' BEDROOM	N5	Chris and Jina argue about Anthony	1, 3	1 2/8	
8:30p				WRAP			
					TOTAL:	10 4/8	

CHARACTER	CAST	STATUS	ON SET	CAR	CHARACTER	CAST	STATUS	ON SET	CAR
01. Chris	MacLeod Andrews	W	8:00AM	15P					
03. Jina	Kelly Sullivan	W	8:00AM	15P					

POSITION	NAME	CONTACT	CALL	CAR	POSITION	NAME	CONTACT	CALL	CAR
DIRECTOR	Arthur Vincie	XX-XXX-XXX	7:30A	Cargo	BOOM OP.	Kevin Tadge	XX-XXX-XXX	8:00A	15P
DP	Ben Wolf	XX-XXX-XXX	8:00A	15P	GAFFER	Simeon Moore	XX-XXX-XXX	8:00A	15P
Key HMU	Janis Lozano	XX-XXX-XXX	8:00A	Self	SET PA	Alina Andranikian	XX-XXX-XXX	8:00A	Self
COST. DES.	Ghislaine Sabiti	XX-XXX-XXX	8:00A	15P	SET PA	Denzil Thomas	XX-XXX-XXX	7:30A	Self
MIXER	Anthony Viera	XX-XXX-XXX	8:00A	15P	SET PA	Blaine Chou	XX-XXX-XXX	8:00A	15P

PROPS	WARDROBE	SPECIAL
Chris gear and cart Jina mask and laptop display Chris "wall of stuff" Stunt & "dull" knife	Jina "date wear"	

WORD OF THE DAY	TRANSPORTATION	OTHER
Teratology 1. the science or study of monstrosities or abnormal formations in organisms.	15-PASS / Cargo Van / Arthur Vincie	

ADVANCED SHOOTING SCHEDULE

DATE	SCENES	D/N	CAST	PAGES	DESCRIPTION
	EXT. FIELD DAY				
9/20	18	D101	1, 2	5/8	Chris sees Ayana in the field
9/20	37	D101	1, 2	1/8	Chris and Ayana lie in the field, look at the sky
9/20	2	D101	1, 8	6/8	Chris meets Anansi, asks to be pushed back
9/20	28	D101	1, 8	4/8	Anansi visits Chris, Chris tells him to go away
9/20	40, 42	D101	1, 2	5/8	Chris complains to Anansi that he wants a normal life
9/20	73	D101	1, 2	2/8	Chris and Ayana lie on the ground, Anansi walks over
9/20	91	D101	1, 2, 8	5/8	Ayana, Chris and Anansi talk, he "pushes them back"
9/20	110	D101	1, 2, 8	1 pg.	Ayana meets Anansi, he offers to take him with her
9/20	112	D101	1, 2, 8	7/8	Ayana & Chris meet Anansi in the field
9/20	143	D101	1, 2, 8	6/8	Anansi offers one last time to take them with him
	AYANA'S APARTMENT				
9/21	66, 68	N5	2	2/8	Ayana traces her hands across the tapestry
9/21	53, 55	D2	2	5/8	Ayana gets into her apt., washes her hands, spins
9/21	79, 81	D6	1, 2	1 1/8	Chris and Ayana clean up after Jess/Morton murder
9/21	95, 97	D100	1, 2	2 1/8	Chris and Ayana run into her apt. after mine escape
9/21	106, 108	D7	2	4/8	Ayana rearranges her wall-web, washes out the door
9/21	126, 128, 130	D7	1, 2	1 7/8	Ayana shows Chris the wall-web
9/21	134, 136	D7	1	4/8	Chris walks into Ayana's apartment, but it's empty

FIGURE 21.2 A callsheet from *Found In Time*. Phone numbers have been obscured.

Start Packets

Before the shoot starts, you should assemble start "packets" for the cast that contain the following, pre-filled-out forms:

1. SAG cast agreement
2. Cast deal memo (the extended contract)
3. Payroll start forms, W-2 and I-9 (these usually come in one multi-page form)

You'll want three copies of items #1 and #2 in the packet. Then paperclip these forms together and hand them out to the actor at your first or second meeting (or in a worst-case scenario on the first day of the shoot). You'll want them back either on the actor's last day or the last day of their first week of work, whichever comes first.

Your crew start packets may just include the crew deal memo, or that plus the payroll start forms if you're using a payroll company to pay them. The same rules apply – fill them out, hand them out, get them back.

Cast Payroll Paperwork

When you set things up with the payroll company, they're going to expect the following paperwork from you at the very beginning:

1. Estimate of total payroll.
2. A signed payroll services agreement. This is the contract between the production company and the payroll company.
3. Insurance certificate from your insurance company.
4. Deposit check.
5. A copy of the SAG contract you signed with SAG (sometimes they don't want this).
6. Minor's work permit, if you're employing minors.
7. Worker's comp evaluation form, if you have any stunts or hazards in your shoot. This form basically will ask you to list the stunts and may ask you who's going to be supervising them (an armorer if there are weapons on set, a pyrotechnician for explosives, a stunt coordinator for stunts, etc.).
8. A copy of the script.

Then, for each performer they're paying for, they'll also want:

1. A copy of the (1-page) SAG agreement.
2. The original payroll start forms.
3. If the actor is a loan-out (their corporation is getting paid instead of them directly), a W-9 filled out for their company.
4. An agent deposit authorization letter from the actor's agent. This authorizes the payroll company to make out the actor's checks directly to his agent, who will then take the 10 percent fee and pass on the difference to the actor.
5. A child work authorization permit (if the actor is a minor).
6. A Coogan (trust fund) account statement or information sheet, so the payroll company can pay the account directly.

For any crew they're covering, they'll want:

1. The original payroll start forms.
2. A copy of the union contract (if you've signed up with any unions).
3. They *may* ask for a copy of the crew deal memo, but I've never seen this.
4. An invoice if the crew member is being paid as a subcontractor.

In addition to providing the company with this info, you'll be well-served if you come up with a payroll worksheet for each week and send it along as well. This will give them some kind of guide to work from when they're preparing the payroll. Table 21.2 shows a sample worksheet.

This can take a little time to set up (this was in Excel), but it will help you estimate the cast payroll and also keep track of what paperwork you've gotten and/or still need from your actors.

If I'm paying the crew myself, I usually do a simpler version of this worksheet, so that (again) I can keep track of their hours and get a good estimate of total payroll expenses.

The payroll company will hand you a big thick stack of start forms and blank timecards when you finalize your agreement with them. Don't fall behind on the payroll – SAG and/or the unions

TABLE 21.2 Sample cast payroll worksheet

#	Role	First Name	Last Name	SS #	Line Item	Guild	Agent	SAG Deal	Start	I-9/ W-9	W-4	Loan Out	Contract Type	Contract Rate	Rate/ Hour	WEEK #2 TOTALS Reg	OT1	OT2 $25	MP $25	Days	Total + Agent 10%	SAG 15.3%	Fed/St. Fringes 21.0%	Payroll Fee $15.00	TOTAL
1	John	Bruce	Willis	xxx–xx– xxxx	114–01	X	X	X	X	X	X	X	Day	100	12.50	40.0	14.7	0.0	1.0	5.0	880.69	$135	$185	$15	$1,215.38
2	Hans	Alan	Rickman	xxx–xx– xxxx	114–01		X		X	X	X	X	Day	100	12.50	32.0	10.9	0.0	0.0	4.0	664.81	$0	$140	$15	$819.42
3	Red Shirt Lucky #1	Actor		xxx–xx– xxxx	114–02	X	X	X	X	X	X		Day	100	12.50	8.0	0.3	0.0	1.0	1.0	143.69	$22	$30	$15	$210.85
4	Red Shirt Guy #2	Pilot		xxx–xx– xxxx	114–02	X	X	X	X	X	X		Day	100	12.50	40.0	15.9	0.0	0.0	5.0	877.94	$134	$184	$15	$1,211.63
5	Red Shirt Joe #3	Actor		xxx–xx– xxxx	114–02	X	X	X	X	X	X		Day	100	12.50	24.0	0.0	0.0	0.0	3.0	330.00	$50	$69	$15	$464.79
6	Dead Cop #1	John	Playsonlycops	xxx–xx– xxxx	114–02	X	X	X		X	X		Day	100	12.50	40.0	0.0	0.0	0.0	5.0	550.00	$84	$116	$15	$764.65
7	FBI Johnson	Duane	Johnson	xxx–xx– xxxx	114–02	X	X	X	X	X	X		Day	100	12.50	40.0	0.0	0.0	0.0	5.0	550.00	$84	$116	$15	$764.65
8	...	...		xxx–xx– xxxx	114–03	X	X	X	X	X	X		Day	100	12.50	8.0	0.5	0.0	0.0	1.0	109.38	$17	$23	$15	$164.08
9	...	...		xxx–xx– xxxx	114–03	X	X	X	X	X	X		Day	100	12.50	8.0	0.0	0.0	0.0	1.0	110.00	$17	$23	$15	$164.93
10	...	...		xxx–xx– xxxx	114–03		X	X	X	X	X		Day	100	12.50	8.0	0.0	0.0	0.0	1.0	100.00	$0	$21	$15	$136.00
11	...	...		xxx–xx– xxxx	114–03	X	X	X	X	X	X		Day	100	12.50	8.0	0.0	0.0	0.0	1.0	110.00	$17	$23	$15	$164.93
12	...	...		xxx–xx– xxxx	114–03		X	X	X	X	X		Day	100	12.50	8.0	0.0	0.0	0.0	1.0	110.00	$17	$23	$15	$164.93
13	...	...		xxx–xx– xxxx	114–03	X	X	X	X	X	X		Day	100	12.50	8.0	0.0	0.0	0.0	1.0	110.00	$0	$23	$15	$148.10
14	...	...		xxx–xx– xxxx	114–03			X		X			Day	100	12.50	8.0	0.0	0.0	0.0	1.0	100.00	$0	$21	$15	$136.00
	TOTAL:															280.0	42.3	0.0	2.0	35.0	4746.50	$577.07	$996.77	$210	$6,530.33

can fine you if you do. And the agents and managers will hound you. Schedule some time on the "days off" during the shoot for dealing with this.

Setting Up the Production Designer and Costume Designer

These two folks will be doing a lot of purchasing, and will be operating more or less on their own (except for some things which they'll ask you to buy or rent). So when you first hire them, you should hand over:

1. A company credit card (even if it's just a copy), preferably with a large limit
2. Petty cash equal to 30–50 percent of their total purchases + rentals + expendables line items
3. A stack of resale certificates
4. Insurance certificates made out to any big vendors they need to rent from (like a costume or prop rental house)
5. Blank expense forms and envelopes so they can track their receipts (see below for more about this)

Whatever card you give them should have a substantial limit on it, because they'll be doing a lot of buy-and-returns – buying material (props, paint, wardrobe) and then returning it for partial or full refunds after the shoot is over. This is one of the few ways that these departments can actually stay on budget and still deliver the goods.

The resale certificates will help them save you money – they can hand these out to the vendors they're buying from, so you'll pay no sales tax on a lot of items. You'll have to make out the insurance certificates once they give you the names of vendors they'll be renting from.

You should also get *from* them a list of expendables/supplies/gear that they'll need that you can rent or buy from a unit supply house (see Chapter 14 for more details).

During the shoot, you'll have to replenish their petty cash periodically. Try to get them to turn in what receipts they can during the shoot. They won't be able to turn in all their receipts because they'll be hoping for buy and returns on a substantial portion of items, but at least get them to separate out non-design expenses (tolls, gas, off-set meals, cab rides when transporting heavy stuff) from design expenses.

Vendor Packets

When you sign up with each vendor, you'll need to assemble a vendor packet and then store a copy in your file box. The package should contain:

1. Credit card authorization form
2. Credit card deductible form (if they need it)
3. Resale certificate (so they won't charge you tax)
4. Insurance certificate (to cover rented items)
5. Equipment list, so you know what you're getting

Try to get this to the vendors no later than a week before the shoot, if you can. The insurance certificates can always wait until the night before the pickup (or the day of it if absolutely necessary). Sometimes the equipment list changes during the course of the checkout. Do the best you can to track the changes. If it's a PA doing the pickups, make sure s/he turns in whatever "out" sheet the vendor gave him/her.

Run Lists

The day before you need the PAs to do a big run for you – the equipment pickup day is a good example – you'll want to type up a run list and hand it out ahead of time. This breaks down where they're going, including the address, cross street, phone number, and contact person; also some indication of what they'll be picking up and/or dropping off. You may want to include directions as well. These can be handwritten in a pinch, but you're better off typing them up and handing out multiple copies. Be sure to give your PAs a road atlas, in case their smartphones decide to conk out in the middle of giving them driving directions.

Insurance Certificates

When you bind your insurance policy, you'll either be given some online tool for creating new certificates, or you'll have to email your broker to have him/her create and send them to you. Most low-budget film policies include the online tool (after all, it saves the broker effort and therefore money). As soon as you bind the policy, create and print out certificates for your vendors, the cities you're shooting in, locations, payroll company, unions, and cast and crew members (especially if you're renting gear from any of them). This tedious chore can take a little time. Some brokers will make the initial batch of certificates out for you (if they have the insured parties in their database) when you bind the policy. So when you're finalizing the policy, make sure to send the broker a list of people/vendors/locations you know you'll need certificates for.

Expense Envelopes

Whenever I hand someone petty cash, a check for purchases, or out-of-pocket reimbursements, I give them a blank expense sheet, and an envelope with some scrap paper inside. What you want is for the person to tape up their receipts on the scrap paper, then itemize them on the expense sheet (even if it's just a couple) and stick everything inside an envelope. You can email blank expense sheets to your staff as well. What you *don't* want is for the person to give you a ball of crumpled-up receipts and expect you to sort it all out. So have plenty of blank expense sheets and envelopes on hand. Yesterday's callsheets and sides make excellent scrap paper, by the way.

Reimbursements, Petty Cash, and Check Writing

You really want to limit these activities to once a day if you can. Carry an "emergency" check in your wallet just in case, but try to avoid writing a lot of checks on set. You can easily get distracted and write out the wrong amount, or write the wrong payee in, and then you've just wasted a check, or under-or-overpaid someone.

I usually write the checks when sitting down after the day is over, with QuickBooks open and a hardcopy of the budget next to me.

I try to write out reimbursement checks within a day or two of receiving the paperwork, at night before I go to bed. Every check should be matched to a piece of paper from the payee: an invoice, timesheet, credit card slip, expense sheet (if it's for a bunch of receipts), or a purchase order (for something not purchased yet). You should also be able to code either the entire check or the individual receipts to a line item in the budget. Finally, if you're trying to tally up receipts, the total amount the payee is asking for should match up with the receipt totals.

Try to avoid situations where people are going out-of-pocket. I've found that if you give people a certain amount of cash (or a check) up front, they'll spend that amount and then ask for another check or more cash. If you ask them to cover the expenses, they'll spend more, figuring that you'll cover it regardless.

Petty cash is the bane of my existence. It's very hard to track. I've tried every method – having a separate wallet, making sign-out sheets, having people turn in their petty cash before re-upping it. No matter what, I end up with some discrepancy. My file box usually has a mountain of loose change and singles at the bottom by the end of every shoot.

Do your best at the end of each week to reconcile the petty cash you've signed out to your crew with what you've gotten back in receipts so far. But don't give yourself an aneurysm. There's a reason they call it "petty" cash. If someone owes you several hundred dollars in receipts or petty cash, that's one thing. But if someone's $10 short or is missing a receipt, it really, truly, *will not matter* to the film as a whole. What I usually do is add a line item to the budget in the Production Overhead Department, called *Unallocated Petty Cash*. Any petty cash that gets signed out is allocated to this line item. When the receipts start pouring back in I'll take money out of this account and put it into the proper line items (gas, tolls, food, etc.) for the receipts. But I'll usually have a hundred or so dollars in the unallocated petty cash line item. Sometimes this is because someone didn't turn in their petty cash, or the receipts were so faded or their handwriting so garbled I couldn't make it out, or they (or I) lost the receipts. At least you have a record of the petty cash outlay.

Production Reports

The callsheet tells you what should happen that day. The production report tells you what actually happened. This is where you'll record the actual time in and wrap-out for each of the departments; what scenes you shot, owe, deleted, and/or added; how many pages you covered; if anything extraordinary happened on set (an accident or an extra take that rocked); and the in-and-out times of the actors.

I try to keep these forms as dirt-simple as possible. I'm usually absolutely dead tired when recording them, so I'll fill out the bare minimum or even handwrite it in on the way home. While it seems unnecessary, the production report will become invaluable when you're trying to figure out whether you shot a scene or not, or when you want to check on how much the crew went into overtime on a particular day, or when some good or bad event happened.

Hotcost Reports

Whatever accounting system you end up using to keep track of your expenses (Quicken, QuickBooks, or some of the newer film-oriented expense programs such as Gorilla), you'll want to periodically generate hotcost reports (Figure 21.3). A hotcost report is a list of expenses, summarized by department and line item. It compares what was in the budget to what was spent, and tells you if you're *hot* (going over budget) or not.

You should print this out at least once per week, so you can see if you're running out of money in one department or across the entire budget.

Passing the Football

To keep all this paperwork and communication organized, you'll want to keep it in your production file box. If you have a production office with a coordinator or UPM, you'll want to use a "football." This is a filebox or accordion file holder that goes back and forth between the set and the production office (hence, the football). It should be handed off to the production office in the evening at the end of the day, with the day's shooting materials, production reports, and deal memos. The office staff load it up with the next day's callsheets, sides, run lists, and start paperwork for the next day. Either someone takes it home and brings it to set the next morning, or it stays in the office overnight until someone picks it up (usually on the way to the set). The football itself is compartmentalized either by department, form type, or both.

Even if you don't have an office or staff, you can adopt a similar system to keep track of who should get what, or give you what. My production file box has a set of folders in it, one per department, that act as a football.

The Trick to Paperwork

The first week of the shoot is always a bit hectic – one reason to push for a five-day week. Anything you fall behind on during the week you can catch up on during the days off.

Make sure everything goes into the football or into your file box. You can always sort it out later. Callsheets, sides, expenses that have to be paid out, and forms that have to be signed by people who aren't coming back the next day take priority over other paperwork.

HOTCOST REPORT FOR Found In Time   Page 7
As of 07/22/2012 2:27:28 PM

Line Item	Account	Budgeted	HotCosts	Difference
210-00	PRODUCTION SOUND			
210-01	Production Mixer	$2,275.00	$4,702.25	($2,427.25)
210-02	Boom Operator	$0.00	$902.34	($902.34)
210-03	Playback Operator (Music)	$0.00	$0.00	$0.00
210-15	Sound Equipment	$2,275.00	$0.00	$2,275.00
210-16	Addditional Rentals	$600.00	$0.00	$600.00
210-31	Expendables	$453.00	$276.88	$176.12
	PRODUCTION SOUND	$5,603.00	$5,881.47	($278.47)
211-00	SET OPERATIONS			
211-01	Set Medic	$0.00	$0.00	$0.00
211-02	Craft Service	$0.00	$0.00	$0.00
211-03	Craft Services Utility	$0.00	$0.00	$0.00
211-15	Craft Service Package	$650.00	$1,102.45	($452.45)
211-16	Unit Rentals/Expendables	$650.00	$666.60	($16.60)
211-20	Meals	$4,642.00	$5,787.81	($1,145.81)
211-21	Caterer	$0.00	$0.00	$0.00
211-25	Walkie-Talkie Rental	$136.00	$300.00	($164.00)
211-30	Kit Fees	$0.00	$0.00	$0.00
211-31	Expendables (See 211-16)	$0.00	$0.00	$0.00
	SET OPERATIONS	$6,078.00	$7,856.86	($1,778.86)
212-00	COSTUME/WARDROBE			
212-01	Costume Designer	$2,550.00	$2,873.19	($323.19)
212-02	Costume Assistant	$0.00	$0.00	$0.00
212-03	Wardrobe Supervisor	$0.00	$0.00	$0.00
212-04	First Set Costumer	$0.00	$0.00	$0.00
212-05	Costumer/Shopper	$0.00	$0.00	$0.00
212-06	Costume/Wardrobe PAs	$0.00	$0.00	$0.00

07/22/2012 2:27:28 PM

HOTCOST REPORT FOR Found In Time   Page 8
As of 07/22/2012 2:27:28 PM

Line Item	Account	Budgeted	HotCosts	Difference
212-15	Purchases/Rentals	$1,144.00	$2,206.91	($1,062.91)
212-16	Cleaning	$195.00	$16.80	$178.20
212-30	Kit Fees	$0.00	$0.00	$0.00
212-31	Expendables	$130.00	$19.42	$110.58
212-32	Damages	$0.00	$0.00	$0.00
	COSTUME/WARDROBE	$4,019.00	$5,116.32	($1,097.32)
213-00	HAIR/MAKEUP			
213-01	Key Makeup Artist	$2,600.00	$3,501.31	($901.31)
213-02	Key Hair Artist	$0.00	$0.00	$0.00
213-03	Assistant H/MU Artists	$0.00	$0.00	$0.00
213-05	S/FX Makeup	$0.00	$91.77	($91.77)
213-15	Hair/Makeup Expenses	$520.00	$335.93	$184.07
213-30	Kit Fees	$650.00	$0.00	$650.00
213-31	Expendables	$100.00	$0.00	$100.00
	HAIR/MAKEUP	$3,870.00	$3,929.01	($59.01)
214-00	LOCATIONS			
214-01	Location Manager	$0.00	$0.00	$0.00
214-02	Assistant Location Manager	$0.00	$0.00	$0.00
214-03	Location PAs	$0.00	$0.00	$0.00
214-04	Location Scout	$0.00	$0.00	$0.00
214-06	Security	$0.00	$0.00	$0.00
214-10	Scouting Expenses	$25.00	$0.00	$25.00
214-15	Site Rentals	$3,400.00	$4,838.73	($1,438.73)
214-16	Soundstage Rentals	$3,200.00	$4,600.00	($1,400.00)
214-31	Expendables/Location Supplies	$500.00	$98.00	$402.00
	LOCATIONS	$7,125.00	$9,536.73	($2,411.73)

07/22/2012 2:27:28 PM

FIGURE 21.3 A hotcost report from *Found In Time*.

GETTING YOUR SOUND AND VIDEO IN SYNC

As you approach the first day of shooting, you'll be swamped with a variety of concerns, ranging from small to large. All of them will seem urgent, but the truth is that some of them can wait. Deal with the big things first – locations, crew hiring, casting, insurance, bidding on equipment – and let other things slide or delegate them to your staff.

The two most important things you'll want to have worked out *before* day one on set are:

1. Making sure the sound-and-camera recording systems are set up properly
2. Making sure everyone understands the card or tape workflow once the film has been shot

These are the kinds of things we all lose sleep over, since there's no negative to go back to (though that was hardly foolproof). And if your film is out of sync at this point, you're … in real trouble.

Sound and Camera Sync Options

It's remarkable to me that, more than a hundred years after the birth of cinema, and over 80 years since "talkies" came into their own, we are still dealing with the issue of how to sync sound and image. It comes down to four choices:

1. **Recording separate sources, independently.** This is the "default" option. Your sound mixer records sound to his DDR (direct-to-disk sound recorder), your DP records image to her camera. You use a dumb slate – or better, a smart slate that's slaved to the DDR – to mark the takes. If you're shooting film this is pretty much your only option. If you're shooting on a DSLR, this is probably also what you'll end up doing.
2. **Recording separate sources, slaved timecode.** You can rent timecode generators that will slave both the audio and video to a common timecode. If you're shooting on a camera

that has a timecode input, this is a great option – you will be able to sync up your footage easily in post by lining up the timecode numbers. Keep in mind that someone in the sound or camera departments will have to periodically check this device. Also, it means attaching one more thing to the camera.

3. **Recording separate source, reference track "thrown" wirelessly to camera.** The sound mixer sends out a wireless signal containing a mixdown of the audio he's recording on his DDR, to a receiver strapped to the camera. This will not be as good as the DDR audio, but at least you will have a decent-sounding reference. Keep in mind that someone will have to check the batteries on the transmitter and receiver, and it means attaching one other thing to the camera.

4. **Recording single-source.** Your audio is routed through a mixer (hopefully), then straight into the audio inputs on the camera. This is the worst option. It tethers the camera and sound departments, which is not always a good thing. Also, the camera audio input processing circuits are never as good as those of a professional-grade DDR. But if you're in a pinch (or shooting a documentary), you may not have any other option.

Note that you can combine scenarios #2 and #3, which is what we did on *Helena from the Wedding*. Micah Bloomberg, the sound mixer, and Steve Kazmierski, the DP, strapped a little "saddlebag" to the camera, containing the timecode generator and the wireless receiver. Every now and then the power would go out on the receiver or the wireless signal would get wonky, so the editor had to sync up the production audio.

You also need to make sure everyone is recording at the same (or a matching) framerate. If you're shooting video at 23.976fps, the audio should be recorded at either 23.976fps, or 29.97fps with non-drop timecode.

Use a smart slate (synched to the DDR timecode). The smart slate displays timecode when the clapper is open, synchronized to the DDR's timecode. When you close the clapper, the timecode freezes and a red light snaps on for one frame. This will help you sync up the footage later.

Workflow – from Camera and DDR to Drive

Once the memory cards are full on the DDR and camera, the DP should hand them off to … *someone*, who copies them to a hard drive, makes a backup of the copy, wipes them, and hands them back. Six years after tapeless HD was introduced, this still scares me. Even when we shot film more often, occasionally a rookie 2nd AC would screw up and reload a mag with exposed film, resulting in fun psychedelic experiments but little in the way of usable footage.

Don't let this experiment happen on your film. Work out who gets the tape or card or mag (the editor, assistant editor, AC, or the DIT), what happens to the footage, and how the empty cards/drives/mags are kept separate from the full ones.

Bring this up during the production meeting, and again before the equipment check-out, so you know everyone's on the same page. The sound and camera rental houses can help you navigate this issue as well.

DIRECTING AND THE SET

I recommend that you keep your script analysis notes, storyboards, diagrams, and dog-eared, notated script in a binder, and keep the binder on set. If it gets too bulky, keep the diagrams/boards separate from the script. Keep everything in scene order – that way you can always reference the previous and subsequent scenes; it'll remind you of where you are in the story.

I usually look through the analysis and script for the next day just before I go to bed. Sometimes I wake up with new ideas. Then I'll look at the script again over coffee on set.

When you're on set, I recommend you watch at least one or two takes directly instead of through the monitor. While you may miss the framing, you'll be seeing the performances more clearly. The actors, I find, really appreciate it when someone's looking at them, instead of seeing the entire crew watch television. There are times where you'll need to look in the monitor, but you can always play the take back; you will never be able to see it "live" again. This is one reason Steven Soderbergh also operates his own camera – he finds it brings him in closer to the actors.

Another thing I recommend, though it's really up to you: stand up while you're on set, especially if you're the director. Don't sit down too much. Stand up. Move around. I found that when I'm standing, I feel more awake and put out a little more energy. I could be dreaming, but it seems to also have a positive effect on everyone else. The crew takes their cues from you. Of course, it's hard to write checks or fill out paperwork while you're standing up. But when you're not doing something that requires a signature, stay upright.

During the shoot, if everything is going well, you may feel a bit redundant on set. The crew and cast know what they're doing, and you're just kind of … sitting or standing around, waiting. Don't sweat it. Don't try to over-assert control. If you've done your prep work, then this is what *should* be happening. Obviously, if you think things are going off the rails or something is really taking forever, it may be time to crack the whip, but that's what the 1st AD is for.

Stay Cool

Keep arguments off set as much as possible. It can really blow everyone's cool. Having said that, everyone is allowed one freak out per shoot. Thanks to YouTube, everyone saw Christian Bale's rant on the set of *Terminator: Salvation*. But almost no one saw the hours of shooting, stuntwork, and sweat in the desert that preceded it. When everyone's working for long hours with little sleep in tight quarters and under deadline pressure, someone is going to wig out. If you're the one wigging out, get it out of your system, apologize, and move on. If you can, walk off set first. If you can't, keep from insulting anyone in particular. People will *not* forgive you no matter what you say later. You're the boss, so your voice carries weight.

If the person wigging out is a crewmember, take a minute and go off set with the person. Or ask his direct boss (the department head) to go off set together. Don't make too big deal out of it. If he keeps freaking out, find out what's going on. Perhaps he needs a hug or a nap. If he's getting stress from someone else on the crew, then promise to talk to them. If he's just not cut out for independent film, then it may be your cue to look for a replacement. This can happen when people step up in responsibility but aren't really ready for it. I've had to fire a few people (thankfully, very few) because of this. They simply froze instead of doing their jobs, and couldn't get "unstuck." You can't afford to lose too much time if the situation doesn't improve, so keep some resumes handy just in case.

If the person freaking out is a performer, it's usually because they're afraid of looking foolish, or something is really blowing their concentration (see the Bale rant above). If it's a concentration issue, try to solve it (maybe move video village further away from the set, for example). If it's an issue of looking foolish, then you have to do your best to reassure him that you'd never let that happen. Your job is to take the actors out on a highwire, but keep them from falling off it. You may have to work to earn their trust – propose good criticism when they do sub-par work, and push them in a constructive way to do better, and tell them when you're pleased.

WHEN PLANS GO AWRY

> *In preparing for battle I have always found that plans are useless, but planning is indispensable.*
> President (and General) Dwight Eisenhower

Despite your most brilliant plans, something will go wrong. The shot you and your DP came up with that was going to carry you smoothly from one scene to the next – it's not working. The actors aren't gelling in quite the way you anticipated. The lead actor's agent called you to tell you that they just booked their client on a big show. You now have a week to find a replacement, or rearrange your entire shoot.

FIGURE 21.4 When plans go awry.

Over the years, I've read a fair number of books on organization, planning, scheduling, and time management. Almost all of them had some nugget of wisdom to offer. But few mentioned what you should do when, despite deploying their "perfect" planning systems, things still went awry. So let's get into what to do when your plans hit reality head-on.

It Doesn't Matter

Race-car drivers like to walk the course the day before a big race, so they can rehearse their moves and get to know the terrain. You've done something similar in your prep work. You've deepened your understanding of the script, the production process, and your ultimate goals. So if things aren't going according to plan – if the angles indicated by the storyboard or diagram aren't giving you what you want, or a scene is coming out differently than you imagined – don't sweat it. Your knowledge of the material will carry you over the rough patch, and give you the background you need to come up with a new solution.

This is one reason to come up with multiple scene objectives for each of your characters. An actor's performance that was fresh and wonderful in rehearsal is now sounding stale on location and in front of the camera. Well, can changing their objective help? Sometimes, just trying something different, even if it fails, can jolt everyone out of their groove, and they're then back in a more playful state, willing to try new things. If none of those alternate objectives produces results, come up with something on the spot. Trust that your understanding of the script and your cast will carry you through even when your plans won't.

Recognize Human Frailty

Most diets fail because they (or the dieters) assume a superhuman level of self-control. You will still want to eat all the cupcakes in the house, regardless of the fact that you *know* it will set you back. I know from whence I speak. I lost over 70 pounds over a few years, after having developed some bad eating (everything) and exercise (never) habits. Those bad habits didn't disappear overnight. The first thing I did was make sure I didn't have snacks in the house, and I asked my friends not to bring any over.

When you're preparing your schedule, keep in mind that the crew may not be able to keep up a relentless pace every day. If people are having a progressively harder time getting to set and getting warmed up after three days of shooting eight pages per day, is there a way to give them a break? Can you push some things around to create one "slightly lighter" day? Can you reduce the number of setups you'll need? Can you start with a less complicated scene and then dive into the big scene of the day?

This is one reason for sticking with the five-day week, and why having coffee available after lunch is so important. Everyone's natural tendency is to go take a siesta after lunch, so make sure the caffeine, fruit, and other healthy snacks are ready to save people from the sugar dip.

Similarly, if you find you're going over twelve hours a day consistently, then it's time to consider adding another day to your schedule, rather than trying to push the crew to work harder. It's quite possible that they just aren't going to be able to go any faster than they are now.

Lean on Your Team

My cellphone was stolen at the end of the second week of *Found In Time*. I was able to email Ben Wolf, the DP, and the rest of the cast and crew, and asked everyone to contact him in case of emergency, since they wouldn't be able to reach me. Ben and I have been working together for over a decade, so I knew I could count on him. Similarly, there were a lot of times when I was stuck for a shootable master for a scene. But he always came through with a setup that would work great. Or we would just watch the actors rehearse until something came to us.

The point is that you will not be able to provide all the answers, but if you have the confidence of your team, you can lean on them for help. In most cases, the results will be better than what you could have come up with on your own. This kind of *synergy* is invaluable, but it does mean giving up some control. This is okay. As long as you can still keep the film going in the direction you want it to go, it'll be fine.

No One Is Irreplaceable

If someone is actually screwing up your shoot, however – they're bullying you, slacking off, phoning in their performance (if they're in the cast), or are otherwise causing bad mischief – you should very seriously consider replacing that person. Even if they're your lead actor.

Obviously, the first thing to try and do is to patch things up, and/or make sure that the person is in fact causing problems, and not just trying to bring attention to existing ones. Don't shoot the messenger, in other words. Talk to the person in a quiet moment, find out what's going on. But you don't have time to work out the kinks in your relationship, and frankly if this is how it performs under stress, *then it's a bad relationship*. If you let someone stay aboard the team who's abusive or operating with a different agenda, it will send a bad signal to others, that it's okay for them to misbehave.

Now, there are times when you won't be able to fire the person, if, let's say, he's the nephew of your biggest investor. The trick is to get the rest of the team on your side, and isolate him so he can't do too much harm. This may take some serious machinations and patience, but it can keep things from getting out of hand.

Also, keep in mind that what I'm talking about is beyond simply "not getting along." A film set is a work environment, after all. You have to work with people you may not actually like all that much. But if someone is actually not doing her job or actively making yours more difficult, that's a problem that needs to be addressed.

Simplify

If the shot isn't going well because it's too complicated, or your actors are getting stuck in a particular spot in the scene, or you're not finding exactly the location you want, it could be time to try something simpler. This sounds obvious, but we often get fixated on what we have planned – it's like playing a videogame on hardest difficulty and dying in the same spot. Instead of going back to the medium setting and getting through it just once, we become ever more determined to learn that magic technique that will keep us from getting roasted to death by the fireball-wielding demon.

Sometimes practice *does* make perfect. But sometimes you just can't afford to wait for muscle memory to kick in. So break the shot down into simpler components. Give your actors something easier to cope with. Perhaps you've "over-unitized" the scene, breaking it into too many beats. Your actors are trying to keep track of the transitions and are losing their place in the scene. Or you've got an exchange of dialog that could be made simpler.

Kick the Can Down the Road

If today isn't going well, but you're coming back to the same location tomorrow, then perhaps the answer is to just get through the current scene, regroup when you get home, and then shoot everything you'll owe tomorrow. This is dangerous – you're just moving problems instead of solving them – but it can also give you the breathing space to come up with better decisions and for everyone to take a break.

Work in Pieces

If a scene isn't going well – if the performances are off and you can't seem to bring them back, or you don't have time to rehearse a good moving master, or the sound environment is too unstable for a long take – break up the scene into pieces. You're moving in the opposite direction of consolidating setups, but with a specific purpose. Your goal is to create enough material for the editor to build the scene in post. This is not the ideal situation but it can get you out of a jam.

Redundancy

Always have more than one copy of your camera masters. Buy at least two drives, and keep them mirrored as often as possible. This way if one goes down you won't be suffering. Likewise, if you need four walkies, think about renting five. The additional cost buys you some flexibility, in case you need to put one in a car for a driving shot.

Look for redundancy in some non-obvious places. I'm still figuring out what the ideal number of PAs to hire is. I often try to get away with as few as possible, but sometimes this bites me in the butt, when both of them are on runs and I need someone to do a lockup down the block. Again, the additional cost is not huge compared to the flexibility you gain. If you're shooting in a remote area, then definitely contemplate renting a second camera body.

KEEPING PERSPECTIVE

Nothing is as important as shooting the scenes, and doing it well. If you find the paperwork overwhelming, then you need to switch priorities. The audience will never see it. They'll only see the finished film. You can afford to make small mistakes on your paperwork, as long as you're getting the contracts signed and people paid on time.

Don't be afraid to let a little control go. A lot of first-time directors don't want to hand the checkbook over to the producer, line producer, or UPM. But this is short-sighted. You can put mechanisms in place to make sure the money is well-spent. You can schedule time to sit with the check-writer, to approve/disapprove of checks. You can ask for hotcost reports on a regular basis. You can hold back on petty cash until people turn in their receipts. You can hire a part-time production accountant to come in once a week and keep the books in shape. An overage in one line item can be made up with an underage in another.

But whenever you try to watch the money and the movie at the same time, the money wins. It's good to be responsible to your investors (especially if they're related to or sleeping with you), but they invested in you as a filmmaker. So make the film!

Finally, get some sleep every day. Even if it's three or four hours a night, make sure it's consistent. The time will be well-spent.

QUESTIONS/EXERCISES

1. If you have a callsheet template you like, fill it out with your Production Day 1 schedule.
2. Are you a morning or evening person? If you're a morning person, get up a little earlier and do the paperwork first thing.
3. Keep a notebook and pen next to you at night. If you wake up with some insight into a particular scene, write it down right away, before coffee.
4. Put a production file box or "football" together. Make sure it's stocked with plenty of blank forms.

## Chapter 22

Preparing for Post

FIGURE 22.1 Postproduction logging.

"Production is just an assembly-line to get the script onto the screen," said William Goldman in his book *Which Lie Did I Tell?*. Like a lot of Goldman's writing (except for his screenplays), it's both nonsense and completely true at the same time. Production is much more than an assembly line – it really is where the film is forged. Forged is the right word, too – the materials get melted down (along with a scary amount of money), and through the sweat and tears of a lot of talented people, beaten into something wonderful.

What Goldman gets right, however, is that you don't end up with a movie at the end of the shoot. You end up with something that has to be sifted through and cut together, and eventually gets made into a film. Making a steel sword requires heating, folding, and cooling iron over a hot bellows over days or months. The editing process is a lot like this – you'll circle around the material, chipping, trimming, and discovering new things, all the while aiming for something that looks like what you designed in the first place.

However, it helps if you don't throw your post staff under a bus. On a lot of films I've worked on, post just disappeared from everyone's mind (including my own). The objective was to get it shot. It's only when we gave the editor a hard drive full of unlabeled takes, and said "here, cut this" – or tried to do a rough cut ourselves – that we realized that we hadn't prepared for post. So we'll talk about how to prepare for post, both before and during production.

GETTING THE FILM READY FOR POST

Before you shoot, you'll want to work out, as best as possible, what each person in your post "world" needs and at what stage. While every film is different, there is a "standard" post workflow of sorts (Table 22.1).

TABLE 22.1 Post workflow

#	Step	Inputs	Personnel	Gear	Outputs
1	Transcoding Organizing bins	Original clips Production audio	Ass't editor	NLE Transcoding utility	Project file w/bins Transcoded clips in folders on drive
2	Synching	Transcoded clips Audio files NLE project file	Ass't editor	NLE PluralEyes	Synched clips nested in project file
3	Logging clips Script notes	Project Script	Director Ass't editor	NLE	Lined script with notes Logging notes of some kind Binder with notes, sound reports, production reports, etc.
4	Picture edit	NLE project file Binder Hard drive	Editor	NLE	Sequences in reels in project file
5	Feedback screenings	Rough or 2nd cut on DVD	Editor Ass't editor Trusted friends	DVD projector	Notes for next cut
6	Reshoots/ inserts	Wish list of shots	Skeleton crew and cast	Basic gear Props, set dressing	Video/audio footage
	Picture Locked:				
7	F/X and titles	NLE project file F/X plates Add'l computer-generated footage	DP? Ass't editor VFX artist Editor (possibly)	NLE Photoshop Motion After Effects(?)	Locked VFX Quicktimes and titles
8	Transcode for online (if necessary)	NLE sequences (reels) Camera master files	Ass't editor	NLE Transcoding utility	Transcoded hi-resolution selects only (clips that made the final cut) Notes EDL

#	Step	Inputs	Personnel	Gear	Outputs
9	Conform	Final clips Offline sequences (reels) VFX and title sequences EDL	Ass't editor	NLE	NLE sequences, linked to final clips
10	Color correction/ Basic compositing	NLE sequences (reels) Notes	Colorist Director DP	NLE Color Motion After effects	Color corrected reels with all titles and effects in place
Image Conformed/Corrected:					
11	Prep for sound edit	Audio files Reels (preferably color corrected, but at least the final conforms)	Ass't editor	NLE	Quicktimes for each reel per sound designer/ composer specs OMF files per reel Sound design notes in binder
12	Sound design	OMF files Audio files Sound cue sheet Reference Quicktimes Binder	Sound designer Foley artist? Dialog editor?	ProTools or other sound software NLE	ProTools session files ADR/Foley files in session
13	Music	Quicktimes Sound notes Rough music cue notes	Composer	Instruments Music mixing software	Soundtrack, broken into reels, premixed Music cue sheets
14	Mix	Session files Quicktimes Soundtrack files	Sound designer Re-recording Engineer (?) Director	ProTools Mixing hardware	Bounce tracks
Sound Mixed:					
15	Final output	Blank HD and SD stock Final cut reels "Bounce" tracks	Ass't editor Post house editor	Online suite (for tapes)	Projection master – DCP or HDCAM DCP master (files) SD tape master DVD master (Quicktimes)
16	DVD output	DVD master (Quicktime) "Extra" features clips Menu graphics DVD cover/sleeve art DVDs and sleeves	Ass't editor	DVDStudio Pro	DVDs in sleeves

You don't have to work out every last detail of this process before you shoot, and you're likely to make some changes along the way. Your composer may give you some rough cues to edit with, or you may have to do some preliminary VFX as part of the picture edit.

What you want to establish, as clearly as possible, are your choice of formats:

1. Your shooting (or acquisition) format – H264, XDCAM EX, ProRes 444 or 2K/4K RAW, film?
2. Your editing format – 1K proxy files, ProRes, DNxHD files?
3. Your online format – could be the same as your editing format, or you could be going back to your acquisition format.
4. Your output/delivery formats – HDCAM-SR HD tape master, HDCAM/60i projection master, DigiBeta SD master, DVD masters, and/or DCP package?
5. Your final sound mix – stereo, stereo LTRT (left and right encoded together) or Dolby 5.1, or both?

Table 22.2 shows a few sample format workflow scenarios. Each path has its own technical requirements and potential pitfalls.

One thing I absolutely recommend is to buy or lease your own editing workstation, and keep a local copy of all the clips and project files. This way you can troubleshoot problems, make DVDs, prepare material for the sound editor without bumping off the picture editor, and so on. You can amortize the investment by making this your primary computer once the post is done. You'll also have a redundant copy of the film in case something goes wrong with the editor's drive.

What the Editor Needs

In Ye Olde Days of filmmaking an apprentice or assistant editor would work with the production and the lab to get the reels of film, sync them, label them, keep the trims organized, and compare the takes to the script supervisor's notes. As budgets got tighter and non-linear systems got a little

TABLE 22.2 Format workflow

	Scenario #1	Scenario #2	Scenario #3	Scenario #4
Camera:	Canon 5D or C300	Sony F3	Arri Alexa	Red
Acquisition format:	Canon H.264	XDCAM EX	2K ArriRaw	4K RedRaw
Acquisition type:	Highly compressed (35mbps)	Highly compressed (50mbps)	2K per frame Downsampled from 3K	4K per frame
Frame size/rate:	1920 × 1080 / 24p	1920 × 1080 / 24p	2880 × 1620 / 24p	4480 × 2304 / 24p
Editing format:	ProRes LT	ProRes LT	ProRes 422	ProRes Proxy
Transcoding method:	Canon EOS Plug-in	Sony XDCAM ClipViewer	Automatic	RedRushes
Online format:	ProRes HQ	ProRes HQ	DPX	4K RedRaw
Output/delivery formats:	ProRes HQ reels DVD masters	ProRes HQ reels DVD masters	HDCAM-SR/24p DVD masters	HDCAM-SR DVD masters
Theatrical output formats:	Blu-Ray?	DCP package	DCP package HDCAM 60/i	DCP package HDCAM 60/i
DCP frame size:	1920 × 1080	1920 × 1080	1920 × 1080 or 2K	1920 × 1080 or 2K or 4K
Mix format:	LTRT for DVDs	LTRT for DVDs 5.1 files for DCP	LTRT & 5.1 for everything	LTRT & 5.1 for everything

better at organizing material, that job started disappearing. But the work of organizing the footage so that it's actually editable hasn't gone away. So it may be up to you or an unpaid intern to get the film into shape.

What does the editor need to get started? Ideally:

1. A "starter" project file in the editor's choice of NLE (non-linear editor) format (Final Cut, Premiere, Avid, Vegas … whatever).
2. All the video clips from the film, transcoded into an editable format, synchronized with the production audio, and labeled in the project file with the scene, shot, and take number. If the files are also named with the scene–shot–take, that's even better.
3. All the clips should be referenced in the project file, organized however the editor wants them. On *Found In Time*, Dan wanted everything in scene bins.
4. All the sound clips, identified in the NLE with scene–shot–take.
5. A "lined" script and script supervisor notes (if available).
6. Camera and sound reports (if any).
7. Ideally, a log of the clips, giving some kind of indication of the shot duration, the dialog, angle, whether the shot was any good or not. You can create this list in the NLE or separately.
8. Any notes you want to give.
9. A revised vision statement.
10. The production reports and schedule may be helpful.
11. All this on a roomy hard drive, preferably with an eSATA connection.
12. A "dope" sheet that spells out what's where on the hard drive, what your target deliverables are, and what your acquisition and editing formats are.
13. A nice thick binder with printouts of the above (PDFs are great too, but nothing beats paper).
14. A Dropbox or other cloud drive for sharing files (this is good for your entire post staff, actually).
15. Access to your Vimeo account for posting rough cuts for review (password-protected, of course).

If you have someone on the crew preparing this laundry list during the shoot, then that's great. If not, then put aside some time to do this before the editor starts working. It can take a while, depending on your technical expertise. It will not only help your editor but also your sound designer, composer, visual effects designer, and online editor/conformist.

Grab a Hard Drive

The truth is that you can never have enough drives. On *Found In Time*, the camera and audio masters took up about 500GB of space. However, I ultimately ended up getting one external 2TB backup drive, and one internal 2TB editing drive, and two more external 2TB drives, one for the sound designer and VFX artist, and one for the editor and colorist. Since hard-drive prices generally come down over time, I recommend that you only get what you need as you need it.

Start the Spreadsheet

Before you start doing anything, you'll want to put together a master clip list – that's a list of all your video and audio clips (in their original file names). You'll also want to put on each row:

1. The original file name
2. The scene, shot, and take for each clip
3. The frame rate and format (if you shot with multiple formats)
4. What folder each clip lives in on the hard drive (you probably organized the camera master files by shoot day)

5. Timecode start/end
6. Some kind of brief summary of the shot (the angle)
7. A longer description
8. Whether the clip is MOS (without audio) or not
9. The matching audio clip filename
10. The bin inside the NLE project file that the clip was imported into

What you'll end up with will look something like Figure 22.2 (this is a database I built in a program called FileMaker).

When you start out you'll probably just have the filenames filled in with a lot of blank columns. However, as you go through the steps of transcoding, synching, and logging, you'll fill up this information, and it will become a complete clip log which you can present to your editor.

Transcoding and Synching Footage

For films shot on highly compressed formats (like Canon's H264 format, HDV, or XDCAM-EX), or large formats (2K, 4K RAW), you'll usually need to transcode the footage to some variant of DNxHD (Avid) or ProRes (Apple), so your editor can cut it without creating too much drag on her system. There are a number of utilities – most offered by the camera manufacturers – that can do batch conversions of footage. Some can rename your clips along the way. Note that these utilities transcode your clips to copies – they shouldn't replace your camera masters.

If you decide to rename your clips (I recommend the scene–shot–take format), make sure you note the *original* clip name so you can reference back to it if you ever have to go back to your camera masters. Also, make sure that the timecode type and start of your transcoded clips *exactly matches* that of your original clips, or you will be in for some extremely unpleasant surprises when you conform your masters down the road.

Once you've transcoded your clips, you'll bring them into the NLE project file, organized into bins according to your editor's desire. The transcoding process is fairly automatic (it took less than a week to transcode all the clips from *Found In Time*).

FOUND IN TIME

Scene/Shot/Take			TCStart	TCEnd	Action Start	Angle	Edting Bin	MOS
123	B	2	12:28:45:00	12:29:22:20	12:28:57	on Chris	Scene 123	☐
123	B	3	12:30:20:00	12:31:11:04	12:30:37	on Chris	Scene 123	☐
123	B	NG	12:26:52:00	12:26:53:00		on Chris	Scene 123	☒
133	A	1	14:54:41:00	14:55:03:04	14:54:52	master	Scene 133	☐
133	A	2	14:55:38:00	14:56:21:15	14:55:45	Master	Scene 133	☐
133	A	3	14:57:41:00	14:58:38:04	14:57:51	Master	Scene 133	☐
133	A	4	15:01:17:00	15:01:26:02			Scene 133	☐
133	A	5	15:01:49:00	15:02:41:23	15:01:56	Master	Scene 133	☐
134	A	1	15:03:19:00	15:04:26:13	15:03:34	racks	Scene	☐
134	B	2	15:10:17:00	15:11:50:14	15:10:44	on Door	Scene	☐

Clip Name: 134-B-2   Duration: 00:01:33:15

Description: Chris enters. False start @ 15:10:26.   SECOND ATTEMPT @ 15:11:25 Soft focus on Chris

Video:

Audio:

SourceFile: MVI_1720.MOV   AudioSourceFile: FTIME134BT2.   Camera Reel: Day10

FIGURE 22.2 A logging database.

Synching takes longer. Typically, you'll start a new sequence in the project file for each shot, bring in the audio and video clips, line them up (either using the slate, matching timecode, or dialog), trim any leading audio, and either export the results to a new file, or keep the sequence in the project, labeling it with the scene–shot–take. Again, make sure the timecode start of the sequence matches the timecode start of your video exactly. This process can take a very long time, but there a few utilities that can help – Pluraleyes, a plug-in for Final Cut, Premiere, Avid, and Vegas, can take a batch of clips and sync them up.

If you're desperate, you can use the reference audio from the camera to edit with, and just sync up the DDR audio when you've locked picture. The problem is that you could be in for some nasty surprises – something that sounds moderately acceptable with the camera audio is really off when you get the real sound. Or the camera audio is just unusable even for editing. So if you (or your intern) can stand it, just bite the bullet and sync everything. With Pluraleyes, it's not so terrible.

Ideally, someone will do this during the shoot. But if that was just one more thing than anyone could deal with, give yourself a solid week-to-two weeks (if you have nothing else to do) to sync up the footage if you're using a plug-in.

One important note: during the transcode/sync process, you'll want to make sure that the sound *sample rate and bit depth remain the same as that of the original DDR-recorded files.* If the sound mixer recorded the sound at 48KHz, 16-bit, then that's what you want to keep the files at.

(S)logging

Logging footage isn't fun. When you start, it's exciting enough, because you're finally seeing takes from your film! But after about an hour, you start thinking about the shots you didn't get or the performance that was off, or just about everything except an evaluation of *what you have.* However, this is the best way to familiarize yourself with the material, while also preparing the log book for the editor.

What you want to do is watch all the takes and fill in those rows on your spreadsheet with information about each one. What to write down? Apart from the timecode start, you should record the FFA (first frame of action, or "action start"), the angle/summary of the shot, a lengthier description, and a comment on the video and/or audio. If the clip actually contains two takes – because you kept the camera rolling and started over – indicate this somewhere in the description. If you'd prefer, you can write this information in the NLE project file directly – all programs feature columns to put in angle and description data, and some also allow you to create custom columns. I use a spreadsheet because I want to be able to print out the logs independently, and also because I will give them to the sound editor and colorist/conformist later on.

Depending on how many clips there are and how many hours a day you log footage, this could take you anywhere from a week to three weeks. If you're very pressed for time and you had a script supervisor, the editor can rely on his/her notes instead. You can also delegate this task, but if you do you may be missing out on an opportunity to really get to know the footage.

Lining the Script

While you're (s)logging, you also want to create a "lined" copy of the script, if the script supervisor didn't create one already. What's this? It's a version of the script that reflects the dialog actually spoken during the takes (if different), notes which scenes were omitted from shooting altogether, and which parts of each scene are covered by each camera setup and take. As you're logging each shot for a given scene, keep a hardcopy of the script next to you. You want to cross out, amend, or add lines of dialog to reflect what was actually spoken during the shoot. You also want to draw vertical lines indicating what part of a scene is covered by which camera setup. Label each vertical line with the setup letter.

Figure 22.3 shows a copy of a couple of pages of lined script from *Found In Time.* This is immensely helpful to the editor. She can see from looking at the lines just how well or how poorly

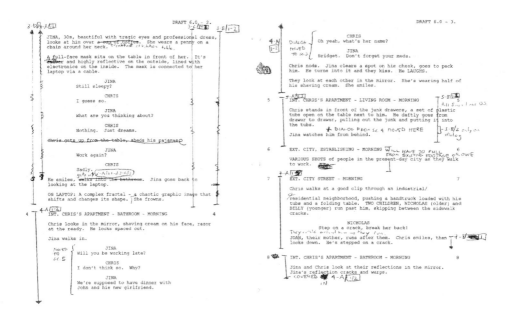

FIGURE 22.3 Lined script from *Found In Time*.

covered a given scene is. It also saves her from having to search in vain for a scene that was omitted. The sound designer will also find it helpful, as he will use it to look through audio takes for superior off-camera dialog.

To save yourself time, do this while you're logging, instead of after. It will slow you down a little bit but it's worth it. If your script supervisor did this on set, you can skip this step.

Vision Statements and Dope Sheets

Just as you did for the cast and crew, you'll want to prepare some inspirational materials and references for your editor, sound designer, composer, and visual effects artist. I like to recommend a few films whose editing style I appreciate, and some music that might make for a good jumping-off point for the score. If you have some previous shorts that the editor can study, include copies of them too.

You also want to write out a one-to-two-page "dope sheet." This should have the following vital information on it:

1. Shooting format, frame rate, frame size, and the camera.
2. Audio sample rate and bit depth.
3. What the *editing* format and frame size is.
4. The intended reel lengths – usually 20 minutes is good; trying to edit the film in one chunk is usually a bad idea; breaking things up into reels helps keep sequences from getting too big/complicated.
5. What you want the editor to deliver – usually sequences in the NLE, starting on the hour.
6. Where files can be found on the hard drive.
7. Any notes, either general or specifically on scenes/sequences, that you think may help the editor.

On *Found In Time*, we often shot several scenes together and simply slated them with the first scene number (so scenes 31 and 34 were slated as scene 31; scenes 20 and 59 were slated as scene 20).

I noted this on the dope sheet. If I hadn't, Dan Loewenthal, the editor, would probably have called me asking what happened to the footage for scenes 34 and 59.

You'll also send out dope sheets and vision statements to the visual effects artist, composer, colorist/conformist, and sound designer as well.

Go Away

Once you've given the material to the editor, you should do something non-film related for a while. The temptation may be there to sit in on the rough cut, but resist it if you can. Your evaluation of the material is too bound up in your experience getting it. You may have spent all afternoon getting a particular shot, but to the editor's dispassionate eye it just doesn't work, so out it goes.

Do something with your friends, family, loved ones (remember them?). Box up all the wrap binders and take care of the inevitable post-shoot hangnails (like wrangling over the missing walkie battery you swore was returned). When the editor's done with the rough cut, come back.

Start Up the Marketing Machine Again

During the shoot, you probably didn't have much time to tweet. But as soon as you catch your breath, you want to get back to updating your web and social media presence. Start posting some production stills, and mock up some DVD artwork/posters.

Post can take a long time and be very energy consuming, in a slow-burn sort of way (as opposed to production, when everything's burning). Send out monthly emails, telling everyone on your team what's going on. These are the hardest times for your hardcore fans, so keep them in the loop. They will go the extra mile for you in promoting the film down the road.

Reshoots/Additional Photography

You'll want to schedule any reshoots or additional photography about two-thirds of the way through the editing process. If you start too soon, you'll probably shoot material you don't need; too late and you'll hold up the rest of post while the editor integrates the new material.

Screenings

It's a good idea to have a rough-cut or second-cut screening, and do it in a real screening room. Looking at the film on the editor's monitor will not give you the same sense of pacing as seeing it projected. Invite some people you trust who'll give you honest feedback. I'd say don't invite the cast and crew, unless you think they'll be able to step away from their involvement in the work. Prepare for it to be an awful experience. You will only see what's wrong. Be open to feedback, just as you were during the initial readings of the script – there are no bad ideas. Look for patterns of feedback. Those are things to bring up with your editor. She will probably know better than you how to filter what people are saying to get to what is really bothering them.

SOUND DESIGNER AND COMPOSER

You may want to involve your composer while the picture cut is still in flux, so she can provide some temp tracks the editor can cut to. And it's a good idea to have a joint spotting session or two, where you, the editor, the composer, and the sound designer watch the film and make notes on where to put certain score/design cues.

Make sure the composer and sound designer talk to each other. Sometimes, a scene may call for a cue that sits right on the border between an ambient sound and a score element. You don't want your composer and sound designer doing duplicate work or, worse, doing no work (since each will figure the other one will do it).

You don't want to start sound design until the picture is really, truly locked. The end credits can change, but if you start mucking with the film after picture lock, you're just going to cause delays and maybe run up your costs. This means that:

1. Visual effects have to be timed to the locked picture – you probably won't have these done by the time you lock picture, but you can't have the shot duration changing on you.
2. Score elements need to line up to the locked picture – the composer will need to be looking at the same locked picture as the sound editor.

Just as with the editor, you'll also be preparing a binder and hard drive for the sound designer and composer. It will contain everything that the editor's drive/binder contains, but also:

1. OMF (Open Media Framework) export files for each reel (ask your sound designer on how he wants these), including all tracks.
2. Quicktime files, in whatever codec and frame size the sound designer works in. Usually the Quicktimes should have timecode burn-in.
3. Another set of Quicktime files in whatever codec and frame size the composer works in.
4. Some kind of preliminary music cue/sound cue sheet. The sound designer may end up working this up with you and the composer.
5. A "dope sheet" as above, but also explaining what you need from the composer and designer.
6. A visual effects cue sheet that lists the shot ins-and-outs and the nature of the shot. This way the designer and composer know that shots will be changed (even though the duration will stay the same). As the VFX designer finishes his work, you may want to regenerate Quicktimes for the affected reels.

VISUAL EFFECTS DESIGNER AND COLORIST/CONFORMIST

Post is a "fairly" linear process, but once the picture is locked you can work in parallel on the sound and visuals. The trick is to make sure they stay in sync. Keep updating the visual effects cue sheet with the progress made by your effects artist. If the VFX shots are simple wire removals or other image fixes, the composer and sound designer don't necessarily need to be "in the loop." However, any time you're going to be *creating* things using VFX, there's a chance that you'll be changing the character of the film somewhat, and the underlying sound should match.

For the VFX artist and the colorist/conformist, you'll want to prepare a drive and binder similar to the one you created for the editor and sound designer. In addition, these folks will also need:

1. An EDL (edit decision list) for each reel (mostly for the conformist)
2. A Quicktime reference for each reel (may include timecode burn-in)
3. The NLE project files
4. Color notes (from you and/or the DP)
5. VFX cue sheet
6. Enough space on the drive for the final VFX files and project files, and for the final reels.

If you finish your color/conform before your sound work is done, make new Quicktimes of the color-corrected final reels, and give them to your sound designer and composer. If there's been any frame slippage (frames that were inadvertently added or deleted during the color correction, VFX work, or the conform), this should be immediately noticeable (and hopefully fixable).

ONE-STOP POST HOUSE VS. *À LA CARTE*

There are a few production and post companies that offer "round-trip" service – picture cutting, VFX, titles, color, conform, sound design, mix, and final output. They're worth bidding out to, but I've often found that they're deficient in one area or another. The sound department often seems to get the short end of the stick; the re-recording "suites" often are tuned for broadcast rather than theatrical mixing. Or the post house subcontracts out some of the services (like hiring the colorist) and then marks up their fee. On the other hand, in an arrangement like this you're getting a de facto post supervisor, which can save you a lot of headaches, especially if tech isn't your thing.

When I put together a budget, I'll talk to a few post houses and then compare them to what I can get by hiring individuals or smaller companies to handle each task separately. If you're technically savvy and you have an editing workstation (or can add it to the budget without breaking it), you could be better off this way, both financially and in terms of control (you'll be on *your* timetable for the most part, not the post house's).

One thing that's just about impossible to do on your own is the final tape output, and while DCP (digital cinema projection) packages are easier to assemble on your own, the post house is the only place likely to rent you a DCP-projection-capable theater so you can make sure it worked. The other issue is that you may have to do the color and conform (what is sometimes referred to as the "online") in a post house because they're the only folks who can handle your requirements. If you shot on 2K or 4K and edited at 1K (*à la* the Red workflow), you may not be able to find an individual colorist with the kind of home computer setup that can handle that data load.

Do make nice with the local post house. The staff are often dying to work on something more creative than the latest shampoo ad, and they're quite talented. They may be good candidates for your picture editor, VFX artist, or colorist.

QUESTIONS/EXERCISES

1. Query some local production and post companies to see what kind of post services they offer. If they have a "one-stop shopping" deal on post, find out what they're offering, and what they can handle. If you're shooting on the Red at 4K, can they handle a 4K online?
2. What do you want to shoot on? What format are you likely to be editing and onlining on?
3. Try logging a little bit of footage – either from one of your projects or someone else's. Use paper-and-pen, a Word document, a spreadsheet – the format doesn't matter. Pay close attention to the first frame of action, any issues in the shooting, or if there were multiple takes done while the camera was still rolling.
4. Start thinking about other films that you could use in your vision statement. Is there a style of editing that you're drawn to?

## Chapter 23

Preparing for Distribution

FIGURE 23.1 The goal.

If a film gets made and no one sees it, it doesn't exist, right? You should be preparing for distribution from the minute you finish the first polished draft of your script. Your distribution goals may change during the course of making the film, but you should always keep in mind that, someday, someone is going to want to pay to see your creation (regardless of the medium or venue). Even if you're just making a "calling card" film, nothing will attract future investors and producers more than being able to demonstrate that yes, in fact, your film found some kind of audience.

The biggest hurdles to distribution are fivefold:

- **Consolidation of distributors.** Despite technological advances that in theory would make it a more "democratic" medium, a relatively small number of distributors hold the keys to the kingdom.
- **The surplus of product out there.** The cost of *making* films has decreased significantly, so more ultra-low-budget movies are being made.

- **Changing landscape.** It's difficult if not impossible to plan for distribution when the landscape may change between the start of preproduction and the end of post.
- **Exhaustion of money.** Usually at this stage of the game, you've burned through all your cash, but you'll still be expected to shell out for promotional material, a producer's rep fee, festival fees and expenses, delivery items.
- **Exhaustion, period.** After years of work (from the writing onward), you're probably itching to get on with your next story.

You can't directly control the first three items, but you have some say in the last two. But even if you can't predict or control something, you can still prepare for it, to a degree.

THE ONLY CONSTANT IS CHANGE

The current state of the film marketplace is a little like a tectonic event, when two continental plates butt up against each other. Mountains are created, populations get separated geographically, and the ocean reflows around the new landmass. Except that it's happening on a much faster timescale. The last two decades have seen the introduction of a host of destabilizing technologies – affordable HD, DVDs, internet streaming, and computers with the horsepower to effectively become media centers (finally).

If you look at the current state of distribution, all the "models" appear to be up in the air. The model that most of us are familiar with – and that the studios use when releasing their own, bigger films – is that each distribution "window" is a discrete entity. The priority is on a large theatrical release, followed by VOD, then DVD and streaming (sometimes at the same time, sometimes streaming trails DVD), with premium cable, basic cable, and broadcast TV following later. Merchandise tie-ins hopefully "synergize" with this strategy, so you can make a pretty penny off the lunchboxes, board and videogames, happy meals, and so on.

This model is predicated on the "big" premiere generating enough buzz to sustain the opening few weeks, when the ticket sales split favors the distributor over the theater owners. Theatrical is not expected to be a big money-maker, but increases the prestige and therefore the perceived value of all the other windows. The studio spends enormous sums on advertising and promotion to grab eyeballs and hopefully lure audiences into theater seats.

Because of the enormous up-front expense associated with this model, films are molded to it rather than the other way around. Unsurprisingly, these films (by and large) fit neatly into genre categories or sub-categories, have broad appeal, and feature A-list stars, directors, and visual flair. Ideally, these films become part of a franchise, one leading to the other, so that customers are hooked onto a "brand." A significant exception to this is the Pixar movie model – they have made sequels but also produce a fair number of original films. However, Pixar is itself a brand, one of the few that exist at the studio level apart from Disney and perhaps Weinstein Bros. (most people never say, "Let's go see a 20th Century Fox movie"). Similarly, some actors and directors become "brands," that then become part of the draw for a film.

It's been clear for a long time that this model doesn't work well for indie films. Of course, independent films are not really set up along the franchise model. They're made mostly by newcomers (often still working out their chops), tend to be character-oriented, and appeal largely to a niche market of one kind or another. They can't compete on the level of spectacle with other blockbusters, and often don't have "stars." However, independent films can be a proving ground for studio-friendly talent, so distributors have looked at them in somewhat the same way they looked at the comics companies (many of which they also own).

In the mid-90s and again in the mid-2000s, studios realized that there could be gold in these movies. Boosted by the returns of some outliers (*El Mariachi*, *The Blair Witch Project*, and later *Paranormal Activity*) they tried to get involved with indies in various ways. In the 1990s they acquired independent distributors or created their own independent arms. But budgets got bigger, the films didn't do so well, and most of these experiments were shut down.

The internet looked like it was going to change the equation somewhat, but the studios now found themselves competing with a group of new players – Amazon, Apple, YouTube, the various streaming aggregator services, and a few other smaller companies (most of which have gone under at this point). The distributors have responded by launching Hulu, making various deals with Netflix and iTunes, and in some cases offering their own streaming services.

At this point, the larger distributors seem to be retreating from the space that independent films occupy. They tend to offer "stingy" deals and don't really promote the films as heavily as they probably could. The economic climate beginning in 2007 didn't help. So a filmmaker who made a film for $600K–$1M could suddenly find themselves receiving offers of $50K–$100K for all rights, with no real expectation of receiving anything more than that down the road.

In contrast, some brave filmmakers are embracing different types of distribution strategies, ranging from piecemeal (split rights) deals, to DIY, to everything in between. And the "windows" are collapsing. Some smaller distributors (IFC Films, for example) use the day-and-date releasing model (the film is available for streaming, on DVD, and in theaters on the same day). The advantage of this model is that the film is launched into the marketplace for the cost of one promotional campaign, and people who want to see it but don't want to pay theater prices can get it right away instead of having to wait (or as is increasingly the case, just downloading a pirated copy from the internet).

All of this seems like a lot to absorb, and, indeed, it is. But film distribution has always been a very volatile medium, as befits one that's barely a century old. At this point, stage plays, music concerts, and novels have come to assume certain core forms, and don't deviate from them very much. But movies used to be shot on black-and-white film and projected to a live musical accompaniment. Initially there wasn't a standard framerate (one reason really old films can sometimes appear jerky). Each change in technology – sound, color, format (35mm, 70mm, DCP), lenses, stock – and the competition from television, cable, VHS, DVD, VOD, and now the internet, has produced seismic shifts.

PREPARING FOR THE UNKNOWABLE

So, how do you plan for distribution, then? First, do the research, and construct a rough strategy as part of the business plan. By the time you're in post, revisit and revise this plan. If the film has changed during the shoot and editing, then the approach you initially came up with may not make sense anymore. Perhaps you should submit to dramatic festivals instead of horror-specific ones. Perhaps you need to find a producer's rep who can help you position your film better. In your research, you'll want to make a list of the following:

1. Festivals
2. Producer's reps
3. Sales agents
4. Distributors
5. Consultants
6. Events (comic conventions, for example) that have some tie-in to your film's subject matter or core audience

This shouldn't be a random list, but based around your film. Is there a producer's rep or distributor who seems to do a good job with the films in your genre? Are there festivals that target your audience? Do a search on withoutabox.com for festivals that might match your genre or niche audience. Make sure to write down festival submission dates! Talk to your war council.

Second, look at what's changed since you went into preproduction. Is the distributor you were thinking about still in business? How are the films in the same genre as yours performing? You can't predict when a genre will peak and then wane for a bit, but you can try to ride "the wave."

Third, be flexible. If festivals aren't responding to your material, go to producer's reps. If you can't get one interested in your film, perhaps you should contact sales agents directly (foreign and domestic). You may have to go backwards and forwards – a producer's rep can help you get into festivals.

Finally, don't do this alone! Consider hiring a producer of marketing and distribution (PMD). On the one hand, you may feel like you just can't afford another salary right now. On the other hand, perhaps it's a worthwhile investment. You may recoup the costs back more easily than if you try to do everything yourself.

TARGET YOUR FESTIVAL RELEASE

Festivals are great for filmmakers and filmgoers. But your main concern is to get the film in front of an audience that contains some sales agents, producer's reps, distribution scouts, or other industry folks. Festivals cost a lot of money to attend. You have to pay for the projection master, screeners, airfare, ground travel, lodging, food, a publicist, and any publicity material you make. Even if the fest helps you out a little bit, you could easily wind up with a five-figure bill.

So make it count. If you feel that you have a shot at one of the top-tier festivals (Sundance, Berlin, Cannes, or Toronto), then try to premiere there, and hold off on applying to others until you've heard back from at least two of them.

If you feel that you'd get more mileage out of one of the larger genre or regional festivals, then aim for these. Festivals are rather unforgiving in some ways. The top-tier ones will not screen your film if it's premiered somewhere else (with few exceptions). Others are more liberal but will bring you less attention. So list your festival deadlines and make some choices. Be aware that after your film is about a year old, it will become ineligible for certain festivals. So don't update your film's IMDb page with a status of "completed" until you get into a festival. Also, make sure the copyright notice on all your publicity materials, website, and the film credits is for the *current* year.

INCLUDE DELIVERABLES IN YOUR BUDGET

When you sign a deal with a distributor, they'll give you a laundry list of items (deliverables) that they expect from you, usually within 30 to 60 days of signing the agreement. Sometimes the advance will not be paid until the distributor receives everything. Since filmmakers are usually broke at this point, they have a hard time coughing up the deliverables.

Avoid this by including as many deliverables in your *post* budget as possible. This means putting in some money for tape and DCP package output (as opposed to just mastering to Quicktimes), errors and omissions insurance, duplication fees and postage for all the screeners, PAL transfers, and DigiBeta standard def masters. Table 23.1 shows a shortlist of the things that you may have to deliver to a buyer. This is not exhaustive – the delivery requirements can run on for three pages – but you get the idea. If you can make sure most of these items are ready by the time you enter the distribution world, you'll be that much better off.

One of the hardest things to put in the post budget is a full music and effects (M&E) mix. An M&E mix is one where the dialog is completely separated from the music and effects. This allows foreign distributors to dub the film into a foreign language. Sounds simple, right? Except that your dialog track will contain some ambient sounds (walking, leaves rustling, traffic, etc.). If you simply turn the dialog track off, these sounds will be gone as well, and the mix as a whole will feel incredibly sterile. So the sound designer has to go in and replace *every* non-dialog sound that happened to get on the dialog track. This is very labor intensive and can sometimes be as expensive as the original sound design. However, with foreign markets being a big part of the distribution landscape, you really have to take this into account. So if your budget is in the $1M and above range, you *really should* put it in.

TABLE 23.1 Deliverables

Type	Item	Reason
Files	Full-resolution Quicktime files of entire film	
	DVD masters (project file and assets)	
	Behind the scenes material (Quicktimes)	
	DCP package	
Tape masters	HDCAM SR-1080/24p	Protection master
	HDCAM SR-1080/60i	Projection master
	DigiBeta	SD master
Sound	Music master tracks	
	Stereo LTRT mix bounce tracks to film	
	Dolby 5.1 mix bounce tracks to film	
	ProTools session files	
For foreign release	PAL masters	For foreign distributors
	Textless titles	For foreign language dubbing
	M&E mix	
Other	Errors & omissions insurance	
	Copies of all deal memos and paperwork	
	Copy of copyright notice	
	Corporate papers (operating agreement, incorporation certificate, etc.)	
	Publicity materials	
	DVD/Blu-Ray glass master	
	Trailer	

STAY THE COURSE, KEEP BUSY

The day you finish your film, you'll feel like a hero. The film looks great, sounds great, and the world is your oyster. The next day, panic and doubt will set in, as you realize that you now have to send your baby off into the world and hope for the best.

This is normal. The best cure is staying busy, especially during the down cycles, when you're waiting for word from festivals or reps. Putting your promotional material together is a great way to stay busy. On *Found In Time*, Simeon Moore, our gaffer, shot some great behind-the-scenes moments, and a number of folks on the crew got some good publicity stills. I used some of the stills in the press kit, and went out and shot some interviews with the crew and cast. It was incredibly therapeutic to stop worrying about the festival applications, and cut Simeon's footage and my interviews into some "making of" shorts.

STAY ORGANIZED

There's a tendency for things to fall apart a bit after the shoot. The pace slows down during post, so it's not as urgent that you keep your books updated every week, or keep your wrap binders updated every month. But as you enter the promotion/distribution phase, things can happen very quickly after months of downtime. If you've slacked off too much, you'll risk misplacing the one piece of paper you need. So stay on top of your paperwork. Make sure your artwork is ready to go – if you get into a festival, you'll need to produce the following materials:

1. Printed DVDs in cases with sleeve art
2. Posters
3. Small posters (letter-sized)
4. Stickers
5. Postcards (these are not as popular as they used to be but they're still standard at festivals)
6. Electronic press kit on a printed CD or DVD, with sleeve art
7. Web-and-print versions of all your graphics
8. An updated press kit

You won't have much time to prepare this material – the average period between filmmaker notification and the festival start is five-to-six weeks, and you'll probably be scrambling to deliver the master to them during that time period. So have this stuff in as ready a state as possible.

STAY CONNECTED TO THE CAST AND CREW

You'll want to stay connected to the cast and crew during the distribution period, because you may want them to help you fill a festival screening, or come to a Q&A, or spread the word to their friends about the upcoming DVD release. Budget some time for putting clips together for their reels. Some agents will call you right after the wrap party to see if they can have some clips for their client. I'd advise against releasing unfinished material unless it's for an imminent audition. But it may be that giving the actor the clips early on is what cements your relationship, and makes him or her want to help you out.

STAY CURRENT

Distribution trends change quite often. There are two online resources – Film Specific (filmspecific. com) and The Film Collaborative (thefilmcollaborative.org) – that offer consulting and education in distribution. They have a fair amount of free material but also offer various levels of paid membership that gets you access to video and audio seminars, consultation services, and contacts. Non-Multiplex Cinema (nonmx.tv) and the Independent Feature Project's site (ifp.org) also feature articles and videos on distribution and marketing.

SPEND WISELY

If you have to go raise money to get through distribution, you'll be putting yourself and your investors in an awkward position. So don't spend money you don't have to. That seems obvious, but it bears repeating. Cast and crew screenings are great, but they can take away money that you might need later on when it's time to do the Blu-Ray masters. Four-walling in a theater might be good for your ego, but can you justify the cost? Going to film markets on your own (without an agent) could be a good way to make contacts, but may not be worth the expense if your film doesn't have traction yet (hasn't been in any fests or hasn't sold). Applying to every festival under the sun is not only a waste of money, but you could give away your premiere to a third-tier festival when you want to premiere at a top-tier one. Since you're not in production, where you have to make fast decisions, weigh and measure your options carefully.

QUESTIONS

1. Do you have a distribution strategy for your film?
2. Is there a distributor that you think has a good track record with films similar to yours?
3. What deliverables have you budgeted for? Which haven't you been able to squeeze in?
4. Do you have a list of festivals that you'd like to get into?

## Chapter 24

Beyond Basic Planning

EMBRACE CONSTRAINTS

I've said this before but it bears repeating: constraints can be turned into a framework rather than a constriction. You have a suboptimal location – where the light is a bit off and one wall is unshootable – and a limited span of time to shoot a complicated scene. You can ask for time (don't have it), a second camera (no money in the budget), or try to stage it in a different location (more money again). Or you can find a way to work the constraints into the equation. Treat it like a poetic structure – the tanka, sonnet, and haiku forms of poetry have very draconian limitations. But working within them becomes a creative challenge, and can lead to real brilliance (apparently Shakespeare thought so). Is there a way you can use the cramped location to your advantage – could it make your characters uncomfortable? On a logistical level, if you only have an actor for a brief period of time, can you shoot all the other angles first? If the location is still being dressed, can you pick a corner that's done and shoot everything there? If you can't get the camera through the open window because it's too big, can you find a cut-point and pick up the shot from inside, or move the actors closer to the window and keep the camera on the other side? Sometimes, by working with what you have instead of what you don't, you can come up with something a lot more interesting and alive.

PICK YOUR BATTLES

Of course you want your film to be perfect. And it's worth holding yourself and the team up to a high standard. But if you expend your energy on winning every battle, you're going to inevitably run out of steam when you need it most. If you get the restaurant owner to lower his fee by 40 percent but not 50 percent so you can shoot there, then ask yourself whether going another round and wearing the owner down is worth it. Are you losing goodwill at that point? Will he kick you out of the restaurant the minute you go over?

Similarly, are you spending an enormous amount of time pouring over every petty cash receipt, only to find that you've spotted $10 of mistakes? It's good to look over things, but scrutinizing everyone's receipts may be the one more thing that you don't have time to do. Arguing over small amounts of money is invariably counterproductive in the larger scheme of things. Get the big things under control first, then sweat the small stuff.

A lot of directors fall back on the Kubrick defense – they've read about what a relentless perfectionist he is, how hard he's pushed everyone. However, he created a structure that allowed him to work that way. He also changed tactics periodically. If you read the stories surrounding *2001: A Space Odyssey*, you'll note that he experimented a lot, and was willing to discard an idea or technique if it clearly wasn't working. So while he might have been a perfectionist regarding his *aims*, he was flexible in terms of his *means*. He also tended to work with smaller crews, picked producers who could shield him from financial pressure (*2001*'s budget went up about 10 times), and, importantly, established a track record earlier in his career working on lower-budget material. So you may have to prove yourself in order to become the next Kubrick.

YOU'RE SHOOTING THE MOVIE, NOT THE BUDGET

It really is the case that two-thirds of a film shot on budget isn't worth as much as a full film that goes over budget. You don't want to have to choose between these alternatives – you want to bring the film in on budget. But if you're shooting on a really low budget to begin with ($200K or less), no one is ever going to know if you go $10K over budget if you need it to finish the film. In a more immediate sense, if you're both the producer and the director and you have to choose between the two roles to get through a difficult day, *direct* the film first and *produce* it later (this is a variant of kicking the can, in a way). This is not an excuse to spend money willy-nilly, but a way out of a tough situation.

HOPE ABOVE ALL ELSE

Skip Blumberg, a pioneering producer (he's been working since the 1970s, largely in documentaries and children's television), once said "There's always a reason to stop shooting." You're tired, the weather is turning against you, the shot isn't coming out right, the ice cream truck won't stop. These are all good reasons to get *upset*, and sometimes being upset is exactly what's called for – it can motivate both you and others to fix the problem. But you can't give up hope. Don't stop shooting.

As a line producer, especially when I was starting out, I used to have a feeling of imminent doom, pretty much constantly. Directors seemed like the ultimate Tarot deck fools, just about to walk over that cliff while singing away quite happily. But fools are also wise! They dare to take leaps that don't seem like they'll work, and somehow make it across to the other side. Sometimes hope flies in the face of evidence. Sometimes it seems like the ultimate luxury. But in fact it's the key ingredient to perseverance. You can temper it with prudent planning and adjustments, but don't let it be extinguished.

CONCLUSIONS

Preproduction often seems like a pretty dense thicket of work, and it may even threaten to suck all the joy out of the process of filmmaking. However, if you look at any profession, the people who excel and come to master their skills are the ones who view prep as an integral part of their work. A musician will play many more notes in his room alone than he ever will in front of a crowd. A writer will discard a forest's worth of drafts for every novel she completes. Most of the actors I know constantly read up on their craft, take classes, work out, and generally keep their instrument (their mind and body) sharp. If you can view prep as just another part of your life, like brushing your teeth, getting dressed, or eating breakfast in the morning, you will find the joy in it. And when you do step on the set, you'll be doing so with real, fully earned confidence.

Good luck and make great films!

QUESTIONS/EXERCISES

1. Go through your schedule. Do you have any lulls or "quiet" days that can make up for the heavy ones?
2. Try reblocking a scene in a tighter space than you'd originally written it for. Can you make it work?
3. Look at your intended master shot for a scene. Can you break it up into smaller pieces?
4. Ask your DP for some help in blocking a scene.

Further Reading, Tools, Resources

SOURCES

Unless otherwise noted, the photographs and line art are by the Author. Thanks to Ben Wolf, Simeon Moore, Alina Andranikian, John Bonafede, and Brendan Mason for contributing photographs and artwork for the book.

The information about *Sita Sings the Blues* comes from several sources, including *Selling Your Film Without Selling Your Soul* (see below) and Nina Paley's own website, www.ninapaley.com.

Information about films I worked on comes from my memories and notes, as well as subsequent conversations with the people involved. Information about films that my friends worked on comes from personal (and professional) conversations with those friends.

ACTING, DIRECTING ACTORS

Ball, William. *A Sense of Direction*. New York: Drama Book Publishers, 1984.
A very skillfully written, direct account of how to work with actors.

Barr, Tony. *Acting for the Camera*. New York: HarperCollins, 1997.
Very exercise-driven, full of good nuggets of wisdom.

Bettman, Gil. *First Time Director: How to Make Your Breakthrough Movie*. Studio City, CA: Michael Wiese Books, 2003.
Some of what he has to say is garbage (he worships Bob Zimeckis), but he does get a lot right and presents it in a very no-nonsense way.

Haase, Cathy. *Acting for Film*. New York: Allworth Press, 2003.
Cathy is a terrific actress and also teaches acting for directors at School of Visual Arts. This is a very practical, exercise-driven guide for actors (and therefore extremely handy for directors).

Shurtleff, Michael. *Audition*. New York: Bantam Books, 1980.
It turns out that film acting is a lot like auditioning – there's very little time to rehearse or memorize, so you have to get to the emotional core of a scene very quickly. An excellent book for writers as well – you can figure out your characters very quickly.

Weston, Judith. *Directing Actors: Creating Memorable Performances for Film and Television*. Studio City, CA: Michael Wiese Books, 1999.
Weston, Judith. *The Film Director's Intuition*. Studio City, CA: Michael Wiese Books, 2003.
Two of the best books I've read about directing actors, and using script analysis techniques to gain insight into the story.

CRITICISM/INTERVIEWS

Harris, Mark. *Pictures at a Revolution: Five Movies and the Birth of the New Hollywood.* New York: Penguin Books, 2009.
This is a fantastic history of the making of the five films that were up for the Best Picture Oscar in 1968 (*The Graduate*; *Bonnie and Clyde*; *In the Heat of the Night*; *Guess Who's Coming to Dinner?*; *Doctor Doolittle*). Each represented, in a way, a different kind of filmmaking business and aesthetic. In many ways, it marked the beginnings of a conflict between studios and independents that continues to this day.

Littger, Stephan (Ed.). *The Director's Cut: Picturing Hollywood in the 21st Century.* New York: Continuum Press, 2006.
Stephan interviewed 21 directors, including some pretty heavy-hitters (Sydney Pollack, Andrew Davis, Bryan Singer, David Fincher, and Andrew Adamson, among others). The interviews were very candid and full of good information.

Lowenstein, Stephen (Ed.). *My First Movie: 20 Celebrated Directors Talk About Their First Film.* New York: Penguin Books, 2002.
Lowenstein, Stephen (Ed.). *My First Movie: Take Two: Ten Celebrated Directors Talk About Their First Film.* New York: Penguin Books, 2008.
In both of these books, Lowenstein conducts some very revealing episodes with a variety of directors, including the Coen Brothers, Mira Nair, Kevin Smith, Tom DiCillo, Ang Lee … Great reading for when you feel like nothing is happening fast enough and that you're *never going to finish your film*. It's inspiring.

Nochimson, Martha. *Dying to Belong: Gangster Movies in Hollywood and Hong Kong.* Malden, MA: Blackwell Publishing, 2007.
Covering the historical and social roots of the gangster film in both Hollywood and Hong Kong, this book does a great job of really capturing the defining notes of a genre, and made me think a lot about what genre does for an audience.

Rothman, Jack. *Hollywood in Wide Angle: How Directors View Filmmaking.* Lanham, MD: Scarecrow Press, 2004.
Jack Rothman is a sociologist, so his perspective is different – and refreshing. Instead of gobs of interviews, he aggregates data and looks at the director's job from the point of view of studio politics, social issues, and artistic and psychological motivations.

DIRECTING/WRITING/DESIGN/FILMING/EDITING

Horowitz, Marilyn. *How to Write a Screenplay in 10 Weeks.* New York: ArtMar Productions. New Edition, 2011.
Full disclosure: Marilyn was my spouse, business partner, and the producer of my first film, *Caleb's Door*. Nonetheless, this is a great book on screenwriting, and I've found it particularly helpful when rewriting and preparing shooting scripts.

Katz, Steven D. *Film Directing: Shot by Shot.* Studio City, CA: Michael Wiese Books, 1991.
A concise and well-written guide to what I've been calling previsualization – including a comprehensive breakdown of angle, movement, and composition choices.

LoBrutto, Vincent. *The Filmmaker's Guide to Production Design.* New York: Allworth Press, 2002.
He really knows how to talk to production designers and get their perspective on the creative process.

Malkiewicz, Kris and M. David Mullen. *Cinematography*, Third Edition. New York: Touchstone, 2005.
A great reference book and beginning guide to cinematography.

Murch, Walter. *In the Blink of an Eye: A Perspective on Film Editing*, Second Edition. Los Angeles: Silman-James Press, 2001.
A terrific short introduction to the craft and theory of editing, written by the editor of *Apocalypse Now*, *The Godfather*, *Cold Mountain*, *Jarhead*, *The English Patient* … amongst others.

DISTRIBUTION

Candler, Sheri, Jon Reiss and The Film Collaborative. *Selling Your Film Without Selling Your Soul*. Los Angeles: Hybrid
  Cinema Publishing, 2012.
In some ways, it's an important update on *Think Outside the Box Office*. In other ways, it's very
much its own beast – a book full of case studies of independent filmmakers choosing their own
distribution path.

Parks, Stacey. *The Insider's Guide to Film Distribution*, Second Edition. New York: Focal Press, 2012.
Stacey Parks is a sales consultant and was a sales agent for many years. This book really delivers
the goods on distribution, film markets, foreign distribution, and sales agents, among other things.

Reiss, Jon. *Think Outside the Box Office*. Los Angeles: Hybrid Cinema Publishing, 2009–2010.
This is one of the best books on distribution out there.

Distribution – Online

Jon Reiss: www.jonreiss.com
Jon is a producer, director, teacher, and writer, with a lot to say and a gift for saying it.

The Film Collaborative: www.thefilmcollaborative.org
I can't say enough good things about these guys. They work as consultants, (non-profit) sales agents,
and educators on distribution. There's a ton of free content, and also several membership options,
which unlock more resources and also various forms of distribution consulting.

Film Specific: www.filmspecific.com
Stacey Parks has a ton of resources on this site. She focuses on financing as well as distribution.
There's a lot of free content, but you can also sign up for a yearly membership, which unlocks a ton
of seminars and materials.

MAGAZINES/ONLINE

CreativeCow: www.creativecow.com
A video/film/creative magazine that also features a very active user forum, a host of great tips/tricks
videos, and other really cool and useful information.

HD For Indies: www.hdforindies.com
A good technical blog on HD, targeted at indie filmmakers.

Independent Filmmaker Project: www.ifp.org
A multi-city resource. They host events and seminars, and offer various kinds of support to independent filmmakers. The site features some good articles and info, but they also have various membership options, each of which comes with some nice perks (free screenings and discounts on events).

Indie Slate: www.indieslate.com
A terrific nuts-and-bolts bimonthly. Features camera reviews, "how I did it" stories, articles on legal,
screenwriting, and distribution issues, and festival guides.

NY Shooting People: www.shootingpeople.org
It started as a listserv, but it's become a very good source of information, event notifier, and networking tool.

ReelGrok: www.reelgrok.com
This site offers a tremendous amount of information for line producers and producers – budgets,
labor rates, "how-to" articles, a jobs board, a forum, seminars … you name it.

SAGIndie: www.sagindie.org
This is *not* the official website of the Screen Actors Guild but that of a separate non-profit dedicated to making SAG's information more readily accessible to people. They have sample contracts and paperwork for all the agreements, a production resource locator, a board for posting casting calls, and articles on filmmaking and working with SAG.

PRODUCING

Entertainment Partners. *Paymaster.* Available online: www.paymaster.com
This is a *giant* compendium of all the current union labor rates, general rules, fringes, and other helpful payroll info. It's available in either book or PDF format. It's updated once a year (smaller updates are sent to you for free once you've bought that year's edition).

Landry, Paula. *Scheduling and Budgeting Your Film: A Panic-Free Guide.* Waltham, MA: Focal Press, 2012.
One of the best books out there on breaking down and budgeting your script.

Levison, Louise. *Filmmakers and Financing: Business Plans for Independents*, Sixth Edition. New York: Focal Press, 2009.
A very comprehensive guide to writing a business plan for your film.

Showbiz Software/Media Services Payroll. *State Tax Incentives Guide.* Available online: http://media-services.com/answers-tax-incentives.html
This is a comprehensive, up-to-date online app that lists all the state (and local) tax incentive programs, and their requirements.

SOFTWARE TOOLS

I've tried to focus on cheap or free, cross-platform solutions wherever possible.

Artrage: www.artrage.com
About $30 buys you a terrific paint program for Mac or PC.

Audacity: http://audacity.sourceforge.net
A free multitrack audio editor. You don't get a ton of frills (it can't lay down MIDI tracks) but it's got enough truly useful tools for you.

CHDK: http://chdk.wikia.com/wiki/CHDK
This is a free, nondestructive firmware replacement for most Canon cameras. It doesn't permanently erase your camera's native firmware, just simply overrides it while the camera is on. You get a host of unlocked goodness with this thing – RAW shooting mode, an intervalometer (for time-lapse work), better exposure control (great for nighttime shots), remote support, and a lot of other features.

GIMP: www.gimp.org
A free, open-source, cross-platform, fully featured photo editor. It takes some getting used to if you've been using Photoshop, but it's pretty awesome.

InkScape: www.inkscape.org
A free, open-source, cross-platform vector drawing program.

MPEG Streamclip: www.squared5.com
A free cross-platform video player and converter. Its specialty is taking MPEG files and transport streams (like DVDs, or H.264 files) and re-wrapping them into Quicktimes, AVI, DV, or MPEG4 files.

Processing: www.processing.org
A free, open-source, platform-independent programming language (don't be scared) oriented towards creating visual work. Somewhat similar to Flash but with a different focus. I've just started playing with it and it has some amazing capabilities.

Video Vegas: www.sonycreativesoftware.com
The red-headed stepchild of non-linear editors, this (much cheaper) PC-only editor does a good job. It comes with a host of decent effects and a really good set of titling tools.

VLC Media Player: www.videolan.org
A free, cross-platform video player/decoder/converter tool. Can pretty much convert and play anything you want to throw at it.

Yellow Tools Independence Free: www.yellowtools.us
A multitrack sound editor/MIDI controller/loop-based tool. Free, for Mac and PC. Plus it comes with 2GB of audio source files.

VARIOUS RELATED

Kawasaki, Guy. *The Macintosh Way: The Art of Guerilla Management*. New York: HarperCollins, 1990.
Kawasaki, Guy. *Selling the Dream*. New York: HarperBusiness, 1992.
Guy Kawasaki was Apple's original Mac Evangelist, and lasted through the end of the first Steve Jobs era before going off to start another software company (4D). These two books are well-written mélanges. In between autobiography and observations of life at a leading computer company is some serious examination of being a leading company and the act of selling your "brand" or service to others. The latter book is especially important to independent filmmakers.

McCloud, Scott. *Understanding Comics: The Invisible Art*. New York: William Morrow Paperbacks, 1994.
An amazing and serious analysis of comics in particular and art in general – told in comic form.

Read, Herbert. *Icon and Idea: The Function of Art in the Development of Human Consciousness*. Boston: Schocken Books, 1965.
Difficult to find, but worth reading if you can. Artists, Read contends, explore the boundaries of consciousness and reality, expand both, and then move on while the priests and scientists and others come after. Includes some very interesting analyses of art from the cave paintings at Lascaux through the time of the publication of the book.

Useful Forms

SCENE ANALYSIS

SCENE #:_____

SCENE _____

DESCRIPTION:_____

_____

_____

Objective:			
Obstacle:			
Moment Before:			
Love in Scene:			
Images:			
Given Circ.:			
Notes:			

FIGURE B.1 Scene-by-scene script analysis.

_____ CHARACTER QUESTIONNAIRE   Page _____

CHARACTER NAME: _____

Age	Gender	Height	Species	Race/ Ethnicity	Sexual Preference	Religion/ Spirituality

Physical description

_____

_____

_____

_____

What does ____ want?

_____

_____

_____

_____

What does _____ need?

_____

_____

_____

_____

How would _____ describe ___ job?

_____

_____

_____

_____

Does _____ want to do anything for a living/work besides the current job?

_____

_____

_____

_____

What's the longest romantic relationship ___'s ever been in?

_____

_____

_____

_____

Who does _____ love?

_____

_____

_____

_____

FIGURE B.2 Cast questionnaire, page 1.

_____ **CHARACTER QUESTIONNAIRE**   Page _____

CHARACTER NAME: _____

Who has _____ been kind to in the past?

_____
_____
_____
_____

Who was kind to _____ in the past?

_____
_____
_____
_____

Educational background

_____
_____
_____
_____

What kind of music does _____ listen to?

_____
_____
_____
_____

What environment did _____ grow up in?

_____
_____
_____
_____

Describe parents/ guardians/mentors

_____
_____
_____
_____

Parents'/guardians' professions?

_____
_____
_____
_____

Preferred clothing

_____
_____
_____
_____

FIGURE B.3 Cast questionnaire, page 2.

_____ **CHARACTER QUESTIONNAIRE**   Page _____

CHARACTER NAME: _____

Favorite color
_____
_____
_____
_____

Addictions, weaknesses, fetishes?
_____
_____
_____
_____

Write down some images that come to mind – they can be from the character's past, or things that are important to him/her, or things that other characters (or you) associate with him/her.

Who in the script does _____ interact with the most?

Describe their first meeting.

Other comments?

FIGURE B.4 Cast questionnaire, page 3.

_____ : CAST BREAKDOWN SHEET

Contact: _____

#	Character	Age	Gender	Race/Eth.	Profession	Physicality	Emotionality	
1.								
2.								
3.								
4.								
5.								
6.								
7.								
8.								
9.								
10.								
11.								
12.								
13.								
14.								
15.								
16.								

FIGURE B.5 Casting breakdown sheet, page 1.

_____: CAST BREAKDOWN SHEET

Contact: _____

#	Character	Age	Gender	Race/Eth.	Profession	Physicality	Emotionality
17.							
18.							
19.							
20.							
21.							
22.							
23.							
24.							
25.							
26.							
27.							
28.							
29.							
30.							
31.							
32.							

FIGURE B.6 Casting breakdown sheet, page 2.

______ STORYBOARD

Page ___ of ___

SCENE#	SETUP	SUB.
INT./EXT.	TIME	MVMT.
Script Pg.	Script Day	

FIGURE B.7 Script breakdown page.

_____: **CAST CONTACT LIST**   Page __

Contact: _____

Name	Role	Address	Email/Phone

FIGURE B.8 Cast contact list.

_____: **VENDOR LIST**   Page ___

Contact: _____

Type	Name	Address/Contact	Email/Phone
Camera			
Catering			
G & E Gear			
Insurance			
Permits/ Film Comm. Office			
Payroll			
SAG			
Unit/Craft			
Sound			
Vehicles			
Walkies			

FIGURE B.9 Vendor contact list.

_____: LOCATIONS LIST   Page ___

Contact: _____

Location (in Script)	Dates	Address	Contact/Email/Phone

FIGURE B.10 Location contact list.

				-CALL SHEET-			DATE:_____

-CALL SHEET-

PRODUCTION CALL:
CREW CALL:

BREAKFAST:
LUNCH:

DATE:_____
SHOOT DAY: __ of __

DIRECTOR: _____
SUNRISE: ____ AM
SUNSET: ____ PM
WEATHER:

HOSP.	
POLICE	
FIRE	

TIME	SCENE #	SET	D/N	SCENE DESCRIPTION	CAST	PAGES	LOCATION
						TOTAL:	

CHARACTER	CAST	STATUS	REPORT AT	ON SET	TRANSPORTATION

POSITION	NAME	CONTACT	CALL	CAR	POSITION	NAME	CONTACT	CALL	CAR

PROPS	WARDROBE	SPECIAL

WORD OF THE DAY	TRANSPORTATION [NO PERSONAL VEHICLES!]	OTHER

ADVANCED SHOOTING SCHEDULE

DATE	SCENES	D/N	CAST	PAGES	DESCRIPTION

FIGURE B.11 Callsheet template.

– PRODUCTION REPORT

Date: Director:
Shoot Day: Producer:
Location: UPM/LP:

SCHEDULE / TIMING: SCENES

	Schedule	Actual
AD Call		
Breakfast		
Crew Arrive On Set		
Crew Call		
Cast Call		
First Shot		
Lunch Out		
Lunch In		
First Shot Post-Lunch		
2nd Meal Out		
2nd Meal In		
Camera Wrap		
HMU Wrap		
Crew Wrap		
Leave Location		

Scene #	Length:

Scenes Sched.:

Scenes Shot:

Scenes Owed:

Scenes Del.:

SHOOTING COMMENTS:

DEPARTMENT TIMING:

	In	Out
Production		
Art		
HMU		
Costume		
Sound		
Camera		
Grip		
Electric		

COVERAGE COMMENTS:

VIDEO MEDIA:

Roll   Duration: Comments

CAST

#	Role	Name	Day	Call	WRAP

SOUND MEDIA:

Roll   Duration: Comments

CAST COMMENTS:

NOTE: OTHER COMMENTS:

FIGURE B.12 Production report template.

PETTY CASH SIGNOUT

_____

DATE STARTED _____

DATE	PO#	To:	Reason	$$ Out	$$ In	Signed By

FIGURE B.13 Petty cash signout template.

EXPENSE SHEET				**SHEET/PO #** _____	

DATE: _____

PAID TO: _____

REASON: _____ **CHECK #:** _____

PAID OUT: _____ **REMAIN:** _____

#	Date	Description/Vendor	Line Item Reason	AMT:
1.				
2.				
3.				
4.				
5.				
6.				
7.				
8.				
9.				
10.				
11.				
12.				
13.				
14.				
15.				
16.				
17.				
18.				
19.				
20.				
21.				
22.				
23.				
24.				
25.				
26.				
27.				
28.				
29.				
30.				
				TOTAL:

FIGURE B.14 Expense sheet template.

PAYROLL WORKSHEET

CONTACT: _____

WEEK ENDING: _____

PAYROLL TYPE: _____

Role/ Position	First Name	Last Name	SS # OR EIN	Line Item	Union	Agent	Loan Out	Con-tract Type	Day/ Week Rate	Hourly Rate	Reg. Hours	1.5x OT	2.0x OT2	MP ___	Other Charge	Agent 10%	Union HP&W	Fed/St. Fringes	Payroll Fee	TOTAL

TOTAL:

FIGURE B.15 Payroll worksheet template.

Union Information

UNIONS AT A GLANCE

TABLE C.1 Overview of union low-budget contracts

Organization	Covers	Low-Budget Agreements	Limits	
WGA (Writers Guild of America)	Writers	Low-budget agreement All monies deferred	< $500K	
		Low-budget agreement All monies deferred *except* $10K fee + $5K publication fee + fringes	< $1.2M	
		Basic low-budget agreement Rates are approximately 50% of standard Approximate cost per script: $40K + additional fees + fringes	< $5M	
DGA (Directors Guild of America)	Directors Assistant directors Unit production managers Location managers (in NYC)	Six levels (1A, 1B, 2, 3, 4A, 4B) Increasing salaries for each level Increasing guaranteed work periods and perks for each level	1A: 1B: 2: 3: 4A: 4B:	$500K $1.10M $2.60M $3.75M $5.5M $8.5M
SAG/AFTRA (Screen Actors Guild/ American Federation of Television and Radio Artists)	Actors Background talent	Three contracts (see Chapter 10) with variations Increasing rates Rates and agreements will probably change once merger has been ratified	ULB: MLB: LBA:	$200.0K $625.0K $2.5M
IATSE Locals (International Alliance of Theatrical Stage Employees)				

Organization	Covers	Low-Budget Agreements	Limits
52 – Studio Mechanics	Grips Electricians Carpenters Propmasters/propmakers Set decorators/dressers Greensmen Sound mixer/boom op./ sound utility Medics VTR (video playback) Set painters, craft service, wardrobe supervisors (outside NYC)	National low-budget agreements Tiers 1–3 Increasing rates at each tier Regional East Coast Council agreements, rates customized Individual ("one-off") agreement possible	Tier 1: $5.0M Tier 2: $8.5M Tier 3: $12M
161 – Production Coordinators/Script Supervisors	Production coordinators Accountants Script supervisors		
600 – Photographers	Director of photography Camera operators Assistant camera Still photographer DIT (digital image tech) Unit publicist		
700 – Editors	Editors Assistant editors Sound editors Music editors/supervisors Foley artists		
764 – Wardrobe	Wardrobe supervisors Wardrobe assistants Wardrobe shop staff		
798 – Hair/Makeup	Hair stylists Makeup artists		
829 – Scenic Artists	Production designers Art directors Art dept. coordinators Scenics Costume designers Costume assistants Computer graphics artists		

Blue-Collar Locals

817 – Theatrical Teamsters	Teamsters (drivers) Captains/coordinators Casting directors	East Coast Council agreement possible One-off agreements possible	

UNION RATES IN MORE DETAIL

This is a very condensed breakdown of each agreement (the SAG agreements are covered in Chapter 10). All the rates are current until at least June 2013.

TABLE C.2 Details of low-budget contracts

Tier	Budget Ceiling	Salary		HP&W	Notes/Other Comments
WGA Low-Budget Agreement					
Super low[a]	$500K	All fees deferred			Deferred doesn't mean *free*. The fees are paid back when the film starts earning money. *Also* you are supposed to release the film theatrically first
Low[a]	$1.2M	$10K for script $5K publication fee Remainder of fees are deferred		14.5%	
WGA Minimum Basic Agreement					
Low[a]	$5M	$43.7K for script		14.5%	Rewrites, treatments, etc. are extra
DGA Low-Budget Side Letter Agreement					
DIRECTORS					
Levels 1–2	$2.6M	Negotiable		14%	At least 20 days' allowance for director's cut
Level 3	$3.75M	$75K per picture		14%	Minimum 13 weeks guaranteed At least 8 weeks' allowance for director's cut
Level 4A	$8.5M	$12,598/week		14%	Minimum 13 weeks guaranteed At least 10 weeks' allowance for director's cut
Level 4B	$3.75M	$15,117/week		14%	Minimum 13 weeks guaranteed At least 10 weeks' allowance for director's cut
UPMS AND ADS					
Level 1A	$500K	Negotiable		14%	
Level 1B	$1.1M	UPM: 1st AD: 2nd AD: Other 2nd:	$1,582/week $1,504/week $1,008/week $649/week	14%	No production fee or completion of assignment
Level 2	$2.6M	UPM: 1st AD: 2nd AD: Other 2nd:	$2,397/week $2,280/week $1,528/week $877/week	14%	No production fee or completion of assignment Salaries are 33% of basic rate

Tier	Budget Ceiling	Salary		HP&W	Notes/Other Comments
Level 3	$3.75M	UPM: 1st AD: 2nd AD: Other 2nd:	$2,876/week $2,735/week $1,834/week $1,052/week	14%	UPM: Production fee $200/week 1st AD: Production fee $200/week 2nd AD: Production fee $150/week Salaries are 50% of basic rate
Level 4A[b]	$5.5M	UPM: 1st AD: 2nd AD: 2nd 2nd AD: Other 2nd:	$4,700/week $4,463/week $2,298/week $2,822/week $1,723/week	14%	UPM: Production fee $867/week 1st AD: Production fee $727/week 2nd AD: Production fee $592/week Salaries are 60% of basic rate
Level 4B[b]	$8.5M	UPM: 1st AD: 2nd AD: 2nd 2nd AD: Other 2nd:	$5,371/week $5,101/week $3,414/week $3,225/week $1,970/week	14%	UPM: Production fee $990/week 1st AD: Production fee $831/week 2nd AD: Production fee $676/week Salaries are 80% of basic rate
Level 4C[b]	$11.5M	UPM: 1st AD: 2nd AD: 2nd 2nd AD: Other 2nd:	$6,043/week $5,738/week $3,841/week $3,628/week $2,216/week	14%	UPM: Production fee $1,114/week 1st AD: Production fee $935/week 2nd AD: Production fee $761/week Salaries are 90% of basic rate

IATSE Low-Budget Theatrical Agreement[c]

Tier	Budget Ceiling	Salary		HP&W	Notes/Other Comments
Tier 1 Ultra low	$1.85M	STN: Keys: 2nd: 3rd:	Higher than key $23.11/hour $20.87/hour $18.64/hour	6% MPIPH or $85/day	STN = Subject to negotiation. Usually refers to higher-paid keys (DPs, art directors, costume designers, editors, sound editors, etc.) MPIPH = Motion Picture Industry Pension and Health Plans. Covers employees from LA, and certain employees from NYC

(Continued)

TABLE C.2 (Continued)

Tier	Budget Ceiling	Salary		HP&W	Notes/Other Comments
Tier 1	$5.5M	STN:	Higher than key	6% MPIPH *or*	Overtime is 1.5× between 8 and 12 hours
		Keys:	$23.11/hour	$92/day	
		2nd:	$20.87/hour		
		3rd:	$18.64/hour		
Tier 2	$8.5M	STN:	Higher than key	6% MPIPH *or*	The rates on Tiers 2 & 3 vary quite a bit from position-to-position, hence the range
		Keys:	$30–$44/hour	$109/day	
		2nd:	$27–$29/hour		
		3rd:	$24–$26/hour		
Tier 3	$12M	STN:	Higher than key	6% MPIPH *or*	
		Keys:	$32–$47/hour	$113/day	
		2nd:	$29–$31/hour		
		3rd:	$28–$29/hour		

Sources: WGA.org (WGA low-budget agreement sample), DGA.org (DGA Rate Card 2012–2013), IATSE-intl.org, *EP Paymaster*, published by Entertainment Partners.

[a] I made these "tier" names up.
[b] These rates are for "location" shoots. Studio shoot rates are lower.
[c] These rates are for production cities. Films shot outside these cities have lower rates and benefit plan contributions. The cities are: New York, Los Angeles, Chicago, Cleveland, Detroit, Orlando, San Francisco, St. Louis, and Washington, DC.

HOW TO CONTACT THE GUILDS AND UNIONS

Each local has an office located somewhere in its jurisdiction. SAG and the DGA have several regional offices. The WGA has two big offices (one in LA and one in NYC).

IATSE: www.iatse-intl.org
Teamsters: www.teamster.org
　　　　www.ht399.org
　　　　Some theatrical teamster locals are part of a joint council of locals; 817 is part of Joint Council 16, www.teamstersnewyorkcity.org
DGA: www.dga.org
WGA: www.wga.org
SAG: www.sag.org
　　　　www.sagindie.org – this is a non-profit that provides info on SAG contracts.

The sites listed above have contracts, ratecards, and contact information. Two of the major payroll companies, Entertainment Partners and Media Services, have payrate guides that include the rates and contact information.

Index

Italic page numbers indicate tables: bold indicate figures, including photographs.

Preparing for Takeoff

You have the camera, time, money (or credit card), so why don't you just start shooting? That's one way to do it. However, be prepared for major mid-shoot changes, unhappy actors, a resentful crew, wasted days, and dwindling finances. This can all be avoided by solid planning – but where do you start?

Preparing for Takeoff will give you the tools you need to fully prepare for your independent film. Arthur Vincie breaks down the entire life cycle of a film, showing how scheduling, previsualization, location scouting, clearing permits, and other preproduction tasks are just as vital to the success of your film as the shoot itself.

- Master the preproduction workflow from the perspectives of both the director and producer, whether you're one or the other – or both.
- Learn the nuts and bolts of planning, such as script analysis, casting prep, location and tech scouting, legal preparation, previsualization, and even postproduction and distribution prep – all from someone who's been in trenches himself.
- The companion website includes a bonus chapter, sample script analyses, storyboards, beat sheets, and more.

Arthur Vincie has over fifteen years of film and television production experience as a line producer, producer, and director. Vincie has line produced or production managed numerous independent films and is very active in the New York City independent filmmaking community. He has done production work for major television networks, including NBC, ABC, and BBC America. He founded and currently runs Chaotic Sequence Inc., a company that produces shorts and features. He recently wrote and directed the feature film *Found In Time*, which premiered at the 2012 Shriekfest Sci-Fi/Horror film festival.